May, 1

DO NOT MARK OR WRITE ON
DO NOT MARK OR WRITE ON
TEXTBOOK LABEL
25¢ credit will be deducted for defacement
25¢ credit will be deducted for defacement
of this label.

TRINITY HIGH SCHOOL
4011 FRANKFORT AVENUE
LOUISVILLE 7, KENTUCKY

NAME OF PUPIL	YEAR	
Charles Hile	69-70	400
Kenny Fante	70-71	280

2 3 4 5

2

Jan 29 Book - 104 pages
Feb 26 Test Rest of Book

The Laidlaw English Program

LANGUAGE — LINGUISTICS — COMPOSITION

- Beginning English
- English 2
- English 3
- English 4
- English 5
- English 6
- Using Good English,
    Junior High School, Book One
- Using Good English,
    Junior High School, Book Two
- Using Good English 9
- Using Good English 10
- Using Good English 11
- Using Good English 12

USING

COMPOSITION
GRAMMAR
LINGUISTICS

GOOD ENGLISH

JOHN E. BREWTON
Chairman, English Department
George Peabody College for Teachers
Nashville, Tennessee

R. STANLEY PETERSON
Head of the English Department
New Trier Township High School
Winnetka, Illinois

B. JO KINNICK
Teacher of Creative Writing
Oakland High School
Oakland, California

LOIS McMULLAN
Formerly Teacher of English, Laboratory School
George Peabody College for Teachers
Nashville, Tennessee

MARION L. STEET
Television Teacher of Linguistics
Philadelphia Public Schools
Philadelphia, Pennsylvania

LAIDLAW BROTHERS · PUBLISHERS

A Division of Doubleday & Company, Inc.

River Forest, Illinois

PALO ALTO, CALIFORNIA   DALLAS, TEXAS   ATLANTA, GEORGIA   TORONTO, CANADA

ILLUSTRATIONS BY: Edwin Lundquist and Dan Siculan

ACKNOWLEDGMENTS: Excerpt from *Statute of Pleading* and from Benjamin Franklin's *A Collection of Essays and Fugitive Writings*, quoted in *A History of the English Language*, 2nd Edition, by Albert C. Baugh: Reprinted by permission of Appleton-Century-Crofts, Inc. / Excerpt from "Crisis in Education" by Bernard Iddings Bell: Reprinted by permission from Mrs. Bernard Iddings Bell. / Excerpt from *Walt Whitman Reconsidered* by Richard Chase, copyright 1955 by William Sloane and Associates: Reprinted by permission from William Morrow and Co., Inc. / Excerpt from the Preface to *A Personal Record* by Joseph Conrad: Reprinted by permission of J. M. Dent & Sons, Ltd. / Excerpt from *The Notebooks of Leonardo da Vinci*, as reprinted in *Artists on Art*, edited by Robert Goldwater and Marco Treves: Reprinted by permission of Harcourt, Brace, & World, Inc. / *Acceptance of the Nobel Prize*. Reprinted from *The Faulkner Reader*, (Random House, 1954). / Excerpt from *The Failure of Communism* by Oscar Handlin: Reprinted from *The Atlantic Monthly*, December, 1961. / Excerpt from a review by Richard Hooker of *Power and Responsibility: the Life and Times of Theodore Roosevelt* by William Henry Harbaugh: Reprinted from the *Springfield Republican*, June 25, 1961. / Excerpt from a review by Alfred Lansing of *No Latitude for Error* by Sir Edmund Hillary: Reprinted from the *New York Herald Tribune Books* section, August 6, 1961. / Excerpt from *The Ordeal of Power* by Emmet John Hughes: Reprinted by permission from Atheneum Publishers. / Excerpt from *Profiles in Courage* by John F. Kennedy: Reprinted by permission from Harper and Row, Publishers, Inc. / Excerpt from "Snobs, Slobs, and the English Language" by Donald J. Lloyd: Reprinted by permission from the author. / Excerpt from *Madison Avenue, U. S. A.* by Martin Mayer: Reprinted by permission from Harper and Row, Publishers, Inc. / Excerpt from *Tradition and Progress* by Gilbert Murray: Reprinted by permission from George Allen and Unwin Ltd. / Excerpt from "In the Country," from *The World of George Jean Nathan* by George Jean Nathan: Reprinted by permission from A. S. Barnes and Co., Inc. / Excerpt from a review by Wilfrid Noyce of *No Latitude for Error* by Sir Edmund Hillary: Reprinted from *New Statesman*, May 19, 1961. / Excerpt from CONVERSATIONS OF GOETHE WITH ECKERMAN, translated by John Oxenford and edited by J. K. Morehead for Everyman's Library: Reprinted by permission from E. P. Dutton and Co., Inc., Publishers. / Excerpt from *Understanding English* by Paul Roberts: Reprinted by permission of Harper & Brothers, copyright 1958. / Excerpt from *KAMONGO, or the Lungfish and the Padre* by Homer W. Smith, copyright 1932, 1949 by Homer W. Smith: Reprinted by permission of the Viking Press, Inc. / Excerpt from *TRAVELS WITH CHARLEY In Search of America* by John Steinbeck, copyright 1961, 1962 by the Curtis Publishing Co., © 1962 by John Steinbeck: Reprinted by permission of the Viking Press, Inc. / Excerpt from *The Elizabethan World Picture* by E. M. W. Tillyard, copyright 1961: Reprinted by permission from the Macmillan Co. / *A Mississippi Pilot:* from *Life on the Mississippi:* Reprinted by permission of Harper & Brothers. / Excerpt from *The Centaur* by John Updyke: Reprinted by permission from the Fawcett World Library. / Excerpt from a review by C. W. Weinberger of *Power and Responsibility: the Life and Times of Theodore Roosevelt* by William Henry Harbaugh: Reprinted from the *San Francisco Chronicle*, August 13, 1961. / Excerpts from *Once More to the Lake* from *One Man's Meat* by E. B. White: Reprinted by permission of Harper & Brothers. / *The Red Wheelbarrow* by William Carlos Williams, copyright 1938, 1957 by William Carlos Williams: Reprinted by permission of New Directions, Publishers. / Review by John T. Winterich of *Secret Service Chief* by U. E. Baughman and Leonard Wallace Robinson: Reprinted from *Saturday Review*, January 13, 1962. / Excerpt from *You Can't Go Home Again* by Thomas Wolfe: Reprinted by permission from Harper and Row, Publishers, Inc.

PHOTOGRAPHS: Cover and page ii: Courtesy of Monsanto Chemical Company. / Page 157: Courtesy of Hofstra College, Hempstead, N. Y. / Pages x, 1, 25, 45, 69, 93, 113, 133: J. Julius Fanta—Colorpix.

CONTENTS

Unit 7   Writing Research Papers—continued

Unit 8   Writing Effective Paragraphs   157

Unit 9   Linguistics—Modern Language Study   183

viii

Unit 12   Mechanics in Writing   363

Unit 13   Style in Sentences   429

Unit 1

Newspapers, Magazines, Books

Perhaps to a greater degree than you realize, you are affected by what you read. Much of what you know today you have learned through your reading, and much of what you will need to find out in the future you will search for in books, magazines, and newspapers. Equally important, your reading affects many of your attitudes and ideals.

It is therefore important that you give some thought to the reading habits you have developed, for the benefit and enjoyment you derive from your reading depend upon them. Are you taking advantage of the best that is offered in reading materials? Are you reading as thoughtfully as you might?

To answer these questions, you should know something about standards for evaluating your reading habits. In this unit you will study some of these criteria. You will also be given some help in improving your ability to choose reading materials wisely and to interpret and analyze carefully what you read.

CHECK YOURSELF

Write brief answers to the following questions. In the pages that follow, you can find the answers to these and similar questions concerning newspapers, magazines, and books.

1. What are the principal functions of a newspaper?
2. What kinds of events are considered newsworthy by news editors?

1

3. In what ways may the news become "slanted"?
4. What are some points that should be considered in judging the worth of an editorial?
5. Why is it desirable to read more than one newspaper?
6. What are some of the factors that affect readers' selections of magazines and articles?
7. What are some criteria for judging the worth of magazines?
8. Why should you read a news magazine in addition to a newspaper?
9. What are some characteristics of an excellent book?
10. What are some aids you can use in selecting books?

1. Newspapers

We have the newspaper, which does its best to make every square acre of land and sea give an account of itself at your breakfast-table.

—RALPH WALDO EMERSON

PURPOSES OF NEWSPAPERS

One of the main purposes of the newspaper is to report the news; but the modern newspaper does much more than report events of current interest. It also provides comments about the news and interpretations of it. In addition, the paper has become an important part of the business life of the nation. Its business and financial pages supply essential information, and its advertising columns, both classified and display, provide a marketplace for buyers and sellers of goods and services. The newspaper also offers many features to inform, advise, and entertain. A large metropolitan paper, for example, often furnishes such diverse features as health counseling; reviews of books, movies, and plays; bridge lessons; investment advice; golf tips; crossword puzzles; and many others.

There is still another, very important, function of the newspaper: to serve as a clearinghouse for the exchange of ideas and opinions. On the editorial page of most newspapers you can find letters written to the editor by the readers of the paper, as well as editorials. When a paper prints such letters about issues of public interest, it furnishes a valuable public forum for the exchange of views, especially when many points of view are included. The newspaper, of course, is not the only medium for such an exchange of views, nor should it be; but it is a very important one, since most adults read at least one newspaper daily.

A newspaper that carries out the purposes that have been discussed thus performs an important public service. Many years ago when Adolph Ochs took control of the *New York Times,* he included in the aims of his paper its public-service functions. His famous words summarize the purposes of any good newspaper, then and now:

> "It will be my earnest aim that the *New York Times* give the news, all the news, in concise and attractive form. . . . To give the news impartially . . . to make the columns of the *New York Times* a forum for the consideration of all public questions of public importance, and to that end, to invite intelligent discussion from all shades of opinion."

 DEVELOPING YOUR SKILL

A. Why is it essential that the masses of the people in a government such as ours be well-informed? Be ready to discuss this question.
B. Discuss some ways in which the newspaper contributes to the business life of the nation.
C. Be prepared to discuss the following statement of Lord Macaulay and relate it to one of the purposes of a newspaper: "Men are never so likely to settle a question rightly as when they discuss it freely."
D. Examine carefully a copy of a large metropolitan newspaper and list the features it provides.

EVALUATING NEWSPAPERS

Although it might be untrue to say that any newspaper is vastly superior in all respects to all others, papers do differ widely in content and quality. They differ in type of news emphasized, in manner of presenting the news, in the completeness and accuracy of the reporting, in editorial policy, in size and make-up, and in the kind of advertising they contain and the amount of space devoted to it. In evaluating newspapers, teachers of journalism and other qualified judges often use the following or similar points.

The selection of the news

In general, anything that people are likely to be curious about or anything that affects the lives of large numbers of people is considered newsworthy. A national election, for example, or an international conference would be considered newsworthy. A dramatic incident, or one involving conflict such as a court battle, is also considered news even though the number of people affected may not be large. Human-interest stories are also rated by news editors as having high reader-interest. The story of a strike might be newsworthy on several counts. It often affects large numbers of people, there are usually some dramatic incidents in connection with it, and frequently there are also some related human-interest incidents worth reporting.

But there are still other factors that affect the selection of items to be printed. To some extent, the policy of the paper determines what is chosen for publication. Some papers give much space to events of national and international interest, while others emphasize sensational stories about personal violence and crime. Still others tend to prefer items that are supporting evidence for the particular viewpoint favored by the paper. Such papers tend to pass by, or treat superficially, news items supporting the other side or sides of a question.

The selection of the news may also be affected by as simple a thing as the availability of an item in time for a deadline. If another item had come in in time, a particular story might not have been chosen. And occasionally a news editor may show a lapse in judgment as to the real significance of a story that has come in. However, a good newspaper publishes the significant news with great regularity, it avoids emphasizing items of a sensational nature, and it presents various sides of issues that are controversial.

In a recent survey, teachers of journalism in some of our larger universities were asked to comment on the way news stories were selected in several large metropolitan newspapers. Many of these teachers thought that too much space was given to sports, gossip columns, comics, and stories of crime and violence, and not enough to events of national and international interest or to helpful interpretations of such events. Some of the teachers felt that some of the news reports would benefit by a sifting out of unnecessary details.

The news that is selected for weekly newspapers usually differs from that chosen for dailies. Since the weekly paper serves smaller communities, it gives more space to local events than do the large dailies. The national and international news is often interpreted and analyzed more thoroughly than time permits in a daily paper, and often the future significance of the news is emphasized.

The manner in which the news is presented

A news story should tell only the facts; it should not give an opinion. In a well-written news article, the essential facts are given in the first one or two, or lead, paragraphs, and subsequent paragraphs give the story in greater detail. Thus, you should be able to read the first few paragraphs of a well-written news article and find its basic points. The writing should be easy to read, interesting, and, of course, grammatically correct.

The amount of space given a news article and the prominence of its position in the paper should be in proportion to its significance. For example, a report of an international conference usually should be found on the front page. Such a report should be given enough space so that all important facts can be treated adequately. Also, the facts should be given space according to their relative importance. By giving too much emphasis to unimportant details, or by underemphasizing important facts, the truth is distorted and the article may be said to be "slanted."

The headline of a news article should summarize the news accurately and impartially. Although by its nature a headline can give only the main point or points of a story, it should not be dishonest or misleading. An example of a misleading headline is one in which one part of the headline is minimized, and a dramatic part of the headline emphasized. In the following headline, for example, if the words *Smith sees no* were put in very small type and the dramatic words *immediate threat of war* were put in very large type, the resulting headline would be very misleading, especially to one glancing at the headline from a little distance.

The completeness and accuracy of the reporting

The degree to which completeness and accuracy are achieved in news stories is another important point of difference among papers. Every effort should be made to include all important facts and to check sources of information carefully; but it is not always possible to get a complete story, and there are many opportunities for inaccuracies to creep in. Stories often must be written under the pressure of a deadline that doesn't permit thorough checking of sources. Thus, from time to time, even in the best of papers inaccuracies and errors of some kind are found. A good paper, however, makes a great effort to give a complete, accurate story; and it will print retractions or corrections of proved misstatements.

The editorial page

The editorial page is the place for the expression of views and opinions —both those expressed in the editorials and those expressed in the letters to the editor. Papers vary widely in the quality of the editorials that they include, as well as in the range of opinions that are allowed expression on that page. As you know, a good paper publishes comments that express many points of view.

Not all editorials are written to persuade you of something. Editorials may also explain, commend, or deride. In editorials written to convince you or to persuade you, the emphasis is often on an appeal to the emotions. Sometimes an appeal is made primarily to the intellect. An editorial also may be slanted to a great degree in favor of a particular political party or in favor of certain policies of the paper. Other papers contain editorial comment that is independent of any political affiliation.

In judging an editorial, you may find the following questions helpful:

Are the opinions of the writer stated as facts? Does the writer say, for example, "My candidate for mayor is the best qualified of the three candidates," without giving sufficient evidence to support his assertion?

What are the sources of the facts used to support an opinion? Whenever possible, the writer should tell where he got his facts.

Who is writing, and what might be his possible motives? Does the writer for a paper known to favor the Republican (or Democratic) party favor their candidate for an office? Does he discredit the candidate of the opposing party?

Are some important facts omitted, and are other facts, supporting the opinion of the writer, overemphasized? For example, in an argument claiming that a certain kind of fire equipment is superior to other kinds in fighting certain types of fires, are many instances given of its successful use and is there no mention of any instances in which it was not successful? Is any comparison made with other equipment designed to do the same thing, and are any statistics quoted to prove the superiority of the equipment in question?

Are the conclusions drawn from too few cases, and are the cited cases typical ones? Are exceptions explained? For example, it might be argued that, on the basis of a poll of riders on a commuter train, most of the riders favored a decrease in service rather than an increase in fare. You should consider whether a sufficient number of riders were interviewed to make this conclusion a sound one, and whether the riders interviewed were those who regularly rode to work and would be greatly inconvenienced by a decrease in service. Are any reasons given to explain the opinions of those who did *not* favor a decrease in service? Since the answers to these questions are not always easily found, one should compare the opinions in this editorial with other sources of information, such as similar reports on television and radio and in other papers.

Does the writer appeal more to your intellect or to your emotions? Does the writer give opinions that are based on sound reasoning? Or does the writer avoid the basic issues and appeal unduly to your sense of fear or other emotions?

The layout and typography

Papers differ also in physical aspects. The type should be easy to read, and the layout of the paper—the arrangement of type and pictures—attractive. The photographs should be in good taste; that is, they should not be exaggerated or used in a sensational way in order to attract attention. They should add something to the understanding of the stories they illustrate.

The advertising

The kind of advertising in a paper and the amount of space devoted to it are other important points to consider in judging papers. Advertising, though necessary and desirable, probably should not take up more than approximately one half of the paper. Advertising is necessary to help pay for the cost of publishing the paper, as well as to help sell goods and services. Every effort should be made to see that the advertising is reliable and honest. If there is a sale advertised, for example, there should be enough items on sale to justify the advertisement. The sale items should be accurately described. The photographs and other art work used in the advertisement should not violate the principles of good taste.

You have seen that papers may be evaluated in regard to the six main points that have been described. It may be helpful to you to ask yourself the following specific questions when you evaluate a paper:

Is the selection of the news fair and impartial insofar as you can determine by a comparison with the news presented by other papers and on radio and television programs?

Is there a balance of news—local, national, and international? (Except in weekly newspapers, in which the news is chiefly local)

Is the manner of presentation of the news accurate and unbiased? Are news stories well written?

Is the amount of space given to news stories, as well as their position in the paper, in proportion to their importance?

Are the headlines honest or misleading? Do they accurately and impartially summarize the news? Or do they overemphasize dramatic events that are of no great significance?

Are the news interpretations helpful to your understanding of the news?

Are opinions reserved for editorial writers, columnists, or writers of signed articles, so that readers may readily distinguish statements of opinion from statements of fact?

Does the paper avoid sensationalism and exaggeration?

To what extent does the editorial page serve as a clearinghouse for the exchange of ideas and opinions?

Are the editorials well written? Use the questions on page 7 in evaluating editorials.

 DEVELOPING YOUR SKILL

A. The class may compare the selection of the front-page news in at least two newspapers of the same date. What items appear on both front pages? Discuss the amount of space given to these articles in each paper.

B. Clip headlines and stories from at least two papers and bring them to class. Be ready to compare and evaluate the headlines. How accurately do the headlines describe the content of the stories? Are any of the headlines misleading? Do the headlines emphasize dramatic but insignificant events?

C. Bring to class news articles on the same subject from at least two papers. Be prepared to discuss the articles in respect to differences in the following:

1. Space allotted to the article
2. Placement of the article in the paper
3. Placement and amount of space given to important facts in the article
4. Omission of facts
5. Differences in relating of the same facts
6. Overemphasis of unimportant details
7. The extent to which the news article reflects the editorial policy of the paper on this particular subject

D. Bring to class clippings of stories and photos from several papers. Be ready to explain whether you consider the photos in good taste and also whether they add to your understanding of the stories they illustrate.

E. Bring editorials to class and be ready to read them and explain whether they appeal more to the intellect or to the emotions.

F. Have a class discussion about the merits and faults of two newspapers with which most students in the class are acquainted. Each speaker should be required to give examples that will support the points that he makes. One purpose of the discussion is to give as many students as possible an opportunity to state differing opinions logically and in a calm, composed manner.

G. Read an issue of a metropolitan newspaper and write a critical evaluation of it. You may wish to use the questions on pages 8-9 in writing your evaluation.

IMPROVING YOUR READING OF NEWSPAPERS

Are you getting the greatest possible benefit from your reading of newspapers? If you are like most people, you can probably improve your newspaper-reading habits. Many people tend to read not only the same paper or papers, day after day, but also the same parts of those papers. They also read chiefly what reinforces an opinion they already have formed. Many do not give enough attention to news about foreign affairs or the relations of our country with other countries.

Have you let yourself fall into habits of reading such as those just described? If you have, you should try to change these habits. In addition, there are some desirable reading habits that you should be cultivating.

You may wish to consider the following points and decide whether you think that you are making the most of your reading of the newspaper.

READING THE NEWSPAPER

1. Read several papers regularly to become acquainted with newspapers of various types and to be able to compare them.

2. Examine all parts of a good newspaper to find out what is in it. You probably will never want to read everything in a paper; however, you should sample all parts to find out what is worth regular reading.

3. Plan your reading time. Are you spending too much time on some parts and too little on others?

4. Use the indexes, news digests, and other devices provided by newspapers to help you find quickly the section or information you want.

5. Read editorials often, and read them critically. In an editorial whose purpose is to convince you, think about the arguments critically, perhaps using the questions on page 7 to help yourself evaluate them.

6. Think about what you read. Compare what you have read with what you have read elsewhere or have heard on television or radio programs. Also ask yourself how you can use this information. Does it help you understand more fully something that you only partly understood before? Does it answer a question you may have had for some time?

7. Take an active part in supporting those newspapers you feel do the best job. Besides buying those newspapers, write letters to the editor commending what you approve of and speaking out against what you believe is wrong.

DEVELOPING YOUR SKILL

A. A poll may be taken of the reading habits of the class. Which of the following parts of the paper are read regularly? Discuss the results of the poll to determine whether the reading is spread over a wide range.

Art Reviews	Drama Reviews	Magazine Section
Book Reviews	Editorials	National News
Business and Finance	Foreign News	News Digest
Cartoons	Health News	Science News
Classified Advertise-	Home Improvements	Society News
ments	Interpretations of	Sports
Columnists	News	Television-Radio
Display Advertise-	Letters to the Editor	Travel
ments	Local News	Women's Page

B. Keep a written record of your own newspaper reading for a week. Include the total time spent in reading each day and the topics covered.

C. Write a paragraph outlining ways of improving your reading of newspapers. You may wish to use the suggestions on this page to serve as a yardstick in determining areas for improvement.

Review Exercises — Newspapers

A. Discuss the ways in which the essential meaning of a news story may become distorted. Give examples.
B. Explain some of the ways in which an argument in an editorial may be slanted.
C. Be ready to give facts in support of this statement by James B. Reston: " . . . perhaps more than any other institution in the country, the newspaper and the press associations create the intellectual climate in which the nation lives."
D. Write a paragraph in which you describe the characteristics of a fine newspaper.
E. Write an evaluation of a paper that you read regularly, explaining how it does or does not carry out the purposes of a good newspaper.

2. Magazines

MAGAZINES AND THEIR READERS

Like newspapers, magazines are read widely and they also have a significant influence on the thoughts and actions of millions of people. A magazine, or periodical, is any publication which is published at regular intervals, or periods, of more than one day—once a week, once a month, or at some other specified period.

Magazines differ greatly in subject matter, style of writing, make-up, and reader appeal. They also differ widely in reading difficulty, ranging from those that require a very limited reading ability to the learned journals of the professions and to quality magazines such as *Harper's, The Atlantic Monthly*, or the *Saturday Review*. The content and style of writing of such periodicals appeal to those with higher-than-average reading ability and a wide range of intellectual interests.

The reader can choose from a great variety of magazines. There are news magazines such as *Time, Newsweek*, and *U.S. News and World Report*, which are devoted chiefly to giving an overview of the week's news and interpretations of current happenings. Such magazines explain relationships between events in greater detail than is found in the daily papers. Magazines such as *Life* and *Look* depict the news of the week primarily in pictures. General publications such as *The Saturday Evening Post* contain stories, articles, verse, and other features that appeal to those with many and varied interests. Periodicals such as *Good Housekeeping, The Ladies' Home Journal, McCall's, Harper's Bazaar, Vogue,* and many others cater to women's particular interests. There are various digest magazines that present in condensed form selections taken from current publications.

There are also many magazines that specialize in particular subjects. Are you interested especially in sports, travel, science, antiques, interior designing, or the theater? Whatever your interest, there are magazines for you. *Sports Illustrated, Holiday,* and *Popular Science Monthly* are only a few examples of such specialized magazines.

Magazines called *trade journals* give information about specific occupations. Some of the larger companies publish their own magazines to keep employees and other interested persons informed about the company and its activities and progress. Such publications are called *house organs.*

As you can see from the large variety of magazines that are published, people differ widely in the periodicals they choose to read. What are some of the factors that determine why readers choose the mazagines and articles they do?

It has been found that readers often do what is easiest for them, as well as what they have become accustomed to doing. For example, they tend to buy magazines that are easily available to them at the corner drug store or nearby newsstand. They tend to buy the same magazines repeatedly. Also, it has been found, men's selections of reading material in magazines are often quite different from women's. Age, reading ability, education, and occupation are other factors that may have an effect on reading selections.

It has been found that as people grow older they tend to read more magazines. They also tend to read more editorials, articles about foreign relations, and similar kinds of selections. It was found, further, that the number of years a reader attends school and his reading ability have an

effect on his choices. Those who have had more schooling and those who have developed a greater reading ability, either in or out of school, show a preference for articles about such topics as foreign relations, social problems, and economic matters. The vocabulary used in such selections is more difficult than that used in some other kinds, and to understand such articles it is necessary that the reader have a high level of reading ability. Those with more education also have a greater range of interests, and they tend to buy and read more magazines than those with less schooling. A person's occupation also seems to affect his reading habits. For example, businessmen and professional men such as doctors, teachers, or lawyers show a strong preference for articles on public affairs.

Men, in general, regardless of occupation or education, tend to read more about public affairs than women do. They also read more sports news than women do. Women are inclined to prefer human-interest stories. It must be remembered, however, that other factors such as age, education, reading ability, and occupation also affect reading habits. Thus, the differences between the reading preferences of men and women are more sharply defined among those who have had only grade-school education than among those with high-school education or higher.

The average reader does not read every article in a magazine. According to one study, the readers who were questioned read at the most only one in seven articles, or at the least one in every ten articles. The average reader is likely to read the same magazine or magazines repeatedly, to the exclusion of many others. And he may also limit himself to the same types of articles. Thus, if the reader wishes to make changes in his reading habits, he will probably have to make a conscious effort to do so.

14

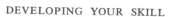

A. Your teacher may wish to take a poll of the magazines with which the class is familiar. Classify the magazines according to the types described on pages 12-13, such as general, news, travel, and other types. With which ones are the members of the class most familiar? Least familiar?

B. Be ready to discuss some of the factors that may affect a reader's selection of reading material in a magazine.

C. Why are the differences in reading interests more pronounced between men and women with grade-school education than between men and women with high-school education or higher? Be prepared to explain this fact in class.

D. Why should you read a news magazine in addition to a daily newspaper? Be prepared to tell why this is a desirable practice.

E. Be prepared to explain the difference between a trade journal and a house organ.

F. List magazines that could be read in your family by most of its members. Then write a paragraph telling why such magazines would appeal to persons of both sexes, of different ages, and diverse interests. How do these magazines differ from magazines devoted to specialized interests?

G. Visit a newsstand or a public library and list some magazines with which you are unfamiliar. Classify them according to type of magazine as described on pages 12-13. Are there any types that you have not read?

GETTING THE MOST FROM MAGAZINES

Magazine reading, when purposeful and selective, can be profitable as well as entertaining. If you are to get the most from your reading, however, you must become familiar with many publications to learn what is available.

The following questions should help you to appraise and select the best magazines from the large number available.

1. Does the magazine provide accurate, helpful, significant information? Fresh inspiration? Wholesome entertainment? A magazine should do one of these three things.

2. If the magazine is designed primarily to give news and interpretations of it, does it fill the following requirements?

  a. Is the information accurate?
  b. Does the writer cite sources of facts? Are the sources reliable ones?
  c. In giving the background for certain events, are relationships between various factors made clear?
  d. Are the interpretations logical, and are they helpful to your understanding of the subject?
  e. Are controversial subjects presented fairly, with more than one point of view presented?
  f. Are important facts omitted or given adequate coverage?

3. If the magazine contains fiction, does the fiction meet the following standards?

  a. Does the story give a true picture of life and people?
  b. Are the themes of the stories concerned with a subject of some significance?
  c. Are the illustrations artistic and appropriate?
  d. Are the illustrations free from vulgarity?

4. In a general-type magazine are the contents—articles, stories, poems—varied in style and subject matter?

5. Is the magazine free from sensationalism and exaggerated emotional appeal?

Fortunately, there are many excellent magazines. There are some, however, that are not worth your time. They contain fiction that gives an untrue picture of life and people. The characters in the stories tend to be stereotyped and unreal. The language used is often unnecessarily crude and vulgar, and the illustrations are garish and exaggerated. Some magazines are not worth your time because they are concerned largely with the insignificant and the superficial. The reading level required to read these kinds of magazines is far below that required of high-school seniors; such magazines should therefore have very little appeal for you.

After you have spent some time in exploring magazines and becoming familiar with the kinds of materials they contain, you will find it increasingly easy to evaluate magazines well. You will also find it easier to know where to look for the kind of information you need. For example, you will discover that informative and helpful reviews of current books are found in such magazines as the *Saturday Review, Time, The Atlantic Monthly,* and *Harper's.*

There will be occasions, however, when you will need help in locating the particular issue of a magazine to give you the specific information you need. A practical help in finding magazine articles is the *Readers' Guide to Periodical Literature,* which you can find in your library. In this guide, articles that appear, or have appeared, in over one hundred magazines are listed by topic and by author. The title and the author of the article are given, together with the name of the magazine and the issue in which the article appears.

DEVELOPING YOUR SKILL

    A. Why is it increasingly important that you learn to evaluate magazines well? Be ready to discuss this statement.

    B. Read at least one of the more informative articles that require a high level of reading ability. Be prepared to discuss in class what you read.

    C. Make a study of your magazine-reading habits for a week. Keep a written record of the following: the amount of time you spend reading magazines; the kinds of magazines you read; whether you have read any new kinds during the week. Then write a paragraph in which you outline ways of improving your reading habits.

    D. Read several articles in a magazine that is new to you. Write a critical evaluation of the magazine, using the questions on pages 15-16 as an aid in writing your review.

Review Exercises — Magazines

A. Discuss five ways in which magazines differ. Give examples to illustrate the various points you make.

B. Choose three topics of current interest and look up references on them in the *Readers' Guide to Periodical Literature.* List at least two references for each topic.

C. List one magazine in each of the following categories that you consider to be an excellent example of that type: news, general, travel, sports, and digest. Write a short paragraph about each magazine, telling why you consider it to be an excellent example of its type.

3. Books

Reading is to the mind what exercise is to the body.

—JOSEPH ADDISON

EVALUATING BOOKS

Books are perhaps the largest single source of solid information. However, just as in any other kind of reading material, books differ in quality, usefulness, and subject matter treated.

To judge the worth of a book, you must first determine its purpose and then judge how well it has carried out this purpose. A good book should make a significant contribution in one or more of these fields—your wisdom, your pleasure, or your appreciation of life.

In evaluating books, you may find the following questions useful:

1. Does the book add measurably to your wisdom, your pleasure, or your appreciation of life?

2. Is the subject matter of some consequence? A good book is concerned with a significant human experience or a significant truth.

3. Is the author qualified to write on the subject? He should have had the education or the background of experience that qualifies him to write with authority and perception on the subject.

4. Is the organization of the book clear? Are the parts arranged so that their relationship to each other is easily seen?

5. Is the presentation such that it provokes thought? Do you find yourself discussing the book with others or using arguments from the book in your conversations? After reading a good book you should often feel impelled to read more about the subject that has been treated, or about a topic related to it.

6. In a treatment of a controversial subject, does the author present more than one point of view? Are important facts omitted or underemphasized? Are unimportant facts overemphasized? Are appeals made to your prejudices?

7. In a book of fiction, is the plot believable and easy to follow? Is your interest in the story caught early and maintained? Are the characters true to life or stereotyped? Are the actions of the characters adequately motivated? Do you feel that you know yourself or others better for having become acquainted with the characters?

 DEVELOPING YOUR SKILL

A. Students may be chosen to give evaluations of a book that many in the class have read, using the questions listed on pages 18-19 to help them. Then the class may wish to discuss the differences in their evaluations.

B. Using book reviews, other sources of information available to you, or your own reading experiences as a guide, list what you consider to be an excellent current book in each of the following fields: a novel; an inspirational book; a humorous book; a book that treats a controversial subject; a book on some aspect of politics, science, or economics. After each title, give the source or sources of the information on which you based your evaluation of that book.

C. Write an evaluation of a book that you have read recently. Use the questions on pages 18-19 and explain to what degree the author met the requirements for excellence in a book as pointed out by these questions.

GETTING PLEASURE AND PROFIT FROM BOOKS

Books used well can contribute significantly to your mental development, your pleasure, and your appreciation of life. But to get the most from books, you must not only select wisely from the many available, you must also form other desirable reading habits. You should learn to become aware of your reading needs. It is equally important to know how to use the available helps in locating the books you need. And, finally, you should know how to evaluate the worth of what you read and make use of the knowledge you acquire through your reading.

As you read the following points, you may wish to check your reading habits with them to see whether you are getting the most from your reading of books.

1. Plan your reading to take care of your needs. What do you need? For example, should you "catch up" on reading that you have missed, in order to be better prepared for college entrance? Do you need to find out more about your chosen career? After you are out of school, you will want to think about whether you are learning all you should about the job you are then doing, or whether you could be preparing yourself for the next step forward in your career. Not all your reading, of course, should be planned. Some of it should be chosen spontaneously, just for sheer enjoyment of reading. But you should make sure that you are including books that will help you reach your goals.

2. Use many helps in finding the best books for your purposes. Book lists and guides have been prepared on various subjects and for various purposes. You should be able to find some of these lists and guides in your public library. Become acquainted with the book reviews in newspapers and magazines, as well as with a digest such as the *Book Review Digest*, which contains condensed reviews of current books by many reviewers. It is also helpful to browse through bookstores and the book sections of department stores, stopping to look at the exhibits and displays of new books. Do not overlook the advantages of visiting your public library frequently and becoming well acquainted with it. Your librarian also will be happy to help you find the books you need.

3. Develop discrimination in your reading. Repeatedly make wise choices in your selections, basing your evaluations on the questions on pages 18-19.

4. Read with a purpose. Keep in mind some questions that you would like to have answered. You are more likely to profit from your reading if you read with the thought of finding answers to questions that you may have.

5. Use the bibliography provided in many informational books to find sources of more information about some aspect of a subject than is given in the book you are reading. Increasingly, as you mature, you will find that you will wish to "follow up" in this way in order to gain a better understanding of a subject.

6. Seek variety in your reading. As your interests develop, you will naturally tend to read books on an increasingly greater range of subjects, but you should also make a conscious effort to increase your range.

7. Balance your reading program. Include biographies, short stories, essays, poems, plays, and novels, as well as books on special subjects such as philosophy, travel, history, economics, science, and many others. Do not confine your reading to the old or to the new alone. Read some of both.

8. Think about what you read. Do you agree or disagree with what the author is saying? Can you think of what he might present next? Do you think that the author's development of a topic is logical and easy to follow?

9. Use what you learn to help yourself think more clearly and make more accurate judgments. Discuss ideas with others. Perhaps try to explain to someone something that you have read.

10. Make a definite effort to develop your mental capacities. Explore new areas or delve deeper into old fields. From time to time think about what you have been reading to find out whether you are developing your capacities as much as you might. Occasionally choose a book for the definite purpose of improving your tastes or of stretching your powers of understanding and imagination.

DEVELOPING YOUR SKILL

A. Be prepared to discuss this statement of John Locke: "Reading furnishes us only with the materials of knowledge; it is thinking that makes what we read ours." Tell in what ways you can make what you read yours.

B. Have a class discussion about the types of books with which the class is most familiar and least familiar. The following list of types of books will help you in your discussion. Which types have been overemphasized? Which have been overlooked?

Adventure	Music	Romance
Art	Mystery	Science
Autobiography	Nature Lore	Short Stories
Biography	Novels	Sports and Recreation
Essays	Plays	Travel
Gardening	Poetry	Vocations
History	Reference	Westerns
Hobbies	Religion	World Affairs

C. Make a list of types of books you should read more of in order to balance your reading.

Review Exercises — Books

A. Discuss various sources of information about books. Evaluate each of these sources in terms of their usefulness to you.
B. Your teacher may appoint a group to hold a round-table discussion on the ways in which one can get the most pleasure and profit from the reading of books. Use the points listed on pages 20 and 21 as a help in your discussion.
C. Write a paragraph in which you tell specific ways in which you can improve your reading of books.

UNIT SUMMARY

In this unit you have been given an opportunity to learn how to get more pleasure and profit from your reading of newspapers, magazines, and books. You have seen how each of these media can be used to enrich your life through adding to your information, your enjoyment, or your appreciation of life. You have become acquainted with some criteria with which to judge the worth of these media. And finally you have studied some ways to improve your own reading.

UNIT REVIEW EXERCISES

DISCUSSION TOPICS

A. How do newspapers differ in respect to the following points?

    1. The selection of the news
    2. The accuracy of the reporting
    3. The manner in which the news is presented
    4. The editorials
    5. The layout and typography
    6. The amount and kind of advertising

B. Why are there so many different kinds of magazines?
C. What are some of the factors that affect readers' choices of magazines and articles?
D. What is the meaning of the following quotation from Ralph W. Emerson: " 'Tis the good reader that makes the good book "?

WRITTEN WORK

A. List three magazines with which you have become acquainted during the study of this unit. Write a brief paragraph describing each, telling why it is or is not a magazine worth reading. Use the questions on pages 15-16 as a help in making your evaluations.
B. Write a short composition on one of the following subjects:

    1. How Newspapers Help to Form Public Opinion
    2. Services Newspapers Render
    3. My Favorite Magazines
    4. Enjoyable Books

VOCABULARY

Some words in this unit may have been unfamiliar to you. In the following sentences some of the words are used in different contexts. Write the numbers 1 to 5 on your paper. After each number write the letter of the word or words that have the same or nearly the same meaning as the italicized word in each sentence. Before making your choice, find the word on the page indicated to see how the word is used in the unit.

1. What *criteria* were used in selecting the essay-contest winner?   [p. 1]
    (*a*) judgments; (*b*) opinions; (*c*) standards; (*d*) skills
2. My friends lived in a *metropolitan* area.   [p. 2]
    (*a*) suburban; (*b*) rustic; (*c*) in or near the city; (*d*) prosperous and sophisticated

3. *Subsequent* events proved that John was right in his decision.   [p. 5]
   (*a*) related; (*b*) succeeding; (*c*) preceding; (*d*) decisive
4. The witness said that he had had a *lapse* of memory.   [p. 4]
   (*a*) good test; (*b*) small error or slip; (*c*) poor; (*d*) superior kind of
5. The jury was composed of people who were *unbiased* in their feelings toward
   the defendant.   [p. 8]
   (*a*) impartial; (*b*) frank; (*c*) honest; (*d*) immovable

SPELLING

The following words appeared in this unit or were chosen because they are
commonly misspelled. Study the list carefully until you can spell each word
correctly.

1. criteria	11. reinforces
2. metropolitan	12. blurb
3. subsequent	13. cater
4. lapse	14. composed
5. unbiased	15. impartial
6. diverse	16. delving
7. enhancing	17. articulate
8. forum	18. typography
9. affiliation	19. profound
10. successive	20. statistics

UNIT SELF-TEST

Write answers to the following questions and exercises.

1. Explain the ways in which news stories and editorials may be slanted.
2. List at least five ways of helping yourself get the most from your reading
   of newspapers.
3. What are some criteria for judging the worth of magazines? Give at least
   five criteria.
4. What are ten questions you might ask yourself to find out whether you are
   getting the most benefit from your reading of books?
5. What are some points to be considered in evaluating the worth of books?
   List and explain at least five such points.

Unit 2

Critical Listening

> . . . many have been harmed by speech,
> Through thinking, few or none.
>
> —SIR THOMAS VAUX

When you listen critically, you attempt to evaluate correctly the worth of what you hear. It is essential that you develop this ability, because every day you are subjected to a barrage of words designed to influence your thoughts and actions. No one, of course, wishes to have his decisions and choices made for him; yet this is precisely what often happens when one is not sufficiently aware of the power of words.

To what extent do you think that you are influenced by what you hear on television, radio, in conversations, and in other ways? Can you tell when someone is trying to influence you?

In this unit you will study ways of increasing your proficiency in critical listening. By improving your ability to think clearly and logically, by learning about the more common propaganda techniques, and by cultivating certain habits and attitudes, you can develop the ability to make better judgments about what you hear.

Before beginning the study of this unit, you will find it helpful to write brief answers to the following questions.

1. Why is it a good plan to suspend judgment about the worth of an important statement?
2. What are some habits and attitudes that hinder your ability to make sound evaluations of what you hear?
3. Is "Bob likes to play tennis" an opinion or a statement of fact?
4. What are fallacies in reasoning?
5. Give an example of a false analogy.
6. What is a hasty generalization?
7. What are some criteria for judging a speech?
8. What is a good definition of propaganda?
9. What are some names that have been given to methods commonly used by propagandists?
10. Can propaganda be used for worthy purposes? Explain your answer.

1. Critical Listening Skills

To evaluate well, it is essential to listen attentively and think carefully *before* coming to a conclusion about what you hear. Often you must suspend judgment until you can find adequate information upon which to base a valid conclusion. This attitude of suspended judgment allows you time to consider more than one point of view; it also helps to keep you from a hasty acceptance of others' opinions without careful scrutiny of them.

An essential skill in listening is the ability to distinguish facts from opinions. You must also learn to think clearly in order to distinguish a logical, impartial presentation of an opinion from one based on half-truths, misinformation, or confused thinking.

DISTINGUISHING FACTS FROM OPINIONS

It is sometimes a relatively simple matter to distinguish facts from opinions. A statement of a mathematical fact, for example, is easy to identify as a fact rather than an opinion. Such a statement can be proved to be either true or false. It is either a statement of fact or it is an untrue statement. Similarly, a statement concerning the number of books published during a certain year in the United States is also quite easily identified as a statement that can be verified as a fact.

A statement such as "Bob is washing the car this afternoon" is one that you may be able to verify as a fact by direct observation; but "Bob is late again, as usual" is a statement of opinion. The words *as usual* tell you that it is a judgment, or statement of opinion, about Bob's habit of tardiness. Another example of an opinion is the following statement: "All sixteen-year-olds should be given driving lessons." This opinion may or may not be based on established facts or the correct interpretation of those facts; but it is an opinion, not a fact.

Some statements, however, are not so quickly identified as either fact or opinion. For example, if one were to say that most inhabitants in a remote village in Africa like American food and clothing, it would probably be difficult to decide quickly whether this is a statement that could be verified as a fact or whether it is an opinion based on insufficient evidence. Reliable reference materials that would verify this statement as a fact might be rather hard to find. You should therefore suspend judgment about such statements until you have an opportunity to find out more about them.

It should be remembered, too, that opinions may or may not be valid ones. To be valid, an opinion must be supported by facts. To substantiate an opinion such as "I believe that Mr. Johnson would make a good mayor," you would have to cite examples of his ability in areas that would show him to be a likely candidate.

DEVELOPING YOUR SKILL

> A. Read each of the following statements and be ready to tell whether each is a statement that can be verified as a fact, a statement of opinion, or a statement that could be either a fact or an opinion.
>
> 1. *David Copperfield* was written by Charles Dickens.
> 2. Charles Dickens was greatly beloved both in Great Britain and in the United States.
> 3. Montpelier is the capital of Vermont.
> 4. Abraham Lincoln was the sixteenth President of the United States.
> 5. Norfolk, Virginia, is one of the nation's busiest port areas.
> 6. This poem is not easy to understand.

7. Mercury is the smallest planet of the solar system.
8. Senator Smith was met at the airport by many of his supporters.
9. An enthusiastic group was on hand at the airport early this morning to welcome Senator Smith to our city.
10. Learning to dance is a pleasant way of gaining new popularity and poise.
11. Viewing television is largely a waste of time.
12. Football is the most popular collegiate sport in the United States.
13. Tom hates to mow the lawn.
14. Some of the nation's best racing horses are found in Kentucky and Virginia.
15. Lincoln was the best liked of all the Presidents.

B. Listen to radio programs or watch television for an hour. Then make a list of statements of fact and statements of opinion. Be ready to discuss this list in class, telling which of the statements of fact you think are verifiable and which questionable. Also be ready to tell whether any of the opinions were stated as if they were facts.

C. Write five statements of fact and five statements of opinion. Label your sentences as statements of fact or opinion. Then write at least three statements that might be either facts or opinions.

LISTENING FOR FALLACIES IN REASONING

Thinking about facts, ideas, or events in a systematic and logical way is called reasoning. You may make use of either *inductive* or *deductive* reasoning. In inductive reasoning you examine a number of specific instances and reason about them in order to arrive at a general truth or a conclusion. For example, you may conclude that a certain item of food was responsible for the food poisoning of a number of people, if all of the people who ate this item of food subsequently became ill, and if there was no other probable cause for their illness at that time. This is an example of inductive reasoning.

In deductive reasoning, you move from the general to the specific. In other words, you attempt to draw a conclusion about a specific instance by relating it to a general truth. An example of deductive reasoning might be as follows: There are many opportunities for jobs for those with a command of French and Spanish; therefore, since I have a command of French and Spanish, there should be many opportunities for me to get a job.

Arriving at an incorrect conclusion may be the result of accepting as a fact something that has not been proved to be a fact. It can also be caused by errors in reasoning about those facts—misinterpretation of facts or the way in which facts are related to each other. Such errors in reasoning are called *fallacies.*

Some of the more common fallacies in reasoning that you will hear will be presented in the pages that follow. Though each type differs in some ways from each of the others, you will notice that they seem quite similar. Each fallacy is, indeed, the result of insufficient or careless observation by the speaker, and/or his inability or unwillingness to consider in a logical manner all the factors affecting the conclusion.

False analogy

One of the most common errors is the assumption that because two persons, objects, or ideas are similar in one or more respects, they must necessarily be similar in some further way. For example, note the false analogy in this statement made by Tom: "Bill is eighteen and he drives a car to school. I'm eighteen, too, and I should therefore be allowed to drive a car to school." According to the statement, there is only one point of similarity between Tom and Bill—the fact that both are eighteen. In order to be a true analogy, there must be more points of similarity or there must be similarity in some important point. Also, points of difference should be unimportant ones.

In order to determine whether Tom should be allowed to drive, you would have to consider other characteristics and circumstances such as these: Perhaps Bill lives a greater distance from school than Tom does, and he may have no other means of transportation. On the other hand, Tom may live on a bus line that services his school, and others in his family may need the car for transportation to work. Also, Tom may not have learned to drive well, whereas Bill may have proved his ability as a driver. There are still other points to consider, such as the reliability of the boys and their ability to take responsibility.

In deciding whether an analogy is true or false, then, consider the following questions:

Are the persons or objects compared similar in more than one respect or in some important respect?

Are the points of difference unimportant ones?

Are the points of difference such as to invalidate the points of similarity?

Hasty generalization

A generalization is an effort to find the connection between facts that *seem* to be related. This kind of reasoning is an attempt to find causes for certain effects. As you may know, scientists make use of generalizations in their work. They observe, make tentative conclusions concerning their observations, and suspend judgment until they have had an opportunity to test their conclusions. It should be remembered, however, that it is easy to make errors in generalizations. Generalizations only point to probable truths; the conclusions reached in this way must be proved.

A common error, for example, is one in which a generalization is made too hastily. If, after talking with a few people from last year's class who disliked college, you were to say, "Everyone from last year's graduating class hates college," you would be making a hasty generalization. To make a conclusion such as this valid, everyone from the class who went to college would have to be queried and found to be unhappy. This is an example of a hasty generalization drawn from too few cases. By changing *Everyone* to *Some*, the conclusion may be made correct. That is, by limiting the statement to include just the ones who were interviewed and who said they were unhappy, the statement could be corrected.

Another example of a hasty generalization is this statement: "Believe nothing that you read in a newspaper. *The Daily Record* made five mistakes in reporting our last football game." As you can readily see, the faulty reporting of just one game by just one newspaper is not sufficient evidence upon which to base a conclusion about the kind of reporting found in all papers. It is not even enough to justify a sound conclusion about the reporting in *The Daily Record*.

In evaluating the worth of a generalization, it is helpful to keep the following questions in mind:

Are enough instances given to justify the conclusion that is reached?

Are the instances cited typical ones?

Are any exceptions cited, or are there any explanations for the exceptions?

False dilemma

The fallacy that is frequently referred to as a false dilemma consists of submitting only two choices when more choices exist, as in the statement, "If we can't have Mr. Stokes as our coach, the team just won't be any good." It isn't always easy to detect this kind of fallacy, since an important, or dramatic, factor is often singled out and said to be the *only* alternative to some disagreeable or undesirable situation. It is, of course, true that a coach usually has much to do with the success or failure of a team; but there are always other factors to be considered, too, such as the skill of the players themselves, their physical stamina, and their mental alertness, as well as the ability of the teams they meet.

It is especially difficult to detect a false dilemma if one's emotions become greatly involved. It is much more difficult to make the effort to find other possible alternatives, too. For example, a feeling of intense loyalty to the coach would make it difficult to try to think of other ways to avoid having a poor team.

Another example of a false dilemma is found in the statement "If you're not for me, you must be against me." It should be somewhat easier to detect the false dilemma in this statement. As you can easily see, the person being addressed may be neither for nor against the speaker, but completely neutral in his attitude toward him.

When you are offered only *one* way "out" of a situation, or when you have only two choices, it is a good plan to think very carefully to find out whether there are not more possibilities. There are, in fact, very few problems that can be resolved in only two ways.

Post hoc, ergo propter hoc

A fallacy which bears a Latin title *post hoc, ergo propter hoc,* meaning "after it, therefore because of it," refers to the incorrect assumption that because one event follows another, the first event is the cause of the second. Suppose that a friend of yours has been driving a beautiful new car recently and seems to have become very popular. You say that the new car is the cause of his new popularity. But there may be other factors involved; such factors are more difficult to see, however, if one is emotionally involved and is, as in this case, perhaps somewhat envious of the car. The car may be only one of many contributing factors such as your friend's pleasant disposition, his helpfulness, his friendliness, or other traits that would tend to make others seek his company. He may also have been more popular than you realized, but the new car seemed to call your attention to the fact.

Most of you can see the fallacy of saying that a piece of "hard luck" such as losing your billfold is the result of having broken a mirror. Such a statement is, of course, based on a superstition about the breaking of mirrors. But an example such as this may serve to help you remember a *post hoc* fallacy.

Begging the question

Begging the question consists of assuming, or taking for granted, that a statement has been proved when it has not. For example, this statement concerning the readers of a magazine begs the question. "Only the most intelligent people read our magazine. We know this because our magazine appeals only to the most intelligent people." What should be proved (that only the most intelligent people read their magazine) is stated as if it were already proved.

Equivocation

A fallacy in which different meanings of the same word are used in the same argument is known as equivocation. Notice that the words *fair* and *right* are used in widely different ways in each of the illustrative sentences below, thus invalidating the arguments that are based on other meanings of those words.

You say that you want to be *fair*.

You must admit that my candidate has a *fair* record; therefore you should vote for him.

I should do what is *right*.

It is my *right* to apply for a driver's license when I am sixteen.

Therefore I should apply for a driver's license when I am sixteen.

DEVELOPING YOUR SKILL

A. Read the false analogies in the following sentences and be ready to tell why they are fallacies.

1. This law has operated successfully in Pennsylvania; therefore, it should work just as effectively in Florida.
2. We should vote for John Smith for President because he is a self-educated man. After all, Abraham Lincoln, a self-educated man from the frontier, was one of our greatest Presidents.
3. In time of war a President who is in office should be re-elected, because it has been proved that it is unwise to change horses in the middle of a stream.
4. Most basketball players are tall. Therefore Ricky should make a good basketball player, since he is over six feet tall.

B. Be prepared to discuss the hasty generalizations below and explain the faulty reasoning in each.

1. I saw a high-school boy with his hat on at a school program last night, and this morning I saw a high-school girl comb her hair on the bus. The modern generation is certainly rude.
2. The governor was found guilty of accepting bribes. All politicians are crooks.
3. The best meal I ever ate was cooked by a French chef. Frenchmen are superb cooks.
4. They have more judges in their criminal courts in that city than we do. They must therefore have more crime than we have.

C. Identify the fallacy that is contained in each of the following statements. Be ready to discuss each fallacy and tell why it represents
an error in reasoning.

1. When I was in Italy, I heard several great Italian opera singers;
   Italians are great singers.
2. It is wrong to steal because it is not right to take things from others.
3. This town has grown and prospered during my administration;
   therefore, you should re-elect me as mayor.
4. I like Poe's "The Raven" because I always have liked poetry,
   and I particularly like Poe.
5. Waste not, want not.
6. I should get an "A" on my English theme; I spent as much time
   in research and writing as Sally did, and she got an "A."
7. Of course everyone in our class likes pizza; we didn't have any
   pizza left after our last class party, did we?
8. There were a lot of penalties given our opponents in last Saturday's game; everyone on that team cheated all the time in that
   game.
9. The Jones family just bought a big, new car; they must be very rich.
10. Unless we can take that trip to Yellowstone Park this summer, our
    vacation will be ruined.
11. To be a good sport, you must take an active part in sports of all
    kinds.
12. That football players are good students is shown by the fact that
    two members of our team are "A" students.

D. Write an example of each of the following fallacies in reasoning: false
analogy; false dilemma; hasty generalization; and *post hoc*.

Review Exercises—Critical Listening Skills

A. Be ready to discuss the following questions.

1. What kinds of facts are easily identified as facts? Tell why they are so
   easily identified.
2. How can you tell that a particular statement is an opinion? Give an
   example of a statement of opinion.
3. What is an example of a statement that might be either a statement of
   fact or an opinion?
4. Why is it a good plan to suspend judgment about a conclusion concerning
   any important subject?

B. Write answers to the following questions.

1. How can you determine whether an analogy is true or false?
2. Why is the following an example of a hasty generalization: "I wasn't invited to last night's party; I'll always be left out"?
3. What is a false dilemma? What is an illustration of one?
4. What well-known superstition also illustrates the *post hoc* fallacy?
5. What is an example of the fallacy called *begging the question?*
6. What is equivocation? Give an example of this fallacy.

2. Detecting Propaganda

All ambitions are lawful except those which climb upward on the miseries or credulities of mankind.

—JOSEPH CONRAD

As defined by the Institute for Propaganda Analysis, an agency that was formed to study propaganda and to help the public analyze it, propaganda is an ". . . expression of opinion or action by individuals or groups deliberately designed to influence opinions and actions. . . ." In a sense, then, each of us is at times a propagandist of sorts. In a broad sense, whenever we try to influence someone to accept our point of view or to take some action that we advocate, we are propagandizing. By means of propaganda worthy goals are often achieved, such as the raising of money for charity or other worthwhile purposes. Some propaganda, however, is used to accomplish unworthy goals by the use of unscrupulous methods. Some of the decisions that you make and the opinions that you form are relatively unimportant; others, though, are of such importance that your whole life may be affected by them.

The degree to which a given message is able to influence the ideas or opinions of listeners or to move them to action is dependent upon factors other than just the strength of the message itself and the skill with which it is projected, though these are important. The situation of the listener at the time he hears the message and his predisposition toward the message also influence its effectiveness. The situation includes such factors as time and place, whether the listener is alone or with others, the attitudes of those who are with him, and similar conditions. The predisposition of the listener toward the message is affected by his needs, ideals, and values, as well as by his education and background of experience—in short, everything that makes him what he is can have an effect on the way an individual is likely to react to a particular message. Clever propagandists make good use of mood and occasion, as well as what they know about the needs, interests, curiosities, fears, doubts, habits of thought, and, often, the ignorance of their listeners.

To protect yourself against being unduly influenced by the rising tide of propaganda that beats against your ears incessantly, you must learn to recognize some of the methods that are frequently used by propagandists.

PROPAGANDA DEVICES

Propagandists know that it is easier for people to react emotionally to a statement than to "think it through"; they also know that many people are disinclined to think carefully, or to think very much at all, about what they hear. They are apt to *react* rather than to *think*. Thus, in much of the propaganda that you will need to analyze, there is an attempt to divert your attention from a logical, calm consideration of the facts by appeals to your emotions. Also, propaganda is often based upon fallacious reasoning.

Emotionally charged and "slanted" words

By his very choice of words, a propagandist can remind you of something pleasant or unpleasant, and in this way influence you for or against a person, group, or idea. Unless you are on your guard, a clever propagandist can manipulate your feelings much like a puppeteer manipulates his puppets, pulling certain wires and causing you to react in just the way he wishes.

Words such as *house, theorem,* or *pencil* are words without emotional tone. That is, they do not stimulate any feelings. Words such as *honor, friend,* and *home* have emotional tone. They are said to be emotionally charged. These words are positively charged; but some may be negatively charged.

As you read the following sentences, note the emotionally charged words in the second and third sentences.

The man refused to change his mind.
The man steadfastly refused to change his mind.
The man obstinately refused to change his mind.

The first statement is a factual report of what took place. In the second statement the word *steadfastly* has a favorable emotional tone and is positively charged. The word *obstinately* in the third statement has an unfavorable emotional tone and is negatively charged.

Consider also the varying effects produced by the following three statements concerning the group that heard a campaign speech.

A *large audience* heard Senator Smith last night.
A *small crowd* heard Senator Smith last night.
A *few hundred people assembled in the huge auditorium* to hear Senator Smith last night.

Each of these statements gives a different picture. To find out which statement is a factual report and which are slanted, you would have to know how many actually were in the audience. *Large* and *small* may express opinions, since what seems large to one person may seem small to another. An example of a factual statement might be the following: Five hundred people (or approximately five hundred people) heard Senator Smith last night.

As a critical listener, you must always be on the alert to recognize the difference between objective, factual statements and statements that are emotionally charged or slanted.

Other commonly used propaganda devices

One method of appealing to your emotions is the use of *name-calling*. In this method the propagandist uses a bad tag or label to encourage you to reject a certain person, group, or idea without taking the trouble to do much, if any, thinking. For example, a propagandist may call someone an apple-polisher, a perfectionist, a slave-driver, or an obstructionist. The names vary with times and places, but an appeal is frequently made either to people's prejudices, their hates, or their fears.

To divert your attention from a close examination of the issues in question and to persuade you to accept or approve a certain person, group, or idea, a propagandist may make use of *glib generalities* such as "man of peace" or similar words suggesting positive ideals or generally accepted principles.

At other times, the propagandist may make use of *transfer* to cause you to accept or reject something. A person, group, or idea generally considered as being worthy is associated with the person, idea, or group that the propagandist wishes you to accept unquestioningly. He may say, for example, "My candidate, *like Lincoln,* believes . . . . " Disapproval also may be transferred. A political leader, for example, may be compared with a despot or a dictator. To sell a product, an advertiser may try to transfer prestige, authority, or sanction to his product in various ways. A connection may be made, for example, between a pretty girl and the kind of lipstick that she is wearing.

By the *stacking of arguments* a propagandist may sometimes try to convince you of something; that is, he may select only those facts, false statements, or half-truths that give the best or the worst possible case for or against a person, group, product, or program.

The *common touch,* or the *plain folks* theme, is frequently used during political campaigns, when it seems advantageous to seem to be "just plain folks." A candidate is likely to say that he enjoys some common or simple foods such as hot dogs or some inexpensive methods of entertainment in order to identify himself with the common people, at least superficially.

Often a propagandist may make use of almost everyone's wish to be on the winning side. He may lead you to think that "everyone" is buying this or that, is voting in a certain way, or is in favor of this or that policy. He encourages you to get on the *bandwagon.*

A knowledge of these commonly used propaganda devices should be helpful to you in keeping yourself from being unduly influenced in forming your opinions and in making your decisions. Once you become aware that a speaker is using one or more of these devices, you can separate the device from the idea and judge the idea on its own merits.

 DEVELOPING YOUR SKILL

A. To find out your own attitude toward certain words, arrange the following words in two columns—those that are positively and those that are negatively charged. Be ready to discuss in class the reasons for your arrangement.

colleague	conservative	dictator
middle-of-the-roader	statesman	spendthrift
social climber	politician	pal
progressive	patriot	radical

B. In your television and radio listening, find examples of the use of *transfer* as a propaganda technique, and be ready to discuss them in class. Explain in each instance whether the transfer was intended to create a favorable or an unfavorable reaction.

C. Be prepared to explain how a speaker makes use of the technique of the stacking of arguments and to give an example of this technique, either one that you make up or one that you have heard.

D. List several examples of propaganda that you hear on television and radio (commercials, political speeches, fund-raising campaign speeches, inspirational talks) and be ready to analyze them in class. You may wish to use questions such as the following to help you.

1. Exactly what is each example trying to make you think or do?
2. Is it for your own good, the good of the people generally, or the good of a few people that you are encouraged to think or do what the propaganda urges or implies?
3. Which examples are subtle in their appeal, and which are obvious?

E. Listen to speeches on television or radio and try to find examples of one or all of the following propaganda techniques: the stacking of arguments; the common touch, or plain folks; glib generalities; name-calling; transfer; or bandwagon. Be prepared to discuss the effectiveness of these techniques as they were employed.

F. Write a short paragraph in which you try to use completely objective words, with no emotional overtones in any of the words. Then ask someone to read your paragraph and point out any such words that you may have included.

G. Select three commonly used propaganda devices and explain them. Give an example of each device.

DRAWING CONCLUSIONS AND MAKING DECISIONS

Fortunately, the ability to make sound evaluations is one that can be cultivated. As you acquire a larger background of experience upon which to base your judgments, and as you gain skill in logical thinking, you should be able to make increasingly better evaluations. As you learn from past errors in judgment, you will form the habit of suspending judgment about matters of importance until you have ample opportunity to investigate thoroughly various opinions and the reliability of sources of information. You will find, too, that certain habits and attitudes are helpful to you.

Controlling subjective factors

It is worthwhile to ask yourself whether or not you are not being completely objective about what you are listening to. That is, are you being impersonal in your judgments, or are you allowing subjective factors such as emotional attitudes or personal bias to influence your judgments? You may know from your own experience how easily you can accept the opinion of someone whom you admire greatly, or how easily you can disagree with an opinion you do not want to hear. To arrive at sound conclusions, you must learn to separate the argument from the person stating it. You must also avoid enlarging the importance of arguments that you approve of, and minimizing the importance of those arguments that you do not like.

Another roadblock to making sound evaluations and drawing valid conclusions is inertia. Many people do not wish to take the trouble to examine facts carefully or search for additional facts that might be pertinent. But to reach a sound conclusion, hard work is often needed.

One of the first steps in arriving at sound conclusions should be to evaluate one's own habits of thought. It is essential not only to cultivate an attitude of suspended judgment, but also to control the subjective factors that could lead you astray.

Some criteria for evaluating what you hear

In trying to come to a logical and sound conclusion about the worth of what you hear, it will be helpful to ask yourself the following questions:

1. Who is the speaker? Does he have a reputation for clear thinking and honesty?

2. What is the speaker's purpose? Does he state frankly at the outset what his purpose is in making the speech?

3. Does the speaker make references to the sources of his information so that the facts that are stated can be checked?

4. Does he give a well-rounded presentation, or does he omit important facets of a problem?

5. Does the speaker label his opinions as opinions, or does he state them as if they were facts?

6. Does he support his opinion with facts and sound reasons, or does he resort to fallacies or half-truths?

7. Is the speaker consistent throughout his speech?

8. Does he play upon your sympathies or prejudices?

9. Does the speaker let you form your own opinions, or does he try to hurry you into accepting his opinions and conclusions? Does he try to frighten you?

10. Are you being fair and maintaining an objective attitude? Are you taking the trouble to make sure of your facts and the correctness of your reasoning?

> DEVELOPING YOUR SKILL

    A. Be ready to discuss some subjective factors that can influence your decisions and opinions.

    B. The class may decide upon a particular speech that they wish to listen to on television or radio. The members of the class may write an evaluation of the speech, using the criteria suggested on page 41.

Review Exercises—Detecting Propaganda

A. Listen to slogans, generalizations, or frequently repeated statements that you hear while listening to television and radio. Make a list of them and be ready to explain the propaganda techniques used in each.

B. Write a speech in which you use one or more of the propaganda techniques that were presented in this chapter.

C. Read accounts of several national political campaigns and select at least three slogans that were used. Write an explanation of the propaganda device used in each slogan.

UNIT SUMMARY

In this unit you have seen why it is important for you to cultivate your ability to listen critically, and you have studied in some detail the skills that are needed to come to sound conclusions about what you hear. You have learned how to distinguish fact from opinion, and you have studied examples of the more common fallacies of reasoning and the more common propaganda techniques. You have also learned the importance of suspending judgment about conclusions and of maintaining an objective attitude while you search for pertinent facts and for information concerning the reliability of those facts.

UNIT REVIEW EXERCISES

DISCUSSION TOPICS

A. Explain the relationship of the following statement of John Dryden to the development of critical listening skills: "With what ease believe we what we wish!"

B. Tell some subjective factors you must control to arrive at sound conclusions.

C. What types of personalities are most likely to be influenced by propaganda? Be ready to give reasons for your answers.

D. Explain each of the following fallacies in reasoning:

1. False analogy	4. *Post hoc, ergo propter hoc*
2. False dilemma	5. Begging the question
3. Hasty generalization	6. Equivocation

E. What are seven commonly used propaganda techniques? Give examples.

F. What are some criteria by which you can judge the worth of a speech?

WRITTEN WORK

A. Write an explanation of the difference between a statement of fact and a statement of an opinion, and give an illustration of each.

B. Explain why propaganda that is based on half-truths is so dangerous.

C. Write a definition of the word *propaganda*.

D. Write a short composition on one of the following subjects:

The Most Persuasive Speech I Have Ever Heard
Uses I Have Made of Propaganda
How I Resist Propaganda
Propaganda in the Movies

VOCABULARY

Some of the words in this unit may have been new to you. To help you remember their meanings, they are used here in different contexts. Write the numbers 1 to 5 on a sheet of paper. After each number, write the letter of the word or phrase that can best be substituted for the italicized word in each sentence. Before making your choice, find the word on the page indicated to see how the word is used in the unit.

1. The lovable professor was also known for his *proficiency* in several languages.   [p. 25]
   (*a*) knowledge; (*b*) adaptability; (*c*) experience; (*d*) superior competency

2. The investigator's *assumption* proved to be correct.   [p. 31]
   (*a*) supposition; (*b*) forecast; (*c*) calculation; (*d*) computation

3. The witness for the prosecution testified that the defendant was *unscrupulous*.   [p. 35]
   (*a*) disloyal; (*b*) unprincipled; (*c*) unfair; (*d*) careless

4. The orator played upon the *credulities* of the people.   [p. 35]
   (*a*) laziness; (*b*) pet beliefs; (*c*) inclination to believe; (*d*) generosity

5. The noise from the street sounded *incessantly* in our ears.   [p. 36]
   (*a*) loudly; (*b*) unceasingly; (*c*) intermittently; (*d*) intolerably

Spelling

These words appeared in this unit or were included in this list because they are often misspelled. Study each word carefully so that you will be able to write all the words correctly when they are dictated to you.

1. proficiency
2. assumption
3. unscrupulous
4. credulities
5. incessantly
6. incoherence
7. facet
8. scrutiny
9. equivocation
10. slogan
11. advocate
12. incompetent
13. predisposition
14. disinclined
15. manipulates
16. obstructionist
17. theorem
18. advantageous
19. fanatical
20. isolationist

UNIT SELF-TEST

1. Explain the difference between a statement of fact and a statement of opinion and give an example of each.
2. List at least five criteria for judging the worth of a speech.
3. Name and explain seven commonly-used propaganda techniques.
4. Explain why you should question the worth of an opinion that gives you only two choices.
5. What is a false analogy? Give an example of one.
6. Why should you seriously question the integrity of a speaker who tries to hurry you into making a decision on a matter of some importance?
7. What are some habits and attitudes that help you to arrive at sound conclusions?
8. What is the fallacy that is called equivocation? Give an example of it.
9. What habits of thought and common weaknesses are made use of by some propagandists?
10. Give an example of a false dilemma.
11. How can you recognize a hasty generalization?
12. Explain the fallacy that is known by the name of *post hoc*.
13. Explain what is meant by *begging the question*.
14. Give an example of propaganda used for worthy purposes.
15. Why is it important to suspend judgment on decisions about matters of some importance?

Unit 3

Speeches to Persuade

"Hello, old chap, you got to work, hey?"

Tom wheeled suddenly and said:

"Why, it's you Ben! I warn't noticing."

"Say—I'm going in a-swimming, *I* am. Don't you wish *you* could? But of course you'd druther *work*—wouldn't you? Course you would!"

Tom contemplated the boy a bit, and said:

"What do you call work?"

"Why ain't *that* work?"

Tom resumed his whitewashing, and answered carelessly:

"Well, maybe it is, and maybe it ain't. All I know is, it suits Tom Sawyer."

"Oh, come, now, you don't mean to let on that you *like* it?"

The brush continued to move.

"Like it? Well, I don't see why I oughtn't to like it. Does a boy get a chance to whitewash a fence every day?"

That put the thing in a new light. . . .

This familiar episode from Mark Twain's *The Adventures of Tom Sawyer* is an example of *persuasion*—the means by which an audience is made to change its thinking or its conduct. Tom Sawyer persuaded Ben and the other boys that what they had thought of as *work* was actually a *privilege*. By the end of the day, you will remember, the fence had three coats of whitewash on it, and Tom had accumulated a store of small boys' treasures. Tom Sawyer knew his audience and used—at a personal level—the techniques of persuasion that would be most likely to appeal to his audience. He depended not only on the use of persuasive language but also on tone, gesture, and attitude.

Persuasion may be as simple as Tom Sawyer's approach, or it may be as complex as speeches to influence national and international policy. Its appeal may be directed to the intellect or to the emotions—or to both. Persuasion is found in conversations between individuals, in group discussions, and in public addresses. It is the language of the man trying to sell a product, of the congressman running for re-election, and of the lawyer defending a life. In this unit the term *persuasion* is used to mean any kind of speech whose purpose is to influence the thinking or actions of an audience.

  CHECK YOURSELF

The following questions will help you to determine how much you already know about the techniques of persuasion. After you have answered the questions, your teacher will give you the correct answers and will discuss them with you.

1. What is the fundamental aim of all persuasion?
2. What is the general purpose of a Mother's Day speech?
3. What is the general purpose of a debate speech?
4. What is the general purpose of a sales talk?
5. What two factors, other than the general purpose, determine the speaker's approach to his subject?
6. What speaking device depends upon pleasant associations?
7. What speaking device uses unpleasant associations?
8. What is the name given to the speaking device that depends upon the prestige and experience of well-known persons for its effect?
9. What speaking device works to make people act together?
10. What are the two basic types of appeals used in persuasion?

1. Planning Your Speech

The story is told that two Chinese laborers were engaged in a heated argument. A visitor standing in the crowd that surrounded the disputants expressed surprise that the men hadn't come to blows. "Ah," said an old Chinese gentleman, "but the one who strikes the first blow will have admitted that he has run out of ideas."

Persuasion is accomplished through the exchange of ideas, not through force. A successful speaker, then, cannot afford to "run out of ideas"; he must hold clearly in mind the purpose of his speech and must have at his command sufficient material, well organized and interestingly presented, to achieve his purpose.

PURPOSE

Speeches to persuade usually have one or more of three general purposes: *to stimulate an audience, to convince an audience,* or *to motivate an audience to take action.* The speech to stimulate is aimed primarily at the emotions. Its goal is usually the revitalizing of an existing emotion or the substitution of one emotion for another. The speech to convince is aimed primarily at the intellect. Its goal is usually the acceptance of a belief or a policy. The speech to motivate an audience to action may arouse emotions and may deal with beliefs. Its immediate goal, however, is direct action.

Commencement speeches, patriotic speeches, and speeches at pep rallies, reunions, and similar occasions usually have stimulation as their goal. The commencement speaker seeks to impress upon his audience the values of education and the high goals for which the graduates should strive. The speaker at a patriotic rally exhorts his listeners to rededicate their allegiance to flag and country. Even the cheerleaders at school pep rallies act as persuaders by appealing to the loyalty and school spirit of the student body. When listening to speeches whose purpose is to stimulate, audiences are aroused to feel deeply about the speaker's subject.

The debater, the attorney building a court case, the political speaker, the head of a government justifying his government's policy—all these speakers use persuasion to convince. They may be dealing with beliefs that are not accepted by the audience, beliefs for which the speakers seek acceptance; they may be dealing with disputed ideas about which an audience is as yet undecided; or they may be dealing with strongly held convictions that they want to change. Since the speech to convince is primarily concerned with ideas—beliefs and policies—the appeal must be made largely to the intellect through logic and evidence.

Every day you are exposed to persuasion whose purpose is to motivate you to take action. You are urged to buy various products, to read specific newspapers, magazines, and books, to visit diverse parts of the country and the world, to join organizations, to vote, to watch, to listen, to believe, to disbelieve, to accept, to reject, and so on. These appeals are often directed to the emotions and may be directed to the intellect, as well. The difference between persuasion to motivate to action and persuasion to stimulate or to convince lies not in the type of appeal made but, rather, in the immediate goal. The speech to motivate to action must, to be successful, result in the specific desired action rather than in the general—and sometimes delayed—response that frequently results from the other types of persuasion.

The differences among the three types of persuasion may be more clearly defined by noting the result of each kind of persuasion as applied to the same situation. In the city of X, a large group of people in the low-income bracket are forced to live in crowded, unsanitary slums. The speech to stimulate would arouse the concern of the audience for the plight of the people forced by circumstance to live in such conditions. The speech to convince would persuade the audience that there is a need for legislation to provide for the alleviation of the situation. The speech to motivate to action would press for the appropriation of funds to provide adequate housing for the people concerned.

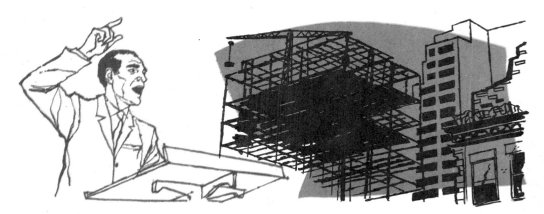

A. Discuss the three kinds of persuasion and the goal of each. Cite examples of situations in which each kind of persuasion might be used.

B. Each of the following statements is to be considered the central theme of a persuasive speech. Read the statement and decide whether the purpose of the speech, is (*a*) to stimulate, (*b*) to convince, or (*c*) to motivate to take action.

1. Your ten dollars a month will provide support for a needy child.
2. Compact cars are more economical to operate than larger models.
3. These men gave their lives for democracy.
4. Man is inspired by the beauty of nature.
5. More stringent laws are needed to control highway traffic.
6. Larry MacArthur's qualifications make him the outstanding candidate for class president.
7. Don't let yourself be misled by the false promises of Mr. Blank.
8. A career in the military service offers many educational and vocational opportunities.
9. On the basis of the evidence you have heard, you have no choice but to find the defendant guilty as charged.
10. As you look back on your four years at Lakeland High School, you will remember these years as among the happiest and most profitable of your life.

C. Listen to recordings of famous speeches. One good source is the album called "I Can Hear It Now" arranged by Edward R. Murrow and Fred Friendly. Determine the basic purpose of each of the speeches to which you listen. If recordings are not available, your teacher may wish to have several students read speeches from the collections in your library.

APPROACH

Before a speaker can prepare an effective persuasive speech, he must analyze the occasion on which he is to speak and the audience to whom he will speak. The purpose of the occasion, the physical characteristics of the place in which the speech is to be given, the place of the speech in the program, the significance of the occasion, and the background and attitude of the audience are factors that will affect the content of the speech.

The following questions will help you decide what approaches to take when preparing a persuasive speech.

1. What is the specific purpose of the occasion?

A speech, to be effective, must conform with the basic purpose of the occasion. Find out, for example, whether the occasion is a dedication, a reunion, a testimonial, the start of a charity campaign, a school budget hearing, or a political rally. Be sure the content of your speech does not violate the basic purpose of the occasion.

2. What are the physical characteristics of the place in which the speech is to be given?

A speaker's approach to his subject will vary according to whether his speech is to be given indoors or outdoors, in a large auditorium or in a small room, in a face-to-face situation or on radio or television. Try to find out whether the appointments in the place in which you are to speak will help you to achieve the response you want or whether they will work against you. For example, an audience that is seated on comfortable chairs in a beautifully appointed room may find it difficult to identify themselves with the homeless and the needy—unless the speaker uses the luxury of the surroundings to point up the contrast.

3. What is the place of the speech in the program?

Before you prepare your speech, you will want to know whether there are other speakers or whether you are to be the only speaker. If there are to be other speakers, determine the significance of their speeches in relation to yours. Is yours to be the major speech or a supporting speech, or are all the speeches of equal significance? Will you be the first speaker or the last? What else has been planned for the program? What effect will the rest of the program have on the response you wish to achieve?

4. Does the occasion have significance beyond its immediate purpose?

Sometimes, the immediate purpose of an occasion is only a part of a broader purpose. For example, a testimonial banquet is given to honor someone for outstanding service or achievement. If that is the sole purpose of the occasion, the speeches would undoubtedly be limited to laudatory comments about the guest of honor's achievements in his particular field. On the other hand, the testimonial banquet might be a means of bringing to the attention of the public not only the man's accomplishments in his field but also those qualities that would make him a good candidate for public office.

When the occasion does have a larger significance, the speaker's approach depends upon factors beyond the immediate purpose. He must know what the larger significance is, who, besides the audience, may be interested in the occasion, and whether the audience senses the extended significance of the occasion.

5. What is the response of the audience likely to be?

In order to achieve the response you want, you must find out as much as possible about your potential audience before composing your speech. A good persuasive speech must be directed to the fundamental wants of mankind: comfort, security, and safety; recognition, dignity, and self-respect; curiosity and adventure; reverence for something higher than himself—hero worship, tradition, the Deity. Try to find out enough about the background of your audience to determine to which of the fundamental wants your appeal should be aimed.

The attitude of the audience toward the speaker, the topic, and the occasion will affect the persuader's approach to the speech. If the speaker is well known and has proved himself, he will probably find the audience ready to listen to him. If the speaker is unknown, he will have to convince the audience of his abilities, in addition to persuading the audience to accept his ideas.

The most successful speakers are usually those who learn as much as they can about the attitude of the audience toward the topic and the occasion and then develop their speeches in terms of what they have learned. Audience attitudes fall into four general categories: favorable, indifferent, doubtful, and opposed. It is not likely that all the members of an audience will have exactly the same attitude, but if you can determine the prevailing attitude, you can plan the development of your speech more effectively.

An analysis of the factors that help determine your approach to a persuasive speech is not always easy, but it is sufficiently important to the success of your speech to be worth the time and effort involved. Information about the occasion, the physical characteristics of the place, the program, and the significance of the occasion can usually be learned from the person who extends the invitation to speak. Persons associated with the organization or the group arranging the occasion can usually tell you something about the audience to whom you will speak.

DEVELOPING YOUR SKILL

    A. Discuss the following statement: "Before a speaker can prepare an effective persuasive speech, he must analyze the occasion on which he is to speak and the audience to whom he will speak." In your discussion consider the various aspects of the analysis, the purposes of the analysis, and the methods of getting information.

    B. Select a topic for a persuasive speech. Write a statement of purpose for the speech and tell for what occasion the speech is to be prepared. Then list the five questions for analysis that were discussed in this section of the unit. Under each question indicate the procedures you would follow in carrying out that aspect of your analysis of the occasion and the audience. .

Review Exercises—Planning Your Speech

A. Write the numbers from 1 to 3 on a sheet of paper. After each number write the general purpose of the kind of persuasion that would be used in the situation described.

    1. A TV announcer presenting a commercial
    2. A minister preaching a sermon
    3. A speaker defending the proposition that every high-school student should take part in some extracurricular activity

B. Write a composition in which you discuss the importance of analyzing the occasion and the audience before composing a persuasive speech. Include in your discussion the specific aspects that must be considered when you make such an analysis.

2. Composing the Speech

DEVICES

The fundamental aim of persuasion is to influence the thinking or actions of others. Four basic devices are used by speakers to achieve this aim: the acceptance device, the rejection device, the testimonial device, and the bandwagon device. Speeches to persuade may include any one or any combination of these devices.

The four basic devices used in persuasion are geared to trigger automatic acceptance or rejection responses in listeners. They are directed to the fundamental wants of mankind and are based upon symbols and word connotations that are common to most people. These devices are usually used honestly and sincerely; unfortunately, they are sometimes used dishonestly and insincerely. Learning how these devices are applied will not only help you to compose speeches of persuasion but will also enable you to analyze persuasion techniques that are directed at you. Once you understand the devices of persuasion, you will be better protected against their use for dishonest purposes and will recognize their value in persuasion for beneficial purposes.

Persuasion by means of the acceptance device uses words and symbols that have pleasant associations: *mother, devotion, love, kindness, humility, confidence, security, prestige,* and so on. Any symbol that automatically evokes a pleasant picture may be employed as an acceptance device. Franklin D. Roosevelt's now famous "Four Freedoms" message to Congress employs the acceptance device. It is filled with words and promises whose connotations are pleasant. The following excerpt is taken from this address. Notice particularly the expressions in italics.

> In the *future days, which we seek to make secure,* we look forward to a world *founded upon four essential human freedoms.* The first is *freedom of speech and expression*—everywhere in the world. The second is *freedom of every person to worship God in his own way*—everywhere in the world. The third is *freedom from want . . .* everywhere in the world. The fourth is *freedom from fear . . .* anywhere in the world.
>
> —FRANKLIN D. ROOSEVELT, "Message to Congress," January 6, 1941

However, this device can have an ultimate effect opposite to the one intended if the fair words and promises are not proved through performance. For example, the man who has been persuaded to vote for a tax increase in the belief that the higher taxes will provide for community improvements, will, in the future, react unfavorably to the promise of "community improvements" if the original promise is not kept. In this way terms that have pleasant connotations may develop unpleasant connotations. In the same way words that have unpleasant connotations may develop pleasant associations. The word *science* is a good example of this kind of change. At one time all things scientific were associated with black magic and evil. Today *science* is associated with accepted, approved, and beneficial methods.

The rejection device uses words and symbols whose unpleasant associations will cause the listener automatically to reject the idea or thing that the persuader wants him to reject. Words such as *rattlesnake, poison, scorpion, germs,* and *carbon monoxide* suggest danger, disease, and death. Symbols such as a skull and crossbones and a flashing red light warn of danger. As a result of the use of the rejection device, people have been saved from trouble, injury, and even death.

In the hands of a dishonest or insincere persuader, the rejection device may endanger the well-being of individuals or of large groups of people. This misuse of the rejection device is sometimes evident in political campaigns when words such as *liberal, Tory, plutocrat,* and *capitalist* are used in such a manner as to insinuate that certain candidates are dangerous to the welfare of the community, the state, or the nation.

Individuals are protected by the libel and slander laws against the flagrant misuse of the rejection device. However, these laws cannot protect groups of people or ideas. It was for this reason that Hitler, for example, could successfully carry out his hate campaigns. By using words that triggered the automatic responses he desired, he was able to win the support of people of all economic and educational backgrounds.

The testimonial device is one with which you are probably familiar. The persuader using this device cites testimonials—supporting evidence —of well-known persons to give prestige to the point of view he is expressing. When the testimonial is based upon actual experience, it is a helpful and valid device. In this sense testimonials are reports made by persons whose background and experience qualify them to judge the worth of a product, an idea, or a belief.

Sometimes, however, the testimonial device is misused and must be closely analyzed. By what authority does the baseball star say that a particular hair tonic is the best on the market? Has he tried all the hair tonics available? Do his background and experience qualify him to judge hair tonics? The example given here does not illustrate a serious misuse of the testimonial device, but it does point up the ease with which the word of well-known persons can influence the public. Advertisers would not use such testimony were it not effective.

The fourth device used in persuasion—the bandwagon device—is used to influence mass action. It is the device of causes and crusades. At a simpler level it is the device used by cheerleaders at a football game. By getting masses of people to act together, the persuader hopes to achieve his purpose. He may be successful—as Susan B. Anthony was in her fight for women's suffrage—or he may be unsuccessful—as political parties often are in promoting their candidates. It is only when people have the same responses to the persuader's proposals or ideas that the bandwagon technique is successful. The persuader's goal determines whether the device is good or evil. In the hands of a Hitler, the bandwagon device results in catastrophe; in the hands of a persuader dedicated to good, it may result in reforms and a better way of life.

DEVELOPING YOUR SKILL

A. Read the following excerpt carefully and then point out and discuss the devices Marc Antony used to persuade his audience.

ANTONY. Friends, Romans, countrymen, lend me your ears;
I come to bury Caesar, not to praise him.
The evil that men do lives after them;
The good is oft interred with their bones;
So let it be with Caesar. The noble Brutus
Hath told you Caesar was ambitious:
If it were so, it was a grievous fault,
And grievously hath Caesar answer'd it.
Here, under leave of Brutus and the rest,—
For Brutus is an honourable man;
So are they all, all honourable men;
Come I to speak in Caesar's funeral.
He was my friend, faithful and just to me:
But Brutus says he was ambitious;
And Brutus is an honourable man.
He hath brought many captives home to Rome,
Whose ransoms did the general coffers fill:
Did this in Caesar seem ambitious?
When that the poor have cried, Caesar hath wept:

Ambition should be made of sterner stuff:
Yet Brutus says he was ambitious;
And Brutus is an honourable man.
You all did see that on the Lupercal
I thrice presented him a kingly crown,
Which he did thrice refuse: was this ambition?
Yet Brutus says he was ambitious;
And, sure, he is an honourable man.
I speak not to disprove what Brutus spoke,
But here I am to speak what I do know.
You all did love him once, not without cause:
What cause withholds you then to mourn for him?
O judgment; thou art fled to brutish beasts,
And men have lost their reason. Bear with me;
My heart is in the coffin there with Caesar,
And I must pause till it come back to me.

 FIRST CITIZEN. Methinks there is much reason in his sayings.

 SECOND CITIZEN. If you consider rightly of the matter, Caesar
has had great wrong.

 THIRD CITIZEN. Has he, masters?
I fear there will a worse come in his place.

 FOURTH CITIZEN. Mark'd ye his words? He would not take the
crown;
Therefore 'tis certain he was not ambitious.

 FIRST CITIZEN. If it be found so, some will dear abide it.

 SECOND CITIZEN. Poor soul! his eyes are red as fire with weeping.

 THIRD CITIZEN. There's not a nobler man in Rome than Antony.

 FOURTH CITIZEN. Now mark him, he begins again to speak.

 ANTONY. But yesterday the word of Caesar might
Have stood against the world: now lies he there,
And none so poor to do him reverence.
O masters, if I were disposed to stir
Your hearts and minds to mutiny and rage,
I should do Brutus wrong and Cassius wrong
Who, you all know, are honourable men.

I will not do them wrong; I rather choose
To wrong the dead, to wrong myself and you,
Than I will wrong such honourable men.
But here's a parchment with the seal of Caesar;
I found it in his closet; 'tis his will:
Let but the commons hear this testament—
Which pardon me, I do not mean to read—
And they would go and kiss dead Caesar's wounds
And dip their napkins in his sacred blood,
Yea, beg a hair of him for memory,
And, dying, mention it within their wills,
Bequeathing it as a rich legacy
Unto their issue.

FOURTH CITIZEN. We'll hear the will; read it, Marc Antony.

ALL: The will, the will! we will hear Caesar's will.

—WILLIAM SHAKESPEARE, *Julius Caesar*

B. Decide on a topic for a speech to persuade. Write the topic on a sheet of paper and write a statement indicating the occasion for which the speech is to be given and the purpose of the speech. Then list as many of the four devices as could be used in achieving your purpose. Illustrate each of the devices you list by writing a sentence or two in which you show how you would use the device.

DEVELOPMENT

The development of a speech to persuade depends upon the purpose of the speech and upon your analysis of the occasion and the audience. When these steps have been completed, you are ready to gather material and outline the speech. The techniques involved in gathering material and in outlining are those you have learned to use when doing research. In the preparation of a speech to persuade, interviews and correspondence are sometimes used as sources of information more often than they are in preparing other types of discourse.

As you prepare your speech, keep your purpose clearly in mind. Every idea and every device you use must lead directly to the purpose you want to achieve. Find out what time limit has been set for your speech and work within that limit. List all the points you would like to make and then cut less important ideas until you have only the number of key points that can be developed in the time allotted to you.

As was discussed in the section on the purpose of speeches to persuade, the aim of the speech to stimulate is to arouse an emotional response in the audience. To achieve such a response the speaker will have to include appeals to the emotions and basic wants of his audience. When composing a speech to stimulate, you must first determine, through audience analysis, what motivates that particular audience most strongly. That motive or attitude or emotion should then be the direct appeal of the speech. All other appeals should contribute to achieving the desired response.

Do not overlook the importance of logic and of factual material in the speech to stimulate. Statistics, examples, comparisons and contrasts, and authoritative testimony are frequently the bases upon which speeches to stimulate are built. Statistics to prove that automobile accidents claim more lives than do wars are sure to achieve an emotional response. A factual comparison of the amout of food a Korean orphan receives daily as opposed to the amount consumed by an American child is filled with emotional appeal. Weave together emotional and factual material so as to achieve the purpose of your speech.

Since the speech to convince aims to make an audience accept, reject, or change a belief, its chief appeal must be to the intellect rather than to the emotions. The speech to convince must be developed through strong evidence and logical reasoning.

The first step in composing a speech to convince is the statement of the proposition to be developed in the speech. After the proposition has been clearly defined, the materials for the speech are developed as for a debate: determine the main issues of the speech, state your contentions in terms of those issues, gather material to support your contentions, and outline or brief the speech.

Although the predominant appeal of the speech to convince is based on logic, do not overlook the importance of appeals to the emotions. It may be necessary to demonstrate to the audience that their personal wants will be advanced by the proposition you are developing.

The speech to motivate to action should also be developed through appeals both to the emotions and the intellect. Remember that the goal of such a speech is to make the audience take definite action. The materials, then, should be so developed as to result in the immediate desired action. All the appeals must be clearly directed to this goal.

 DEVELOPING YOUR SKILL

A. The occasion of the following speech was the acceptance of the Nobel Prize for literature. Read the speech and then answer the questions that follow it.

I feel that this award was not made to me as a man, but to my work—a life's work in the agony and sweat of the human spirit, not for glory and least of all for profit, but to create out of the materials of the human spirit something which did not exist before. So this award is only mine in trust. It will not be difficult to find a dedication for the money part of it commensurate with the purpose and significance of its origin. But I would like to do the same with the acclaim too, by using this moment as a pinnacle from which I might be listened to by the young men and women already dedicated to the same anguish and travail, among whom is already that one who will some day stand where I am standing.

Our tragedy today is a general and universal physical fear so long sustained by now that we can even bear it. There are no longer problems of the spirit. There is only the question: When will I be blown up? Because of this, the young man or woman writing today has forgotten the problems of the human heart in conflict with itself which alone can make good writing because only that is worth writing about, worth the agony and the sweat.

He must learn them again. He must teach himself that the basest of all things is to be afraid; and, teaching himself that, forget it forever, leaving no room in his workshop for anything but the old verities and truths of the heart, the universal truths lacking which any story is ephemeral and doomed—love and honor and pity and pride and compassion and sacrifice. Until he does so, he labors under a curse. He writes not of love but of lust, of defeats in which nobody loses anything of value, of victories without hope and, worst of all, without pity or compassion. His griefs grieve on no universal bones, leaving no scars. He writes not of the heart but of the glands.

Until he learns these things, he will write as though he stood among and watched the end of man. I decline to accept the end of man. It is easy enough to say that man is immortal simply because he will endure: that when the last ding-dong of doom has clanged and faded from the last worthless rock hanging tideless in the last red and dying evening, that even then there will still be one more sound: that of his puny inexhaustible voice, still talking. I refuse to accept this. I believe that man will not merely endure: he will prevail. He is immortal, not because he alone among creatures has an inexhaustible voice, but because he has a soul, a spirit capable of compassion and sacrifice and endurance. The poet's, the writer's, duty is to write about these things. It is his privilege to help man endure by lifting his heart, by reminding him of the courage and honor and hope and pride and compassion and pity and sacrifice which have been the glory of his past. The poet's voice need not merely be the record of man, it can be one of the props, the pillars to help him endure and prevail.

—WILLIAM FAULKNER, "Acceptance of the Nobel Prize"

1. What is the general purpose of the speech?
2. What is the specific purpose of the speech?
3. Does the speech have significance beyond the immediate occasion?
4. What appeals are evident in the speech? Give specific examples.
5. What devices does the speaker use? Give specific examples.

B. Susan B. Anthony was arrested for voting in the presidential election of 1872. She was fined one hundred dollars, which she refused to pay. The following excerpt is taken from her famous speech on women's right to suffrage. Read the speech and then answer the questions that follow it.

Friends and Fellow Citizens:—I stand before you to-night under indictment for the alleged crime of having voted at the last presidential election, without having a lawful right to vote. It shall be my work this evening to prove to you that in thus voting, I not only committed no crime, but, instead, simply exercised my *citizen's rights,* guaranteed to me and all United States citizens by the National Constitution, beyond the power of any State to deny.

The preamble of the Federal Constitution says:

"We, the people of the United States, in order to form a more perfect union, establish justice, insure *domestic* tranquillity, provide for the common defense, promote the general welfare, and secure the blessings of liberty to ourselves and our posterity, do ordain and establish this Constitution for the United States of America."

It was we, the people; not we, the white male citizens; nor yet we, the male citizens; but we, the whole people, who formed the Union. And we formed it, not to give the blessings of liberty, but to secure them; not to the half of ourselves and the half of our posterity, but to the whole people—women as well as men. And it is a downright mockery to talk to women of their enjoyment of the blessings of liberty while they are denied the use of the only means of securing them provided by this democratic-republican government—the ballot.

For any State to make sex a qualification that must ever result in the disfranchisement of one entire half of the people is to pass a bill of attainder, or an *ex post facto* law, and is therefore a violation of the supreme law of the land. By it the blessings of liberty are forever withheld from women and their female posterity. To them this government has no just powers derived from the consent of the governed. To them this government is not a democracy. It is not a republic. It is an odious aristocracy; a hateful oligarchy of sex; the most hateful aristocracy ever established on the face of the globe; an oligarchy of wealth, where the rich govern the poor. An oligarchy of learning, where the educated govern the ignorant, or even an oligarchy of race, where the Saxon rules the African, might be endured; but this oligarchy of sex, which makes father, brothers, husband, sons, the oligarchs over the mother and sisters, the wife and daughters of every household—which ordains all men sovereigns, all women subjects, carries dissension, discord and rebellion into every home of the nation.

Webster, Worcester and Bouvier all define a citizen to be a person in the United States, entitled to vote and hold office.

The only question left to be settled now is: Are women persons? And I hardly believe any of our opponents will have the hardihood to say they are not. Being persons, then, women are citizens; and no State has a right to make any law, or to enforce any old law, that shall abridge their privileges or immunities.

—SUSAN B. ANTHONY, "On Woman's Right to Suffrage"

1. What is the general purpose of the speech?
2. What is Susan B. Anthony's proposition?
3. What devices does she use to develop her proposition? Give specific examples.
4. What appeals are evident in the speech? Give specific examples.
5. How do the devices and appeals used in the speech show that the speaker analyzed the occasion and the audience?

C. Emile Zola's defense of Captain Alfred Dreyfus, who had been falsely accused of having sold military secrets to Germany, resulted in a libel charge against Zola. The following excerpt is taken from Zola's speech at his own trial. Although Zola was supposedly speaking in his own defense, notice that his appeal was for Alfred Dreyfus. Read the speech and then answer the questions that follow it.

The Dreyfus case! ah, gentlemen, that has now become a very small affair. It is lost and far-away in view of the terrifying questions to which it has given rise. There is no longer any Dreyfus case. The question now is whether France is still the France of the rights of man, the France that gave freedom to the world, and that ought to give it justice. Are we still the most noble, the most fraternal, the most generous nation? Shall we preserve our reputation in Europe for equity and humanity? Are not all the victories that we have won called in question? Open your eyes, and understand that, to be in such confusion, the French soul must have been stirred to its depths in face of a terrible danger. A nation cannot be thus upset without imperiling its moral existence. This is an exceptionally serious hour; the safety of the nation is at stake.

And when you shall have understood that, gentlemen, you will feel that but one remedy is possible,—to tell the truth, to do justice. . . .

Dreyfus is innocent. I swear it! I stake my life on it—my honor! At this solemn moment, in the presence of this tribunal, which is the representative of human justice: before you, gentlemen, who are the very incarnation of the country, before the whole of France, before the whole world, I swear that Dreyfus is innocent. By my forty years of work, by the authority that this toil may have given me, I swear that Dreyfus is innocent. By the name I have made for myself, by my works which have helped for the expansion of French literature, I swear that Dreyfus is innocent. May all that melt away, may my works perish, if Dreyfus be not innocent! He is innocent. All seems against me—the two Chambers, the civil authority, the most widely-circulated journals, the public opinion which they have poisoned. And I have for me only the ideal,—an ideal of truth and justice. But I am quite calm; I shall conquer.

I was determined that my country should not remain the victim
of lies and injustice. I may be condemned here. The day will come
when France will thank me for having helped to save her honor.

—ÉMILE ZOLA, "Appeal for Dreyfus"

1. What is the general purpose of the speech?
2. What is the specific purpose of the speech?
3. What appeals are evident in the speech? Give specific examples.
4. What devices does the speaker use? Give specific examples.
5. How does the organization of the speech show the speaker's awareness of his purpose, the occasion, and the audience?

Review Exercises—Composing the Speech

A. Select a topic for a speech to stimulate, a speech to convince, and a speech
   to motivate to action. Prepare an outline for each speech. Work within a
   three-minute time limit.
B. Your teacher may wish to have you deliver one of the speeches you outlined for Exercise A.

3. Delivering the Speech

METHODS OF DELIVERY

There are four methods of delivering persuasive speeches: impromptu,
extemporaneous, manuscript, and memorized. The value of each type
of delivery depends upon the occasion for which it is used.

The impromptu speech is the speech that is given with no prior planning of appeals and devices or of their sequence. The impromptu speech
must be based upon previous knowledge and experience. Impromptu
speaking usually takes place in small, informal groups. Its success depends upon the ability of the persuader to "think on his feet" and to adapt
himself to the responses of his audience.

The extemporaneous speech requires detailed preparation of a speech for a specific occasion and a specific audience. The appeals and devices are planned, evidence is gathered, and the outline is written. The actual wording of the speech is left to the moment of delivery when the speaker selects the words that seem best to fit the mood and attitude of his audience. Most direct speaker-audience persuasion is extemporaneous.

In situations in which time and exactness of speech are important, speaking from manuscript is advocated. This method of delivery is used most often in radio and television addresses. The greatest difficulties in reading a speech from manuscript are achieving the effect of spontaneity and maintaining eye-contact with the audience. Both can be achieved if the speaker practices reading his speech until he knows it well enough that he can concentrate on interpretation and on his audience rather than on the manuscript.

The memorized speech is used most often in situations in which the same speech is to be delivered more than once and must be exactly the same each time. Lecture series, sales talks, and some political campaign speeches are situations in which this method of delivery is used. As with the manuscript speech, the difficulty with a memorized speech lies in making it sound spontaneous. Again, practice is the solution. The matter of eye-contact with the audience, however, is easier than with the manuscript speech, since the speaker is not hampered by having to read.

DEVELOPING YOUR SKILL

Write a composition in which you discuss the four methods of speech delivery and the advantages and disadvantages of each. If possible, make specific reference to speakers whom you have heard use each of these methods.

65

DRAMATIC IMPACT

In order for persuasion to achieve its goal, it must have some dramatic impact to hold the attention of the audience. A mere recital of ideas, however good the ideas may be, is not enough to stimulate, convince, or motivate the audience.

Dramatic impact can be given a speech through the use of vivid narrative, word pictures, moving illustrations, striking comparisons, appropriate quotations, specific instances, and impelling argument. Whenever possible, introduce the element of suspense through the use of occasional periodic sentences and the question form. Such devices, added to the effective use of voice and gestures, will gain and hold the attention of your audience throughout the speech.

DEVELOPING YOUR SKILL

    A. Discuss the importance of dramatic impact to the success of a speech to persuade.
    B. Select a speech from a collection in your library. Write an analysis of the speech in terms of the devices used to give dramatic impact to the speech.

Review Exercises—Delivering the Speech

Prepare a three-minute extemporaneous speech to persuade to be delivered at a time scheduled by your teacher. Pay particular attention to the delivery of the speech. Your teacher may wish to have each speech criticized after it has been given.

UNIT SUMMARY

Persuasion is the kind of discourse that is used to inspire audiences or to move them to feel deeply about something; it is the means by which people are convinced of the need for change; it is the motivating factor in bringing about action. The basic appeals in persuasion are to the intellect and to the emotions. The purpose of the speech, the occasion on which it is to be given, and the background and attitude of the audience determine the kinds of appeals used.

Four basic devices are used by persuaders to achieve their goals: the acceptance device, the rejection device, the testimonial device, and the bandwagon device.

There are four methods of delivering persuasive speeches, each of which is suited to particular situations: impromptu, extemporaneous, manuscript, and memorized. Regardless of the method used, the persuader must at all times be conscious of his audience and must—through voice, gesture, and dramatic impact—strive to gain and hold the attention of his listeners.

UNIT REVIEW EXERCISES

DISCUSSION TOPICS

A. Discuss the following statement: Persuasion is an important motivating factor in a modern society.
B. Discuss the reasons for using both appeals to the emotions and appeals to the intellect in each of the three kinds of persuasive speeches.
C. Discuss the four methods of delivering a persuasive speech and the relative values of each in given situations. Be specific.

WRITTEN WORK

A. Decide on a proposition for a speech to convince. Write a sentence outline for the speech, showing the issues and the development of the issues. Label the appeals and devices you would use.
B. Assume that you are to be class valedictorian at your commencement exercises. Write the speech that you would deliver.

VOCABULARY

The italicized words in the following sentences were used in other contexts in this unit. Write the numbers 1 to 5 on a sheet of paper. After each number write the letter of the word that could best be substituted for the italicized word. The numbers in brackets indicate the pages on which the words can be found in the unit.

1. The doctor prescribed medicine for the *alleviation* of the pain. [p. 48]
   (*a*) cure; (*b*) treatment; (*c*) relief; (*d*) remedy
2. The *ultimate* strain ripped the wing from the plane. [p. 53]
   (*a*) heavy; (*b*) maximum; (*c*) best; (*d*) minimum

3. Our teacher constantly *exhorts* us to read test questions carefully.   [p. 47]
   (*a*) tells; (*b*) directs; (*c*) instructs; (*d*) warns
4. The *commencement* of the activities was the cutting of the ribbon that extended across the expressway.   [p. 47]
   (*a*) beginning; (*b*) end; (*c*) culmination; (*d*) occurrence
5. No one could corrupt his *tranquillity*.   [p. 61]
   (*a*) laziness; (*b*) calmness; (*c*) shiftlessness; (*d*) privacy

SPELLING

The following spelling words appeared in this unit or were chosen because
they are commonly misspelled. Study these words so that you will be ready
to write them from dictation.

1. alleviation	11. minute
2. ultimate	12. ninety
3. exhorts	13. all right
4. commencement	14. altogether
5. tranquillity	15. mathematics
6. posterity	16. sophomore
7. persuasion	17. sergeant
8. testimonial	18. diving
9. predominant	19. eighth
10. impromptu	20. equipped

UNIT SELF-TEST

1. What is meant by *persuasion?*
2. Name the three general purposes of persuasion.
3. What two factors must be analyzed before a speaker can prepare an
   effective persuasive speech?
4. What are the two kinds of appeals used in persuasion?
5. List the four basic devices that are used in speeches to persuade.
6. Which device depends on words and symbols with pleasant associations?
7. Name the four methods of delivery used in persuasive speaking.
8. List five devices that add dramatic impact to a speech to persuade.
9. What factor, in addition to dramatic impact, will help you gain and hold
   the attention of your audience?
10. List in order the five steps that must be followed in preparing a speech
    to persuade.

Unit 4

English and Your Career

For some time now, you probably have been thinking in a general way about your plans for the future, and some of you may have made choices of a school or a career, or both. Now you must make more definite plans, if you have not already done so. How can your use of English help you to carry out your plans? Effective use of your language is an essential part of your basic equipment. You will always be expected to meet certain standards in the use of English.

Whether you plan to continue your education or whether you plan to go to work immediately after graduation, you will need to be able to communicate effectively with others. Increasingly, applicants for admission to college are being required to show their ability to organize their thoughts and to express those thoughts clearly and correctly. Employers, too, are looking for applicants who can use English correctly and effectively.

In this unit you will practice writing the letters that you will need to write in applying for admission to college or for a job. You will also study ways of using your language effectively in a personal interview. In addition, you will study such aspects of career planning as finding information about training opportunities and jobs, deciding upon a college and a career, and similar topics.

Before reading the rest of this unit, ask yourself the following questions. The answers to them will help you find out how much you know about careers and career planning and how much you still have to learn about them.

1. In choosing a college or university, is its accreditation the most important factor to be considered?
2. What are at least three sources of information about various kinds of jobs?
3. What kinds of information should you include in a letter of application for a job?
4. Why should a letter of application for a job be concise?
5. How do you apply for admission to a college or university?
6. Where can you find out about scholarships and other types of financial aid?
7. Why is it often advisable to choose more than one college or university?
8. Should you make any specific preparations for taking College Entrance Board examinations?
9. What should you take with you when you apply for a job?
10. How should you dress for a personal interview?

1. Choosing Your Career

It is important for you to make plans for your career and set goals for yourself now, even though as time passes and circumstances change you may wish to change your plans. It often happens that plans must be altered, or even completely changed. You will make more progress, however, if you decide on definite goals now and work consistently toward them. If you are going to college immediately after graduation and haven't yet decided on your career, it is probably wise to choose broad areas of interest and arrange to take courses that would prepare you for a number of jobs. If you are to take up a career immediately after graduation, it will be necessary to make a more detailed study of specific jobs at this time.

Often it is necessary to make several decisions and take several steps at the same time in regard to your career. For example, your long-range goal may be to become an architect or a lawyer, and your immediate goals may be to find a job for next summer and to be accepted by a college for next year.

Making decisions, especially about your long-range goals, is not easy. First of all, you must know yourself and your abilities and lasting interests. Then you must study the various ways in which you can use these abilities to the best advantage.

STUDY YOURSELF

Approach your decision about your goals honestly and sincerely. Ask yourself: What kind of work do I really want to do? What aptitude do I have for successfully doing the job? In making your decision, you should consider your preferences and your abilities, though there are also other factors to be taken into account.

Suppose, for example, that you are thinking of a career as an electrical engineer. You might consider the answers to the following specific questions:

1. What evidence is there that you have ability in this field? Have you taken aptitude tests or worked as a helper in this or a related field during vacations?

2. Have you read about the work in this field so that you have a good idea of what the work entails? Have you observed anyone at work?

3. Have you taken courses that would enable you to be accepted for training in this field? If not, can you arrange to make up such courses?

4. Could you enjoy doing this kind of work for a long time?

5. Do you have enough financial backing to permit you to enter the period of preparation required? If not, can you see how you could make arrangements to secure the necessary money?

(The last of these points is probably the least important; for if you have ability, there are many ways of securing the needed funds.)

Discovering one's aptitude is sometimes difficult, but it is often helpful to look back upon your activities of the last few years. What kinds of summer jobs did you have? What hobbies did you pursue? What community activities or Junior Achievement projects did you take part in?

What school clubs and activities interested you? Taking part in the publication of a school paper, for example, may point to any of a number of talents—an aptitude for writing, skill in organizing and directing activities, or perhaps sales ability. What subjects in school held the greatest interest for you?

Your grades may offer some indication of your present or potential abilities. You can also take aptitude tests to find the fields of greatest opportunity for you. If your school has a vocational adviser, you can get valuable help from him.

In thinking about a career, you must consider your physical make-up, since certain jobs require greater physical stamina than others. Good health, of course, is vital to success in almost any job.

All your characteristics must be taken into account. Some traits, such as reliability or accuracy, of course, can be cultivated. Others, such as the preference for working alone or with other people, are individual traits that you should consider carefully when you make a choice of vocation.

Be realistic about your abilities and your limitations, but do not underestimate your potential capacities. It is important that you study yourself, realistically but with imagination and perspective, to find out what goals you should set for yourself. Don't "sell yourself short" and take the easiest thing. You will find that there is great satisfaction in trying to develop your abilities to their fullest extent.

DEVELOPING YOUR SKILL

    A. Be ready to discuss the following questions in class.

        1. How may one go about deciding on his career goals? What factors should be considered?

        2. What are some examples of long-range goals? Immediate goals?

        3. In what ways can one go about discovering one's abilities?

    B. Select an occupation that you feel you might be able to fill, and be ready to explain why it might be a good choice for you.

JOBS AND JOB REQUIREMENTS

In finding out about jobs, requirements for jobs, and opportunities for receiving training for jobs, you will want to make use of as many sources of information as possible. Often you can get valuable information through informal conversations or interviews with older people.

Sometimes it is possible to visit various places of employment and see people at work. Your current reading may even be a rich source of information if you are reading the biography of someone who has worked in a field in which you are interested. And, of course, there is much helpful literature.

In exploring the whole field of possible occupations, you will find that the *Occupational Outlook Handbook,* compiled every other year by the United States Department of Labor, is very helpful. It lists various jobs and gives information as to the areas in which there are the best opportunities. You may also wish to explore the *Dictionary of Occupational Titles,* put out by the United States Employment Service. It lists over forty thousand jobs under five large divisions of work. These five divisions are as follows: Professional and Managerial; Clerical and Sales; Service Occupations; Agricultural, Fishery, Forestry, and Kindred; and Skilled, Semiskilled, and Unskilled Occupations. Both of these books may be found in most public libraries.

To find information in your library about specific jobs, look in the card catalogue under the heading *Vocational Guidance,* or under the heading of a specific job. Encyclopedias also have short descriptions of various selected careers, as well as an over-all view of vocational opportunities.

Some libraries have a special file listing all the books, pamphlets, and other vocational materials available in that library. Sometimes a special place in the library is set aside for books and pamphlets about careers and career planning. Some of this literature, you will find, tells about the jobs themselves, the education and training required, the working conditions, salary, and similar topics. Other literature gives special help in self-appraisal and job planning.

Some sources of vocational literature are listed on the next page. You may find some of the materials they publish in your school or public library. Or you may write to these sources directly for literature about the job or jobs you are interested in.

Bellman Publishing Company, Box 172, Cambridge, Massachusetts 02138

Chronicle Guidance Publications, Inc., Moravia, New York 13118

Institute for Research, The, 537 South Dearborn Street, Chicago, Illinois 60605

Personnel Services, Inc., Peapack, New Jersey 07977

Science Research Associates, Inc., 259 East Erie Street, Chicago, Illinois 60611

Superintendent of Documents, United States Government Printing Office, Washington, D. C. 20025

Vocational Guidance Manuals, Inc., 1011 East Tremont Avenue, New York, New York 10060

 DEVELOPING YOUR SKILL

A. Select three career possibilities for yourself and be ready to discuss them in class. Be prepared to tell about the education and training required, the working conditions, the salary, and other factors that make these jobs appeal to you.
B. Read a trade journal or find examples in the classified advertisements in a newspaper in which there is an opportunity to "earn while you learn." Be ready to describe the job, telling of salary, hours, special requirements or benefits, and other pertinent information.

OPPORTUNITIES FOR EDUCATION AND TRAINING

Many careers that you investigate will require college training, and you may feel that you do not have enough money to go to college; but if you have the ability to do college-level work and you really want to go to school, it is likely that you can find ways of going, even with very little money. There are many scholarships and loans available to those who can qualify for them. Such scholarships are especially helpful when supplemented with part-time and summer jobs, and perhaps loans also. A large privately sponsored program is the National Merit Scholarship program. Some large corporations also have plans to help the sons and daughters of their employees. There are scholarships available through many other sources—clubs, civic groups, college alumni groups, and religious and other organizations. The federal and state governments also have various plans to help qualified applicants. Some local banks, in co-operation with the United Student Aid Funds, Inc., help students by lending them money at nonprofit interest rates. Students begin to pay back such loans five months after graduation. Some schools permit students to pay their tuition in installments while going to school.

Colleges vary widely in costs, too, and you may be able to find one that you can afford, even if you do not qualify for a scholarship or for another type of aid. There are colleges in which the students alternate periods of study and work. In such co-operative schools, the students go to classes for a certain length of time and then work for the same period. An effort is made to place the student in a field closely related to the one being studied, thus affording him an opportunity to gain practical knowledge. In addition to providing valuable work experience, such plans also lower college costs for students. Costs can be held down in other ways, too; for example, some schools have co-operative dormitories, where a student can cut costs by helping to cook meals and care for his own room.

It is probably a good plan to choose the schools you are interested in and write them for detailed information about financial aid available to you in their school, either through scholarships, loans, work opportunities on or near campus, or in other ways. The following publications also will be helpful to you in finding information about various educational opportunities.

Brownstein, Samuel C., *College Bound: Planning for College and Career*. Great Neck, New York: Barron's Educational Series, Inc., 1957.

Brownstein, Samuel C. and Weiner, Mitchel (Kaplan, Stanley, ed.), *You Can Win a Scholarship*. Great Neck, New York: Barron's Educational Series, Inc., 1956.

Burckel, Christian E. and Huber, William Hurt (editors), *College Blue Book*. Ninth Edition. Yonkers, New York: Christian E. Burckel and Associates, 1959.

Educational Testing Service, College Entrance Examination Board, *College Handbook*. Princeton, New Jersey: Educational Testing Service, 1959.

Eskow, Seymour and Jarvie, Lawrence L., *Barron's Guide to Two-Year Colleges*. Great Neck, New York: Barron's Educational Series, Inc., 1960.

Feingold, S. Norman, *Scholarships, Fellowships, and Loans,* Three Volumes. Cambridge, Massachusetts: Bellman Publishing Company, 1949-1955.

Irwin, Mary (ed.), *American Universities and Colleges,* Eighth Edition. Washington, D. C.: American Council on Education, 1960.

Lovejoy, Clarence E., *Lovejoy's College Guide.* New York: Simon and Schuster, 1959.

United States Office of Education, *Scholarship and Fellowship Information.* Washington, D. C.: United States Government Printing Office, 1960.

If, after examining many possibilities, you decide that you cannot continue your education but must go to work immediately, there are still a number of ways in which you can continue your education. Evening and correspondence courses help many to continue their education while working at full-time jobs during the day. Many industries and trades pay small salaries while they give free training for specific jobs. There are courses offered on television on a number of subjects. Credits gained in this way may be applied toward a degree in some colleges.

Opportunities for extending your education and for receiving training in many fields are constantly being increased. Make good use of your public library and other sources of information to keep up-to-date on the latest offerings.

DEVELOPING YOUR SKILL

A. The class may wish to hold a panel discussion in which various students tell about the kinds of scholarships and loans available to high-school graduates. Use the references listed on pages 75-76 or other such sources of information. Each member of the panel might discuss opportunities in a selected field.

B. Write a paragraph or two that you might include in a letter to an uncle, an aunt, or other relative who is interested in your activities. In two hundred words or less, tell of your plans and hopes for the future, giving details about a long-range goal or an immediate one.

C. Look in one of the reference books listed on pages 75-76 or in others similar to them and find the names of at least three colleges that offer co-operative, or work-study, plans. Then write paragraphs summarizing the way the plan operates in those schools. Assume that the one reading your summaries knows nothing about such schools.

Review Exercises—Choosing Your Career

A. Discuss the importance of the following points in choosing a career: abilities and interests, scholastic and work records, personality traits, and financial backing.
B. What are some personality traits that are helpful in almost any kind of work that you might undertake?
C. Write a short paragraph telling about the kinds of information you can find in the *College Handbook* and *Lovejoy's College Guide.*
D. Write a paragraph in which you describe at least three ways of obtaining information about various jobs.

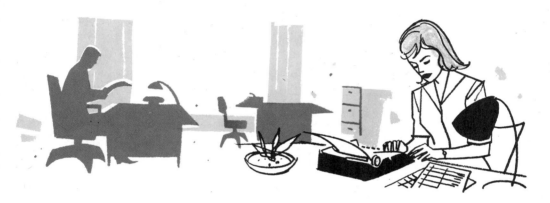

2. Your Job-Finding Campaign

In finding a job, you may have to write letters of application in which you present your prospective employer with his first, all-important impression of yourself. It is important that this letter be written in the correct form and that it contain the necessary information. There will be other written forms that you must be able to complete accurately. You will also need to know how to conduct yourself in a personal interview.

LETTERS AND FORMS

When you find a job that you would like to apply for, either through the placement department of your school, through an employment agency, through the classified advertisements in the newspaper, or other means, it will often be necessary to write a letter of application. The letter of application should be written in the same form as any other business letter. (See Rules 73a to 73k in the Handbook.) Such a letter should include all the necessary facts but no unnecessary or irrelevant details. Your prospective employer has many letters and other papers to read; consequently, he does not have time to read a long letter. He needs a clear, concise presentation of pertinent facts.

Below are listed some points to remember in writing a letter of application.

1. Give the source of information of the vacancy and a direct statement of the position you are applying for.

2. State your reasons for your interest in the position.

3. List your educational qualifications and experience that qualify you for the position. Emphasize those facts that show how you can be helpful to your prospective employer.

4. Give personal qualifications honestly, without boasting or being too modest. Tell age, marital status, school and community activities, and other information pertinent to the position.

5. Include references—names, positions, and addresses of people who will speak well of your ability and your character. Do not list members of your family. This list of references may be on a separate sheet of paper included with your letter, if you wish.

6. Request an interview. Be sure to give your address and telephone number.

7. Do not use trite, or overworked, expressions such as "Thanking you in advance," "Assuming this will meet with your satisfaction," or "I beg to remain."

8. Observe carefully the conventional forms for a correct business letter.

9. Proofread your letter, checking to see that there are no errors in spelling or sentence structure.

10. Make a carbon copy so that you will have a record of your application.

As you read the model letter on the next page, ask yourself these questions: Is it persuasive? Is the necessary information presented clearly and concisely? Does the writer appear to have confidence in his ability without seeming to be conceited? Is the letter in the correct form?

128 Kenner Avenue
Nashville, Tennessee   37215
July 1, 19--

Mr. W. A. Carwell
Carwell Construction Company
Nashville, Tennessee   37203

Dear Mr. Carwell:

Because I am looking for a job this summer, I was very much interested when my father told me that you were offering summer jobs in your construction company to boys of eighteen or nineteen who have had at least one year of industrial arts in high school.

I am eighteen years old and in good health. I am unmarried. I attended grammar school and high school at Peabody Laboratory School, and I plan to enter Vanderbilt University in premedicine this fall.

In my junior year in high school I had an extensive course in industrial arts. During the following summer I worked in the carpentry shop at Peabody College and found that I liked the work very much.

If you wish to know something of my character and ability, you may contact the following people, both of whom have known me for at least five years:

> Dr. R. O. Beauchamp
> Peabody Laboratory School
> Edgehill Avenue
> Nashville, Tennessee   37204
>
> Mr. R. A. Appleton
> Peabody College
> Nashville, Tennessee   37204

I hope you will be interested in talking to me about the job. If you wish to call me for an interview, my telephone number is Cy 2-2961.

Sincerely yours,

Robert Pritchard

Robert Pritchard

You will notice that the preceding letter of application does not include detailed information such as place of birth, height, weight, details of education, details concerning hobbies and skills, and other such information. To include all this information in the body of the letter would make the letter long and less persuasive. Such information is ordinarily included on a separate sheet, called a Personal Data Sheet. Such a data sheet, or résumé, can easily be filed by your prospective employer, and this is the usual procedure. If you do not enclose a data sheet, your application letter may not receive as much consideration as letters that do include them.

In filling out your Personal Data Sheet, be honest and accurate about your personal qualifications, but make the most of your true qualifications that show you to be dependable and efficient. Experience as an officer in a school organization is valuable, as is any work experience. Any skills such as typing or operating other office machines also are valuable and should be noted.

Before you list anyone as a reference, be sure that you have his permission to use his name. A letter requesting such permission need not be long, but it must contain enough information so that the person receiving the letter can carry out your request. You may wish to call the person and tell him of your plans before you write your letter.

A letter requesting a letter of recommendation should follow the steps below, though not necessarily in the same order.

1. Ask courteously for the personal favor of a letter of recommendation.

2. State definitely the position that you are applying for, and give the name and address of the person to whom the letter of recommendation should be sent.

3. Remind the person of your former contacts with him, if this seems necessary.

4. Include a stamped envelope addressed to the person to whom the recommendation is to be sent.

 DEVELOPING YOUR SKILL

    A. Be ready to list and discuss in class the points you should remember in writing a letter of application for a job.

B. As a class, review the items to be included on a Personal Data Sheet. Make up a form for one in class, and put it on the board.

C. Write a paragraph that could be a part of a letter of application in which you try to convince a prospective employer that you have the educational qualifications and interests that fit you for a particular job.

D. Write a letter applying for a position that you know about or one that you find in the classified advertisements of your local paper. Choose one that seems to be suitable for you. Before you begin to write, visualize the employer, evaluate the position, and decide upon your qualifications and aptitudes for the work. Fold your letter properly and write the mailing address on one side of it.

E. Write a letter to the personnel manager of a large corporation or business, setting forth your qualifications and asking about vacancies in positions for which you are qualified. Also fill out a Personal Data Sheet for his files.

APPLYING IN PERSON

Before you are hired for a job, you will be interviewed by at least one person, and sometimes by more than one. If you are prepared for such an interview and know what to expect, it will be much easier for you, and you are likely to be more successful. Then, too, if you feel prepared for an interview, you can give your full attention to it, and you will be more at ease. Do not be overconfident, but remember that you do have certain skills that your prospective employer has need of, and perhaps you can provide just the help that he needs.

It will help you to keep in mind the following points as you prepare for an interview.

1. Pay special attention to your personal appearance. Dress neatly and conservatively. If you are a boy, wear a suit or a jacket and slacks, a white shirt and a tie, and dark-colored socks. If you are a girl, wear something tailored and neat; also use discretion in hair style and good taste in applying make-up.

2. Be on time for your appointment.

3. Wait to sit down until you are asked to.

4. Be careful of your posture. Look alert. Do not lounge in your chair or slouch when you walk.

5. Be courteous, attentive, and pleasant. Look at the interviewer, but do not stare at him.

6. Speak distinctly and in a pleasant, low-pitched voice. Use correct English.

7. Anticipate some questions that you may be asked, and have factual answers ready. Take a copy of your Personal Data Sheet with you, or have some notes handy.

8. Know the requirements for the job you are applying for and something about the company.

9. Show purposive behavior by being able to tell why you have made certain plans and why this job will fit in with your plans. Show a willingness to do all that the job asks.

10. Answer questions briefly but fully enough to be accurate.

11. Be confident about your ability, but be scrupulously honest about the importance of the jobs you have held. Do not brag or exaggerate.

12. Do not try to "steer" or prolong the conversation. Be alert for signs that the interview is over.

During the interview you will be observed carefully to see whether you measure up to the standards of the company. The interviewer will be alert for evidences in your speech and actions of personality traits that he considers important. After you leave his office, he may check a rating sheet similar to the one that follows. Such a rating sheet is filed with your application.

Study the personality traits listed on the rating sheet. How do you rate yourself? You can increase your confidence and self-assurance by working seriously toward the improvement of any personality traits that may be a liability to you in your work.

RATING SHEET FOR INTERVIEW

Name of Applicant_____ Date_____

1. Personal Appearance

Dressed in poor taste; untidy	Acceptably dressed	Suitably dressed	Very well dressed

2. Poise

Awkward, ill at ease	Irresponsive, apathetic	Responsive, well-controlled	At ease, excellent self-control

3. Speech

Unpleasant speaking voice; very poor English	Fairly good speaking voice; fair vocabulary	Well-modulated voice; good vocabulary	Agreeable voice, expresses himself well

4. Information

Poor command of facts	Adequately well-informed	Well-informed	Exceptionally well-informed

5. Mental Alertness

Slow to comprehend	Appears interested	Attentive, interested listener	Keen perception and understanding

6. Health

Low vitality; appears to be in poor health	Appears to be in fair health	Good health and average vitality	Exceptional health and high vitality

When you apply for a job personally or go for an interview, you may be asked to fill out a detailed application blank. You will be expected to fill out such forms accurately, quickly, and completely. Therefore you should take with you the proper information and the following:

1. A pencil and a pen. (Use blue, blue-black, or black ink, never red or green.)
2. Your birth certificate.
3. Your social security card, if you have one.
4. A recent, small photograph.
5. A correctly-filled Personal Data Sheet that includes the following:

   a. List of references, their addresses, telephone numbers, and occupations
   b. Names and addresses of any former employers
   c. Schools attended, diplomas received, and dates
   d. Names and addresses of the members of your immediate family

Before beginning to fill out an application blank, read it through to be certain that you understand the questions. Be sure to follow the directions exactly. Be self-reliant and do not ask unnecessary and annoying questions. Read instructions carefully. Write legibly, adjusting the size of your writing to the space given. Do not abbreviate unless absolutely necessary. Give honest answers to all questions and check all dates and facts to see that you have given them accurately. Proofread your work before handing it in.

Sometimes it is advisable to write a follow-up letter after you have been interviewed for a job. If there is no appointment made for further interviews, you may wish to write a short letter to the personnel manager, thanking him for the courtesy of the interview and assuring him of your continued interest in the position. Remember what you have learned about the writing of business letters. Make your letter brief and courteous, and be sure that it is perfect in every detail.

DEVELOPING YOUR SKILL

    A. Discuss the job applicants that are described on the next page and tell whether, as an employer, you would hire any or all of these applicants, and if so, under what circumstances. If you would not hire them, give the reason or reasons for your decision in each instance.

1. Donna presented herself for an interview for a job as clerk-typist for an insurance company. Her clothing had been well selected and she was well-groomed. She was ten minutes late, but she explained that she had had to wait for a bus. She didn't know anything about insurance offices or what kinds of typing would be required, but she was confident that she could do the work. Responsive and pleasant, she talked at length about her high-school activities and her grades.

2. Sam reported on time for a job as salesman at an automobile show-room. He was wearing slacks, a sports shirt, and white socks. He greeted the interviewer pleasantly, sat down before he was asked to, and continued to chew gum. When asked about his summer and part-time jobs, he told the interviewer about them in great detail, making them sound very important. He said that he was considering any number of jobs, and that he thought he should start at a pretty good salary.

3. Lisa was beautifully groomed, conservatively dressed, and on time for her interview for a job as a receptionist for an employment agency. She spoke barely above a whisper, and the interviewer frequently had to keep asking her to repeat what she had said. From time to time, she looked away from the interviewer and at her watch or out the window. She answered all questions as briefly as possible, sometimes with as little as just *yes* or *no*. She couldn't remember dates and places but said she would be glad to look them up.

B. On a sheet of paper number the items on the Rating Sheet for Interview and assume that you have just been interviewed for a job and the interviewer has filled out a rating sheet for his files. Check the items as you think he might have checked them. Be honest.

C. Write a follow-up letter for Robert Pritchard, using the information given on page 79.

Review Exercises—Your Job-Finding Campaign

A. Discuss the information that should be included in a letter of application.
B. Review the procedure for listing references, and be ready to write the points on the board.

C. Discuss the ways in which your study of English can help you in your job-finding campaign.

D. You may wish to write a dramatization of an interview, showing either correct or incorrect conduct in an interview. If you illustrate incorrect behavior, it may be more interesting if the blunders are small but telling, such as an applicant who sits down before he is asked to or wears white socks.

3. The College for You

In an earlier part of this unit you learned about some sources of information about colleges, and you probably have done some preliminary work in trying to find the right school. Since there are so many applying for admission, it is probably wise to consider more than one school in case you are not accepted by your first choice.

In making your final selection, you should consider the opportunities each school offers in your special field of interest. Schools often are better in one field than in another; therefore, the one that is best for someone else may not necessarily be the best one for you. You should also take into account the accreditation of the school, the reputation of its faculty, its library and laboratory facilities, and its location and the advantages or disadvantages of the location. A most important consideration, also, is whether or not you can meet the entrance requirements.

ENTRANCE REQUIREMENTS

More and more schools are requiring that you take one or more entrance examinations. The most widely used are those given by the College Entrance Examination Board through its Educational Testing Service. Such tests are given at various times during the year at central locations throughout the country, and you must file applications to take them. The tests usually required are the Scholastic Aptitude Test and the Achievement Tests in various subjects. The aptitude test is a measure of your ability to reason. The achievement tests are a measure of what you have learned in specific subjects.

In addition to these two, many schools require that you also take a test of your ability to write compositions. It is frequently called a Writing

Sample Test. In this test you are given a topic and are required to write an essay on it. You must complete this test in an hour, without the use of dictionaries or other reference books. This test is not scored by the Educational Testing Service, as are the other two kinds of tests, but it is forwarded to your college for their records. The scores on the Scholastic Aptitude Test and the Achievement Tests are sent to the college or colleges you specify, as well as to your high school.

The catalogues of the various colleges tell you which tests you need to take and how to go about getting application forms. The *College Handbook* published by the College Board also gives this information. The application forms must be completed and returned with your fee prior to the test dates. Be sure to get your applications in on time. It takes time for applications to be processed, and, as you know, there are many others also sending in applications.

Although tests are widely used by colleges, they are not the only criteria used to determine who shall be admitted. Tests are used by admissions officers to help them make the judgments concerning admissions as fair as possible. As you can understand, not all high-school grades are comparable. An A grade in School A may not mean the same as an A grade in School B. Tests are used, therefore, but your grades and other factors are also considered. Your rank in your high-school graduating class, the recommendations of principal and teachers, and your participation in school and community activities are all taken into account.

There is a great variation also in scholastic averages and courses required for entrance. To enter many schools, you must be in the upper half of your high-school graduating class. Others require that you be in the upper third, or even in the upper tenth. At the other extreme, some ask only that you be in the upper two thirds. Some have no requirement in this matter.

You will find it helpful to talk over your choices of schools with your vocational counselor, if you have one, with someone who has attended that school, if possible, and with your parents and teachers. Sometimes colleges employ counselors to answer questions of prospective students. If there are such counselors in your area, it is usually helpful to arrange an interview with them. If the schools you are considering are in your area, you may wish to visit the campuses.

DEVELOPING YOUR SKILL

  A. Assume that you are a vocational counselor in a large high school. Be ready to tell what advice you would give to a group of students about a choice or choices of colleges.
  B. Find the entrance requirements for five different schools and be ready to tell them to the class. Find out what high-school courses are required, whether or not entrance examinations are required, the terminal date for submitting applications, the required high-school scholastic average, and other pertinent data.
  C. Using the *World Almanac* list of colleges and universities or a reference such as those listed on pages 75-76, choose a school and find out the following information about it. Be ready to discuss this information with the class.
    1. Location, year organized, number of students and faculty
    2. Reputation of faculty
    3. Library and laboratory facilities
    4. Accreditation
    5. Advantages or disadvantages of location
  D. Write an essay of about two pages on what you hope to achieve in your four years at college, or in the next four years in a career. Make this exercise serve as a preparation for the composition test that you may have to take in college entrance examinations by limiting yourself to one hour for organizing your essay and writing it. Do not receive any help from anyone, and do not use dictionaries or other reference materials.

MAKING APPLICATION FOR ADMISSION

After you have decided upon several colleges, the next step is to write to the Director of Admissions of each school, asking for application forms and other materials you may need. Be specific about the materials you wish sent to you—application forms, catalogue, materials on scholarships, information about financial-aid opportunities, housing, or other such topics. Make your letter concise and to the point. Be sure to write it in the correct form for a business letter. Neatness and accuracy are of the utmost importance also.

In most schools such letters should be addressed to the Director of Admissions, but sometimes they should be addressed to the Dean of Admissions or the Registrar. If you consult the catalogue of the school in question, you can find out how to address your letter. Any letter addressed to the Director of Admissions will reach the proper office, however.

After you receive the application forms, you must fill them out carefully. Though they vary somewhat from school to school, there are several things that you should keep in mind in filling them out. Before beginning to write, read the whole form through carefully. You may need to assemble some information or discuss some of your answers with your family or with your counselor or teachers. Take time enough to fill each blank accurately, and be sure to follow the directions to the letter.

In many application forms you will be asked about your reading interests. The Director of Admissions wants to know what you read, and he also wants to know how well you can write English. In many application forms you will be asked to write a paragraph about your reading interests in current literature. You may also be asked to write a brief paragraph telling your reasons for wishing to attend that school. It is a good idea to practice writing paragraphs on another sheet of paper until you are satisfied that you have written good ones. This part of the application form is important and deserves your careful attention.

Sometimes you will be asked to write a short autobiography. It is best to make an outline before you begin to write. Be sure to write carefully, including, of course, information about your hobbies and special interests, as well as your hopes and plans for the future. This is a most important part of the application, and you should give it your careful attention. You may wish to have someone read what you have written before you make your final copy.

In addition to your application form, there are other records required by the college. The director of your school or your principal will send a complete statement about you, which is usually a composite of the opinions of all your teachers. A transcript of your scholastic and other school records will be sent to the college you choose. Your physician will be asked to vouch for your health. The college authorities want to know if you are physically fit and emotionally adjusted to do college work. In some schools you may be interviewed before you are admitted.

DEVELOPING YOUR SKILL

A. Make an outline and write an autobiography that would be suitable for use with an application form.
B. Write letters to the Director of Admissions of each of three schools that you would like to enter, asking for a catalogue, an application form, and other materials you may wish.

Review Exercises—The College for You

A. Your class may wish to hold a panel discussion in which you consider at least six important points that affect choices of schools. Tell why such considerations are important.
B. Write a paragraph in which you explain why you selected a certain occupation or school. Then exchange papers with a classmate for criticism. Evaluate the content as well as the structure and form of the paragraph. Consider the following points: Are the reasons for the choice good ones? Are they clearly stated? Is the paragraph correct in its organization and in the mechanics such as grammar, spelling, indention, and punctuation?

UNIT SUMMARY

In this unit you have practiced using English in ways that will be helpful to you in your immediate future. Specifically, you have learned how to write the kinds of letters that you will be required to write, whether you are entering an occupation or going to college. You have learned what to include in such letters, how to organize your thoughts, and how to write your letters in the correct form. You should now be familiar, also, with the types of forms that you will be expected to use in giving factual information about yourself. You have practiced taking part in personal interviews; thus you should be able to approach this experience with more poise and self-assurance. In addition, you have learned about some of the qualities employers desire in employees, and you have been encouraged to evaluate your own fitness for your chosen career by honestly appraising your own abilities and qualifications. As you do the review exercises that follow, you will help yourself fix more firmly in mind what you have learned about the effective use of English in carrying out your plans for your career.

UNIT REVIEW EXERCISES

DISCUSSION TOPICS

A. How would you go about getting information about colleges?
B. If a person had the ability to do college work, a good scholastic average, and had taken the necessary courses to enter a school of his choice but didn't have enough money, what kinds of financial help may be available to him? Name as many kinds as you can, and tell where he might find out details about such helps.
C. What are some criteria for choosing the best college for yourself?
D. What things should you mention in a letter asking someone to recommend you for a job?
E. Explain the difference between a Personal Data Sheet and a Rating Sheet for Interview.

WRITTEN WORK

A. List the information that should be included in a letter to the Director of Admissions of a college.
B. In a short paragraph, explain how to go about filing applications for College Board examinations.

VOCABULARY

Write the numbers 1 to 5 on your paper, and after each number write the letter of the word or phrase that could best be substituted for the italicized word in each sentence. Before making your choice, find the word on the page indicated to see how the word is used in this unit.

1. Mr. Townsend asked particularly about the *accreditation* of the school. [p. 70]
   (*a*) prestige; (*b*) stability; (*c*) certification; (*d*) reputation
2. The winner of the race had great *stamina*. [p. 72]
   (*a*) determination; (*b*) physical vigor; (*c*) skill; (*d*) drive
3. The efficient secretary should give information to her employer's callers with *discretion*. [p. 82]
   (*a*) discrimination; (*b*) cautious reserve; (*c*) disdain; (*d*) deliberation
4. You should consider your *potential* abilities before making the decision. [p. 72]
   (*a*) actual; (*b*) best developed; (*c*) latent; (*d*) most valuable
5. His writings were filled with *trite* expressions. [p. 78]
   (*a*) unusual; (*b*) sparkling; (*c*) worn-out; (*d*) droll

SPELLING

The following spelling words appeared in this unit or were chosen because they are commonly misspelled. Study each word carefully so that you will be able to write all the words correctly when your teacher dictates them.

1.	accreditation	11.	occupational
2.	stamina	12.	asset
3.	discretion	13.	succeed
4.	potential	14.	conventional
5.	trite	15.	knowledge
6.	personnel	16.	physically
7.	vocational	17.	mentally
8.	qualifications	18.	minimum
9.	transcript	19.	inaccurate
10.	legibly	20.	scholastic

UNIT SELF-TEST

Write answers to the following questions and exercises.

1. Name the principal ways in which entrance requirements for the various colleges differ.
2. What are some of the other criteria, besides tests, that are used by admissions officers in determining who shall be admitted to colleges and universities?
3. Name at least six things that you can do to help yourself feel poised in a personal interview.
4. Explain the difference between a Personal Data Sheet and a Rating Sheet for Interview.
5. Name, in the order of your choice, three careers that you are considering, and explain the reasons for this order.
6. Give three adverbs that tell how you should fill in an application form for a job or for admission to college.
7. What things should you take with you when you apply for a job?
8. What are some trite expressions to avoid in writing a letter of application?
9. Write a letter in which you apply for a position or ask for admission forms for college entrance. Be especially careful of the form of your letter and the placement of its parts.
10. How can you best prepare yourself for College Entrance examinations?

Unit 5

English Words

You can never know too much about your native language. Knowledge is power. And the more you know about the English language, the greater will be your power to write and speak it effectively.

In this unit you will obtain a detailed overview of the nature and development of the English language. You will learn of the origins of English and of the forces that have shaped it during each of its three major periods of growth. You will study the differences between English as it was originally spoken and English as it is spoken today in Great Britain and the United States. Moreover, in studying these differences you will gain a knowledge of the structure of English and its relation to other languages, both ancient and modern. You will see something of the resourcefulness of English in absorbing foreign influences. Lastly, you will see how English emerged from a welter of dialects to become a unified language capable of enormous flexibility in expressing a wide range of thoughts.

Your answers to the following questions will help you to evaluate your knowledge of the history and structure of English.

CHECK YOURSELF

Write the answers to the following questions.

1. What are the names of the three periods in the development of the English language?
2. What are the dates of these periods?
3. Does Modern English rely more on a fixed word order or on a system of inflections to indicate the relations between words?
4. What is meant by the term *grammatical gender?*
5. Has English orthography always been uniform?

1. Origins and Growth of English

The English language is traditionally divided into three historical periods. The first of these is called the Old English or Anglo-Saxon period, and it extends from A.D. 450 to 1100. The second period is called the Middle English period, and it extends from 1100 to 1500. The years from 1500 to the present day are known as the period of Modern English.

Before A.D. 450 the language spoken by the people who lived in Britain was Celtic. Though dialects of Celtic are still spoken there today, very few Celtic words are found in Modern English. Those Celtic words that are preserved in Modern English are chiefly the names of places, like *Dover, Kent,* and *York, Aberdeen, Dundee,* and *Carlisle.* In 43 B.C. Roman troops invaded the island in force. From that time until A.D. 410, when the Roman occupation ended, Latin and not Celtic was the language in which official business was conducted.

Shortly after the withdrawal of Roman troops, Teutonic tribes from what is present-day Denmark, northwestern Germany, and the Netherlands began the conquest and settlement of England. In the face of these new invasions, the native Celts gave ground and took refuge in the outlying districts, in Scotland and in Wales. By 550 the Teutonic invaders had entirely subdued the native population and settled in their place. And it is at this point in time that the story of the English language properly begins.

OLD ENGLISH

The languages spoken by the Angles, Saxons, Jutes, and other Teutonic tribes that settled in England during the fifth century were closely related. In a relatively short time these languages fused into a single language known today as Old English or Anglo-Saxon. The most numerous of the invading tribes, the Angles, gave the island its name—*England* means "land of the Angles."

In 597 Augustine, together with a party of forty monks, was sent from Rome to convert the English to Christianity. In less than a hundred years the entire island was converted. Along with this conversion came the building of monasteries and schools, the introduction of Latin as the language of ecclesiastical and secular learning, and the establishment of England as an important center of culture.

The introduction of Christianity had a profound effect upon the English vocabulary. Many of the Latin words in current use in English date from this time. Few Latin words date back to the time of the Roman occupation. Words like *abbot, alms, altar, candle, cleric, martyr, priest, relic,* and *temple* were introduced at this time and show the influence of the new religion. Words from the fields of literature, medicine, and law show the influence of Latin culture.

It might seem at first that Old English, simply because of its antiquity, would be less complicated than Modern English. Actually the reverse is true. And though Old English is the parent of Modern English, it differs considerably from Modern English both in structure and in pronunciation. In Old English, for example, to show case, the adjective changes its form four times in the singular and four times in the plural. Moreover, the Old English adjective has separate forms for each of the three genders. In Modern English the adjective has only a single form.

A comparison of the definite article in Old English with the definite article *the* in Modern English will illustrate two things: (1) the relative complexity of Old English; (2) the process of simplification the English language has undergone. In Old English the definite article has the following forms.

SINGULAR

	MASCULINE	FEMININE	NEUTER
Nominative	sē	sēo	þæt
Genitive	þæs	þǣre	þæs
Dative	þǣm	þǣre	þǣm
Accusative	þone	þā	þæt

PLURAL

ALL GENDERS

Nominative	þā
Genitive	þāra
Dative	þǣm
Accusative	þā

The Old English dative case is used for indirect objects. The genitive and accusative cases correspond respectively to the possessive and objective cases in Modern English. The symbol þ (called a "thorn") is pronounced *th*.

In Modern English the definite article *the* may be used to modify nouns in the nominative, objective, or possessive case; in the singular or plural number; in the masculine, feminine, or neuter gender. In Old English, however, the definite article changes with the case, number, and gender of the noun it modifies. These elaborate changes in form, which are called *inflections,* are an unnecessary burden in a language, and English has gained in clarity and felicity in discarding them.

The nouns in Old English were also inflected. To a lesser extent nouns are still inflected. The noun *stone,* for example, has a singular and a plural form—*stone* and *stones*—and two possessive forms—*stone's* (singular), *stones'* (plural). In Old English, however, the noun *stone* is inflected as follows.

SINGULAR

Nominative	stān
Genitive	stānes
Dative	stāne
Accusative	stān

PLURAL

Nominative	stānas
Genitive	stāna
Dative	stānum
Accusative	stānas

In addition to discarding many cumbersome inflections, English has also discarded grammatical gender in favor of natural gender. In Old English, as in Modern German, the noun *foot* is masculine, the noun *hand* is feminine, and the noun *eye* is neuter. The noun *stone* in Old English is masculine. The nouns *mægden,* meaning *girl,* and *wīf,* meaning *wife,* are neuter. *Wīfmann,* meaning *woman,* is masculine. Clearly the designation of gender in Old English was inconsistent. In Modern English the designation of gender is natural—*boy* is masculine, *girl* is feminine, *book* or *snow* is neuter.

The weakening of inflections and the shedding of grammatical gender resulted in a fixed word order for Modern English. In a highly inflected language, such as Latin, the order of words in a sentence is not fixed, but free. In Latin you may write *Puer puellam amat,* "The boy likes the girl," and *Puerum puella amat,* "The girl likes the boy," without changing the position of the nouns in either of these sentences. By changing the inflections of the nouns, you can show which is the subject and which is the object. In Latin you may also vary the word order within a sentence and the sentence will retain its basic meaning. Consider the first Latin sentence above. *Puer puellam amat, Amat puer puellam,* and *Puellam puer amat* all mean basically the same thing.

In Old English the word order may also be varied, but to a lesser extent, since Old English is not so highly inflected as Latin. In Modern English the word order of a sentence may not be changed without changing the meaning—or destroying the meaning altogether. "The boy likes the girl" is different in meaning from "The girl likes the boy," and "Likes the girl the boy" is simply not English.

Since there are no inflections in Modern English to indicate whether a noun is in the nominative or objective case (and hence a subject or an object), these relations must be indicated by the position of the noun in the sentence. In a typical sentence in Modern English, the subject comes first, the verb second, and the object last. The position of a word in a sentence will thus frequently tell you the word's function:

Henry bought one *stanasfram.*

Even though you do not recognize the meaning of the word *stanasfram,* you recognize by its position in the sentence that it functions as a direct object, telling what Henry bought.

DEVELOPING YOUR SKILL

A. The following passage is in Old English. Directly after it is a translation into Modern English. Study these passages and be prepared to answer the questions regarding them.

Sē hlāford, þe on his earmum hringas hæfde, dǣlde tō his folce þæt gold fram þǣm horde. Þæt fȳr bǣrnde, and þā sweord and þā seax scinon þǣr hīe hēngon on þǣm wealle þæs hūses. Sē scop sang þæt lēoþ. Þǣr waes sē sang and þæt giedd.

In þǣm tūne wǣron þæt hūs and þæt būr þæs eorles. Þǣr druncon hē and his ymbsittendas þæt wīn. Hē þā word sægde tō his folce: "Nimaþ gē þā sweord and þā gāras."

Þā geongan eorlas hæfdon seolfor and gold, and bohton þā seax and þā helmas. Þā lǣddon hīe hira frēondas tō hira hāmum.

The lord, who wore rings on his arms, dealt out to his folk gold from the hoard. The fire burned, and the swords and the knives shone where they hung on the wall of the house. The bard sang lyrics. There was song and story.

In the town were the house and the chamber of the earl. There he [the lord] and his neighbors drank wine. He spoke these words to his people: "Take up the swords and the spears."

The young earls had silver and gold, and bought swords and helmets. Then they led their friends to their homes.

1. What words in the passage of Old English have been preserved in Modern English? Name the Old English words and their modern equivalents.
2. Translate the following phrases from the passage of Old English quoted above: *þæs huses, þæs eorles.* In what case are the words in these phrases? How is this case used differently in Modern English? In giving your answer consider the use of inflections for both the noun and the article.
3. Translate literally the second sentence in the second paragraph of the Old English passage. Be ready to comment on the word order used here and that used in Modern English.

B. Translate the italicized words in the following sentences into Old English. Label the case and number of each translation.

1. *The stones* in her necklace are real.
2. Ted dumped *the stones* into the pond.
3. Only two *of the stones* he lifted weighed under a hundred pounds.
4. Frank gave *the stone* a kick with his foot.
5. Mark hurled *the stone* through the window.

MIDDLE ENGLISH

Most of the differences between Old English and Modern English appeared during the Middle English period. Of these differences, three are chief: (1) the loss of numerous inflections; (2) the discarding of grammatical gender for natural gender; (3) the influx of a great number of French words into the English vocabulary. These three changes are the direct result of the victory of William of Normandy over the English forces at Hastings.

For some time before the death of Edward the Confessor, William had put forth a claim to the throne of England. His claim, like many others before and since, rested a good deal more on his ability to enforce it than on any legitimate legal foundation. In September of 1066, shortly after the death of Edward, William of Normandy crossed the channel from France and defeated the army that Harold, the elected king, had gathered to repel invaders. In the course of the battle at Hastings, Harold was killed and virtually all the English nobility were wiped out. After the Conquest, Norman-French became the everyday language of the governing class, though Old English continued to be spoken by the native population—artisans and peasants.

Old English was thus released from the restraint exercised upon it when it was spoken by the educated and noble classes. This release from a conservative influence hastened the changes that were taking place in the language. Inflections slurred over in speech were dropped. In their place, auxiliary words, prepositions, and a fixed word order were adopted to indicate meanings and to show the relations between words in a sentence. Gradually over the next two hundred years both Norman-French and Old English gave place to Middle English. Middle English was Old English with its grammar simplified and its vocabulary enriched by Norman-French. By 1300 English was the domestic language of both upper and lower classes.

Because French "was so much unknown" in the realm, English became the official language of the courts in 1362 by the enactment of the *Statute of Pleading.*

> Because it is often shewed to the king by the prelates, dukes, earles, barons, and all commonalty, of the great mischiefs which have happened to divers of the realm, because the laws, customs, and statutes of this realm be not commonly known in the realm; for that they be pleaded, shewed, and judged in the French tongue, which is much unknown in the said realm; so that the people which do implead, or be impleaded, in the king's court, and in the courts of others, have no knowledge of that which is said for them or against them . . . . [all pleas] shall be pleaded, shewed, defended, answered, debated, and judged in the English tongue.

By 1500 the process of change had modified English to the degree that it became what most people today would easily recognize as English.

In addition to supplying the right social conditions for acceleration of grammatical change, the Norman Conquest supplied the English vocabulary with a great number of new words. Most of these words have been retained in Modern English. In some cases the French word introduced at this time replaced the English word. For example, *justice* replaced *gerihte* and *judgment* replaced *dom*. But in more cases the French word supplied the English vocabulary with a new concept or the name of an object previously unknown. A study of the French words introduced at this time shows in which areas the Norman influence was heaviest on English culture.

The following is a categorical listing of the French words introduced into the English language during the Middle English period.

Government: administer, baron, count, crown, duke, exile, noble, parliament, prince, rebel, servant, traitor, treasurer

Church: abbey, baptism, cathedral, charity, clergy, convent, prayer, religion, sacrament, sermon, theology

Law: crime, defendant, heritage, judgment, jury, justice, plead, suit, warrant

Military: army, captain, enemy, lieutenant, navy, peace, retreat, soldier, spy

Art and Science: anatomy, art, chamber, chimney, geometry, physician, poet, romance, stomach, sulphur

Dress and Food: apparel, appetite, coat, dinner, dress, fashion, feast, gravy, lace, sugar, supper

DEVELOPING YOUR SKILL

A. Unlike Modern English, Modern German has retained most of its inflections and grammatical gender. Be ready to discuss in class which language you think would be easier for a foreigner to learn —German or English? Give reasons for your opinion.

B. Look up the following words in a dictionary and write their origin. If you have access to a set of *The Oxford English Dictionary,* look up the period each of these words entered the language.

mouth	sin	honey
tax	food	house
earth	pheasant	frost
hound	mansion	sergeant

Review Exercises—Origins and Growth of English

A. Write a short composition explaining in your own words what an inflected language is. Cite examples of words that are inflected in English. If you are familiar with a foreign language, cite examples from that language and make comparisons with English.
B. Explain the differences between a sentence having a fixed word order and a sentence having a free word order. What is the chief characteristic of a language having sentences of a fixed word order? Of a language having sentences of a free word order?

2. Modern English

ONE LANGUAGE

During the Middle Ages several distinctly different dialects of English were spoken in England. The differences between one dialect and another were sometimes so great that a person from one region had great difficulty in making himself understood by a person from another region. Though noticeable variations in grammar, pronunciation, vocabulary, and even spelling exist in Modern English, communication between all English-speaking peoples today is relatively easy in comparison to that of the Middle English period. The chief characteristic of the Modern period is the emergence of a *standard English* from a welter of dialects.

Dialects

Until the fourteenth century no single dialect served as the official medium for the conduct of public business. For official purposes, either French or Latin was used. However, by the early fourteenth century this situation had changed, and one dialect emerged as the standard for the correct writing and speaking of English. This was the dialect spoken in and around the area of London. Gradually, even those whose native dialect was not London English—for example, the poet John Gower—wrote in the London dialect.

One of the most important forces working for the dominance of this dialect was the flourishing printing and publishing industry established in London. In 1477 William Caxton introduced into England the process of printing from a movable type. By 1500 over 30,000 books had been published in London. Though not all these books were in English, those that were were in the dialect of London. In a relatively short time London became the center of English literary culture, and the London dialect, the standard of correct English.

Orthography

The dominance of the London dialect occurred almost accidentally. But other changes in the English language were a good deal more deliberate—if not so thoroughly successful.

During most of the Middle English period, English orthography, or spelling, had transcribed the spoken language with a fair degree of accuracy. However, as the Middle Ages drew to a close, English pronunciations began to change radically, and the discrepancies between sounds and their written symbols greatly increased. By the sixteenth century it seemed as though each writer had his own system of spelling and that he applied it rather inconsistently. Letters were frequently added to words, not because the letters were pronounced, but because they had appeared in the original form of the word. For example, the letter *b* was added to the word *doubt* simply because it had appeared in the original

Latin word *dubitare.* Even considerations with less scholarly basis entered into the spelling of English words. It was common practice among typesetters to add or delete letters from the final word in a line to make all lines on a page the same length.

The first attempts at reforming English spelling aimed at securing a phonetic alphabet. These attempts usually involved adding accent marks and new letters to the existing alphabet. These additions were rather complicated, and they received little or no popular support. The first truly influential reform of English spelling was brought about by Richard Mulcaster toward the end of the sixteenth century. In his book *Elementarie,* Mulcaster modified the goal of a phonetic alphabet and attempted to fix the spelling of a great number of words by printing them in authorized lists. Though the goal of attaining a wide acceptance for a phonetic alphabet is as far away today as it was in Mulcaster's time, his idea of setting up a conventional standard for the correctness of English spelling has endured to our own time.

As a result of accepting a conventional standard of correctness, there is today almost universal agreement on how words should be spelled —and there is also great variation in the number of sounds a single letter of the alphabet may represent. For example, there is no logical reason why the word *speech* should not be spelled *zgheaghte: z* as in *quartz; gh* as in *hiccough; ea* as in *meat;* and *ghte* as in *righteous.* Convention, not logic, dictates the spelling of the word *speech—*as it does the spelling of most other words in English. As a result English spelling is often difficult to learn. Only a few general rules can be applied to determine correctness, and great numbers of words simply have to be memorized.

Vocabulary

Other conscious attempts to influence the course of the English language occurred in the area of vocabulary. During the sixteenth and seventeenth centuries England experienced a cultural renascence. A profound interest in the past, especially in classical writings, was aroused, and the desire to experiment in the present, in language and in science, grew strong. At the time, scholars began to feel the English vocabulary inadequate. Since they wished to express in English the refinements and subtleties they had acquired from their classical studies, they sought to enlarge the English vocabulary.

Modern English

While virtually all writers felt the necess
some writers felt that these terms should
ing elements of English. Many others felt
to borrow freely from other languages.
example, that instead of referring to a
library, which term was derived origin
it would be better to call this structure a
native English words. The argument be
heated and prolonged. But as the argumen
of words were being borrowed from Latin and Greek
over 12,000 words of classical origin were permanently "natural
into the English vocabulary. A partial, random listing of these words
will suggest their range: *absurd, allusion, capsule, circumspection, dictionary, education, exist, extinguish, paragraph, scheme, tantalize, ther-
mometer.*

DEVELOPING YOUR SKILL

A. Be ready to comment in class on the ideas in the following excerpt.
   This excerpt is taken from Paul Roberts' book *Understanding English.*
   Mr. Roberts is writing here about the discrepancy between the sounds
   of English and the way they are written.

   Perhaps the trouble is that English spelling is not quite bad
   enough. If it were a little worse, nobody could manage it, and
   we would either reform it or all be bad spellers together. As it
   is enough people can learn to spell English to make things hard
   for those who can't. . . . if you spell *separate* "seperate," people
   who spell it "separate" will think you're a jerk, and don't think
   they won't.

B. List at least three ways in which each of the following sounds may be
   spelled: *t, k, ē.* Give examples of these different spellings in actual
   words.

C. Consult up-to-date encyclopedia articles and histories of the English
   language for information about one of the following men: King
   Alfred, Geoffrey Chaucer, William Caxton, Richard Mulcaster. Write
   a report about your subject's relation to the development of the English language.

...ND BRITISH ENGLISH

English is the official language of the United States—the ... in which its laws and public documents are written, the language ... more or less well by nearly all of its citizens—it differs in some ...ects from the English spoken in England.

Sometimes this difference has been exaggerated by those who wished to emphasize a cultural, as well as a political, independence from Great Britain. One anecdote, dating from the founding of our nation, tells of a rabidly nationalistic representative to the Continental Congress who proposed that the new nation invent its own language. This proposal was topped by that of another delegate who wished his countrymen to keep English. He thought that the British ought to be forced to learn to speak Greek.

These early expressions of bluster have given place today to a calm assurance of accomplishment. Many American writers—writers like Hawthorne, Melville, Henry James, Ernest Hemingway, and William Faulkner—have attained an international prominence and stature. And in many countries of the world English is taught as a second language largely because of the influence of the United States in world affairs. What was true at the time of the Greek city-states and again at the time of the Roman Empire is equally true today: The importance of a language is greatly dependent upon the importance of the people who speak it.

The remarkable fact about American English is not that it differs from British English, but that it is still so close to the parent language. The years 1790 to 1860 in America saw a tremendous influx of German and Irish immigrants. From 1865, the end of the Civil War, to the present, even greater numbers of Scandinavians, Slavs, and Italians settled in this country. It might be expected that these waves of immigration would exert an influence on the development of English in America. Yet the opposite occurred. The immigrant and his descendants discarded their native language and adopted English whole. Often, by the second generation only the family name remained to indicate a foreign origin. The English language in America seems to have a capacity for absorbing new influences without changing its own course of development.

An American, upon first arriving in England, might be confused by words with which he is familiar, but which are used in senses unfamiliar to him. For example, if he takes a train from London to Leeds, he will not *check his baggage,* but *register his luggage.* His bags are placed in a *luggage van,* not a *baggage train,* and when he reaches his destination, he may claim them at the *left-luggage office,* not at the *check room.* He may be met at the station by a British friend driving a *motor car.* And he may notice further that his friend refers to the *windshield* of his car as the *windscreen,* and the *hood* as the *bonnet.* His friend may stop for *petrol,* but not for *gas.*

The following is a list of common terms that will illustrate further some of the differences between American and English vocabularies. The American term appears in the left-hand column; the British equivalent appears in the right-hand column.

AMERICAN TERM	BRITISH TERM
baby carriage	pram
billboard	hoarding
bumper (of a car)	buffer
can (of food)	tin
candy	sweets
car (of a railroad)	carriage
conductor (on a train)	guard
cracker	biscuit
druggist	chemist
elevator	lift
flashlight	torch
grade (in a school)	form
grain	corn
legal holiday	bank holiday
letter box	pillar box
molasses	treacle
newspaper reporter	pressman
overcoat	greatcoat
policeman	constable
radio	wireless
shoe	boot
streetcar	tram
subway	tube
suspenders	braces
truck	lorry

MUSIC   THEATER   PUBLIC

The differences which exist today between American spelling and British spelling are largely the result of the efforts of one man—Noah Webster. Webster's volume *The American Spelling Book* was first published in 1783. In less than a hundred years, an estimated eighty million copies of this book were sold. Its influence was enormous.

Webster saw the need for an American dictionary and, at the same time, believed that superfluous, unpronounced letters should be dropped from many words. Though Webster would have liked to reform spelling drastically, he contented himself with the modifications he thought most likely to be adopted.

In some cases Webster's efforts modified not only American spelling, but British spelling as well. For example, largely through Webster's efforts the final *k* in words like *musick, logick,* and *publick* was dropped both in the United States and in Great Britain. But oddly enough Webster failed to apply his own rule consistently and spelled *traffic* and *almanac* with a final *k.* Today, his rule is applied more consistently.

Because of the strength of Webster's influence, we in the United States today write *labor* instead of *labour, judgment* instead of *judgement, check* instead of *cheque,* and *theater* instead of *theatre.* British spelling retains the older forms.

This divergence in spelling—as well as that in vocabulary—is really more striking than it is profound. An American in England, or an Englishman in America, needs only to master a comparatively small number of basic words, and he can then communicate with the residents with little or no risk of confusion.

> DEVELOPING YOUR SKILL

A. Be ready to discuss the following statement in class: "The importance of a language is greatly dependent upon the importance of the people who speak it."
B. Select a few pages from a recent British book or publication for analysis of vocabulary. List the specifically British expressions that you notice. Indicate on your list what the American equivalent of each British expression is.

Review Exercises—Modern English

A. Select a passage of about fifty words from some modern book that you have enjoyed reading. List all the words in this passage in separate columns according to the language from which they are first derived. Use your dictionary in determining a word's origin. On the basis of your findings be ready to discuss in class the make-up of the English language.

B. Benjamin Franklin was an early and a staunch advocate of reforming American spelling. But few of his proposals were ever adopted. The following excerpt is an example of how Franklin wished English were spelled. It is from his *A Collection of Essays and Fugitive Writings.* As you read this excerpt, note the innovations in spelling. Be ready to discuss in class some of the reasons behind his innovations. Is Franklin always consistent? Tell why you think the innovations were not adopted. Do you feel that any of them should be adopted today?

In the essays, ritten within the last yeer, a considerable change of spelling iz introduced by way of experiment. This liberty waz taken by the writers before the age of queen Elizabeth, and to this we are indeted for the preference of modern spelling over that of Gower and Chaucer. The man who admits the change of *housebonde, mynde, ygone, moneth* into *husband, mind, gone,* and *month,* iz an improvement, must acknowlege also the riting of *helth, breth, rong, tung, munth,* to be an improovment. There is no alternativ. Every possible reezon that could ever be offered for altering the spelling of wurds, stil exists in full force; and if a gradual reform should not be made in our language, it wil proov that we are less under the influence of reezon than our ancestors.

UNIT SUMMARY

The history of the English language is usually divided into three periods. The first of these, which extends from 450 to 1100, is known as the period of Old English. During this time the natives of Britain spoke a language that was Teutonic in origin and highly inflected. The chief characteristics of an inflected language are the relatively free order of words in a sentence and the numerous changes in word-forms necessary to indicate meaning.

During the period of Middle English, from 1100 to 1500, radical changes began to occur in the language. The most significant of these was the tendency to discard inflections. This discarding of inflections had two important effects on the English language: (1) the replacement of grammatical gender by natural gender; (2) the fixing of the order of words in a sentence.

The third period of English is known as the period of Modern English. It begins in 1500 and extends to the present. This period is chiefly notable as a period of consolidation. One dialect, the dialect of London, emerged as the standard of correct English. Individual systems of spelling gradually gave way to the acceptance of a uniform, if arbitrary, system.

At each of the three stages of its development, the English language absorbed a great number of foreign words. This ability to incorporate and utilize foreign influences has made English a flexible instrument for the expression of a wide variety of thoughts.

Though American English has been subject to a unique series of influences, and has consequently developed almost independently of British English, it has nevertheless remained remarkably close to the parent tongue. Americans and Englishmen usually have little difficulty in communicating with each other.

UNIT REVIEW EXERCISES

DISCUSSION TOPICS

A. In the first chapter of his novel *Ivanhoe,* Sir Walter Scott observed the fact that while the names of live animals—*ox* and *calf,* for example— are Anglo-Saxon in origin, the names for the cooked meats are French in origin—*beef* and *veal.* Discuss the implications of Scott's observation. Do you think the type of words borrowed from another language indicates a cultural indebtedness also?

B. Mild reforms of orthography have always been more generally acceptable than drastic reforms. Why, do you think, is this so? Do you think drastic reforms are called for today?

WRITTEN WORK

A. Write a paper telling of the effects of the Norman Conquest on the English language.

B. Write a short paper on words in the English language you would like to see respelled. Give reasons for your suggestions.

C. Using encyclopedia articles and biographies, prepare a short biography of Noah Webster. Tell what influence he had on both American and English orthography.

VOCABULARY

The italicized words in the following sentences have been used in this unit. From the choice of words given after each sentence, select the word that most closely approximates the meaning of the italicized word. You may wish to refer to the page in the text where the word was first used.

1. The window in the pawnshop contained a *welter* of articles. [p. 93]
   (*a*) great number; (*b*) mixture; (*c*) confused assortment; (*d*) attractive display
2. The disc jockey on our local radio station received an *influx* of criticism about the type of music he played. [p. 99]
   (*a*) an inpouring; (*b*) wide variety; (*c*) assortment; (*d*) small amount
3. Last week the auditors found several *discrepancies* in the books of our firm. [p. 103]
   (*a*) errors; (*b*) falsifications; (*c*) instances of disagreement; (*d*) mistakes
4. Henry is *rabidly* interested in politics. [p. 106]
   (*a*) fundamentally; (*b*) fanatically; (*c*) seriously; (*d*) hardly
5. *Divergence* of opinion is usually a mark of a healthy society. [p. 108]
   (*a*) difference; (*b*) unity; (*c*) clashes; (*d*) consolidation

SPELLING

Study the following spelling words carefully so that you will be prepared to write them correctly when your teacher dictates them to you.

1. welter	11. accommodate
2. influx	12. carrying
3. discrepancies	13. chosen
4. rabidly	14. corner
5. divergence	15. despair
6. antiquity	16. emphasize
7. enactment	17. forty
8. dominance	18. omitted
9. orthography	19. scarcely
10. drastically	20. vigorous

UNIT SELF-TEST

The answers to the following questions are to be found in the unit which you have just finished. If there is any question you cannot answer, turn back to the unit and review.

1. What are the dates of the Middle English period?
2. What are two important differences between Modern English and Old English?
3. What does the word *England* mean literally?
4. What is *natural gender?*
5. How many inflections does the definite article have in Modern English?
6. From what language and during what period were the following words introduced into English: *gravy, lieutenant, crime?*
7. Who was William Caxton?
8. If an Englishman asked you where the chemist's shop was, what would he be asking for?
9. Has English a free word order or a fixed word order? Explain.
10. What is the significance of the year 597 in the history of the English language?

Unit 6

Your Reading Ability

The need for good reading habits is evident everywhere. To succeed in college and in whatever vocation you may choose, and to get the most enjoyment from life, you must be able to read at an adequate rate and with a high level of understanding. To read well, you must also be able to remember and evaluate what you read.

Colleges have stepped up their requirements to the point where the slow and unskilled reader faces almost certain trouble; without good reading habits, students have difficulty in completing the required reading and in making the necessary reports on what they have read. Business and professional men, too, say that they find it difficult to do even the essential reading required to keep up with the trends in their fields. Good reading ability is needed also to help you extend your understanding and enjoyment of life.

Anyone can improve his reading ability. In the pages that follow, you will learn about some ways to develop your ability to read and to understand and evaluate what you read. You will also learn how to report on your reading in summaries and in critical reviews.

Write answers to the following questions. Your answers will help you find out how much you know about reading ability and how much you still have to learn about it.

1. Which is more important, rate of reading or comprehension?
2. Should you adjust your reading rate to the kind of material you are reading?
3. What is the difference between a summary and a critical review?
4. Is outlining a good study technique?
5. Should you read word-for-word or by word groups?

1. Improving Your Reading Skills

The primary purpose of reading, of course, is to get the thoughts that are expressed in the words. But if you are to become a good reader, you must read at an adequate rate. What is considered an adequate rate depends upon the kind of material that is being read. For example, you would read an account of a football game much faster, usually, than the President's State of the Union message. On material of average difficulty, the average adult reads only about 200 to 250 words per minute, which is not a fast rate. The good reader reads from 400 to 600 words a minute. And some excellent readers average from 600 to 1000.

In trying to attain an adequate reading speed, you must not lose sight of the primary purpose of reading—comprehension. Fortunately, however, faster reading and better comprehension tend to go together. Furthermore, as your speed and comprehension improve, you will have less fatigue when you read.

HOW WELL DO YOU READ?

Maybe you think that you read fairly well now, and perhaps you do. But no matter how well you read now, you can improve your ability. The following test will help you find out how fast you read material of average difficulty and how well you comprehend and remember what you read. Time yourself or have someone else time you for one minute.

After you have finished reading, you will be asked to answer some questions about what you have read.

Read "A Mississippi Pilot" by Mark Twain as fast as you can but carefully enough so that you can answer questions about its content.

There used to be an excellent pilot on the river, a Mr. X., who was a somnambulist. It was said that if his mind was troubled about a bad piece of river, he was pretty sure to get up and walk in his sleep and do strange things. He was once fellow-pilot for a trip or two with George Ealer, on a great New Orleans passenger packet. During a considerable part of the first trip George was uneasy, but got over it by and by, as X. seemed content to stay in his bed when asleep. Late one night the boat was approaching Helena, Ark.; the water was low, and the crossing above the town in a very blind and tangled condition. X. had seen the crossing since Ealer had, and as the night was particularly drizzly, sullen, and dark, Ealer was considering whether he had not better have X. called to assist in running the place, when the door opened and X. walked in. Now, on very dark nights, light is a deadly enemy to piloting; you are aware that if you stand in a lighted room, on such a night, you cannot see things in the street to any purpose; but if you put out the lights and stand in the gloom you can make out objects in the street pretty well. So, on very dark nights, pilots do not smoke; they allow no fire in the pilot-house stove, if there is a crack which can allow the least ray to escape; they order the furnaces to be curtained with huge tarpaulins and the skylights to be closely blinded. Then no light whatever issues from the boat. The undefinable shape that now entered the pilot-house had Mr. X.'s voice. This said:

"Let me take her, George; I've seen this place since you have, and it is so crooked that I reckon I can run it myself easier than I could tell you how to do it."

"It is kind of you, and I swear I am willing. I haven't got another drop of perspiration left in me. I have been spinning around and around the wheel like a squirrel. It is so dark I can't tell which way she is swinging till she is coming around like a whirligig."

So Ealer took a seat on the bench, panting and breathless. The black phantom assumed the wheel without saying anything, steadied the waltzing steamer with a turn or two, and then stood at ease, coaxing her a little to this side and then to that, as gently and as sweetly as if the time had been noonday. When Ealer observed this marvel of steering, he wished he had not confessed! He stared, and wondered, and finally said:

"Well, I thought I knew how to steer a steamboat, but that was another mistake of mine."

X. said nothing, but went serenely on with his work. He rang for the leads; he rang to slow down the steam; he worked the boat carefully and neatly into invisible marks, then stood at the center of the wheel and peered blandly out into the blackness, fore and aft, to verify his position; as the leads shoaled more and more, he stopped the engines entirely, and the dead silence and suspense of "drifting" followed; when the shoalest water was struck, he cracked on the steam, and carried her handsomely over, and then began to work her warily into the next system of shoal-marks; the same patient, heedful use of leads and engines followed, the boat slipped through without touching bottom, and entered upon the third and last intricacy of the crossing; imperceptibly she moved through the gloom, crept by inches into her marks, drifted tediously till the shoalest water was cried, and then, under a tremendous head of steam, went swinging over the reef and away into deep water and safety!

Ealer let his long-pent breath pour in a great relieving sigh, and said:

"That's the sweetest piece of piloting that was ever done on the Mississippi River! I wouldn't believe it could be done, if I hadn't seen it."

There was no reply, and he added:

"Just hold her five minutes longer, partner, and let me run down and get a cup of coffee."

A minute later Ealer was biting into a pie, down in the "texas," and comforting himself with coffee. Just then the night watchman happened in, and was about to happen out again, when he noticed Ealer and exclaimed:

"Who is at the wheel, sir?"

"X."

"Dart for the pilot house, quicker than lightning!"

The next moment both men were flying up the pilot-house companion-way, three steps at a jump! Nobody there! The great steamer was whistling down the middle of the river at her own sweet will! The watchman shot out of the place again; Ealer seized the wheel, set an engine back with power, and held his breath while the boat reluctantly swung away from a "towhead," which she was about to knock into the middle of the Gulf of Mexico!

By and by the watchman came back and said:

"Didn't that lunatic tell you he was asleep, when he first came up here?"

"No."

"Well, he was. I found him walking along on top of the railings, just as unconcerned as another man would walk a pavement; and I put him to bed; now just this minute there he was again, away astern, going through that sort of tightrope deviltry the same as before."

"Well, I think I'll stay by next time he has one of those fits. But I hope he'll have them often. You just ought to have seen him take this boat through Helena crossing. I never saw anything so gaudy before. And if he can do such gold-leaf, kid-glove, diamond-breastpin piloting when he is sound asleep, what *couldn't* he do if he was dead!"

To find your reading rate for this selection, simply count the number of words that you have read. Count every word, including articles *a, an,* and *the*. This is your reading rate per minute.

To test how well you have understood and remembered what you have read, read and complete the following test. Number from 1 to 5 on your paper, and after each number write the letter that corresponds to the words that best complete the sentence.

1. The somnambulist was (*a*) Ealer; (*b*) Mr. X.; (*c*) the night-watchman.

2. The sleepwalker was most likely to perform (*a*) when he was troubled about a bad piece of river; (*b*) when he was overtired; (*c*) when he and his co-pilot had had an argument.

3. The crossing above (*a*) Vicksburg; (*b*) Helena, Ark.; (*c*) New Orleans was in a very blind and tangled condition.

4. The somnambulist told Ealer (*a*) that he was asleep; (*b*) that he would take over for a while; (*c*) that it was so dark that he couldn't tell which way she [the boat] was swinging.

5. After the boat was in safe water, Ealer (*a*) went down for some coffee and pie; (*b*) drank some tea; (*c*) fell asleep.

If you marked the correct answers to all the statements, your score is 100 per cent. For every incorrect answer, subtract 20 per cent.

DEVELOPING YOUR SKILL

    A. What is the relationship between rate of reading and comprehension?
    B. What is a good reading rate on reading material of average diffi-culty? What is the range?

LEARNING TO READ IN WORD GROUPS

A good reader reads in word groups. He is intent on getting the thought, and does not center his attention on words as such. Did you ever think what it would be like to watch a motion picture, seeing only one frame per second instead of the normal twenty-four? What a jerky picture it would be! The result would not be a complete picture of an action but a distorted, disjointed series of movements. The watcher would become so interested in watching the individual actions that he

would lose sight of the complete picture. So it is with word-by-word reading. The individual word becomes the center of interest, and as a result the idea (or the complete picture) is lost sight of.

As the eye travels across a line of print, it moves from left to right, pausing slightly at intervals and then moving along to the end of the line, where it makes a return sweep to the beginning of the next line. It is during these pauses that actual reading takes place. Naturally, the fewer pauses, the faster the rate of reading. The fewer the pauses, the less fatigue there will be, too, since the eye does not have to stop and go so many times.

The number of words that your eyes take in during one of these pauses is called the *recognition span*. To develop greater speed, you should try to widen your recognition span and pause for a shorter time. You can see more than just one word at a time. Practice seeing a whole phrase such as *in the morning, beside the waterfall, after the beginning of autumn.* Practice also with whole clauses, beginning with short clauses such as *when he came, if he were here,* and *since the day you left.* As you read groups of words, let your eyes look at the center of the group. You will see more and see it better.

Punctuation can help you see thought groups quickly. So can directional words such as *the following, at this point,* and *nevertheless.* Such words help you to follow the direction of the writer's thought.

As you read the excerpt from E. B. White's "Once More to the Lake" in the exercise section that follows, you will notice that the word groups are also units of thought. If you are not now accustomed to reading in such groups, doing so may seem to slow you down temporarily; any change in habit is accompanied by slight tension. But in time you will be reading faster and with more comprehension.

119

A. Glance briefly at each line below as you hold a pencil in your hand and move it down the column as fast as you can and still understand it. *Do not slow down and do not stop.* If you notice that you are looking at one word at a time, speed up. If you lose the meaning, go back and read the material again, but only in word groups.

One summer,
along about 1904,
my father rented a camp
on a lake in Maine
and took us all there
for the month of August.
We all got ringworm
from some kittens
and had to rub
Pond's Extract
on our arms and legs
night and morning,
and my father rolled over
in a canoe
with all his clothes on;
but outside of that
the vacation
was a success,
and from then on
none of us ever thought
there was any place
in the world
like that lake in Maine.
We returned
summer after summer—
always on August 1st
for one month.
I have since become
a salt-water man,
but sometimes in summer
there are days
when the restlessness
of the tides
and the fearful cold
of the sea water
and the incessant wind
which blows
across the afternoon
and into the evening
make me wish
for the placidity
of a lake
in the woods.
A few weeks ago
this feeling got so strong
I bought myself
a couple of bass hooks
and a spinner
and returned to the lake
where we used to go,
for a week's fishing
and to revisit old haunts.

B. Read an article in a newspaper or a digest magazine in which the columns are narrow. Practice reading in word groups.

C. Find a selection in a magazine or a book and write it in narrow columns as in Exercise A. Make your word groups also thought groups. Practice reading the material that you have grouped in this way.

SOME HABITS TO AVOID

Perhaps you have some reading habits that are holdovers from the habits you formed when you first learned to read. One such habit that is quite common among adults is that of unconsciously forming words with the lips or in the throat. Such a habit is called *subvocalizing*. Your eye can see words faster than you can say them or form them with your lips; thus you are slowed down if you have this habit.

To find out whether you are subvocalizing, place your fingers on your lips while you are reading silently. You should not feel any movement at all. Also, place the thumb and forefinger of your left hand on your Adam's apple as you read a sentence or two silently. You should not feel any tension in your throat, or any vibration.

As you become a more rapid and efficient reader, the habit of subvocalizing tends to take care of itself. When you are reading at home, you may wish to check yourself from time to time as you read by placing your fingers on your lips or to your throat. If you find that you are subvocalizing, try to increase your speed.

Another habit to avoid is that of "going back over your tracks." Almost everyone is guilty of this habit of regression, to a degree. If you are reading very difficult material, you may need to return and reread passages that prevent you from understanding what comes next. But such a return should be a deliberate one, and it should not be frequent in ordinary reading. Do not let yourself jump back and forth and lose the thread of what you are reading. Often, too, if you keep reading, the next sentence or paragraph may clear up what was puzzling you.

To keep yourself on the track, you may wish to try the method suggested here, or you may wish to invent a method of your own. Try using a regular 3- by 5-inch library card and sliding it down the page in such a way that it covers up the material you have just read. Keep the card moving down the page, and do not allow yourself to return to what you have passed over. As your ability improves, gradually move the card down the page at a faster rate. Speed is not the important part of this practice, but you will find that your rate of reading will increase when you stop going back over what you have already read. You will adjust yourself to getting the idea the first time, and your comprehension also will increase.

DEVELOPING YOUR SKILL

A. Read the selection below, which continues Mr. White's essay "Once More to the Lake." Occasionally touch your fingers to your lips or hold your throat lightly to see whether you are subvocalizing.

I took along my son, who had never had any fresh water up his nose and who had seen lily pads only from train windows. On the journey over to the lake I began to wonder what it would be like. I wondered how time would have marred this unique, this holy spot—the coves and streams, the hills that the sun set behind, the camps and the paths behind the camps. I was sure that the tarred road would have found it out and I wondered in what other ways it would be desolated. It is strange how much you can remember about places like that once you allow your mind to return into the grooves which lead back. You remember one thing, and that suddenly reminds you of another thing.

B. Continue reading from E. B. White's "Once More to the Lake," this time moving a 3 x 5 card down the page so that it covers what you have just read. Read as quickly as you can, and do not go back.

I guess I remembered clearest of all the early mornings, when the lake was cool and motionless, remembered how the bedroom smelled of the lumber it was made of and of the wet woods whose scent entered through the screen. The partitions in the camp were thin and did not extend clear to the top of the rooms, and as I was always the first up I would dress softly so as not to wake the others, and sneak out into the sweet outdoors and start out in the canoe, keeping close along the shore in the long shadows of the pines. I remembered being very careful never to rub my paddle against the gunwale for fear of disturbing the stillness of the cathedral.

The lake had never been what you would call a wild lake. There were cottages sprinkled around the shores, and it was in farming country although the shores of the lake were quite heavily wooded. Some of the cottages were owned by nearby farmers, and you would live at the shore and eat your meals at the farmhouse. That's what our family did. But although it wasn't wild, it was a fairly large and undisturbed lake and there were places in it which, to a child at least, seemed infinitely remote and primeval.

I was right about the tar: it led to within half a mile of the shore. But when I got back there, with my boy, and we settled into a camp near a farmhouse and into the kind of summertime I had known, I could tell that it was going to be pretty much the same as it had been before—I knew it, lying in bed the first morning, smelling the bedroom, and hearing the boy sneak quietly out and go off along the shore in a boat.

IMPROVING YOUR STUDY-TYPE READING

No matter how well you think you use your time in study-type reading, you can probably improve your ability. The average adult, for example, understands only about 70 per cent of what he reads. Consequently, when he wishes to use what he has read, he often finds it necessary to reread, sometimes more than once, to get the full meaning.

There are many things you can do to improve your study-type reading. The following suggestions can help you to get the most from your time.

Adjust your speed to the kind of material you are reading. Learn when to read at your average rate, when to read deliberately, and when to skim. In general, read along as fast as you comfortably can and still get the thought. When you come to something that is unfamiliar to you —something for which your background of information and experience has not prepared you—slow down and read more carefully.

Skimming, too, is a useful reading tool. In skimming, you do not read every word, every sentence, or every paragraph; you look quickly across or down a page to find the specific information you wish. Most reference books have an index and a table of contents to guide you to the page where you can find the information you want. Then, using your technique of skimming, you can locate what you need quickly. Skimming also can help you decide whether you want to read a certain book— whether it contains the information you are looking for. Skimming the preface and the table of contents, and reading snatches here and there throughout the book can give you an idea of the content quickly.

It is also helpful to analyze the author's organization of a chapter or a unit. Most chapters or units are divided into parts—an introduction, a body, and a summary, or conclusion. These parts are usually clearly defined in some way, by a heading or by the use of different kinds of type. In the introduction you will find the main points to be discussed. The body contains a discussion of these points. In the summary there is a brief summation of what has been discussed. To keep the general organization in mind, it is often helpful to make a simple outline of the main topics.

Some parts of a chapter or a unit will be harder for you to understand. Spend more time on those parts. Some parts contribute more to the development of the main idea, and they also deserve more of your time.

Learn to recognize the main, or important, idea and distinguish it from the subordinate ideas. The main idea in each paragraph is usually contained in a topic sentence. This sentence should be obvious to the careful reader. Occasionally, you will find that the main thought may be contained in two or even more sentences. With practice, you should be able to find the main thought quickly and easily, and differentiate between the principal thought and the subordinate thoughts.

Use your dictionary when you need to in order to get the thought. Read to the end of a sentence or paragraph before looking up a word.

In reviewing for a test, it is sometimes helpful to make up a list of questions that you think might be asked and read to find the answers to them. After you have finished reading, close the book and try to recall the main points or the answers to the questions you made up. Or try explaining to someone the main points of what you have read. Then go back and reread if necessary.

The reading techniques set forth here will be helpful to you if you decide that you really want to improve your reading. As you practice reading carefully and skillfully, you will find that all your reading will become easier too; for the more you read, the better prepared you are to do further reading. By reading, you are building up a background of information that will help you understand new material. You are also helping to build a vocabulary that will speed up your reading and comprehension.

DEVELOPING YOUR SKILL

    A. Be ready to list and discuss some ways that you can improve your study-type reading.
    B. Read a chapter or a unit in a textbook that you use for another class and write an outline of it that could be used in reviewing.

Review Exercises—Improving Your Reading Skills

A. Tell the relationship between an improved rate of reading and increased comprehension and ease in reading.
B. Bring to class a chapter or a unit in another textbook that you are studying, and be ready to explain the organization of that chapter or unit.
C. Be ready to explain the terms *regression* and *subvocalizing* as they apply to reading, and tell of some ways in which these habits may be overcome.
D. Write a paragraph in which you summarize the suggestions given in this unit for improving study-type reading.

2. Reporting on What You Read

To be able to read well includes the ability to interpret and summarize accurately the content of what you read. Careful analysis and evaluation are also an important part of good reading. Such abilities are needed, especially in college work. From time to time you will be asked to summarize the content of a book, a chapter, or an article in an objective manner. At other times you will be asked to write critical evaluations.

SUMMARIES

In a summary you tell briefly, in your own words, what the book, chapter, or article is about. You also include the title of the work, the name of the author, and perhaps a few words about the author. Before you can write a summary, you must know exactly what is in the material to be summarized, and you should be aware of the author's purpose. Knowing something about the author also helps you to understand a piece of writing. Often the author states his purpose in so many words—usually in the preface or in the opening chapter. Sometimes, however, the purpose is implied or referred to obliquely.

In writing a summary you should make no mention of whether or not the author accomplishes his purpose or of the thoroughness or competency of his treatment of the subject. A summary is primarily a summarization of the content of a book, a chapter, or an article.

U. E. Baughman has devoted his whole working life to the United States Secret Service. He joined up in 1927, when he was twenty-two years old, as a clerk-stenographer in the Philadelphia office; he recently retired as top man, and now, like many retired persons, he is in reminiscent mood.

And in his record, *Secret Service Chief,* with Leonard Wallace Robinson, there are events and personalities to be reminiscent about. Presidents Truman, Eisenhower, and Kennedy have been his personal charges. Chief Baughman got along very well with all of them, though he didn't like all the things they did: Truman's early morning saunters ("they represented the kind of 'habit' that was hand-picked for the assassin"), Eisenhower's passion for the putter ("a golf course is almost a perfect place for an assassination attempt"), Kennedy's sociability ("at this juncture an assassin could very easily join the festivities unaccosted"). There is entertaining anecdotage about all three Presidents—more, naturally, about the first and the second than about the third.

. . . .

The Secret Service, as everybody knows, has another job. It nabs counterfeiters. Chief Baughman has some good stories to tell here. A highly amusing one concerns perhaps the smallest of counterfeiting small fry. This chap (theatre of operations not identified) used to ask shop salesmen or restaurant cashiers to let him have a five-dollar bill for five singles. Glad to oblige. One—never more—of the singles was phony. Actually, the smallest operation in the counterfeiting field is the manufacture of coins. Even nickels are occasionally turned out on a do-it-yourself basis.

Other bits from Chief Baughman's recollections: There are 132 rooms in the White House. A Secret Service man is present at every purchase of food for the Presidential table; he places it in a special receptacle, locks the receptacle, and delivers it to the executive mansion's chef. When President Eisenhower went to Balmoral Castle to attend a royal picnic, Queen Elizabeth greeted him in slacks. (And her sister came over to the Secret Service shack and introduced herself: "My name is Margaret.") When Chief Baughman asked Caroline Kennedy how her brother Jack was, she replied, "It's not Jack, it's John. Jack is my father's name."

—JOHN T. WINTERICH, *Saturday Review*

You will note that this summary tells clearly and succinctly what the book is about. It also gives enough detail to show the kind of material in the book, but not so much that you lose interest in reading it.

DEVELOPING YOUR SKILL

    A. Be ready to discuss the following questions:

        1. What kinds of comments are not included in a summary?
        2. Why should you know something about the author's purpose in writing the material being summarized?
        3. Where in a book are you likely to find a statement of the author's purpose in writing the book?

    B. Find an article in a magazine and write a summary of the salient points made in that article. The article should deal with a subject of some significance. Or write a brief summary of a book that you have recently read.

CRITICAL REVIEWS

A critical review is an attempt to evaluate the worth of a piece of writing. A thorough understanding of what the author really means to communicate is, of course, a requisite for any worthwhile estimate of a work. A reviewer then tries to judge how well the author has accomplished his purpose and to assess the book's good points and its deficiencies. A reviewer also attempts to evaluate the relative value of a piece of writing. What does this book contribute that is unique or valuable? How does it compare with other treatments of the same subject?

Before attempting to evaluate a piece of writing, one might well give some thought to questions such as the following.

1. Is the subject of some significance?

2. What is the author's purpose, and to what extent does he carry it out?

3. What are the qualifications of the author for writing on this subject?

4. Are the author's sources of information reliable ones?

5. Are facts or ideas treated in accordance with their significance?

6. Is the presentation acceptable? Is it lively, monotonous, orderly?

7. Is the organization of the material clear?

8. Does the author make use of propaganda techniques, such as those discussed on pages 35-39?

9. How do the author's interpretations compare with interpretations in other, recognized works?

10. To what extent does the piece of writing make a unique contribution to one's understanding of oneself or one's world?

The nature of the work being reviewed and the reviewer himself determine, to some extent, which of these questions are most important. In two of the reviews of Sir Edmund Hillary's book *No Latitude for Error,* which are given below, note that the reviewers emphasize different points.

> Hillary's characteristic drive and enthusiasm, as well as his capacity for understatement, come out even in the colloquial and sometimes archaic phrases. . . Some chapters tread old ground and some, among the crevasses, tend to monotony because the brink of one crevasse, however perilous, is much like the brink of another. But the final dash to the Pole in Ferguson tractors (is it still heresy

to doubt the value and emphasise the risk of this feat?) moves at superb speed, and the story is held together by the author's intense interest in everything that happened.

—WILFRID NOYCE, *New Statesman*

In the following quotation from a review by Alfred Lansing, which appeared in the *New York Herald Tribune Books,* the reviewer points to a lack of depth and insight, though his over-all judgment of the book also is favorable, and he, too, is aware of limitations imposed by the subject matter.

> The book suffers from what might be termed a literary 'white-out' because of the seemingly interminable sameness of the subject matter. Rather more important from the standpoint of the reader is that Hillary's account lacks depth and insight because it is told entirely from his own point of view. And Hillary does not even plumb his own feelings very deeply. In fact, he draws such a super-ficial picture of his companions on this undeniably rugged journey that this reviewer, for one, felt no compulsion whatever to refer to the accompanying photographs to get an idea of what these fellows looked like. Yet in spite of this, and almost surprisingly, the book somehow achieves a degree of interest which holds the reader's attention.

In these reviews of William Henry Harbaugh's *Power and Responsibility: the Life and Times of Theodore Roosevelt,* notice the kinds of things the reviewers single out for their attention. Richard Hooker, in his review which appeared in the *Springfield Republican,* says, in part:

> Prof. Harbaugh's book, in many of its appraisals, is sound. Its summing up of Roosevelt's contribution to the progress of American government is just. Its chief fault is that in quoting the comments of conflicting witnesses Prof. Harbaugh often does not make clear what comment seems to him most worthy of acceptance and that, when he does so indicate, his preference is occasionally mistaken. With that qualification this book must be recognized as a mine of information and highly valuable.

C. W. Weinberger, writing in the *San Francisco Chronicle,* is less enthusiastic about the book.

> Professor Harbaugh's biography is not a bad one, but there is
> little that is new in it. Both the material and his interpretation of
> it are familiar, and the anecdotes have been told many times. . .
> By using most of the available source material, [it] provides a
> convenient starting place for a study of Roosevelt's life, although
> Henry Pringle's one-volume biography is better in this area; and,
> of course, there is no substitute, for those who would know Roose-
> velt, for his letters and his own writings.

Before writing your own critical reviews, you may find it helpful as
well as interesting to read other reviews such as those given here. Any
review that is valuable must, of course, be based upon a sound understanding of the material to be reviewed. As you read, you will find that
you are able to understand some parts of a piece of writing better than
others because of the background of information that you have acquired,
partly through your reading. Thus you are more capable of evaluating
correctly those parts. As you read more and more widely, you will be
able to make increasingly better evaluations of what you read.

 DEVELOPING YOUR SKILL

    A. Bring to class examples of book reviews that you think are good
       ones, and tell why you find these critical reviews good. Be ready
       to read parts from them to substantiate the points that you make.
       What points of those listed on page 128 are discussed? Are there
       any other criteria that the reviewers use?
    B. Write a critical review of a book that you have read recently. Use
       some of the criteria listed on page 128 in making your evaluation.

Review Exercises—Reporting on What You Read

A. Be ready to discuss some of the criteria that reviewers use in writing their
   reviews. Explain why the subject matter of a piece of writing determines,
   in part, the direction of the criticism.
B. Write a paragraph in which you explain the difference between a summary and a critical review.

UNIT SUMMARY

Your reading ability is important to your future accomplishment. Whether in college or in business, you will need to be able to read at an adequate rate and with a high degree of comprehension.

In this unit you have learned about some habits of good readers, and you have practiced using these habits. Some habits that would prevent you from attaining your maximum reading skill have been pointed out, and you have learned of some ways to overcome these shortcomings.

You have also seen that the ability to read well includes the ability to interpret what you read and to evaluate it well. You have learned the difference between a summary and a critical analysis. You have read some examples of critical reviews and have tried your hand at writing summaries and critical reviews.

UNIT REVIEW EXERCISES

DISCUSSION TOPICS

A. Discuss the following questions:

1. How can you help to widen your eye span?
2. What are some ways to help yourself develop speed in reading?
3. How can you help yourself avoid regressing and subvocalizing?

B. The class may wish to find critical reviews of a book that many in the class have read. These reviews may be brought to class and analyzed.

WRITTEN WORK

A. Write a composition in which you analyze a particularly good critical review of a book of nonfiction. Tell why you feel that it is a good review.
B. Choose a book of nonfiction and write both a summary and a critical analysis of this book. Make the distinction between these two types of report clearly evident.

VOCABULARY

The italicized words in the following sentences were used in this unit. To help you remember their meanings, they are used here in different contexts.

Number from 1 to 5, and after each number write the letter corresponding to the word or phrase that can best be substituted for the italicized word. Check the pages indicated to see how the words were used in the unit.

1. The lake was known for its *placidity*.   [p. 120]
   (*a*) coolness; (*b*) great depth; (*c*) calmness; (*d*) storminess
2. The habit of *regression* should be overcome.   [p. 121]
   (*a*) looking ahead; (*b*) looking back; (*c*) vocalizing; (*d*) daydreaming
3. He briefed us on the *salient* points that had been made.   [p. 127]
   (*a*) salubrious; (*b*) outstanding; (*c*) precise; (*d*) salable
4. The young lawyer seemed to be acutely aware of his *deficiencies*. [p. 128]
   (*a*) shortcomings; (*b*) privileges; (*c*) good points; (*d*) prerogatives
5. The *intricacy* of the pattern fascinated me.   [p. 116]
   (*a*) laciness; (*b*) delicacy; (*c*) complex character; (*d*) simplicity

SPELLING

The following words appeared in the unit or were chosen because they are commonly misspelled. Study these words so that you will be prepared to write them from dictation.

1. placidity	11. undulating
2. regression	12. primeval
3. salient	13. orientation
4. deficiencies	14. condensation
5. intricacy	15. unique
6. requisite	16. compulsion
7. imperceptibly	17. limitation
8. subvocalization	18. adequacy
9. obliquely	19. retention
10. heresy	20. vicarious

UNIT SELF-TEST

1. Explain why it is important to achieve your maximum reading ability.
2. Name and explain at least five criteria for evaluating a piece of writing.
3. Tell what is meant by *recognition span, word-by-word reading, regression,* and *subvocalizing.*
4. Explain the difference between a summary and a critical review.
5. Explain why it is often a good plan to read more than one critical review of a piece of writing.

Unit 7

Writing Research Papers

At the highest level, research aims at discovery—at revealing a new chemical process, for instance, or a previously unknown historical document. But the methods of research at all levels are fundamentally the same. The researcher always shows where and how the results of his work were obtained. He never asserts as true something for which he offers no evidence. And the evidence he offers is documented so that his reader may refer to it himself and determine how well it has been used.

The research papers that you write will show the results of intelligent reading—rather than announce discoveries. But the methods you acquire in obtaining your results will be of use to you for the rest of your life. Whatever career you choose, knowing how to find facts and organize them into a logical presentation will always prove an asset to you.

Before reading further in this unit, answer the questions in the following Check Yourself section. Your answers will indicate your familiarity with the methods of preparing research papers.

Write the answers to the following questions.

1. Which of the following would make a suitable topic for a research paper of ordinary length? Explain your answer.

    The Government of the United States
    The President of the United States
    A Third Term for the President?

2. What is a *working bibliography?*
3. How are bibliography cards related to note cards?
4. What are two common methods for taking notes?
5. What are the four main parts of a research paper?

1. Doing the Research

THE TOPIC

Finding a suitable topic is perhaps the most important step you will take in writing your research paper. If you select a topic in which you have no interest, writing the paper will prove a difficult and boring task. If you select a topic that is too complicated or too broad, your paper will be superficial. In looking for a suitable topic, then, you should bear in mind your interests, your capacities, and the amount of time and space at your disposal.

It is probably best if you begin your search for a topic by selecting some general subject that interests you—architecture, the contemporary novel, water polo. Next, and very important, narrow down this subject. You might find, for example, that novels of the Second World War have a strong appeal for you. At this point you should consider the amount of time and space available for writing your paper. If your paper is to be relatively short—seven or eight pages—you may wish to do research on only one novel, or on only a single aspect of a novel. If you were to diagram this narrowing down process, it might be represented as follows:

the contemporary novel

novels of the Second World War

The Caine Mutiny by Herman Wouk

Wouk's handling of the conflict between authority and individual freedom

The last item of the diagram would make a suitable topic for a research paper.

Before you actually begin work on the paper, you should do some preliminary reading on your topic. Consult an encyclopedia to see if your topic is treated there. Whether it is or not, you should glance through some periodical indexes like *The Readers' Guide to Periodical Literature* to determine the amount of material written about your topic. If very little has been written, you may wish to select another topic. If you find that a fair amount has been written, you may proceed with your research.

DEVELOPING YOUR SKILL

A. The following is a list of subjects too general to be treated in a research paper of ordinary length. Be prepared to show in class how two of these subjects may be narrowed down to manageable topics.

advertising
athletics in high school
censorship
construction of buildings
Eskimos
federal housing
frozen foods
high-school slang

mining
photography
plastic surgery
Revolutionary War battles
sports cars
television
the United Nations
universal languages

B. Select a general subject for a research paper. Your subject may come from the list above or from a list that your teacher assigns. It might be one selected entirely by you. Narrow down this subject to a suitable topic and hand it in to your teacher for approval.

THE WORKING BIBLIOGRAPHY

Once you have decided on a topic for research, you should begin to compile a record of possible sources of information. Compiling this record will entail a trip—and perhaps several trips—to the library to examine encyclopedias, the card catalog, indexes of periodicals, and the vertical file. As you examine these materials, you should keep a record of possible sources of information on your topic. This record is called a *working bibliography*. It will become, after much pruning, the final bibliography of your research paper.

Each potential source of information should be recorded on a separate card. Cards 3 x 5 inches are commonly used. Each card should be numbered (its *source number)* and filed alphabetically by the author. The source number will be needed to identify each card throughout your research. The information on your cards should be complete and approach as closely as possible the form of the entries on a final bibliography. (See pages 147 and 153.) By filling out your bibliographical cards properly, you will be able to save much time later on.

The form for your entries will vary somewhat with the type of source noted. For example, an entry for a book will differ slightly from an entry for an article. The standard information you should include on your bibliographical cards is given below.

BOOK	ARTICLE
1. source number	1. source number
2. call number	2. author's name
3. author's name	3. title of article
4. title of book	4. name of periodical or book
5. city of publication	5. volume number (if any)
6. name of publisher	6. time of publication
7. year of publication	7. pages included in article

The following sequence of bibliographical cards show typical entries for books and articles.

BOOK ENTRY

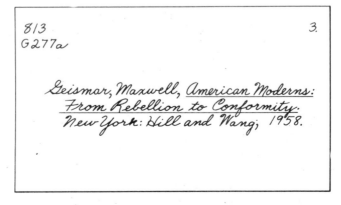

8/3
G277a   3.

Geismar, Maxwell, *American Moderns:*
From Rebellion to Conformity.
New York: Hill and Wang; 1958.

ARTICLE FROM A BOOK

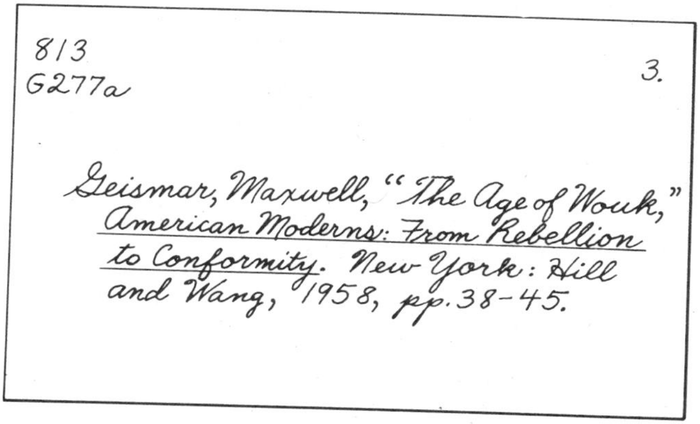

813
G277a   3.

Geismar, Maxwell, "The Age of Wouk,"
*American Moderns: From Rebellion
to Conformity.* New York: Hill
and Wang, 1958, pp. 38-45.

ARTICLE FROM A JOURNAL

2.

Carpenter, Frederick I.,
"Herman Wouk," *College
English,* vol. 17, January
1956, pp. 211-215.

In compiling your working bibliography, you should follow these
two rules: (1) If you are uncertain about recording an item of information concerning a source, record that item. The few seconds it will
take you now to make the note may save you much time later on. (2)
If you are uncertain whether a source is relevant to your topic, make
out a card anyway. Only after you have begun to read your sources
and take notes will you be in a position to say what is relevant and what
is not. Remember that you must accustom yourself to a high percentage
of looking for a low percentage of finding in any research project.

A. Be prepared to discuss the following questions in class.

   1. Why should the form of the entries of the working bibliography be as close as possible to the form of the entries of the final bibliography?
   2. What is the difference between an entry for a book and an entry for an article in a journal?
   3. Why is the call number for a book entered on the bibliographical card? Why is there no call number entered for an article in a journal or magazine?
   4. Why should each card have its own source number?

B. Prepare a working bibliography for the topic you selected for research.

NOTE TAKING

After you have compiled your working bibliography, the next step in your research is reading the sources and taking notes. Do not try to give each source in your working bibliography a full and careful reading. Doing so will only waste much time. You should, however, look up each source to determine its suitability. Sometimes, by simply reading the table of contents you will be able to tell whether a book contains information relevant to your topic. But more often than not, you will have to skim through a few pages of the source.

If your skimming indicates that a source has no bearing on your topic, you may set aside that bibliographical card, and proceed to the next source. If a source seems relevant, reread it—this time carefully and thoroughly, taking notes as you go along. You will find that lined index cards 4 x 6 inches in size are more convenient for taking notes than loose-leaf sheets or smaller index cards. As you take your notes, a central purpose for your research should begin to form in your mind. As this purpose becomes more definite, it will help you to determine which sources are really relevant.

If a cursory reading indicates that an article has a bearing on your topic, you should copy the source number onto your note card. By doing this you avoid having to repeat the bibliographical information. The note itself should be limited to a single aspect of your topic. Never use a single card for more than one source. And do not be skimpy in your note taking. You will find it much easier to write your paper from an abundance than from a scarcity of notes.

After you have transcribed a note, you should decide on a heading for it that accurately describes the information contained on the card. Write this heading in the upper left-hand corner of the note card. Be sure also that you have written down the exact page or pages of the source from which your note is taken. These headings on your note cards will help you later in preparing an outline for your paper. The page numbers of the sources will be needed when you make up your footnotes.

When you have finished taking your notes, you will probably find that you have several note cards for each heading and each source. You should not, however, have one card with several headings or several sources on it.

There are two methods commonly used for transcribing notes. The first of these methods is to quote directly. You transcribe the source exactly as it was written, duplicating the author's spelling and punctuation —even when they are wrong. After an error in a source, place *sic* in brackets to show that the error is not yours. For example, "It was in Cinciniti [*sic*] that he first held public office." However, do not place the term *sic* after older forms of words or after British forms. For example, do not place *sic* after the word *herte* in the following line by Chaucer, "Hard is the herte that loveth nought in May."

> "The Philipines (sic) became a charter member of the U.N. in 1945"

The second common method of transcribing notes is to paraphrase. In paraphrasing a quotation, you reproduce the author's thoughts, but in your own words. Generally, you summarize at the same time.

A third and less common method of note taking combines paraphrase with direct quotation. In using this method, you must be very careful to distinguish your own words from those of the author. Placing the author's words in quotes should enable you to keep the distinction clear.

The following sequence of notes illustrates the methods for taking notes.

DIRECT QUOTATION

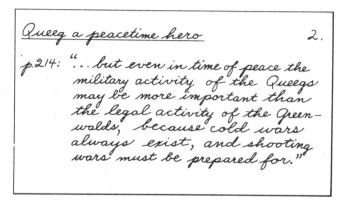

> *Queeg a peacetime hero*   2.
>
> p.214: "... but even in time of peace the military activity of the Queegs may be more important than the legal activity of the Green-walds, because cold wars always exist, and shooting wars must be prepared for."

PARAPHRASE AND DIRECT QUOTATION

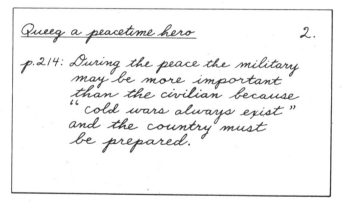

> *Queeg a peacetime hero*   2.
>
> p.214: During the peace the military may be more important than the civilian because "cold wars always exist" and the country must be prepared.

At times you may not need the entire original quotation and may wish to omit some part of it. In a direct quote, you must indicate where material is deleted by using points of *ellipsis*—a series of three dots. If material is deleted at the end of a sentence, you add a period, making four dots in all. Ellipses should never be used to distort the meaning of a source. Never, for example, omit the word *not* from a sentence.

At other times you may wish to insert something into a quotation, usually by way of explanation. In such cases you must indicate what is added by enclosing it in brackets. For example, "The Secretary [of State] then arranged for the conference to be held in Vienna." In adding to a direct quotation, again be careful not to distort the meaning of the original.

 DEVELOPING YOUR SKILL

A. Be ready to discuss the following questions in class.

1. What are the differences among the three methods for taking notes? What advantages, do you think, does each method have?
2. To what uses may brackets be put in citing quotations? In your explanation, be sure to mention the use of the term *sic*.
3. Why is the source number of the bibliography card written on the note card?
4. What are *ellipses* and when are they used?

B. Be prepared to write a bibliography card and a note card paraphrasing the following quotation. The quotation is from an article which appeared in the December 1961 edition of the *Atlantic*. Its title is "The Failure of Communism." Its author is Oscar Handlin. The volume number of the magazine is 208 and the quote is from page 41.

The workers and the peasants are as poorly off with regard to the clothes they wear or their chance of owning an electric appliance. The planners paid but the scantiest attention to their desires, and a creaky distribution system raised the cost of such goods beyond their reach. Of the immense increase in productivity in the past thirty years, only very meager crumbs have come to them.

C. Take notes from the sources listed in the working bibliography that you have prepared for your research paper.

Review Exercises—Doing the Research

A. Be prepared to discuss in class why you should only skim some sources listed on your bibliography cards and read others thoroughly.
B. Give your opinion of why the term *sic* should not be used after older forms and British forms of words. What implication is there in this rule concerning modern American spellings and word forms?
C. Hand in to your teacher the bibliography cards and note cards that you prepared for your research paper.

2. Writing the Paper

THE FIRST DRAFT

If you have selected your topic well and have done a thorough job of research, you should have little difficulty in writing your paper. Do not attempt, however, to go directly from your notes to a final draft. Instead, first prepare an outline of your paper, using the headings on your note cards. (For the correct forms for outlines, see rules 72-72b in the Handbook of this text.) Next, working from both outline and notes, prepare a first draft of your paper, documenting your quotations.

This first draft may have to be revised substantially, but it will serve as the basis of your final draft. As you revise the first draft, you will probably have to revise your outline, too. This revised outline will become your table of contents. Your bibliography cards, pruned of irrelevant sources, will become your final bibliography.

Outlining

Read carefully the notes you have taken. Then decide on the central purpose of your research. Write out this purpose in sentence form. With the central purpose in mind, go through your note cards and lay aside those that are not relevant. Do not proceed hastily. This sorting of the notes requires the exercise of logic and common sense. Take your time, weigh all the alternatives, and choose carefully.

Once you have sorted out the irrelevant notes, arrange the remaining notes into separate piles according to their headings. Look through these headings and decide which ones represent major divisions of your central purpose. Write these headings on a sheet of paper. You should find that the remaining cards tend to group themselves under one of these major headings.

The following is an outline, in finished form, of a research paper. Notice that the title comes first, then the statement of the central purpose, then the outline itself.

HERMAN WOUK AND THE DILEMMA OF AUTHORITY

Though <u>The Caine Mutiny</u> is a well-written story of the sea, the author's handling of the conflict between authority and individual freedom is contradictory and immature.

  I. Background of <u>The Caine Mutiny</u>
 II. Summary of the plot
    A. Character, personality, and skill of Captain Queeg
    B. Removal of Queeg from command of the <u>Caine</u> by Maryk
    C. Court martial of Maryk
    D. Defense of Queeg by Greenwald
III. Arguments against removal of Queeg from command
    A. Queeg a peacetime hero
    B. Removal of commander jeopardizes authority
 IV. Arguments for removal of Queeg from command
    A. Queeg incompetent in wartime
    B. No evidence of Queeg's peacetime competence
    C. Incompetence jeopardizes authority as much as removal from command

The making of an outline will enable you to see clearly the relations among the materials you have gathered. The outline itself will provide you with a plan for writing your paper and will insure that your paper is logically organized.

Documentation

In a research paper, you must give the source of each quotation and paraphrase that you use. The listing of these sources is known as *documentation*. Anyone who reads your paper should be able to check all your sources to determine how well you have used them.

Documentation in research papers is usually accomplished by means of footnotes. As you write your first draft, you should number each paraphrase and quotation. You should place a corresponding number at the bottom of the page and supply your reader with information about the source. This information is called a *footnote*. Footnotes are usually numbered consecutively throughout the paper, rather than beginning again on each new page.

There are several accepted styles of writing footnotes. The style used in the following examples is thus not the only correct way for writing footnotes. In studying the following specimens, you will notice that the form of the footnote varies with the type of source. The forms of the sources you are most likely to encounter in writing your paper are listed here.

BOOKS

One author, first edition:

    [1]F. O. Matthiessen, <u>American Renaissance</u> (New York: Oxford University Press, 1941), p. 5.

More than one author, more than one edition:

    [2]C. K. Ogden and I. A. Richards, <u>The Meaning of Meaning</u>, 8th ed. (London: Routledge & Kegan Paul, Ltd., 1946), pp. 24-26.

More than one volume:

    [3]Edgar Johnson, <u>Charles Dickens: His Tragedy and Triumph</u> (New York: Simon and Schuster, 1952), vol. 2, pp. 972-979.

Prepared by an editor:

    [4]J. William Hebel and Hoyt H. Hudson, eds., <u>Poetry of the English Renaissance: 1509-1660</u> (New York: Appleton-Century-Crofts, Inc., 1929), p. 472.

A translation:

    [5]Albert Camus, <u>The Plague</u>, trans. Stuart Gilbert (New York: Alfred A. Knopf, 1950), p. 61.

ARTICLES

Unsigned, from a magazine:

    [6]"Children Run Longer Than Plays," <u>Time</u>, vol. LXXVII, April 14, 1961, p. 82.

Signed, from a magazine:

    [7]Charles F. Cooper, "The Ecology of Fire," <u>Scientific American</u>, vol. 204, April 1961, p. 151.

Unsigned, from a newspaper:

> ⁸"Postal Rate Rise Voted by House," New York Times, January 24, 1962, p. 1, col. 1.

Signed, from a newspaper:

> ⁹Robert Cromie, "The Bystander," Chicago Sunday Tribune, January 28, 1962, pt. 4, p. 4, col. 3.

Unsigned, from an encyclopedia:

> ¹⁰"International Dateline," Encyclopaedia Britannica, 1958 ed., vol. 12, p. 515.

Signed, from an encyclopedia:

> ¹¹Ernest E. Wahlstrom, "Geyser," World Book Encyclopedia, 1962 ed., vol. 7, p. 163.

From a collection:

> ¹²H. G. Wells, "Stephen Crane From An English Standpoint," The Shock of Recognition, ed. Edmond Wilson (New York: Farrar, Straus and Cudahy, 1955), pp. 661–662.

If you refer to the same source more than once, you need not repeat the entire footnote. If the second reference to a source occurs immediately after the first reference, you may use the term *ibid.* and the page number. This term is an abbreviation of the Latin *ibidem* and it means "in the same place."

> ¹F. O. Matthiessen, American Renaissance (New York: Oxford University Press, 1941), p. 5.

> ²Ibid., p. 73.

If the second reference to a source has other references intervening between it and the first reference, use the term *op. cit.,* meaning "in the work cited," and the author's last name.

> ¹F. O. Matthiessen, American Renaissance (New York: Oxford University Press, 1941), p. 5.

> ²Stephen E. Whicher, "Ralph Waldo Emerson," World Book Encyclopedia, ed., vol. 5, pp. 208–209.

> ³Matthiessen, op. cit., p. 73.

Do not use *op. cit.,* however, if more than one source by the same author is referred to in the paper.

A. Be prepared to discuss in class the advantages of making an outline of your research paper. What are the steps involved in making this outline?

B. Be ready to explain to the class the differences between the terms *ibid.* and *op. cit.* Also describe the situations in which each term may be used correctly.

C. Type or write a copy of the outline of your research paper and submit it to your teacher.

D. Write the first draft of your research paper.

THE FINAL DRAFT

All revisions should be made before the final draft is prepared. The final draft should be as nearly perfect as you can make it and free from any major corrections. Rather than make corrections on a page of the final draft, it is better to rewrite or retype that page.

Mechanics

Your final draft should be typed, or written in ink, on only one side of unruled white paper. The customary size of the paper is 8½ x 11 inches. You should leave margins at the top, bottom, and sides of 1 to 1½ inches. If you type your paper, the text should be double spaced—except where quotations of longer than three lines are used. Such quotations are usually set off from the body of the text—that is, they are indented four spaces from the left-hand margin, single-spaced, and written without quotation marks.

The first line of each paragraph is indented seven spaces. The first line of each footnote is also indented seven spaces; subsequent lines are even with the margin and single-spaced. A double space, however, should be left between the footnotes. Footnotes should be separated from the text by a line about twelve to sixteen spaces long. After each citation and before each footnote there should be a superior numeral—a numeral raised slightly above the line of type or writing—which shows the reader which citation belongs with which footnote.

You begin the numbering of your paper on page two and end on the page the bibliography appears. Place each number in the upper right-hand corner of the page.

When you have finished the final draft of your research paper, you will find that it consists of four main sections. These are as follows:

1. The title page, on which appears the title of the paper, the name of the course, the teacher's name, the date, the student's name
2. The table of contents, which is the final outline with the proper page numbers inserted alongside the headings
3. The body of the paper
4. The bibliography

Bibliography

Every source that is quoted or paraphrased in your paper should be listed in your bibliography. The form of the entries in your bibliography should match that of the entries in your working bibliography.

The sources in your bibliography should be arranged alphabetically according to the author's last name. If the author of the source is unknown, list the source according to the first word in the title, unless the first word is *the, a,* or *an.*

If more than one source by the same author is included in your bibliography, you do not have to repeat the author's name. Instead, simply place a seven-space line in the subsequent entries where his name would appear. For example:

```
Matthiessen, F. 0., American Renaissance. New York: Oxford Uni-
     versity Press, 1941, pp. 221-229.

_____, Henry James: The Major Phase. New York: Oxford Univer-
     sity Press, 1946, pp. 131-151.
```

If a source has two authors, only the order of the first author's name is reversed for the purposes of alphabetizing. The name of the second author is written in the normal order.

Sample research paper

By studying the following sample research paper, you will be able to resolve most of the problems of form you encounter in the course of writing your paper.

HERMAN WOUK AND THE DILEMMA OF AUTHORITY

Herman Wouk's novel The Caine Mutiny was published in 1951 and received at the time almost uniformly favorable reviews. The same year it became a best-seller and was awarded the Pulitzer prize for fiction. In less than four years, five million copies of The Caine Mutiny were sold in the United States and Great Britain, and the book was translated into seventeen languages.[1] Wouk's novel deserves special consideration because it differs from many other best-sellers in two important respects. It is well written, and it deals with a serious theme.

Wouk took as his theme the conflict between established authority and individual freedom in time of crisis. In the last few years Wouk's handling of this theme has been the subject of a critical controversy. The reactions of the critics will be surveyed in this paper. The purpose of this paper is to draw certain conclusions about the value of Wouk's novel in the light of these reactions.

The Caine in the title of the novel is a U. S. Navy mine sweeper, converted from an old 1918-model destroyer, on duty in the South Pacific during the Second World War. As the story begins, the Caine is commanded by Captain De Vriess, a skilled and experienced seaman. De Vriess is also a lax disciplinarian concerning matters of minor importance. "All De Vriess cared about was results," says Tom Maryk, the executive officer and second in command of the Caine.[2] When De Vriess

---

[1]"The Wouk Mutiny," Time, vol. LXVI, September 5, 1955, p. 48.

[2]Herman Wouk, The Caine Mutiny: A Novel of World War II (Garden City, N. Y.: Doubleday & Company, Inc., 1951), p. 48.

is transferred, he is replaced by Captain Queeg. The atmosphere aboard ship suddenly changes. Queeg insists that every minor detail be carried out "by the book," but refuses to admit his own mistakes, blaming them instead on others. Morale and efficiency quickly decline under his command. Says one critic: "His [Queeg's] nagging and vindictive discipline, his antagonism of crew and wardroom, and his eccentric seamanship are the outward manifestation of a man who is inwardly a paranoiac and a coward."[3] Other critics agree on Queeg's basic character. One calls him "a martinet, a liar, a petty tyrant, and, when the chips were down in combat, a coward."[4] Another refers to him as a "testy incompetent."[5]

Gradually, as Queeg's blunders become more frequent and more well known, opposition to Queeg forms and hardens. Tom Keefer, the communications officer, is the leader and the articulate spokesman for this opposition. Finally, during a typhoon in the Philippine Sea, when the ship seems about to be destroyed and Queeg seems on the verge of a mental collapse, he is removed from command by Tom Maryk, and the ship is saved.

Back in port in San Francisco Maryk is put on trial for mutiny. In a devastating cross-examination by Barney Greenwald, Maryk's defense counsel, Queeg becomes hysterical and reveals himself to be suffering from severe delusions of persecution. Maryk is acquitted by the court.

At a celebration party given that night by Tom Keefer,

[3]Edward Weeks, "The Peripatetic Reviewer," The Atlantic, vol. 188, August 1951, p. 79.

[4]"Realism Without Obscenity," Time, vol. LVII, April 9, 1951, p. 110.

[5]Lee Rogow, "Review of The Caine Mutiny," Saturday Review of Literature, vol. 34, March 31, 1951, p. 17.

Barney Greenwald, presumably speaking for Wouk, denounces
Keefer as the instigator of an unnecessary mutiny and defends
Queeg as a kind of hero. Queeg's peacetime service in the
U. S. Navy helped his country be prepared when war came, Green-
wald says, and for that "Queeg deserved better at my hands."[6]
A little later in the novel the alternative to the mutiny is
stated by Willie Keith, through whose eyes the action of the
novel is seen. Wouk has Keith say:

> The idea is, once you get an incompetent . . . skip-
> per—and it's a chance of war—there's nothing to do but
> serve him as though he were the wisest and the best, cover
> his mistakes, keep the ship going, and bear up.[7]

Wouk is saying, in effect, that the authority of a commander does not depend upon his competence, but is absolute.
And yet—and here is where the contradiction arises—Articles
184, 185, and 186 of Navy Regulations provide that a commander
may be removed by a subordinate under certain "unusual and ex-
traordinary circumstances."[8] The mental instability of the
commander in time of crisis would be such a circumstance. Wouk
quotes these articles and has Maryk act in accordance with
them.

Why then, at the end of the book, is the reader asked
to sympathize with Queeg? Some critics have accepted the author's answer that Queeg's peacetime service was a heroic contribution to his country's preparedness.[9] Other critics have
supplied Wouk with an additional answer. They say that the

---

[6]Wouk, op. cit., p. 448.

[7]Ibid., p. 468.

[8]Ibid., pp. xi-xxi.

[9]Frederick I. Carpenter, "Herman Wouk," College English, vol. 17, January 1956, p. 214.

removal of a captain from his command establishes a dangerous precedent—that such an action jeopardizes the authority of all commanders. In a cover story on Wouk, the writer for _Time_ magazine even implied that the defense of Queeg was an affirmation of the author's belief in "hallowed institutions like the U. S. Navy."[10]

The argument about jeopardizing authority by allowing the removal of a commander to go unpunished seems to have much force—especially when it stands alone. It should be remembered, however, that there is more than one way to jeopardize authority. Maintaining an incompetent commander would seem to be an equally good way. In the case at hand, there is also the safety of the ship's company to be considered. If Wouk had shown Queeg anywhere in the book possessed even of a grain of common sense, Queeg's removal during the typhoon would have seemed less necessary. But Wouk has not shown this. By contrasting Queeg's ability with that of De Vriess, Wouk has shown Queeg to be highly undependable. Thus, when one considers, first, the safety of the ship and, second, the lack of respect for authority generated by an incompetent commander, the argument against setting a dangerous precedent loses its force.

Queeg's contribution to wartime preparedness is even harder to accept. From the beginning Queeg is unable to cope with even routine matters. What is worse, he refuses to accept responsibility for his decisions. The first time he takes the _Caine_ out to sea, he scrapes another ship alongside and runs the _Caine_ up onto a mud-bar. And each time Queeg blunders, he tries to shift the blame to one of his subordinates

---

[10]"The Wouk Mutiny," _op. cit._, p. 48.

in order to save face. It is hard to believe that such a man
ever had anything to contribute. Says one critic:

> But if Queeg is no good in the active period of World War
> II, which is the case, there is little reason to suppose
> that he was any good before. His great achievement, we
> learn, in his early career, was in catching a cheese
> thief.[11]

Considered solely as a story of the sea, The Caine Mutiny is an excellent novel. Wouk's descriptions, his charac-
terizations, and his dialogue, his ability to write clearly
and interestingly are matched by few other novelists of this
period. Almost every critic who has reviewed this novel rates
Wouk's narrative skill very high. But when Wouk's handling of
the conflict between authority and freedom is considered, there
remains what Lee Rogow calls "an undigested immaturity."[12]
In fact, Wouk's handling of this theme is very close to Tenny-
son's "Theirs not to reason why,/ Theirs but to do and die."
Wouk seems to be equating unreasoned submission to authority
with personal honor.

Such an equation is surely wrongheaded. "Most serious
writers," says Maxwell Geismar in an essay on Wouk, "do have
an inherent belief in decency and honor. But it is just this
belief that so often made them rebel against empty discipline
and blind, dangerous, or evil authority."[13] It is just this
belief that Wouk lacks. And, in my opinion, it marks Wouk as
one who treats serious themes, but is not himself a serious
writer.

---

[11]James R. Browne, "Distortion in The Caine Mutiny,"
College English, vol. 17, January 1956, p. 216.

[12] Rogow, op. cit., p. 17.

[13]Maxwell Geismar, "The Age of Wouk," American Moderns:
From Rebellion to Conformity (New York: Hill and Wang, 1958),
p. 43.

BIBLIOGRAPHY

Browne, James R., "Distortion in The Caine Mutiny," College
    English, vol. 17, January 1956, pp. 216-218.

Carpenter, Frederick I., "Herman Wouk," College English, vol.
    17, January 1956, pp. 211-215.

Geismar, Maxwell, "The Age of Wouk," American Moderns: From
    Rebellion to Conformity. New York: Hill and Wang, 1958,
    pp. 38-45.

"Realism Without Obscenity," Time, vol. LVII, April 9, 1951,
    p. 110.

Rogow, Lee, "Review of The Caine Mutiny," Saturday Review of
    Literature, vol. 34, March 31, 1951, p. 17.

Weeks, Edward, "The Peripatetic Reviewer," The Atlantic, vol.
    188, August 1951, p. 79.

Wouk, Herman, The Caine Mutiny: A Novel of World War II, Gar-
    den City, New York: Doubleday & Company, Inc., 1951.

"The Wouk Mutiny," Time, vol. LXVI, September 5, 1955, p. 48+.

▶ DEVELOPING YOUR SKILL

A. Be prepared to discuss in class the steps to be taken in preparing the first draft of your paper for the final draft.

B. Prepare the final draft of your paper for submission to your teacher. Before you hand it in, proofread the paper very carefully. Check details of form with the recommendations made in this section.

Review Exercises—Writing the Paper

A. Examine the sample research paper and be ready to explain the use of *ibid.* and *op. cit.* on pages 150 to 152. If these two terms were not used, how would the references then read?

B. Write a short theme explaining the necessity of documenting all quotes and paraphrases in your research paper. In connection with this theme, look up the word *plagiarism* in the dictionary.

UNIT SUMMARY

Putting together a good research paper requires that you systematically carry out six steps. First, you should choose a general subject that interests you and narrow this subject down until you have a suitable topic.

Next, you should compile a working bibliography—a record of possible sources of information on your topic. Third, you should take notes from those sources that have a direct bearing on your topic. Fourth, you should make an outline as a guide to writing your paper. Fifth, using this outline and your notes, you should prepare a first draft of your paper, documenting your sources. This first draft will serve as the basis of the final draft you hand into your teacher. Writing a research paper can be either an interesting or a burdensome task—depending on how you go about it.

UNIT REVIEW EXERCISES

DISCUSSION TOPICS

A. Discuss how one should go about selecting a topic suitable for research. What factors are involved? Be ready to give examples of poorly chosen topics and well-chosen topics.
B. Why is it necessary to list more sources in your working bibliography than you can probably use? Why should you take more notes than you can probably use?

WRITTEN WORK

A. Write a short composition discussing the values of research. How can the techniques learned doing research help you later on?
B. Using the form recommended on page 147, compile a bibliography of seven to ten sources from one of the subjects listed on page 135.

VOCABULARY

Write the numbers 1 to 5 on a sheet of paper. After each number select the letter of the word or phrase that most closely approximates the meaning of the italicized word in each sentence. Before indicating your choice, turn to the page in this unit where the word was used first.

1. He could not *accustom* himself to such a radical change of environment. [p. 137]

   (*a*) tolerate; (*b*) get used to; (*c*) thrive on; (*d*) believe in
2. His examinations were always *cursory*. [p. 138]
   (*a*) thorough; (*b*) superficial; (*c*) difficult; (*d*) exhaustive

3. It was *substantially* the same excuse she had been giving for years.

[p. 142]

  (*a*) basically; (*b*) exactly; (*c*) generally; (*d*) precisely

4. Their testimony was highly *contradictory*.   [p. 143]

  (*a*) controversial; (*b*) sympathetic; (*c*) stimulating; (*d*) conflicting

5. A *vindictive* judge cannot administer justice.   [p. 149]

  (*a*) biased; (*b*) indifferent; (*c*) vengeful; (*d*) hostile

SPELLING

All of the following words were chosen because they are commonly misspelled. Some of these words were used in this unit. Study these words and be prepared to write them correctly when your teacher dictates them to you.

1. accustom	11. competition
2. cursory	12. continually
3. substantially	13. decided
4. contradictory	14. disappeared
5. vindictive	15. gardener
6. manifestation	16. intelligence
7. documentation	17. lightning
8. burdensome	18. portrayed
9. disciplinarian	19. preparations
10. devastating	20. restaurant

UNIT SELF-TEST

1. Which of the following would make a suitable topic for a research paper of ordinary length?

  (*a*) Shakespeare's plays;   (*b*) *Julius Caesar;*   (*c*) motivation of Brutus

2. List the four parts of a research paper.

3. List in their order the steps taken in preparing a research paper.

4. Name the three parts of a final outline of a research paper.

5. What is the difference between the sequence in which footnotes are presented and the sequence in which the items in the bibliography are presented?

Unit 8

Writing Effective Paragraphs

The secret to writing effective prose rests upon one's ability to construct effective paragraphs. Anyone who can put together a good paragraph can write a good multiparagraph composition, for the criteria for the long composition are, on a larger scale, the same as those for the paragraph. You will learn in this unit what these criteria are, and you will practice constructing paragraphs that meet the criteria.

Your own experience tells you that not all paragraphs are alike. For example, a paragraph that relates an incident is different from a paragraph that describes a scene or explains a process. Not all paragraphs are developed in the same way, either. This unit will help you to recognize the purposes of paragraphs, the methods of developing paragraphs, and the ways in which paragraphs are held together.

 CHECK YOURSELF

Write short answers to each of the following questions.

1. What are the basic purposes of paragraphs?
2. What are some methods by which paragraphs are developed?
3. What qualities hold a paragraph together?
4. What is paragraph unity?
5. What is coherence?
6. In what ways can the items in a paragraph be arranged?

157

1. The Purposes of Paragraphs

Paragraphs may be classified in various ways depending upon their purposes. The purposes may be either *narration, description, exposition,* or *argument.* These are commonly called the four *forms of discourse.* You will seldom find a piece of writing that is one kind exclusively. Most narration, for example, contains some description and explanation. But in all writing, one of the forms must dominate. Using the forms together is a skill that you can develop after learning to use each of them individually.

NARRATION

The purpose of narration is to relate to a reader something that has occurred. It may be an author's personal experience, an experience of a friend, or an experience that the author has imagined. As a reader, you have your own standards for narration. The narrative must make some effort to gain your attention. It must be interesting from the outset. The language must be clear, and the events of the narrative must be well chosen so that your interest is maintained. It must proceed in an orderly fashion from beginning to end, and it must have a logical outcome.

Examine the following narrative excerpt. Does it meet your requirements for a good narrative?

> I got thoroughly lost in Bangor, what with traffic and trucks, horns blaring and lights changing. I vaguely remembered that I should be on U. S. Highway 1, and I found it and drove ten miles in the wrong direction, back towards New York. I had been given written directions on how to go, detailed directions, but have you ever noticed that instruction from one who knows the country gets you more lost than you are, even when they are accurate? I also got lost in Ellsworth, which I am told is impossible. Then the roads narrowed and the lumber trucks roared past me. I was lost almost all day, even though I found Blue Hill and Sedgwick. Late in the despairing afternoon I stopped my truck and approached a majestic Maine state trooper. What a man he was, granite as any

quarried about Portland, a perfect model for some future equestrian statue. I wonder if future heroes will be carved in marble jeeps or patrol cars?

—JOHN STEINBECK, *Travels with Charley in Search of America*

DEVELOPING YOUR SKILL

A. Be prepared to discuss the following in the Steinbeck paragraph.

1. The purpose
2. Words or phrases that keep the reader aware of time
3. Kinds of writing other than narrative

B. Locate the sentences that narrate the experience Steinbeck is writing about. Be prepared to discuss whether he gives either too many or too few details of the experience.

C. Write a narrative paragraph about a trip you have taken. Be certain to include the following items in your paragraph.

1. An interesting beginning
2. Logical order of events
3. Lively language
4. Rapid movement of the narrative

DESCRIPTION

Very often you are asked to describe something you have seen—a painting, a room, the exterior of a building, a person. You can probably recall hearing someone describe someone or something for you. You know that some descriptions you hear are good and that some are bad. What makes a description good is the describer's attention to important details—details that you might miss even if you saw the thing being described.

Suppose that you were asked to describe a person to a friend. You would probably first make a generalization: "He is really good looking" or "His looks are nothing to get excited about." After you had made the generalization, you would begin to list the details that support the generalization. You would limit the details to those that support your general statement. Some authors arrange their details to support a generalization that follows the details.

There are many fine descriptions in the world of literature. Read the following brief description carefully. Locate the author's generalization and the details that support it.

> I turned my head, as sleep's heaviness lifted from it, and looked through the window. A few frost-ferns had sprouted from the lower corners of the upper panes. The early sun lay tan on the stubble of the big field beyond the dirt road. The road was pink. The bare trees took white on their sun side; a curious ruddiness was caught in their twigs. Everything looked frozen; the two strands of telephone wire looked locked into place in the sky's blue ice.
>
> —JOHN UPDYKE, *The Centaur*

A. Be prepared to discuss the following questions about the preceding excerpt.

   1. In what position is the author?
   2. Is the order of the details natural?
   3. Which details are most memorable?
   4. What is the generalization?

B. Select a view that you can visualize, a scene looked down upon from a high hill, a cabin in the woods, or a part of a garden. Write a paragraph of description about the view you select. Begin your paragraph with a generalization. Choose the salient details and arrange them in a logical order. Try to avoid using forms of the verb *to be*.

EXPOSITION

The aim of exposition is to explain. This book is almost completely expository. If you wanted to give directions, explain how to change a tire, tell someone the uses of aluminum, or explain how rain is made, you would use exposition. Exposition is used to explain abstract ideas such as communism, materialism, or existentialism. It is the form of discourse used in newspaper editorials and by news commentators. Exposition is, in short, a broad term for any writing that conveys facts and ideas to make a reader better informed.

Every expository paragraph contains a main idea that may be either explicit or implicit. The main idea is supported by specific information.

Read carefully the following expository paragraphs. Look for the main idea in each and list the specific items of information that support the main idea in each paragraph.

Whitman was born into a declining family which tended in the poet's generation to suffer neurosis, idiocy, poverty, sickness, and hard luck. He was the second of nine children. Of these one brother, Jesse, . . . died after years in an insane asylum. The youngest brother, Eddie, was an imbecile and epileptic. Walt's favorite sister, Hannah, though gifted, became squalid, eccentric, and unbalanced during a long and harrowing marriage to an indigent painter who tried to make an artistic career in Burlington, Vermont, and was given to spells of drunkenness and paranoia. The family life which nourished so much human failure seems to have been characterized in Walt's boyhood by a kind of moral and psychic squalor, anxiety, restlessness, and vagrancy, and there can be no doubt that Whitman's lifelong concern with cleanliness and health, which borders sometimes on the crankish and forms also a part of his prophetic program for democracy, was a response to his family life. The wishful image one remembers from Whitman's newspaper editorials of Manhattan surrounded by thousands of healthy citizens bathing in the rivers is a utopian compensation for the squalor he had known. And the history of his brothers and sisters lends a certain concreteness to the word "sane" in the well-known phrase from "When Lilacs Last in the Dooryard Bloom'd." "O sane and sacred death."

—RICHARD CHASE, *Walt Whitman Reconsidered*

The course of evolution is full of monstrous and absurd beasts so erratically fashioned that they proved to be their own undoing. Animals have repeatedly gone off in the direction of specializing some part of themselves until they have reduced the thing to futile absurdity. Some of the dinosaurs got bigger and bigger until their size became an outright handicap; the elephant, the hippopotamus, the gorilla are going the same way. The tusks, the horns, the teeth, the jaws of many animals have become so specialized that they bind these animals down to living a very limited kind of life. Many adaptations start out by being useful but end up through excessive development in being a disadvantage. It is so common to find excessive specialization just preceding the extermination of a race that one comes to associate them together, and to accept the one as a sign of senescence presaging the other. The highly specialized animal is reaching the end of its blind alley.

—HOMER W. SMITH, *Kamongo, or The Lungfish and the Padre*

DEVELOPING YOUR SKILL

A. Be prepared to tell why each of the preceding paragraphs is an example of good exposition.

B. Write a 150–200 word expository paragraph on one of the following topics. Be sure to make the purpose of your paragraph clear and to support your main idea with specific facts.

   1. A political figure of our time
   2. A concept you have learned in history or science
   3. The literary works of an author you have read

ARGUMENT

The fourth form of discourse, *argument,* is closely allied to exposition. Whereas the general purpose of exposition is to explain, that of argument is to convince. You use argument every day, especially in your speech. In your efforts to convince your parents or your friends of some idea you have, you use this form of discourse.

Paragraphs of argument usually begin with a specific proposition—a statement proposed for ultimate acceptance by the reader. Authors of paragraphs of argument must assume that there is opposition to their proposition and must, therefore, offer an abundance of logical reasoning to support the proposition.

If your purpose in a paragraph is to convince your readers that football is America's number one sport, you will have some opposition. Once the facts are known, your readers may agree with the proposition. The important thing to remember is that you must include only the items that logically support your proposition while remaining aware of the possible opposition to it.

Read the following paragraph about language. Notice how certain the author is of his conviction.

> In the first place, language is basically speech. Speech comes first in the life of the individual and of the race. It begins in infancy and continues throughout our lives; we produce and attend to a spoken wordage much greater than the written. Even the mass of writing which floods in upon us today is only the froth of an ocean of speech. In history, also, speech comes first. English has been written for only about fifteen hundred years; before this, it is of incalculable antiquity. In speech its grammar was developed; from changes in the sounds of speech, changes in its grammar come. The educated are inclined to feel that the most important aspect of language is the written form of it, and that the spoken language must and should take its standards from this. Actually, the great flow of influence is from speech to writing. Writing does influence speech somewhat, but its influence is like the interest a bank pays on the principal entrusted to it. No principal, no interest.
>
> —DONALD J. LLOYD, "Snobs, Slobs, and the English Language"

 DEVELOPING YOUR SKILL

A. Be prepared to discuss the following about the preceding paragraph.

1. What is the specific proposition?
2. Is the support logical and clear?
3. Does the author show awareness of opposition?

B. Write a 150-word paragraph of argument on a topic about which you feel very strongly. Limit the support for your proposition to logically derived facts. Remember to allow for the opposition that may exist to your proposition.

Review Exercises—The Purposes of Paragraphs

A. From a short story or novel that you have read, select several paragraphs that demonstrate one or more of the forms of discourse. Be prepared to read the paragraphs in class and to discuss them in class.
B. Write a short paragraph in which you consciously include sentences of narration, description, exposition and argument. Be prepared to explain which sentences are of which type.

2. Paragraph Development

Almost infinite variety exists in the ways in which paragraphs can be developed. An author determines how he can best accomplish the purpose of his paragraph, and then he sets about writing it. He determines his method before he begins writing so that he knows in what direction his paragraph is heading.

Most good paragraphs include a general statement, which can appear anywhere in the paragraph but which usually comes at either the beginning or the end, and some manner of support for that generalization. The differences in paragraph development are in the methods of supporting generalizations. Many paragraphs are developed by one or a combination of the following methods: *example and illustration, detail,* and *comparison and contrast.*

EXAMPLE AND ILLUSTRATION

Example and illustration are similar methods of paragraph development. Both are used to support a generalization in a paragraph. The following paragraph uses numerous examples that support a generalization, which appears at the end of the paragraph.

If the painter wishes to see enchanting beauties, he has the power to produce them. If he wishes to see monstrosities, whether terrifying, or ludicrous and laughable, or pitiful, he has the power and authority to create them. If he wishes to produce towns or deserts,

if in the hot season he wants cool and shady places, or in the cold season warm places, he can make them. If he wants valleys, if from high mountaintops he wants to survey vast stretches of country, if beyond he wants to see the horizon on the sea, he has the power to create all this; and likewise, if from deep valleys he wants to see high mountains or from high mountains deep valleys and beaches. Indeed, whatever exists in the universe, whether in essence, in act, or in the imagination, the painter has first in his mind and then in his hands. His hands are of such excellence that they can present to our view simultaneously whatever well-proportioned harmonies real things exhibit piecemeal.

—LEONARDO DA VINCI, "The Painter's Hands," *Artists on Art*

The examples in this paragraph are numerous and brief. They all lead to and support the last two sentences in the paragraph.

The difference between example and illustration is slight. An illustration is simply an extended example. A typical paragraph developed with illustrations might have only one or two items of support, while a paragraph developed by examples would have many more. Examine the following paragraph, which is developed with two illustrations.

A nation which has forgotten the quality of courage which in the past has been brought to public life is not as likely to insist upon or reward that quality in its chosen leaders today—and in fact we have forgotten. We may remember how John Quincy Adams became President through the political schemes of Henry Clay, but we have forgotten how, as a young man, he gave up a promising Senatorial career to stand by the nation. We may remember Daniel Webster for his subservience to the National Bank throughout much of his career, but we have forgotten his sacrifice for the national good at the close of that career. We do not remember--and possibly we do not care.

—JOHN F. KENNEDY, *Profiles in Courage*

In this paragraph the generalization comes first and is followed by the two illustrations. Illustrations must be especially carefully chosen because there are fewer of them. If one example of five or six is not a strong one, a paragraph could still be a good one because of the four or five good examples. If one illustration is bad, the paragraph would probably fail.

DEVELOPING YOUR SKILL

A. The general statements in the two example paragraphs are in opposite positions in their paragraphs. Be prepared to discuss whether either author might successfully have changed the position of his general statement.

B. Write the following paragraphs.

1. A two-hundred-word paragraph of description in which you use four or five examples.
2. A two-hundred-word paragraph of exposition in which you use two illustrations.

DETAIL

Accumulating pertinent detail is another method of supporting a generalization in a paragraph. Detail is especially important in paragraphs of description. As you saw earlier in this unit, detail is what makes a description complete. Merely to say that a building is impressive tells the reader nothing about the building. Details must be added to support the generalization about the building.

Detail is also important in expository and narrative paragraphs. To explain something to a reader requires considerable attention to detail. To relate an incident interestingly also requires that the author include enough detail so that the reader can follow the action easily.

Read the following paragraph, paying close attention to the amount of rich detail amassed in so small a description. While the basic purpose of the paragraph seems to be description, there is an element of narration.

> From top to bottom the service stairs provided an astounding spectacle. Doors were opening now on every floor and other tenants were coming out to swell the tide of refugees. They made an extraordinary conglomeration—a composite of classes, types, and characters that could have been found nowhere else save in a New York apartment house such as this. There were people in splendid evening dress, and beautiful women blazing jewels and wearing costly wraps. There were others in pajamas who had evidently been awakened from sleep and had hastily put on slippers, dressing gowns, kimonos, or whatever garments they could snatch up in the excitement of the moment. There were young and old, masters and servants, a mixture of a dozen races and their excited babel of strange tongues. There were German cooks and French maids, English butlers and Irish serving girls. There were Swedes and Danes and Italians and Norwegians, with a sprinkling of White Russians. There were Poles and Czechs and Austrians, Negroes and Hungarians. All of these poured out helter-skelter on the landing stages of the service stairway, chattering, gesticulating, their interests all united now in their common pursuit of safety.
>
> —Thomas Wolfe, *You Can't Go Home Again*

A. In the preceding example paragraph many descriptive details are given. Be ready to point out some of the details and to tell how they contribute to the development of the paragraph.

B. Recall an event that you have witnessed—a large meeting, a political convention on television, a football game that you have seen. Choose an event that you could see all of, not just one small portion. Write a generalization about the scene and then list at least six or eight details that contributed to the scene. Then write a two-hundred-word descriptive paragraph about the event, using details to support your generalization.

COMPARISON AND CONTRAST

Other commonly employed methods of paragraph development are comparison and contrast. You use these methods often in your casual conversation. In comparing or contrasting things or ideas, you may choose to make an item-by-item comparison or contrast, or you may choose to present all the information about one part of the topic first and all information about the other part second.

Note how the author of the following paragraph toys with contrast. He does not state that he will contrast two elements, but the contrast is still a successful one. Does he employ an item-by-item contrast, or does he give information about the two ideas separately?

All ruthless intrusions of chance aside, the truth would seem to be that the man who would lead his people, boldly and democratically, must perform—perhaps even live—an almost endless series of marvelous conjuring acts. By these feats, he strives to neutralize and to pacify the crude contradictions of political life. He must proudly know and profess principle—yet sometimes keep his greater purposes from being blunted by his lesser scruples. He must summon his people to be with him—yet stand above, not squat beside, them. He must respect the opinions and the powers of others—but not too much. He must question his own wisdom and rightness—but only a little. He must appease the doubts of the skeptic and assuage the hurts of the adversary—sometimes. He must be aggressive without being contentious, decisive without being arrogant, and compassionate without being confused. He must respect ideas—without adulating them as substitutes for acts. He must respect action—without unharnessing it from thought and reason. He must respect words—without becoming intoxicated with his own. He must have a dramatic sense of history that inspires him to magnify the trivial, fleeting event to serve his distant goal— and to grasp the gravest crisis as if it were the merest nettle. He must be pragmatic, calculating, and earthbound—and yet know when to spurn the mean arithmetic of expediency for the act of utter courage, the sublime gamble that holds no hope beyond the audacity of his own imagination.

—EMMET JOHN HUGHES, *The Ordeal of Power*

 DEVELOPING YOUR SKILL

A. Analyze the preceding example paragraph closely. Do you think the paragraph would have been as effective if the author had chosen to develop the contrast by treating all the things a leader must be and then all the things he must not be? Be ready to defend your position.
B. Select two novels or short stories or poems that you have read recently and compare or contrast one small element in the two works. You could choose elements like characterization or setting or use of language. Write a 150-word paragraph comparing or contrasting the element you choose.

ORDERING OF IDEAS

In almost every paragraph there is a system for ordering the examples, illustrations, or details. Items can be ordered chronologically, as they usually are in narration, or spatially, as they normally are in description. They can go from least important to most important, from smallest to largest, or from simple to complex. There is, in short, almost no limit to the ways in which the ideas in paragraphs may be ordered. The important point is that the author must have an order in mind and must keep his reader informed of it.

What determines the order of the details in the following excerpt from a description of a painting? Is the paragraph clear? Does the reader know where the writer is taking him in the description?

> "I begin from the distance," said I. "I see in the farthest background a very clear sky, as if after sunset. Then, still in the far distance, a village and a town, in the light of evening. In the middle of the picture there is a road, along which a flock of sheep is hastening to the village. At the right hand of the picture are several haystacks, and a wagon which appears well laden. Unharnessed horses are grazing near. On one side, among the bushes, are several mares with their foals, which appear as if they were going to remain out of doors all night. Then, nearer to the foreground, there is a group of large trees; and lastly, quite in the foreground to the left, there are various laborers returning homewards."
>
> —JOHANN ECKERMANN, *Conversations of Goethe with Eckermann*

The place in a paragraph in which you present ideas can give greater *emphasis* to those ideas. A speaker or writer wishing to appeal to an audience might choose to make his strongest appeal at the beginning of his speech or essay, or he might wish to reserve it for the end. The author must decide which way he thinks would be more effective.

Read the following two paragraphs, which might well have been combined into one. Pay especially close attention to the emphasis given to the main idea of the excerpt.

Democracy is the worst form of government. It is the most inefficient, the most clumsy, the most impractical. No machinery has yet been contrived to carry out in any but the most farcical manner its principles. It reduces wisdom to impotence and secures the triumph of folly, ignorance, claptrap, and demagogy. The critics of democracy have the easiest of tasks in demonstrating its inefficiency.

But there is something even more important than efficiency and expediency, namely, justice. And democracy is the only social order that is admissible, because it is the *only one consistent with justice*. The moral consideration is supreme. Efficiency, even practical wisdom and success must go by the board. They are of no account beside the categorical imperative of justice. Justice is only possible when to every man belongs the power to resist and claim redress for wrongs. That is democracy—and that is why, clumsy, inefficient, confused, weak, and easily misguided as it is, it is the only form of government which is morally plausible.

—ROBERT BRIFFAULT, *Mankind in the Making*

 DEVELOPING YOUR SKILL

A. Be prepared to comment on the emphasis given important ideas in the excerpt on democracy. Is it an effective piece of writing? Why?
B. Do you think the description of the painting in the first example paragraph might have been ordered differently? Would it have been as effective as it is?
C. Write five ways in which paragraph items can be ordered.

Review Exercises—Paragraph Development

A. Select from a novel, short story, or essay a paragraph that exemplifies one of the methods of paragraph development. Be prepared to analyze for the benefit of the class the paragraph you choose.
B. Be ready to discuss in class the methods of paragraph development you would use for the following topics.

1. The Right to Strike   4. One Recipe That Can't Miss
2. One of My Happiest Moments   5. Tensions in Modern Life
3. The Challenge of College   6. A Painting of a Battle Scene

3. Holding the Paragraph Together

THE TOPIC SENTENCE

No one need tell you by now that good writing does not just happen. A writer must plan his paragraphs carefully so that the reader can follow his thinking. One essential part of that plan is the topic sentence, which directs the paragraph and gives it body and unity.

If you have ever flown over a city, looked down on country roads from a mountain, or peered from a high building down on the streets of a city, you know that the outline of what you see is quite clear. A well laid out paragraph can be just as clear to the reader who is looking at it if the writer has made his plan clear. On the other hand, if you suddenly found yourself in the middle of a large city or on a strange mountain trail, you would not know where you were or how to proceed. If a writer does not give his reader a clear perspective, the reader will not know how to proceed.

A good writer might write the following sentences to begin a paragraph.

An individual's attitude is composed of so many moods and humors, some blurred and blended with others, some sharp and distinct, that to describe the moods of only one day would be to write pages and pages of not too interesting material. However, *it is comparatively easy to take one definite mood and tell of its effect on you.*

This is the writer's plan. The italicized sentence, the topic sentence, leads the reader on. He is never in doubt about what the writer is going to do or where he is going. He is going to describe one definite mood and its effect.

Although most often the topic sentence is the first sentence in a paragraph, it may be placed anywhere, depending upon the method of development for the paragraph. A writer may begin his paragraph with certain pieces of information that lead to a logical conclusion, the statement of which may be the last sentence. Or he may wish to give some information, state his conclusion, and then give the rest of the information.

In some paragraphs the development of an idea may make the actual statement of a topic sentence unnecessary. Such paragraphs have an *implied topic sentence.* Only very skillful writers can handle such paragraphs well.

 DEVELOPING YOUR SKILL

A. Select the topic sentence in each of the following paragraphs and be prepared to defend your choice and to explain why each topic sentence is placed where it it.

Whether he were scrupulously orthodox or inclined to instinctive superstition, the Elizabethan believed in the pervasive operation of an external fate in the world. The twelve signs of the zodiac had their own active properties. The planets were busy the whole time; and their fluctuating conjunctions produced a seemingly chaotic succession of conditions, theoretically predictable but in practice almost wholly beyond the wit of man. Their functions differed, with the moon the great promoter of change. Though there were skeptics like Edmund in *Lear* and though the quack astrologer was hated and satirized, the general trend was of belief.

—E.M.W. Tillyard, *The Elizabethan World Picture*

On the outside, unfortunately, the new buildings are mostly very much alike; on the inside, it is every man for himself. Appearance (the pejorative word is "front") means a great deal in advertising. At the agencies, especially, décor is a means of expression; the agency tries to say something about itself by its use of space, color and design. At Young & Rubicam, for example, the spaces are large, the upholstery material is leather, and the color is green—walls, carpets, chairs and couches are green, and the name plaques opposite the elevators on the twelve floors that Y & R occupies announce the agency by means of white letters against a green leather background. A visitor to the executive floor of Y & R could be pardoned the feeling that he was in a bank: a long, spacious, deeply carpeted hall broken by a few counter-height partitions to establish areas for the widely spaced secretaries, doors opening into obvious (and almost identical) distinction, the monochrome green enforcing an impression of solidity. McCann-Erickson, more strongly oriented toward sociological and psychological studies, uses a collection of correctly restful pastels in the halls and offices of its spanking-new fourteen-floor New York office, and a visitor to the executive floor of McCann could be pardoned the feeling that he had stumbled into a movie set: a vast center area almost as wide as a city street with secretarial desks of luxurious modern design,

elaborately simple chairs and couches in black, red and yellow
scattered for the ease of important people who have personal appointments but will have to wait.

—MARTIN MAYER, *Madison Avenue, U.S.A.*

B. List the items of support in each of the paragraphs in Exercise A. Do
the items support what you think is the topic sentence in each paragraph?

UNITY

Many students whose paragraphs and compositions are criticized because they lack *unity* simply do not understand what unity actually is.
When you select a subject for a paragraph, you also select a purpose that
you hope to accomplish in the paragraph. In addition, you determine
which method of paragraph development you will use. When you begin
writing, you have only one goal: to accomplish your purpose in the paragraph. If you relate all the elements of your paragraph directly to your
purpose, and if you do not include other extraneous elements, then your
paragraph will have unity. A clearly defined purpose and an orderly
means of achieving that purpose will help you to write unified paragraphs.

Read carefully the following paragraph. Note how clearly the author
develops his purpose and how methodically he supports it in the rest of
the paragraph. He stays within the boundaries set by his purpose.

Any realistic person who hasn't been influenced in his view of
country life by New England naturalists knows that once you leave

the city, you leave behind you all the true peace and comforts of civilized man. As to the comforts, there isn't, I take it, much doubt, except maybe on the part of such fish as prefer cornhusk mattresses to Ostermoors, love the exercise involved in trying to open wardrobe drawers that, once they get to the country, refuse to open unless you reward them with a strained back, a sprained wrist and a bruised toe. And as for the peace there can be even less doubt, save perhaps in the case of those who think it is infinitely more peaceful to lie in bed at night and listen to the rain pour down romantically on a tin roof and then drip through the ceiling and all over your sheets than to roll over quietly in town and sleep dry.

—GEORGE JEAN NATHAN, *The Theatre World of George Jean Nathan*

DEVELOPING YOUR SKILL

A. The first extended example that the author uses in the preceding paragraph has within it several very effective details. Be ready to discuss the effect of these details upon paragraph unity.
B. Select a paragraph from a newspaper editorial. Apply the tests of unity to it. Is its purpose clear? Do all the supporting items actually support the purpose? Is there any extraneous material in the paragraph? Write on a sheet of paper the following about the paragraph you select: (1) the purpose; (2) the method or methods of paragraph development used; (3) a list of the supporting items.

COHERENCE

Like unity, *coherence* is a nebulous term to many students. While unity demands that all the sentences of a paragraph must relate directly to the purpose of the paragraph, coherence demands that there be a clear relationship among the supporting ideas in a paragraph. Coherence assists the reader in following the progression of the ideas. It makes things clear for the reader. Words and phrases that join ideas are especially helpful in accomplishing coherence. Such words as *and, but, or, for, yet, moreover, however, therefore,* and *nevertheless* aid coherence. So do expressions like *In the first place, On the other hand,* and *finally.* Words and phrases that refer to other words and sentences are also helpful.

Note how the author of the following passage helps the reader to follow the paragraph by the use of words and phrases that hold the sentences together and that refer to other parts of the paragraph. Some of the effective words and phrases that contribute to coherence are in italics.

> Think of life as a vast picture gallery, or museum; *or better, perhaps,* as a vast engineering workshop. It is all *those things, among others. Then* think of oneself walking through *it.* You know how the average man walks *through a museum or a workshop* when he knows nothing particular about *it.* You try hard to be intelligent; *failing in that,* you try to conceal your lack of intelligence. *You would like* to be interested, but you do not know *what is interesting* and what is not. *Some of the specimens* strike you as pretty; *some of the engines* seem to you very powerful; *you* are dazzled and amused by the blaze of the fires, *you* are secretly interested in the men and wish *you* could talk to them. *But in the main* you come out at the other end tired and rather dispirited and having got remarkably little out of it. *That is the way* a stupid and uneducated man, with no one to help him, goes through life.
>
> —Gilbert Murray, *Essays and Addresses*

In order to make his writing read smoothly and clearly, any good writer attempts to vary the sentences in his paragraph. For a special effect, some writers repeat sentence patterns throughout a paragraph, but it is a good general rule to vary the kinds of sentences you use. A paragraph in which every sentence begins in the same way and has the same basic construction is dull for the reader. By varying your sentences, you will help your reader to understand the purpose of your paragraph.

DEVELOPING YOUR SKILL

    A. Select a narrative paragraph and be ready to discuss with the class some of the most effective devices the author uses to gain coherence.

    B. Write a paragraph on one of the following topics. Be especially careful to make the sentences and the ideas flow together easily so that your reader can follow the paragraph.

1. An Honor System for Our School
2. The Fly That Buzzed in Study Hall
3. Raising Boxer Puppies
4. Delivering the Goods

Review Exercises—Holding the Paragraph Together

Analyze the following paragraph. Pick out the topic sentence and be ready to discuss the method of paragraph development. Does the paragraph have unity and coherence? Is there good sentence variety? Be prepared to discuss these aspects of paragraph development as they appear in this paragraph.

As a class, literary men do not shine in conversation. The scintillating and playful essayist whom you pictured to yourself as the most genial and entertaining of companions turns out to be a shy and untalkable individual, who chills you with his reticence when you chance to meet him. The poet whose fascinating volume you always drop into your gripsack on your summer vacation—the poet whom you have so long desired to know personally—is a moody and abstracted middle-aged gentleman, who fails to catch your name on introduction, and seems the avatar of the commonplace. The witty and ferocious critic whom your fancy had painted as a literary cannibal with a morbid appetite for tender young poets— the writer of those caustic and scholarly reviews which you never neglect to read—destroys the unlifelike portrait you had drawn by appearing before you as a personage of slender limb and deprecating glance, who stammers and makes a painful spectacle of himself when you ask him his opinion of "The Glees of the Gulches," by Popocatepetl Jones. The slender, dark-haired novelist of your imagination, with epigrammatic points to his mustache, suddenly takes the shape of a short, smoothly-shaven blond man, whose conversation does not sparkle at all, and you were on the lookout for the most brilliant of verbal fireworks. Perhaps it is a dramatist you have idealized. Fresh from witnessing his delightful comedy of manners, you meet him face to face only to discover that his own manners are anything but delightful. The play and the playwright are two very distinct entities. You grow skeptical touching the truth of Button's assertion that the style is the man himself. Who that has encountered his favorite author in the flesh has not sometimes been a little, if not wholly, disappointed?

—THOMAS BAILEY ALDRICH, *The Writings of*
Thomas Bailey Aldrich

UNIT SUMMARY

There are four basic kinds of paragraphs: narration, exposition, description, and argument. All paragraphs are units in themselves and can serve as parts of a multiparagraph composition. Paragraphs may be developed by many methods and combinations of methods. Some of the most common methods are example and illustration, detail, and comparison and contrast. Supporting elements in a paragraph are ordered according to an arrangement that the author chooses.

The skillful writer will plan his paragraphs well. He will develop a good topic sentence and be sure to preserve unity and coherence. By so doing he will be assured that the reader can understand the purpose of each of his paragraphs.

UNIT REVIEW EXERCISES

DISCUSSION TOPICS

Discuss these questions about the paragraph that follows.

1. What is the topic sentence? Is it stated exactly in the paragraph?
2. Is there sufficient sentence variety in the paragraph?
3. What is the general purpose of the paragraph and by what method is it developed?

The late Albert Jay Nock used to remark that the most acute observers of the cultural pattern in America have been not social scientists, educators, clergymen, jurists, philosophers, but humorists. A strong case may be made out for this opinion. One can gain a good deal of pertinent information not to be found elsewhere about eighteenth-century New England, for example, from perusing the *Johnnycake Papers* and about colonial New York from Irving's *Knickerbocker's History*. The Civil War period and what preceded it and its immediate aftermath are illuminated by the comment of James Russell Lowell and even more by that of Artemus Ward. For the true significance of the eighteen-seventies and -eighties one may not omit a careful reading of Mark Twain. The turn of the century is most cannily interpreted by George Ade, by Bert Leston Taylor, most of all by Finley Peter Dunne, who for many years spilled a weekly column of pungent social analysis from the lips of Mr. Dooley, philosopher of Archey Road. The age of normalcy is revealed by the gentle irony of Booth Tarkington.

—BERNARD IDDINGS BELL, *Crisis in Education*

WRITTEN WORK

1. Write in your own words a topic sentence for the preceding paragraph.
2. List on a sheet of paper the items that support the topic sentence.
3. Rewrite the paragraph in your own words, using your own topic sentence and rephrasing the other sentences.

VOCABULARY

The italicized words in the following sentences are used in other contexts in this unit. Write the numbers 1 to 5 on a sheet of paper. After each number write the letter of the word or phrase that could best be substituted for the italicized word. The numbers in brackets are the numbers of the pages on which the words appear in the unit.

1. The mayor spent twenty minutes *deprecating* organized crime.   [p. 179]
   (*a*) threatening; (*b*) expressing disapproval of; (*c*) prosecuting; (*d*) explaining the merits of
2. The performer was in one *ludicrous* situation after another.   [p. 165]
   (*a*) explosive; (*b*) dangerous; (*c*) laughable; (*d*) derisive
3. The critic used one *pejorative* word after another in his review of the play.   [p. 175]
   (*a*) disparaging; (*b*) complimentary; (*c*) nonsensical; (*d*) alliterative

4. The attorney's argument did not seem *plausible*.   [p. 172]
   (*a*) permissible as evidence; (*b*) accurate; (*c*) credible; (*d*) well thought
   out
5. The pitcher's delivery was not at all *orthodox*.   [p. 174]
   (*a*) conventional; (*b*) effective; (*c*) irregular; (*d*) hesitant

SPELLING

   The following words appeared in this unit or were chosen because they are
commonly misspelled. Study these words so that you will be prepared to write
them from dictation.

deprecating	gossamer
ludicrous	heinous
pejorative	imprecate
plausible	juxtaposition
orthodox	lassitude
avatar	lithe
nebulous	matriculate
perspective	lucrative
pervasive	milieu
senescence	montage

UNIT SELF-TEST

   Write on a sheet of paper the answers to the following questions.

1. What are the general purposes of paragraphs?
2. What are two methods of developing paragraphs?
3. Which method is especially useful in description?
4. What is spatial arrangement?
5. Which kind of paragraph is usually arranged chronologically?
6. Is there a fixed position in the paragraph for the generalization?
7. For what reason might an author write the topic sentence last?
8. What two qualities help hold paragraphs together?

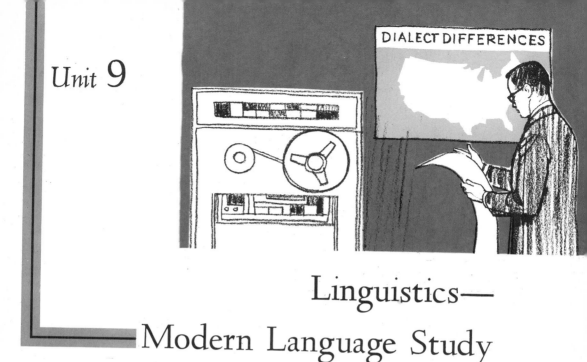

Linguistics—
Modern Language Study

In the past several years linguistic scientists have been responsible for a substantial broadening of language study. They have made it possible for students to understand more about language than was previously thought possible. Understanding of language concepts had always been less than complete because the subject was not approached scientifically. The scientific method is basic to the modern study of language.

This unit will help you to understand the basic nature of language. Not only will you discover how languages are organized, but you will also learn about the general areas of language study. Another unit in this book, Unit 5, deals more extensively with one area of language study—the history and early development of English.

You will be interested to learn the linguistic attitude about grammar and usage and about the purpose and function of a modern dictionary. You will also enjoy studying English dialects—why they exist, where they come from, and whether they will always exist.

The kinds of words in English and the ways in which they form sentences constitute another fascinating part of this unit. You will gain some insight into the structure of your language, and you will learn how and why you use your language as you do.

CHECK YOURSELF

Write answers to the following questions. If there are some that you cannot answer now, return to them after you have completed the unit.

1. What are the four major areas of linguistic study?
2. What is the difference between descriptive and prescriptive grammar?
3. How do some modern dictionaries differ from traditional dictionaries?
4. What are dialects?
5. What determines one's dialect?
6. How do authors represent dialect in fiction?
7. What are sentence patterns?
8. What are transformations?
9. What are the two classes of English words?

1. Areas of Linguistic Study

Because language is so broad and so complex a tool of man, it has occasioned much study and research on the part of linguistic scholars. In order to study language meaningfully, scholars break it down into its component parts and then study those parts as they constitute the whole. The parts of language that scholars study and the areas of linguistic study are of interest to anyone who uses any language, and that, of course, excludes no one.

SOUND, SYMBOL, SYSTEM

All the languages of men are composed of three basic and related parts. The most basic and most simple of these parts is *sound*. Since every language began as a spoken language, sound is the most obvious component of language. If you have ever heard someone speak a foreign language that you are not familiar with, you have, despite your inability to comprehend the substance of what the speaker was saying, recognized that he was using language. You recognized it because the speaker was using the first component of language, sound.

The study of the sounds of a given language is called *phonemics*. The name is derived from the name given to the sounds of a language, *phonemes*. Perhaps the single most important truth of phonemics is that the sounds of a language are not the same as the letters of a language. When you speak of a letter of the alphabet, you are not speaking of a sound but of a letter used to represent that sound. Unfortunately, the letters of English do not accurately describe the sounds of the language. You know that the English alphabet has twenty-six letters. There are thirty-three phonemes in English, with many variations that together more than double in number the letters of the alphabet. This means that some letters represent more than one sound, and that alone causes much difficulty. The English alphabet letter *e,* for example, has several different pronunciations. The letter *e* in b*e*t, b*e,* and *e*nough is actually three different phonemes, and yet all three are represented by the same letter, *e.*

To solve this problem, linguists have developed a phonemic alphabet. In the phonemic alphabet there is a letter to accurately represent each sound in the language. At this time the phonemic alphabet is used by only scholars and students of the language. If it were used by everyone who used English, much of the spelling difficulty that exists today would not exist.

Sounds in a language operate to form the second component of language, *symbols.* Symbols are either complete words or parts of words. For example, the word *man* is a symbol that stands for an adult male. The letters *ed* are a symbol when attached to such words as *watch* and *look.* They indicate past tense.

The symbols of a language are selected arbitrarily. This means that at some time the symbol *man* was selected to represent an adult male. Any other symbol might have been chosen. It could have been *gol* or *schnorp* or any other combination of sounds. But since *man* is the accepted symbol, you must use it when referring to an adult male if you hope to be understood.

If a group of people select their own symbol for an item, they can use it meaningfully within that group only. Suppose that your class decided to change a particular symbol. Suppose you changed *book* to *humlas*. Speaking among yourselves, you could use *humlas* when referring to a book. Outside your class it would be thought rather curious if you asked a student if you could read his *humlas*. As speakers of a language with over 600,000 word symbols, you must conform to the symbols already selected.

As you know, word meanings change, and new words, or symbols, are constantly being added to the language. The word *cool,* for example, has taken on new meanings. So have the words *sharp* and *neat*. In addition, modern science and technology have added many words to the language. It is fascinating to realize that you are directly affecting the language both by changing the meanings of words and by adding new words to the language.

The third component of language is the *system,* more commonly known as the *grammar,* of a language. When you speak or write a sentence, you place the words in a certain order, an order that you learned very early in life. This order is natural to you, and you seldom err in your adherence to the system of your native language. This means, surprisingly enough, that few people ever make true grammatical errors. Most language problems are in the realm of *usage,* not grammar.

DEVELOPING YOUR SKILL

    A. Be prepared to defend the statement that few people ever make grammatical errors in using their native language.
    B. Be ready to discuss how you could tell that someone who is speaking a language you do not know is actually using language.
    C. Write an explanation of the statement that the letters of the alphabet do not accurately represent the sounds of the language.

HISTORICAL LINGUISTICS

Many books and articles have been written about the origin of language and about the history and development of particular languages. Scholars who are primarily concerned with these aspects of language are called *historical linguists*.

For decades historical linguists have been hard at work attempting to determine the origin of language. Theories on the subject abound, and yet none is accepted as the proved one. Even though they cannot definitely determine the origin of language, historical linguists can trace the development of a particular language from a time when it was first known to exist. They believe, for example, that the mother of English and of nearly all modern languages was a language that scholars now call Indo-European. Exactly where and when it came into existence is not known.

There are two methods by which scholars study the development of languages. They can start with languages spoken today and trace their development back to the language or languages from which they came. Or they can begin with the earlier language or languages and trace their development to the language spoken today. In Unit 5 this latter method is employed to help you understand the development of modern English.

A diagram can be constructed demonstrating how certain languages evolved. The first dot below represents English and the second, German. Both came immediately from a language no longer spoken called West Germanic, represented by the lowest dot.

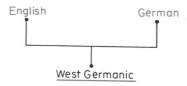

Retaining this diagram, we can add dots representing Danish, Swedish, Norwegian, and Icelandic. These descend from North Germanic, which, along with West Germanic, the mother of English, descends from Proto-Germanic.

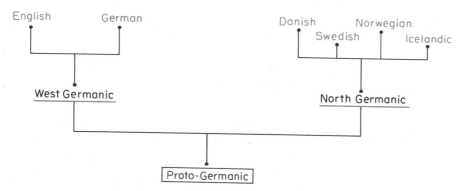

We can add to this diagram dots for French, Italian, Spanish, Portuguese, and Romanic, all of which descend from Latin, which itself comes from Italic. Italic and Proto-Germanic are progenies of Indo-European.

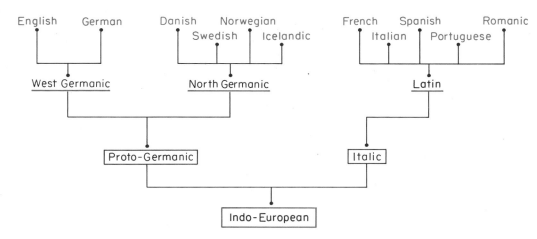

Historical linguistics is of interest primarily to language specialists. All speakers of language, however, should be aware of the role of history in language and especially of the development of their own language.

 DEVELOPING YOUR SKILL

    A. Be ready to discuss the importance of historical linguistics to language study.

    B. Write answers to the following questions.

       1. By what two methods do linguists study the development of a language?

       2. What language is thought to be the mother of English and most other modern languages?

       3. What, according to the illustrations on the ancestry of languages, is the relationship between English and Latin?

COMPARATIVE LINGUISTICS

The branch of linguistics in which the structures of one language are compared with those of another is *comparative linguistics*. Linguistic scholars frequently employ this branch of the science of language for historical reasons. They may compare the development of a particular structure in one language with the development of a similar structure in another language. Or, for the purpose of determining the common ancestry of two languages, linguists may compare certain other aspects of the languages. In this sense comparative linguistics is closely allied with historical linguistics.

Not all comparative linguistics is historical, however. Linguists often compare two or more modern languages without any reference to their historical evolution or ancestry. They may wish to compare them simply to determine the similarities and differences in their present-day structures.

Like historical linguistics, comparative linguistics exists primarily for the linguistic scholar, but it is also of considerable interest to all speakers of language. Since foreign language study has become so important, everyone should have at least some knowledge of languages other than his own. Even a scant knowledge of the general structure of other languages is helpful, and the more knowledge one has of other languages, the better student of language one will be.

DEVELOPING YOUR SKILL

A. Be prepared to discuss the importance of knowing something about the structures of languages other than your native language.
B. Explain in writing the connection between comparative and historical linguistics.

GEOLINGUISTICS

Sometimes called *geographical linguistics, geolinguistics* is the branch of linguistics that describes, scientifically and objectively, the distribution of languages in the regions of the earth. It also describes the variations within a particular language and determines the causes, both geographical and cultural, for such variations.

Geolinguistics deals with modern languages, which are products of certain historical factors and events, and is therefore related to historical linguistics. Its present-day aspects, however, are more pervasive than its historical aspects. It is concerned primarily with describing the variations in languages as they are presently used. It deals directly with current geographical and cultural factors.

Probably the most practical area of linguistic study, geolinguistics offers much interesting information about languages. A geolinguist might wish to study a particular language about which very little is known. His research would hopefully reveal the number of speakers of the language. He would learn of its distribution geographically and of the many varieties that exist in the language. He would learn much about the cultural and political and religious influences upon the language. All these factors would be of interest to the geolinguist and to anyone who wishes to be informed about language and about the great number of factors that influence language.

The study of dialects in language is an important part of geolinguistics. A section later in this unit concentrates exclusively upon dialects and upon their use in imaginative writing.

 DEVELOPING YOUR SKILL

    A. Be ready to discuss the relationship between geolinguistics and historical linguistics.

    B. Explain in writing some of the things a geolinguist would want to learn about a language he is studying and about the people who speak it.

STRUCTURAL LINGUISTICS

Perhaps the most well defined of the areas of linguistic study is *structural linguistics*. As the name tells you, it concerns the structure of a living language—the sounds, symbols, and system—as it is currently being used by its speakers. Structural linguists *describe* language structure; they do not write rules that speakers are expected to follow.

The sounds of most languages are represented by an alphabet of some sort. Structural linguists study both the pronunciations of the sounds of a language and the system for representing the sounds in writing. Sometimes, as with English, they invent means for more accurately representing the sounds of a language in writing. American linguists, realizing that the English alphabet does not accurately describe the sounds of English, have constructed a phonemic alphabet, which describes all the sounds of English.

Another part of the structure of language is the words of a language. By scientific observation, linguists determine the kinds of words there are in a language, and they study the ways in which they are used to make sentences. This latter area of study is the grammar, or system, of language. It concerns the sentence patterns that exist in a language and the ways that the patterns can be expanded and transformed.

The most important thing to remember about structural linguistics is that structural linguists describe the language as it is used. You will study more thoroughly the descriptive nature of the science of linguistics later in this unit.

DEVELOPING YOUR SKILL

A. Be prepared to discuss generally the structural linguist's role in language study.
B. Explain in writing the most important thing to remember about structural linguistics.

Review Exercises—Areas of Linguistic Study

Write answers to the following questions.

1. All languages are composed of what three elements?
2. Which existed earlier, the spoken or written language?
3. Linguistic scholars who speculate on the origin of language are called what?
4. Which area of linguistic study compares the structures of two or more languages?
5. Which area of linguistic study deals with the distribution of languages in the regions of the earth?

2. Descriptive Linguistics

As you saw earlier in this unit, linguists describe the way language is used by its speakers. This approach to grammar and usage is called the *descriptive* approach. It is gradually replacing the *prescriptive* approach to grammar and usage that has been taught for many years.

The prescriptive approach to grammar is based on the assumption that the grammar of English is an outgrowth of the grammar of Latin. Prescriptivists have attempted to make the English language fit the grammatical structures of Latin. In the earlier section on historical linguistics you saw that English does not descend from Latin.

Modern linguists, recognizing that English is a unique language with its own grammatical structure, have attempted simply to describe English as it exists today. Their efforts have met with much opposition from the prescriptivists. But as understanding of the descriptive linguists' position has grown, opposition to descriptive linguistics has diminished.

GRAMMAR AND USAGE

One of the accomplishments of descriptive linguists is that they have made clear the distinction between grammar and usage. When you speak or write a sentence, you use the words in an order that is perfectly natural to you as a native speaker of English. You learned the word order very early by imitating others who used it. You know automatically that *puddles never through he big walks mud* is not an English sentence. On the other hand you know, just as automatically, that *He never walks through big mud puddles* is an English sentence. You recognize, too, that *He don't read very well* is also an English sentence, though you probably recognize that the *He don't* construction is not considered good usage.

The presence of a construction like *He don't* in a sentence does not make the sentence ungrammatical. It is a variety of usage not uncommon among some speakers of English. The primary requirement for an English sentence is that it have normal English word order. If it does, it is grammatical even if it violates socially accepted usage rules. This demonstrates the difference between grammar and usage. Descriptive linguists recognize that many usage rules that have existed for centuries are not followed by all speakers of English. For example, few speakers distinguish between *lie* and *lay* or *who* and *whom*. Yet they speak perfectly grammatical English. The point is that grammar and usage are not the same things and that few speakers ever make truly grammatical errors. The reasons for the varieties of usage are treated in a later section of this unit.

Another contribution of descriptive linguists has been to demonstrate the uniqueness of the grammar of every language. For example, Latin, which is now dead, was a language dependent largely upon *word endings* for meaning. Many adjectives had to have the same ending as the nouns they modified, and verbs had to have endings like their nouns. Languages that depend largely upon word endings are *inflectional languages.* English, on the other hand, depends more upon *word order* for meaning and therefore has a *distributive grammar.* Distribution of words in the sentence is more important than word endings.

Contrary to some traditional notions, linguists maintain that one cannot be expected to understand and use the grammar of English better only because he has studied Latin. Each language has its own distinct grammatical system. This is not to say that there is no benefit to be derived from studying foreign languages. On the contrary, knowledge of a foreign language can substantially broaden one's understanding of another culture and of that particular language. But knowing a foreign language will not help one to understand the grammar of one's own language unless that foreign language has a grammar very much like that of one's own language.

DEVELOPING YOUR SKILL

    A. Be prepared to discuss how a sentence could have a usage problem and still be grammatical.

    B. Write the terms that describe the grammars of Latin and English.

    C. Defend in writing the following statement: Studying the grammar of Latin will not help one to understand English.

THE MODERN DICTIONARY

Nowhere has the voice of the descriptive linguist been heard more clearly in recent years than in the modern English dictionary. Until 1961, when *Webster's Third New International Dictionary* was published, all dictionaries had been written from a prescriptive point of view. Words were listed, "correct" pronunciations and meanings were presented in order of preference, and other pertinent *etymological,* or historical, information was given about the word. Pronunciations and meanings given were those that the editors of the dictionaries thought to be the "correct ones." How the words were being pronounced and how speakers of the language were currently using the words were items that dictionary makers did not consider. They believed their job was to establish standards of pronunciation and usage that all speakers of the language should follow.

Recognizing that the language used by speakers was quite different from that being prescribed in the dictionaries, the editors of *Webster's Third* determined that a dictionary should not presume to set standards of usage but, rather, should report how the language is currently being used. The task of reporting how language is used is a gargantuan one. It requires scientific observation of language and literally millions of samples of language usage.

When their sampling of language was completed, the Webster editors put together the first descriptive dictionary. Most of the same words contained in older dictionaries are still listed, but no one "correct" pronunciation or meaning is given for words. Instead, all the popular pronunciations and meanings are included, as far as space permits. For many of the word meanings, quotations from speakers are included to demonstrate how the word was used by the speakers. Use of these quotations, called *citations,* lends credence to the meanings the editors use for certain words.

The war between prescriptivists and descriptivists over the new descriptive dictionary is still being waged. The new descriptive dictionary has not yet achieved total acceptance, though respect for it is growing. It is clearly a major manifestation of the descriptive movement and will, many scholars believe, set the standard for future dictionaries.

DEVELOPING YOUR SKILL

    A. Be ready to discuss the basic difference between prescriptive and descriptive dictionaries.

    B. Explain in writing what citations in a descriptive dictionary are.

    C. Write a paragraph in which you state your beliefs about the function of a dictionary. Should it set standards or report usage? Defend your belief with logical reasons.

Review Exercises—Descriptive Linguistics

Write answers to the following questions.

1. Why will studying the grammar of a foreign language not directly increase your knowledge of the grammar of your own language?

2. In a sentence or two explain the difference between grammar and usage.
3. What does the term *distributive grammar* mean?
4. Why do few people ever make truly grammatical errors?

3. American Dialects

The field of linguistic study most popular among many students of language is that of dialects. Everyone knows from experience that not all speakers of English in America speak the language in the same way. For that matter, in nearly all living languages there is considerable variety in the ways the languages are spoken. The varieties of speech are called *dialects*. A dialect may be defined as *the speech of any definite cultural or geographical group that has common language habits*. In this section you will learn some of the important characteristics of both geographical and cultural dialects.

GEOGRAPHICAL DIALECTS

That there are definite speech characteristics of certain geographical areas in the United States is undeniable. If you have traveled in other

areas of the country or watched and listened to news programs on television and radio, you have heard the speech of different geographical groups. On the linguistic map on page 195 you can see the general geographical dialect areas in this country. Doubtlessly there are many varieties within each area, but those are too numerous and too scattered to show on a general map.

Common sense tells you that no single geographical dialect is either better or worse than any other. Geographical dialects exist because the people who settled a certain area of the country spoke or learned to speak English in certain ways and because most of these people remained in the area where they first settled. They pronounce certain sounds in particular ways, and they use some words that are characteristic of their area. Because each person is accustomed to hearing the dialect of his area, he naturally thinks that other dialects are unusual. Naturally, people from other areas think his dialect unusual too.

In recent years people have become increasingly cognizant of geographical dialect differences. Because it is so easy to travel from one area of the country to another, people are directly exposed to other dialects. Television, radio, movies, and the other communications media also serve to expose people to the variety in American dialects.

This exposure of people to geographical dialects is taking its toll on the dialects. Linguistic experts believe that the differences between dialects are diminishing rapidly, mainly because people are more mobile than they once were. When people move from one area to another, they retain something of their old dialect and pick up something of that of the new area. The natural result of such mixing of geographical dialects on a large scale will be that one vast general dialect will result. No area will be so isolated as to develop speech peculiarities. The more mobility the people have and the more widespread the communications media become, the more similar will be the language of all the people. While there is no standard geographical dialect now, there may be no geographical dialect differences at all in years to come.

 DEVELOPING YOUR SKILL

> A. Be prepared to discuss the validity of the following statement: Speech that does not adhere to the national standard is inferior.

B. Explain in writing what two factors are affecting geographical dialects and tell how the dialects are being affected.

CULTURAL DIALECTS

Just as the persons in a particular geographical location may have characteristic speech habits, so also may persons in a definite cultural group. *Cultural groups* is an omnibus term. There are, of course, no intact cultural groups per se, but there are large groups of people in America with similar cultural backgrounds. These people can be considered as a group. One's cultural background influences to a large degree the speech one uses. People with similar backgrounds have similar speech habits.

One's education, economic status, and social and family relationships make up one's cultural background. National heritage sometimes affects dialect, too. The first three factors are closely related. One with little education usually has a comparatively low economic status. One's social relationships are customarily with people very much like oneself. As long as these cultural factors remain constant, one's dialect will not change very greatly.

In recent years linguists have made exhaustive studies in and have done intensive research on cultural dialects. One of the conclusions they have drawn is that one cannot claim that one cultural dialect is superior or inferior to another. They maintain that a construction like *He ain't done nothin' to ya'* cannot be condemned solely on the grounds that it does not comply with the traditional rules of usage. Whether the construction conveys meaning and whether the listeners comprehend what is being said are the criteria for determining the appropriateness of speech. Linguists believe that speech should not be labeled *correct* or *incorrect* but, rather, *appropriate* or *inappropriate*. That which is appropriate for one person in one situation may be inappropriate for another person in another situation.

The important thing to remember about cultural dialects is that they do really exist, although, as with geographical dialects, there are certain factors that will cause the differences between cultural dialects to deliquesce. Experts believe that the root of cultural differences is education. In America today more people are receiving more quality education than ever before. As both the numbers of people educated and the quality of education increase, the general economic status will improve. One's social relationships will, of course, be with equally well-educated people. If the present trends continue, there will eventually be no discernible cultural speech habits and no linguistic basis for determining social class.

DEVELOPING YOUR SKILL

    A. Be prepared to discuss the three related cultural factors as they influence dialect. Which do you think most important? How does it affect the other two factors?

    B. Explain in writing why linguists do not use the terms *correct* and *incorrect* in connection with usage.

EYE DIALECTS

As a writer and a speaker of English, you know that the letters of the English alphabet do not accurately describe the sounds of the language. You know, too, that the English spelling system does not allow for the tremendous variety in pronunciation that exists in the words of English. The discrepancy between the alphabet and the sounds of the language and between the spelling system and pronunciation makes it very difficult for writers of fiction to depict accurately the speech of characters in their writings.

Very few people, whether real or fictional, speak words and sounds as they are spelled. Recognizing this discrepancy between spelling and pronunciation, many writers of fiction have chosen to attempt to report accurately the pronunciations used by their fictional characters. This accurate portrayal of the speech of characters is called *eye dialect*. It consists primarily in running certain words together, in omitting certain letters, and in deliberately misspelling certain words altogether.

While eye dialect is often exaggerated, it can also be a very useful device. You have probably read many novels and short stories in which the authors make use of eye dialect. If you have read some of Mark Twain's stories or those of William Faulkner, you have seen the device skillfully employed. The following excerpt is taken from Twain's *The Adventures of Huckleberry Finn*. Do you think Twain's use of eye dialect aids or detracts from your understanding of the characters and of the story?

When they got aboard, the king went for me and shook me by the collar and says:

"Tryin' to give us the slip, was ye, you pup! Tired of our company—hey?"

I says:

"No your majesty, we warn't—*please* don't, your majesty!"

"Quick, then, and tell us what *was* your idea, or I'll shake the insides out o' you!"

"Honest, I'll tell you everything, just as it happened, your majesty. The man that had aholt of me was very good to me, and kept saying he had a boy about as big as me that died last year, and he was sorry to see a boy in such a dangerous fix; and when they was all took by surprise by finding the gold, and made a rush for the coffin, he lets go of me and whispers, 'Heel it, now, or they'll hang ye, sure!' and I lit out. It didn't seem no good for *me* to stay—I couldn't do nothing, and I didn't want to be hung if I could get away. So I never stopped running till I found the canoe; and when I got here I told Jim to hurry, or they'd catch me and hang me yet, and said I was afeard you and the duke wasn't alive, now, and I was awful sorry, and so was Jim, and was awful glad when we see you coming, you may ask Jim if I didn't."

A. Select examples of eye dialect from a novel, short story, or poem that you have read. Be prepared to point out these examples to the class and to discuss their effectiveness.
B. Explain in writing the inadequacy of the English writing system to represent dialects.
C. Listen to the casual speech of two of your friends or family members. Using eye dialect, try to represent their spoken language in writing.

Review Exercises—American Dialects

A. Be ready to discuss how geographical location affects dialect.
B. Explain in writing why geographical dialects may some day disappear.
C. Is there a standard geographical dialect? Write an explanation for your answer.
D. In two or three sentences tell what determines cultural dialect and why differences between cultural dialects are diminishing.

4. English Words

One major part of the descriptive linguist's job is to describe the kinds of words that are in a language and how these words are used in that language. In this section you will study form class and structure words. You will learn how to determine kinds of words, and you will learn how the two kinds of English words function in the language.

FORM CLASSES

Linguists have determined that there are two basic kinds of English words—*form class words* and *structure words*. There are four kinds of form class words, which have the traditional names—noun, verb, adjective, and adverb. For convenience, personal pronouns are included under the noun group. As you know, these are the principal words in English sentences, and they constitute the bulk of the words in the language. The form classes are constantly changing. New nouns, verbs, adjectives, and adverbs are continuously being added to the language. Other words are being dropped as they become meaningless or are replaced by other new words.

The most obvious characteristic of form class words is that they can have several forms. Often when the form of a word is changed, so is its form class. The word *beauty,* for example, is clearly a noun, but another form of the word, *beautiful,* is an adjective. Yet another form, *beautify,* is a verb, and *beautifully* is an adverb. Not all forms of a given form class word belong to a form class different from that of the basic word. Most nouns change form with the addition of *s,* and they remain nouns. The letters *er* or *est* are added to many adjectives, and the words are still adjectives.

Many form class words, even in their simplest form, do belong to several different form classes. A word that is a noun in one situation may be another kind of word when used in another sense. For example, the word *book* is a noun in *He found the book,* a verb in *He will book the suspect on three charges,* and an adjective in *His father is a book salesman.*

The following test frames will help you to determine the kind of form class word a particular word is. Notice that there is a test sentence for each form class. If you are in doubt about the form class of a word, you can test it in each of the test frames. If a word tests out as a noun, that is, if the sentence makes sense when the word is placed in the blank in the noun test frame, test the word in the other frames too, because it may also be able to serve as another form class word. The (*s*) at the end of the noun frame indicates that you may have to test the plural forms of some nouns for the sentence to make sense. The (*it*) after the verb frame indicates that some verbs require a completing word. The verb *make,* for example, would require that you use the (*it*). When testing words with the endings *s, es, ed, ing,* or *est,* drop the endings before testing. You would not test *does,* but *do,* not *walking,* but *walk,* and so on.

NOUN FRAME	He talked about _____ (s).
VERB FRAME	He will _____ (it).
ADJECTIVE FRAME	They seemed _____.
ADVERB FRAME	They walked _____.

By testing certain words in the test frames, you will not only determine the form class or classes to which they can belong, but you will also get a better idea of the flexibility of these words in the language. You will see that many words fit several form classes. You can also notice, in working with some of the words, that different forms of them can serve different functions in sentences.

DEVELOPING YOUR SKILL

A. Be ready to discuss whether the following statement is true: When the form of a form class word is changed, its form class automatically changes.

B. Write the traditional names for the four form classes and tell what the most obvious characteristic of form class words is.

C. Write the appropriate symbol for the form class words—*N* for noun, *V* for verb, *Adj* for adjective, or *Adv* for adverb—above each of the italicized words in the following sentences.

1. *Cows* are *large* animals that *chew* their cuds *constantly*.
2. *Scarecrows frighten* crows from corn *fields*.
3. After the *game* the baseball team *rushed* to the *busiest* airport.

STRUCTURE WORDS

English words that do not change in either form or function are *structure words*. All words that are not form class words are structure words. The number of structure words in English never changes. You know all the structure words and probably use most of them regularly.

While structure words themselves are not new to you, some of the names linguists have given to them may be. The structure words are divided into four groups—*determiners, auxiliaries, prepositions,* and *intensifiers.*

One of the jobs of structure words is to help you determine to what form class a particular word in a sentence belongs. Determiners are structure words that signal nouns. In the sentence *The boy reads many books,* two words, *The* and *many,* are determiners. In both cases nouns directly follow the signal words. When used in sentences, words like these two will always precede nouns, although there may be other words between the determiner and the noun. Determiners are the largest of the structure-word groups. The symbol for determiners is *D.*

Prepositions are other structure words that signal nouns. You are familiar with prepositions and know how they operate in sentences. A noun usually follows a preposition, coming either directly after it, as in *to John,* or coming several words later, with determiners and modifiers in between, as in *to the tall boy.* The preposition, the determiners, the modifiers, and the noun make up a *preposition group.* The symbol for a preposition is *P.* The symbol for a preposition group is *P-group.*

A third kind of structure word that signals another form class word is *auxiliaries.* They signal verbs in sentences. Just as determiners and prepositions signal the appearance of a noun in a sentence, auxiliaries signal the appearance of a verb. Words like *can, will, did,* and *were* are common auxiliaries. You will notice that these and some other auxiliaries can also serve as verbs by themselves. The symbol that represents auxiliaries is *Aux.*

The final kind of structure word is *intensifiers.* They signal both adverbs and adjectives in sentences, though they do not help you to decide whether a word is either an adjective or an adverb. The purpose of intensifiers is to intensify, or strengthen, the meaning of a sentence. *Rather, quite, much,* and *somewhat* are commonly used intensifiers. The symbol for intensifiers is *I.*

DEVELOPING YOUR SKILL

    A. Be ready to discuss the basic difference between form class words and structure words.

B. Write answers to the following questions.

  1. What are the four kinds of structure words?
  2. Which ones signal nouns?
  3. Which one signals verbs?

C. Write the appropriate symbol over each of the italicized structure words in the following sentences.

  1. *An* explosion gave us *quite* a shock while we *were* eating *in the* back yard.
  2. Her aunt always *was* helping *the* nurses *at* our hospital.
  3. It is *rather* difficult to remember the *many* names.

Review Exercises—English Words

A. Write answers to the following questions.

  1. What is the function of test frames?
  2. What is the chief characteristic of form words?
  3. Which is the largest of the structure word groups?
  4. What is the function of intensifiers?

B. Write the appropriate symbol for form class words or structure words over each word in the following sentences.

  1. The people at the theatre were rather tired at the end of the first act.
  2. Bob seldom asked any serious questions.
  3. Carol was telling her story. Then Barbara entered abruptly.
  4. The game was quite close until the final minutes.

5. Sentence Pattern Variations

As a speaker and writer of English you use the language in a very systematic way. Without realizing it, you adhere to certain basic sentence patterns in your use of language. That is, you follow the system, or grammar, of English. Linguists have shown that it is easier and more logical to describe the language in terms of sentence patterns than in the terms that have traditionally been used.

Seven basic sentence patterns make up the system of English. In this section you will see what those seven patterns are, and you will learn how they are varied, through expansion and transformation.

EXPANSIONS

There are several ways in which all sentence patterns are expanded by users of the language. In this section you will analyze the devices by which sentences are expanded. The devices are one-word modifiers, P-groups, S-groups, compounds, or a combination of these devices.

You have already studied one-word modifiers and P-groups earlier in this unit. An *S-group,* or subordinator group, is a group of words that contains a sentence pattern that is a part of one of the seven basic sentence patterns. The italicized words in the following sentences are S-groups.

> *When he returned,* he called Mary.
> He is the man *who called Mary.*

S-groups are introduced by words called *subordinators.* S-groups like the one in the first example sentence expand the verb structure. They are introduced by subordinators like *when, while, as, since, whenever,* and *because.* The symbol for subordinators is *S.* S-groups like the one in the second example sentence expand a noun structure. They are introduced by words like *who, which,* and *that.*

Any part of a sentence can be expanded by compounds. A compound occurs when words like *and, but,* and *or,* commonly called conjunctions, are used to join two elements. Notice how conjunctions join two elements in the following sentence.

> Bob *and* Joe threw *and* kicked the football.

Sometimes entire sentence patterns are joined together. This does not actually produce an expansion, but two separate sentence patterns. Conjunctions are often used to join two patterns, as in the sentence *Harry likes baseball, but Marvin likes football.* Structures called *sentence connectors* also join sentence patterns. They are words like *therefore, however,* and *moreover.* The two parts of the following sentence are joined by a sentence connector: *He said he would not play; therefore we asked another student.*

Sentence pattern one consists of a noun structure tied to a verb structure.

PATTERN 1   **N¹   V**

Girls study.

In sentence patterns where there are additional independent noun structures, they are marked N² or N³ to show that they are not related to the N¹ structure. When two nouns in one pattern are related, they have the same symbol.

The following sentences are expansions of the first basic sentence pattern. The expansion device used is in parentheses after each sentence.

Wise girls study *hard.* (one-word modifiers)
Girls *in our class* study *at night.* (P-groups)
Girls *who want to pass* study *whenever they can.* (S-groups)
Girls *and boys* study *and work.* (compounds)
Wise girls *and boys in our school who want to pass* study *hard at night whenever they can.* (combination of all methods)

In the expansion of Pattern one, notice that any part or parts of the sentence can be expanded. The noun can take modifiers, as can the verb. The noun and the verb can be compounded. Finally, the entire sentence can be compounded, as in the sentence *Girls study, and the results are rewarding.*

Following is a list of the remaining six basic sentence patterns with sample sentences that follow each pattern. After each basic pattern appear some of the possible expansions of the italicized word in the sentence. It is impossible to list all possible expansions of the sentence because the possibilities are infinite. The devices by which the sentences are expanded are in parentheses after each expanded sentence.

PATTERN 2 **N¹ V N²**

Success requires effort.

Success for all requires effort. (P-group)
Success, which everyone desires, requires effort. (S-group)
Success and happiness require effort. (compound)
Great success requires effort. (one-word modifier)
Great success and happiness for all, which everyone desires, require effort. (combined devices)

PATTERN 3 **N¹ V N² N³**

Cars give *drivers* trouble.

Cars give *all drivers* trouble. (one-word modifier)
Cars give *drivers who drive fast* trouble. (S-group)
Cars give *drivers and mechanics* trouble. (compound)
Cars give *drivers in all states* trouble. (P-group)
Cars give *good drivers and mechanics in all states* trouble. (combination of devices)

PATTERN 4 **N¹ LV N¹**

Seniors are *people.*

Seniors are *mature people.* (one-word modifier)
Seniors are *people on the go.* (P-group)
Seniors are *people who need recognition.* (S-group)
Seniors are *mature people on the go who need recognition.* (combination of devices)

PATTERN 5 **N LV Adj**

They seemed *worried.*

They seemed *seriously worried.* (one-word modifier)
They seemed *worried and upset.* (compound)
They seemed *worried about their grades.* (P-group)
They seemed *seriously worried and upset about their grades.* (combination of devices)

PATTERN 6   **N¹**   **V**   **N²**   **N²**

They elected him *president.*

They elected him *class president.* (one-word modifier)
They elected him *president or chairman.* (compound)
They elected him *president for one year.* (P-group)
They elected him *president, which is an important office*
(S-group)

PATTERN 7   **N¹**   **V**   **N²**   **Adj**

She *believed* me intelligent.

She *really believed* me intelligent. (one-word modifier)
She *believed and reported* me intelligent. (compound)
In spite of my grades, she *believed* me intelligent. (P-group)
When she was younger, she *believed* me intelligent. (S-group)

In reading the various expansions of the seven basic sentence patterns, you can recognize that they are more complete and interesting than the sentences that are not expanded. Most of the sentences you speak, write, and read are expansions of the basic patterns. In the preceding expansions, only one part of each sentence is expanded. Normally several words in each sentence will be expanded.

DEVELOPING YOUR SKILL

A. Be ready to discuss the function of modifiers in English sentences.
B. Write the names of three forms of modifiers used in English.

C. Number 1 through 5 on a sheet of paper. Write the name of the italicized sentence expanding device in each of the following sentences.

1. *Because Jack was late,* Judy would not talk to him.
2. The apple *at the top* is the ripest one.
3. Jersey Joe knocked out the *young* boxer.
4. Malcolm was appointed captain *immediately*.
5. *Tim and Geoffrey* looked quite frightened.

TRANSFORMATIONS

You have seen that the basic sentence patterns in English are expanded in a number of ways so that they can express more complete ideas more interestingly. Each of the sentence patterns is a pattern of a positive declarative statement written in the active (as opposed to the passive) form. Yet many English sentences are questions. Some express negative ideas, and some are written in the passive form. These kinds of sentences are not provided for in the seven basic sentence patterns. They are *transformed* from the basic patterns and are called *transformations* of the sentence patterns.

The process and the rules whereby you transform the sentence patterns into questions, negative statements, and passive forms are extremely complex. And yet you make these transformations automatically. When you want to ask a question, you do not have to stop to think how you will transform a basic sentence pattern into a question. This applies for the other transformations as well. Nevertheless it is interesting to see what some of the transformations are and generally how you make them.

Each of the following sentences adheres to one of the basic sentence patterns. The number of the pattern is in parentheses after the sentence.

He is my brother. (4)
Mary was quiet today. (5)
That was an unkind thing to do. (4)

To make questions of these sentences you change the positions of two words, the subject and the verb, in each sentence:

Is he my brother?
Was Mary quiet today?
Was that an unkind thing to do?

Some transformations are more complex. When an auxiliary is used with a verb, the transformation is different. *They should try to do the work* becomes *Should they try to do the work?* The auxiliary, not the verb, moves in front of the subject.

In some transformations there are other considerations you automatically make in addition to mere word position. The sentence *Jack writes to her every day* is transformed as follows: *Does Jack write to her every day?* Note that the verb *writes* becomes *write,* and the auxiliary *does,* which is added in the transformation, determines the number and tense of the verb. Similarly, the sentence *Those who are able to do so read a book every week* becomes *Do those who are able to do so read a book every week?* The auxiliary *do* tells tense and number.

The question transformations treated so far require answers of either *yes* or *no.* Some questions require more lengthy answers. Questions that begin with *question words,* for which the symbol is *Q,* require longer answers. Note how the transformations occur in the following sentences.

> He is coming.
> *When* is he coming?
> Margaret called.
> *Why* did Margaret call?
> Frank drove.
> *Where* did Frank drive?

You make similar transformations when you make negative sentences from the basic sentence patterns. You know where to place the negative construction—*not* or *n't*—in each of the following sentences.

> I am your best friend.
> She was the right girl.

Transforming sentences into the passive form is another automatic ability of users of English. Unlike the other transformations, passive sentences cannot be formed from all the basic patterns. Patterns one, four, and five do not form passives. The other four patterns do transform into passives, however. For each of the other patterns a sentence follows. Note the way that each becomes passive.

> PATTERN 2   Children like candy.
> *Passive*   Candy is liked by children.

PATTERN 3	Jack sent me gifts.
Passive	Gifts were sent to me by Jack.
	or
	I was sent gifts by Jack.
PATTERN 6	They elected John captain.
Passive	John was elected captain.
PATTERN 7	Frosting makes cakes beautiful.
Passive	Cakes are made beautiful by frosting.

From your brief study of transformations you can see that they offer users of the language no particular problem. Like so many facets of language, they are far easier to use than to explain. It is, however, interesting to see how the transformational processes occur in the language.

DEVELOPING YOUR SKILL

A. Be prepared to discuss the meaning of the word *transformation* as it applies to grammar. Prepare your own definition for the word.

B. What are three constructions in English that occur as a result of transformations? Write your answer on a sheet of paper.

C. On a sheet of paper transform sentence 1 into a passive, sentence 2 into a question, sentence 3 into a negative and sentence 4 into a question beginning with a *Q*-word.

1. Jon finished his work three hours early.
2. Bernie ran into the opposing player.

3. Clarence feels strongly about the world situation.
4. Gene telephoned yesterday.

Review Exercises—Sentence Pattern Variations

A. Explain in writing how you know how to expand sentence patterns and how to transform them into questions, negative statements, and passive forms.

B. Each of the following sentences is either an expansion or a transformation of one of the basic sentence patterns. Indicate the number of the basic sentence pattern of each sentence.

1. The tall boy did not give her the book.
2. Elizabeth's father thought my car unsafe.
3. Any good job demands hard work.
4. Did Jerry really look hungry?
5. Wasn't that a sports car?

UNIT SUMMARY

Linguistic science has come a long way toward providing a clear organization and set of terms that will help many people to understand their own language better and to gain an understanding of and appreciation for language generally. In this unit you have studied the fundamental organization of the language—its sounds, symbols, and system. You have seen how linguists study the language and how they describe it from structural, comparative, historical, and geographical points of view. The descriptive nature of linguistic study has led to a new approach to language teaching and learning, especially in the modern dictionary.

You already knew that there are various dialects, but you have learned that geographical location and cultural background determine one's dialect. Writers of fiction sometimes use a device called *eye dialect* to describe accurately the speech of their characters.

Finally, you have come to understand some of the important structural elements of your language, ranging from the kinds of words there are—form class words and structure words—to the kinds of sentences you use. You have seen how you employ the seven basic sentence patterns, expanding them to make them more precise and interesting, and transforming them to form questions, negations, and passive forms. You have, in short, learned a great deal about how your language is used by its speakers.

UNIT REVIEW EXERCISES

DISCUSSION TOPICS

A. In what respect is the English alphabet inadequate?
B. What is meant by the statement that the symbols of a language are chosen arbitrarily?
C. Is it true that few people ever make grammatical errors?
D. Is the use of eye dialect helpful to a reader?

WRITTEN WORK

Write a sentence for each of the basic sentence patterns. Then expand each of the sentences by adding P-groups, one-word modifiers, S-groups, or compounds. Be prepared to explain the use of the sentence-expanding devices that you employed.

VOCABULARY

The italicized words in the following sentences appear in other contexts in this unit. Number a sheet of paper 1 through 5 and write the letter of the word or words that could best be substituted for the italicized word in each sentence. The numbers in brackets are the pages on which the words appear in the unit.

1. Trout *abound* in the streams of Maine. [p. 187]
   (*a*) die; (*b*) swim; (*c*) leap in the air; (*d*) are plentiful
2. He was not even *cognizant* that he had scored the point. [p. 196]
   (*a*) aware; (*b*) certain; (*c*) pleased; (*d*) congratulated
3. Mike's presence gives *credence* to his earlier story. [p. 194]
   (*a*) uncertainty; (*b*) believability; (*c*) trouble; (*d*) complication
4. His plan for the parade was an *omnibus* one. [p. 197]
   (*a*) stupid; (*b*) unbelievable; (*c*) all inclusive; (*d*) incomplete
5. One would not think that these two were his *progenies*. [p. 188]
   (*a*) offspring; (*b*) enemies; (*c*) ancestors; (*d*) disciples

SPELLING

Some of the words in the following list are commonly misspelled words that appear in this unit. Others are chosen from among lists of words that you should know and use.

1.	abound	11.	officiate
2.	cognizant	12.	opulent
3.	credence	13.	pastoral
4.	omnibus	14.	patriarch
5.	progenies	15.	redress
6.	evolution	16.	repository
7.	gargantuan	17.	succumb
8.	pervasive	18.	solstice
9.	etymological	19.	sonorous
10.	err	20.	surveillance

UNIT SELF-TEST

A. Write answers to the following questions.

1. What are the four major areas of linguistic study?
2. Which area deals with dialects?
3. What is the difference between prescriptive and descriptive grammar?
4. How do some modern dictionaries differ from traditional dictionaries?
5. What determines the dialect one speaks?
6. How do authors accurately represent the speech of their fictional characters?
7. What are sentence transformations?
8. What are the two kinds of words in English?
9. Of what three parts are all languages composed?

B. Write the appropriate symbol for each form class word and each structure word in the following sentences.

1. That handsome gentleman in the rear is the nicest person on the trip.
2. He very graciously was helping Alice with her groceries.

C. Write the appropriate symbol for each P-group, S-group, and sentence connector in the following sentences.

1. Jack ran over the hill and caught the ball that Frank hit.
2. Our house is the one on the corner, but we don't like the location.
3. After we moved in, the plaster cracked; nevertheless we are going to stay.

HANDBOOK

FOR

STUDY AND *REFERENCE*

KEY TO HANDBOOK

217

218

Capitalization

Spelling

219

Punctuation

220

221

Unit 10

Sentence Mastery

You have undoubtedly heard it said that when you write, you must write as though your reader were looking over your shoulder. This statement applies not only to the content of your writing, which must hold your reader's interest, but also to the mechanics of your writing, which must make what you say readily comprehensible.

Written English, even more than spoken English, requires careful organization. Spoken language can rely partially on gesture, pitch, pauses, stress, and varying degrees of loudness to convey meaning. Written language, lacking these characteristics, must rely primarily on the fixed word order, or patterns, of English for clarity.

The study of the classifications of words and of the ways words work together to build sentences is called *grammar*. Mastery of the terminology and of the principles of grammar is necessary to sentence mastery. Without an understanding of the terminology, you cannot discuss the principles; without an understanding of the principles, you cannot make full use of your language resources.

Before you begin your study of grammar, complete the following Check Yourself section to determine how much you already know about the aspects of grammar covered.

A. Write on a sheet of paper the simple or compound subjects and predicate verbs in the following sentences. Underline the subjects once and the predicate verbs twice.

1. There are several new courses being offered this year.
2. Mr. Lawrence and his secretary are working on the reports now.
3. The river begins in the mountains and empties into the gulf.
4. Have the newspapers been notified of the change of date?
5. The girls will meet in room 201; the boys, in room 303.

B. Write on your paper the complements in the following sentences. Label each complement according to whether it is a *Direct Object,* an *Indirect Object,* a *Predicate Nominative,* a *Predicate Adjective,* an *Objective Complement,* or a *Retained Object.*

6. Despite the differences among the disputants, the negotiators settled the matter amicably.
7. Participation in the athletic program gives students the exercise they need for physical fitness.
8. When his speech sounded familiar, I believed it a trick of my memory; but it was a case of plagiarism.
9. Both management and labor representatives were sent notices of the special meeting.
10. She doesn't believe that others consider him better qualified than she.

C. Write in a column the italicized words in the following sentences. After each word write its part of speech.

11.-13. *As* I sat looking *out* the window, I saw Mrs. Dimworthy go *out.*
14.-18. *Oh, that* is too *bad;* I hope *that* he isn't *seriously* ill.
19.-20. *Leaving* the scene of the accident *was* his mistake.

1. Basic Sentence Units

Every English sentence is made up of single-word and word-group units, all of which function in relationship to each other to make up the pattern of the sentence. Because, as you learned to speak English, you automatically learned to arrange the various sentence elements into acceptable English patterns, given the words *car, the, embankment, an,* and *struck,* you would undoubtedly arrange the words in the following pattern:

The car struck an embankment.

You might even try the following arrangement:

An embankment struck the car.

Although the second sentence lacks clarity, the relationships among the various elements in both examples are such that you sense that each example is a sentence. You would not, however, call the following arrangements sentences:

The struck an car embankment.
Struck the an embankment car.

While it is true that you tend automatically to arrange sentence elements in the patterns of sentences and can usually sense whether a group of words constitutes a sentence, understanding of language and skill in using language come only with an awareness of how language operates. It is the fundamental operations of language that you will learn in this unit.

SUBJECTS AND PREDICATES

Most English sentences are built on the framework of a subject tied to a predicate. It is this relationship that gives a sentence its basic meaning. If someone were to walk up to you and say, "Don," you would have no idea as to what was meant, unless the word *Don* were some kind of code between you. You would be equally confused if someone were to say only, "Left." However, the words "Don left," spoken in that order, would have meaning for you, even if you didn't know who Don was. You would know that someone named Don had been present but was no longer present.

The subject–predicate pattern is the first of several patterns that are basic to the English language. In the subject–predicate pattern, the subject is always a noun structure or a noun substitute; the predicate is always a verb structure. The pattern may be written with the formula N^1–V. Whenever you have a subject–predicate pattern that expresses a complete thought, you have a sentence.

A sentence is a word or a group of words conveying a completed thought and, normally, containing a subject and a predicate.   [1]

Sentence mastery begins with mastery of the fundamental elements in a sentence—the subject and the predicate.

The simple subject of a sentence is a word or a group of words that names whom or what the sentence is about.   [1a]

The predicate verb in a sentence is a word or a group of words that tells what is said about the simple subject.   [1b]

Lions roar.

The preceding example is an N^1–V sentence in its simplest form. The sentence is about lions; therefore *lions* is the simple subject. Remember that the simple subject of a sentence will usually be a noun or a noun substitute. *Roar* tells what is said about the lions; therefore *roar* is the predicate verb. Throughout this unit, unless otherwise indicated, one line under a word denotes a simple subject; two lines, a predicate verb.

The sentence *Lions roar* may be expanded by the addition of other words without changing the basic pattern of the sentence.

The restless lions in the zoo were roaring menacingly at the people.

As in the preceding example, the predicate verb of a sentence may be a *verb phrase;* that is, it may consist of a main verb and one or more auxiliaries. Some common auxiliaries are *have, has, had, can, do, shall, will, may, must,* and forms of the verb *be: am, are, is, was, were,* and *been.*

The example sentence also illustrates the possible expansion of the simple subject and the predicate verb. The simple subject is *lions;* however, the words *the* and *restless* and the word group *in the zoo* are directly related to *lions.* The words *the restless lions in the zoo* make up the complete subject, with *lions* as the chief word, or headword, of the entire cluster of words.

The complete subject of a sentence is the word group that tells whom or what the sentence is about. The most important word in the complete subject is the simple subject.   [1c]

Similarly, the predicate verb may be expanded by the addition of related words. In the example sentence, *menacingly* and *at the people* are directly related to *were roaring;* the complete predicate, therefore, is *were roaring menacingly at the people.*

The complete predicate of a sentence is the word group that tells what is said about the subject of a sentence. The most important word in the complete predicate is the predicate verb. [1d]

The following shows the example sentence with the complete subject separated from the complete predicate. The simple subject and the predicate verb are underscored.

The restless <u>lions</u> in the zoo people. <u>were roaring</u> menacingly at the

Subjects and predicates may be further expanded by compounding—by combining two or more elements to form an expanded unit. A sentence that contains two or more subjects that relate to all the verbs in the predicate is said to have a compound subject.

A compound subject contains two or more nouns or pronouns as subjects of a predicate verb. The parts of a compound subject are usually connected by *and*, *but*, or *or*. [1e]

The restless <u>lions</u> and <u>tigers</u> <u>were roaring</u> menacingly at the people. (Both the lions and the tigers were roaring; therefore *lions* and *tigers* are the two parts of the compound subject.)

A sentence contains a compound predicate if more than one assertion is made about the subject.

A compound predicate contains two or more predicate verbs. [1f]

The restless <u>lions</u> in the zoo <u>were pacing</u> in their cages and <u>were roaring</u> menacingly at the people. (*Were pacing* and *were roaring* both make assertions about the subject *lions;* therefore, *were pacing* and *were roaring* together form a compound predicate.)

Both the subject and the predicate of a sentence may be compound.

The restless <u>lions</u> and <u>tigers</u> in the zoo <u>were pacing</u> in their cages and <u>were roaring</u> menacingly at the people.

Remember that all the parts of a compound subject are tied to all the predicate verbs in a sentence and that all the parts of a compound predicate are related to all the subjects. Contrast the following sentence with the preceding example sentence:

The restless <u>lions</u> in the zoo <u>were roaring</u> menacingly at the people, and the <u>tigers</u> <u>were pacing</u> in their cages.

In the example immediately preceding, there are two subjects and two predicates; however, only *lions* is tied to *were roaring* and only *tigers* is tied to *were pacing*. Neither subject or predicate, therefore, is compound. The example illustrates a compound sentence.

Compounding subjects and predicates can help you to eliminate choppiness from your writing. Read the following sentences:

The restless <u>lions</u> in the zoo <u>were pacing</u> in their cages. <u>They</u> <u>were roaring</u> menacingly at the people. The <u>tigers</u> also <u>were pacing</u> in their cages. <u>They</u> <u>were roaring</u> too.

By compounding the subjects and predicates of the preceding sentences, you can combine all four sentences into the single sentence with which you have been working.

The <u>lions</u> and the <u>tigers</u> in the zoo <u>were pacing</u> in their cages and <u>were roaring</u> menacingly at the people.

Compound elements do not change the basic pattern of a sentence. The sentence *Lions roar* is an N^1–V sentence. The sentence *The restless lions and tigers in the zoo were pacing in their cages and were roaring menacingly at the people* has the same basic N^1–V pattern expanded to N^1–C–N^1–V–C–V. The *C* in the expanded formula stands for the conjunction *and* that links the parts of the compound subject and the compound predicate.

DEVELOPING YOUR SKILL

A. Be ready to name the complete subject and the complete predicate in each of the following sentences. Then name the simple and compound subjects and predicate verbs.

1. Both nominees for the office of class president have equally good qualifications.
2. The directions for the test were written in concise terms.

3. Recalling the difficulties inherent in a test of this kind, we read carefully and outlined in detail before writing our answers.
4. The model on the poster and the one on the magazine cover must have been posed by the same photographer.
5. Several new magazines and many new books have been received in the school library and are being circulated now.

B. Rewrite the following paragraph in a smoother, more mature style by compounding subjects and predicates wherever such compounding will improve the style.

International tastes in TV programs are not so different as one might think. Quiz programs of all kinds are universally popular. Also popular are panel shows. Situation comedies draw large viewing audiences. So do American westerns. In direct contradiction to the claim that TV is sponsoring a generation of illiterates, many countries offer educational programs. Millions of people watch TV teachers. Many of these people learn to read and write in their native tongues. Some gain fluency in other languages. Some earn credit in advanced courses. Others broaden their knowledge of various aspects of the arts and sciences. Studies of international TV viewing habits point up the cultural similarities among the peoples of the world. They also tend to minimize the cultural differences among the world's population.

ORDER IN SENTENCES

Most English sentences pattern in *natural order,* with the subject preceding the predicate. In some sentences, however, the pattern is varied so that all or part of the predicate verb precedes the subject. Such sentence patterns are said to be in *inverted order.*

The subject usually follows the predicate verb in sentences beginning with *there.*
[1g]

There <u>was</u> no apparent <u>reason</u> for his brusqueness.
There <u>go</u> our <u>plans</u> for the carnival.

In each of the preceding examples, the word *there* is used to introduce an idea. In such usage *there* is an *expletive.* An expletive is an independent element in a sentence; it is never the subject of the sentence.

Inverted order is usually used in questions.

The subject frequently separates parts of the verb phrase in a question.

[1h]

> <u>Has</u> she <u>completed</u> the report yet?
> When <u>did</u> he <u>leave</u> for the airport?

Not all questions, however, are in inverted order; many are in natural order, as in the following examples:

> <u>Who is going</u> with you? (The interrogative word *Who* is the subject.)
> Which <u>plan is being recommended</u>? (The interrogative word *Which* is used as a modifier of the subject *plan.*)

Inverted order is also used in sentences beginning with words that express or imply negative ideas, and is sometimes used in sentences that begin with an adverbial prepositional phrase.

> *Never* <u>have</u> I <u>waited</u> so long for anyone. (Beginning with a negative word)
> *On the table* <u>stood</u> several freshly baked <u>pies</u>. (Beginning with an adverbial prepositional phrase)

Inverted sentence patterns are only variations of the basic sentence patterns. In an N^1–V sentence, writing the predicate before the subject does not change the basic N^1–V pattern. When an auxiliary precedes the subject, the pattern becomes (Aux) N^1–V. The symbol for the auxiliary is written in parentheses to indicate that it may or may not occur in the pattern.

Another variation of the basic sentence pattern occurs in sentences in which the subject is not expressed. In such sentences the subject is *you*, understood.

The subject is understood in a sentence that gives a command or makes a request. [1i]

> Come here immediately! [(You) come]
>
> Think through the problem clearly. [(You) think]

In some sentences the subject is not followed directly by the predicate verb but is separated from it by a modifying phrase. The subject is never a part of such a phrase.

A phrase may come between the subject and the verb. The subject is never within the phrase. [1j]

> One *of the executives* arranged for a special meeting.
>
> Much *of the discussion* centered around the drop in sales.

Problems in subject–predicate recognition occur primarily in sentences in inverted order. Remembering that sentences do not have to be in natural order will help you to overcome a basic problem in subject–predicate recognition.

A sentence in *inverted order* is one in which all or part of the predicate precedes the subject. [1k]

DEVELOPING YOUR SKILL

Write the following sentences on a sheet of paper. Draw one line under the simple subject of each sentence and two lines under the predicate verb. Write *N.O.* in the margin beside the number of the sentence if the sentence is in natural order; write *I.O.* if the sentence is in inverted order.

1. Will you send a reply to his inquiry?
2. Not one of the delegates has the proper credentials.
3. There have been no unusual signs of discomfort in the patient.
4. Seldom does one have an opportunity like that.
5. When making your decision, consider all aspects of the question.
6. For what purpose did you call this committee meeting?
7. What in the world prompted your decision?
8. At the end of the concert, the audience cheered the performers.
9. Never before has the winter seemed so long.
10. At the end of the corridor stands a statue of Abraham Lincoln.

ELLIPTICAL SENTENCES

If someone were to say to you "Where are you going?" you would be more likely to reply, "To the store," than "I am going to the store."

To the store is not a grammatically complete sentence when judged out of context. In context, however, the subject *I* and the predicate *am going* are understood, and the sentence becomes complete. Such a sentence is called an *elliptical sentence.*

An elliptical sentence is one in which the complete thought is implied but not stated. [11]

The elliptical response to a question should be restricted to informal speaking situations or to informal dialogue in writing. However, there are elliptical sentences that may correctly be used in all speaking and writing.

Sentences of command or request in which the subject is understood but is not expressed are elliptical sentences.

Close the door quietly. (The subject *You* is understood.)

As you study the following examples of elliptical sentences, notice that the subjects and predicates in parentheses could be omitted without destroying the meanings of the sentences.

Did you visit England? (Did you visit) France? (Did you visit) Italy?

My father prefers spicy foods; my mother (prefers), bland foods. (The comma indicates that a word has been omitted.)

 DEVELOPING YOUR SKILL

The following sentences are elliptical. Rewrite them, adding the understood words. Put parentheses around the words you add.

1. Miss Wendell is our new Latin teacher; Miss Kendall, our new French teacher.
2. Leave the tickets with Robbie, the programs with Len, and the special invitations with Barbara.
3. Does he plan to be a doctor? A dentist? A pharmacist? A laboratory technician?
4. Agnes's mother brought a meat casserole; Geri's, a salad and rolls; Tom's, coffee, sugar, and cream; and David's, a cake.
5. No, this poem was written by Robert Frost; that one, by Frances Frost.

ABSOLUTE EXPRESSIONS

Many sentences include structures that amplify or clarify the meaning of the sentence but that have no grammatical relationship to the other sentence elements. Such structures are called *independent elements.* One kind of independent element is an *absolute expression,* sometimes called a *nominative absolute.*

At first glance, an absolute expression may seem to include a subject and a predicate. It contains a noun or a pronoun, which may be used as a subject, and it contains a verb form. Close examination, however, will show that the verb form in an absolute expression is a *participle—* a form of a verb used as an adjective. Do not be misled into calling the elements of an absolute expression a subject and a predicate.

An absolute expression, or nominative absolute, is a phrase that is composed of a noun or a pronoun and a participle. [1m]

The absolute expressions in the following examples are in italics. The subjects and predicates of the sentences are underscored.

The storm having abated, <u>we</u> <u>went</u> out to determine the amount of damage.

<u>Ron</u> <u>decided</u> to attend State University, *his brother having recommended it highly.*

DEVELOPING YOUR SKILL

Write the following sentences on a sheet of paper. Underline the simple and compound subjects once and the predicate verbs twice. If a sentence contains an absolute expression, enclose the expression in parentheses.

1. Helen and Bob hurried to class, the bell already having rung.
2. His mother having described Aunt Ellen in detail, Reese recognized her immediately and hurried to her side.
3. Jet travel being so fast, Mr. Bennett and his staff were in New York for lunch, completed their business, and returned to Chicago in time for dinner.
4. His question being unanswered, Tim looked back and saw Nora almost a half block behind him.
5. The old seaman, his yarn having ended, lighted his pipe and, with a satisfied grunt, settled back in his chair.

DIAGRAMING SUBJECTS AND PREDICATES

Sentence analysis involves an understanding of the relationships that exist among the various elements in a sentence. A mechanical device that depicts these relationships clearly is diagraming.

Since the simple subject and the predicate verb constitute the framework of English sentences, these two sentence elements should always be the first ones diagramed. Both the simple subject and the predicate verb are diagramed on a horizontal line called the *base line*. They are separated by a short vertical line that bisects the base line. The simple subject is always written to the left of the vertical line; the predicate verb, to the right.

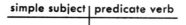

Mr. Stanton arrived early.

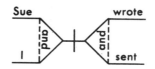

Compound subjects and predicates are diagramed on parallel lines that are connected by perpendicular broken lines. The word that links the compound parts is written along the broken line.

Sue and I wrote the program notes and sent them to the printer.

Sentences that are in inverted order are diagramed in natural order.

Have there been any new developments in the case? (Since the expletive *there* is an independent element, it is diagramed on a line separate from the rest of the diagram.)

there   developments | Have been

The understood words in an elliptical sentence are diagramed in parentheses in their normal positions in the diagram.

See him tomorrow.

Did you mean Louise? Lucille?

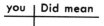

> DEVELOPING YOUR SKILL

Diagram the simple and compound subjects and predicate verbs in the following sentences.

1. Both lectures are scheduled for next week.
2. In addition to bequests to various museums, Mr. Weber left a scholarship fund and made numerous personal bequests.
3. Rice is the staple food in many parts of the world.
4. The ascent being extremely hazardous, take only experienced climbers with you.
5. Rice, chicken, and Spanish sausage are combined in this recipe.
6. The new art gallery already houses some of the world's finest paintings and is rapidly acquiring an outstanding collection of sculpture.
7. Applicants for positions must be capable, intelligent, and personable, the competition being very keen.
8. In the president's office hung a mural depicting the growth of the company.
9. During the last five years there have been constructed two new schools and a fully equipped hospital.
10. Before turning down his proposal, consider it from the point of view of efficiency, as well as economy.

Review Exercises—Basic Sentence Units

A. Do as directed in each of the following. Draw one line under each subject and two lines under each predicate verb in the sentences you write.

1. Write five sentences that have compound subjects.
2. Write five sentences that have compound predicate verbs.

3. Write five sentences that have compound subjects and compound predicate verbs.
4. Write five sentences that are in inverted order.
5. Write five grammatically correct elliptical sentences.

B. Diagram the subjects and predicate verbs in ten of the sentences you wrote
for Exercise A. Select two sentences from each of the five groups. Write
out each sentence and below it write the diagram.

2. Word Functions in Sentences

Words—used either singly or in groups—fulfill specific functions in
sentences. Certain classifications of words may be used as subjects and
predicates; others may be used as modifiers, complements, connectives,
appositives, and independent elements. An understanding of the ways in
which words function in sentences will enable you better to understand
the structure of English sentences.

VERBS

A word used as the predicate in a sentence is classified as a verb.

A verb is a word that expresses action or state of being.   [2]

The architect *destroyed* the blueprints. (Action)
I *was* in the house all day. (Being)

If you have difficulty determining whether or not a word is a verb, try
it in the following test sentence, called a *test frame*. Words that fit this
test frame may be used as verbs. Words that have irregular past forms
are always verbs and need not be tested in the frame. If they are tested,
the present form is used.

He will _____(it).

Before testing words in the frame, drop any *s, es, ed, ing,* or *est* endings. The word *it* in parentheses is used only when it is necessary to the
sense of the sentence. For example, if you were testing *taking,* you would
drop the *ing* and test *take. Take* requires a completing word; therefore
it is used in the test frame.

Another means of recognizing verb structures is by learning to recognize auxiliaries. Auxiliaries signal the beginning of a verb phrase—a group of words consisting of a main verb and one or more auxiliaries. The most commonly used auxiliaries are *can, do, does, did, may, might, must, shall, should, will, would,* and all forms of *be* and *have.*

The auxiliaries *be, do, have,* and *can* may also be used as main verbs. When they are used with other verbs, these words, and other forms of them, are auxiliaries; when they are used alone, they are main verbs. Study the following examples:

Aux V	Aux V
He <u>has called</u> twice.	She <u>is working</u> late.
V	V
He <u>has</u> my book.	She <u>is</u> my friend.

DEVELOPING YOUR SKILL

List on a sheet of paper the verbs and verb phrases in the following sentences. Label each verb according to whether it shows *action* or *being.*

1. Nothing has been decided yet about a band for the dance.
2. When did you last write to your brother in Korea?
3. Does it seem to you that she has become very distant?
4. My mother has been canning fruit all morning and is rather tired now.
5. I have no idea as to what his plans are, nor do I care.
6. At the end of this week, I shall have been working for Mr. Lewis for six months.
7. Why does she insist that she is right when she has been proved wrong?
8. More and more pre-cooked foods are now available.
9. Anyone who can read and follow directions can be a good cook.
10. If he were going with us, he would have been here by now.

NOUNS AND PRONOUNS

The subject of a sentence must always be a noun or a noun substitute. Single words that substitute for nouns are classified as pronouns.

Nouns

A noun is a word that names a person, place, or thing. [3]

The *students* in our *class* studied the *government* of our *city.*

Words may be tried in a test frame to determine whether or not they are nouns. Remember that the endings *s, es, ed, ing,* and *est* must be dropped before a word may be tested in any frame. The test frame for nouns follows:

He talked about _____ (s.)

Sometimes it is necessary to express a word in its plural form in order for it to make sense in the noun frame. The *s* in parentheses in the noun frame stands for any plural. For example, *candle* doesn't make sense in the frame, but *candles* does. *Knife* doesn't make sense, but *knives* does. *Ox* doesn't make sense, but *oxen* does.

You may also recognize nouns in sentences by looking for words that signal noun structures. One such group of words is called *determiners*. Determiners are words such as *a, an, the, this, that, these, those, my, your, his, her, its, our,* and *their* that occur with nouns or noun substitutes in sentences. Sometimes a determiner appears directly before a noun; sometimes it is separated from the noun by other words. The determiners in the following sentence are in italics:

This book contains *several* unusually beautiful illustrations.

Nouns are divided into two general classifications: *proper nouns* and *common nouns*.

A proper noun is a word that names a particular person, place, or thing. A proper noun is always capitalized. [3a]

Gloria visited the *Cloisters* when she was in *New York*.

A common noun is a word that names any one of a class of persons, places, or things. A common noun is not capitalized. [3b]

The *tourist* visited the special *branch* of the art *museum* when she was in that *city*.

Nouns may be divided into three additional classifications: *abstract, concrete,* and *collective* nouns

An abstract noun names an idea, a quality, or an action.   [3c]

> *Patriotism* may be manifested in various ways.
> Bill has proved himself capable of *leadership.*
> Mr. Chester made his money in *manufacturing.*

A concrete noun names an object.   [3d]

When the referent of a noun—that for which the noun stands—exists in the physical world, the noun is said to be *concrete.*

> She has two *closets* filled with *sweaters* and *blouses.*
> The *poodle* walked proudly on its *leash.*

A collective noun names a group, or a collection, of persons or things that is regarded as a single unit.   [3e]

> The *committee* met for three hours yesterday.
> A *flock* of wild geese flew overhead.

Sometimes words that fit the noun classification do the work of adverbs in sentences; that is, they tell *when, where, how much,* or *to what extent.*

A noun used as an adverb is called an *adverbial objective.*   [3f]

> I completed my paper last *week.*
> This *year* the tour will extend to Greece.

An adverbial objective fulfills the function of an adverb in a sentence but retains one of its noun characteristics in that it may be modified by an adjective.

> They walked *three miles.*

In the preceding sentences *miles* is an adverbial objective modifying *walked. Three* is an adjective modifying *miles.*

DEVELOPING YOUR SKILL

> A. For each of the proper nouns in the following list, give a corresponding common noun. For each of the common nouns, give a corresponding proper noun.

PART OF SPEECH TUE (handwritten)

OTHER (handwritten)

1. museum
2. Philadelphia
3. Alaska
4. legislator
5. document
6. Carl Sandburg
7. book
8. nation
9. Cary Grant
10. Ontario
11. Mississippi River
12. island
13. church
14. Leonard Bernstein
15. actress
16. Michelangelo
17. emperor
18. dictator
19. Frank Lloyd Wright
20. queen

B. Divide a sheet of paper into two columns headed *Proper Nouns* and *Common Nouns,* making the second column wider than the first. Subdivide the column headed *Common Nouns* into three columns headed *Abstract, Concrete,* and *Collective.* List each noun in the following sentences under the appropriate heading.

1. The council takes its responsibilities seriously.
2. The convention is to be held at McCormick Place in Chicago beginning on Thursday of next week.
3. During the brief layover at Genoa, a group of passengers visited the shops where they purchased shoes, silks, and various examples of local arts and crafts.
4. Jim and his sister excel both in skiing and in skating.
5. My friendship with John helped to break down the antagonism that had existed between his brother and me.

Pronouns

A pronoun is a word that is used in place of a noun. The noun for which a pronoun is used is the antecedent of the pronoun. [4]

I sent Naomi an invitation. *She* accepted *it* promptly.

In the preceding example sentences, the antecedent of *I* is the name of the speaker; the antecedent of *She* is *Naomi;* and the antecedent of *it* is *invitation.*

The most frequently used pronouns are the personal pronouns, which include the following: *I, me, my, mine, we, us, our, ours, you, your, yours, he, him, his, she, her, hers, it, its, they, them, their, theirs.*

Other commonly used pronouns include *who, whose, whom, which, what, that,* and forms of the personal pronouns with *self* or *selves* added (*myself, themselves,* and so on). Many of the words that may be used as determiners of nouns may also be used as pronouns. When they modify nouns, these words are determiners; when they are used alone in place of nouns, they are pronouns. Compare the use of the italicized words in the following sentences:

These apples are delicious. *(These* modifies *apples* and signals a noun structure.)

These are delicious apples. *(These* means *these apples* and is a pronoun.)

DEVELOPING YOUR SKILL

List on a sheet of paper the pronouns and pronouns used as determiners in the following sentences. After each, write its antecedent.

1. That boy in the gray sweater is my best friend.
2. Those cheerleaders are the only ones in the city who have offered their services to the athletic league for its city-wide rally.
3. Marge, I hope you will help Lois with her history.
4. These papers must be delivered to Mr. Peters immediately; he has been calling about them all morning.
5. Janice Hill, who is a new student, misses the school from which she came.
6. Al said he thinks the organization has undertaken more than it can accomplish.
7. Those notes are mine, but I shall be glad to let you borrow them, Tom, if you like.
8. Advice is easy to give, but it is often difficult to follow.
9. Their appeal having failed, the lawyers met again to determine whether to take it to a higher court.
10. Beth herself was surprised at the results of her experiment.

MODIFIERS

Any word or word group that makes the meaning of other words more exact by describing or limiting them is a modifier. Only two classifications of words are used as modifiers–adjectives and adverbs. A word group that modifies fulfills the function of a single adjective or adverb in a sentence.

Adjectives

An adjective is a word that modifies a noun or a pronoun.   [5]

A modifier is a word or a group of words that describes or limits the meaning of another word or of other words.   [5a]

Many girls wore *bright, colorful* costumes.

The following test frame will help you to determine whether a word fits the adjective classification. Any word that fits the frame may be used as an adjective. Determiners, which modify nouns, are a special group of adjectives and must be learned. They do not fit the frame.

They seemed _____.

Adjectives generally tell *which, what, what kind of,* and *how many.* They are classified in two ways–according to their use and according to their position in sentences. According to use, adjectives are classified as *descriptive* or *limiting.*

Descriptive adjectives, as their name implies, describe nouns or pronouns.

She wore a *blue wool* skirt with a *matching* sweater.

Limiting adjectives point out or specify. The articles *a, an,* and *the* are the most commonly used limiting adjectives. Other limiting adjectives include the possessive forms of nouns and of personal pronouns, cardinal numbers (one), and ordinal numbers (first). These limiting adjectives are also the noun markers called *determiners.*

Helene's uncle was *the second* principal of *our* school.

Adjectives are classified according to position as *predicate adjectives, attributive adjectives,* and *appositive adjectives.*

A predicate adjective is an adjective that appears in the predicate part of a sentence but modifies the simple subject. [5b]

Predicate adjectives complete the meaning of linking verbs such as *be, seem, become, appear, smell, taste, feel, grow, remain,* and *sound.*

I become *restless* when I have nothing to do.

Everyone in the room remained *silent* after Pat's outburst.

An attributive adjective is an adjective that precedes the word it modifies. [5c]

Many valuable awards were made.

An appositive adjective is an adjective that follows the word it modifies. [5d]

Notice that appositive adjectives are set off from the rest of the sentence by commas.

The young actress, *eager* and *hopeful,* started out to make the rounds of producers' offices.

Adjectives are frequently derived from proper nouns. Such adjectives are called *proper adjectives.*

A proper adjective is an adjective formed from a proper noun or is a proper noun used as an adjective. A proper adjective begins with a capital letter. [5e]

Their new cook is *French.*

This book has a *Hawaiian* setting.

Words may move from one part-of-speech classification to another, depending upon the functions they perform in sentences.

Some words may be used as adjectives or as pronouns, depending upon their use in a sentence. [5f]

The words in the list that follows may be used either as adjectives or as pronouns. When they are used as modifiers, they are determiners marking noun structures; when they are used alone, they are pronouns.

all	few	one	these
another	many	other	this
any	more	several	those
both	most	some	what
each	much	that	which
either	neither		

Neither of those books is available. (Pronoun)
Neither book is available. (Adjective)
Which of these dresses do you prefer? (Pronoun)
Which dress do you prefer? (Adjective)

Except for predicate adjectives, adjectives are diagramed on slanting lines below the words they modify. Each adjective is written on a separate slanting line.

His dark, deep-set eyes glittered.

Predicate adjectives are diagramed on the base line. They follow the predicate verb and are separated from it by a diagonal line that slants toward the subject, which is modified by the predicate adjective.

Lou is *restless*. (Predicate adjective)

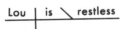

Jack seems *nervous* and *irritable*. (Compound predicate adjective)

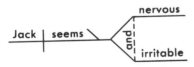

> DEVELOPING YOUR SKILL

A. Write the adjectives in the following sentences. Classify each according to use and according to position.

1. The store has received several new shipments of the designer's latest creations.
2. Two large, formidable dogs guarded the entrance to the vast estate.
3. After a summer during which he worked as a lumberjack, Roy's body was lean and muscular.

4. The children, frightened and tired, were found by one of the search parties after several hours.

5. On our tour of Europe we purchased many Danish and Swiss souvenirs as gifts for our numerous friends and relatives.

B. Write a paragraph in which you describe a memorable sight. Underline the adjectives in your description. Draw an arrow from each adjective to the noun or pronoun it modifies.

C. Diagram the following sentences:

1. The charred, smoky hamburgers tasted good.
2. Those clouds look dark and ominous.
3. Several unusual phenomena have been observed.
4. The criminal's expression was cold and hostile.
5. That large black snake is harmless.

Adverbs

An adverb is a word that modifies a verb, an adjective, or another adverb.

[6]

They *rarely* visit us. *(Rarely* modifies the verb *visit.)*
Everyone was *very* excited. *(Very* modifies the adjective *excited.)*
You tried to work *too* rapidly. *(Too* modifies the adverb *rapidly.)*

The following test frame may be used to determine whether a word may be classified as an adverb:

They walked _____.

Some words that are normally classified as adverbs may pattern with adjectives and adverbs, but never modify verbs. These words are sometimes called *intensifiers* because they strengthen, or intensify, the meanings of the words they modify by showing degree. Some of the most commonly used intensifiers are *very, rather, too, really, somewhat, quite,* and *enough.* Intensifiers do not fit the test frame.

Adverbs fall into five classifications according to their use in sentences.

Adverbs tell time (when), place (where), cause (why), manner (how), and degree (how much or to what extent).

[6a]

He has *often* spoken of you. (Time)
Flowers were *everywhere* in the room. (Place)
The office, *therefore,* was closed. (Cause)
She spoke *distractedly.* (Manner)
I *absolutely* forbid that. (Degree)

Certain adverbs are used to combine two related sentence patterns into a single sentence. Adverbs that are used in this way are called *conjunctive adverbs*. Conjunctive adverbs are sometimes referred to as *sentence connectors* to distinguish them from conjunctions.

An adverb used as a connective is called a conjunctive adverb.   [6b]

The most common conjunctive adverbs are *however, moreover, therefore, consequently,* and *nevertheless.* Notice that a semicolon follows the first sentence pattern when a conjunctive adverb is used as a connective and that a comma usually sets the conjunctive adverb off from the rest of the second sentence pattern.

His career was at stake; *nevertheless,* he bared all the facts.

The words that may be used as conjunctive adverbs may also be used as simple adverbs. When they are used as simple adverbs, no semicolon is used. In the following sentence *moreover* is an adverb modifying *was played*.

The game, *moreover,* was played well.

An adverb that modifies a verb or a predicate adjective is diagramed on a slanting line below the word it modifies.

Andrea has *suddenly* become *rather* angry.

Other adverbs are diagramed on slanting lines connected to the lines of the adjectives and adverbs they modify.

The work was completed *very rapidly*.

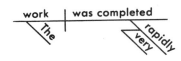

An adverbial objective—a noun used as an adverb—is diagramed in the same way that an adverb is diagramed. If the adverbial objective is modified by another word, the modifier is diagramed on a slanting line connected to the line of the adverbial objective.

His father arrived *home* last *week*.

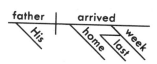

DEVELOPING YOUR SKILL

A. Name the adverbs, including the adverbial objectives, in the following sentences. Name the word each modifies and tell whether the modified word is a *verb,* an *adjective,* or an *adverb.*

1. Yesterday Lisa greeted me rather coolly.
2. The new typist spoke quietly and diffidently.
3. You have apparently forgotten your promise already.
4. His pulse is somewhat rapid but is very steady.
5. Russ came in late last night and banged the door noisily.
6. The banjo can be easily heard over all other sounds in the room.
7. She is talented enough to play the leading role.
8. The somewhat muted tones of a trumpet sounded hauntingly in the background.
9. The child wept plaintively for his mother all afternoon.
10. He overcame seemingly insurmountable obstacles.

B. Divide a sheet of paper into two columns. In the first column list all the adverbs in the following sentences. In the second column opposite each adverb, list the word that the adverb modifies. Write the part of speech of the modified word.

1. Evidently you have not yet heard the news.
2. Recently I saw an unusually excellent movie on TV.
3. The brilliantly costumed dancers performed enthusiastically.
4. I have seldom seen a more enjoyable performance.
5. Nevertheless, it was unusually long and could profitably have been cut somewhat.
6. Undoubtedly, the version you heard was considerably different from the one I heard.
7. When did you leave the party last night?

8. The drummers swayed rhythmically to the beat of the bongos.
9. He spoke rather quietly but still drove his point home convincingly.
10. She has always been willing enough to help.

C. Diagram the following sentences:

1. Melissa has never seemed happier.
2. Where did you go last night?
3. Seldom have I been so disappointed.
4. Your attitude is completely understandable.
5. The sun shone briefly and then disappeared completely.

CONNECTIVES

Two classifications of words—prepositions and conjunctions—may be used as connectives in sentences. The difference between prepositions and conjunctions lies in their specific functions in sentences.

Prepositions

A preposition is a word that shows the relationship of its noun or pronoun object to some other word or words in the sentence. [7]

The book slid *across* the desk.
The book slid *off* the desk.
The book slid *under* the desk.

In each of the preceding sentences, the italicized preposition shows the relationship between the noun *desk* and the verb *slid*. Notice how the change in preposition changes the relationship expressed.

Some of the most commonly used prepositions include the following:

about	beside	in	through
above	besides	inside	to
across	between	into	toward
after	but (except)	near	under
against	by	of	until
among	down	off	up
around	during	on	upon
at	except	out	with
behind	for	over	within
before	from	since	without

Some prepositions are composed of more than one word and are called *phrasal* or *compound prepositions*. The following list includes some commonly used phrasal prepositions:

according to	back of	in front of
ahead of	because of	in place of
apart from	by means of	in spite of
as far as	contrary to	instead of
as to	in addition to	out of

We were delayed *because of* a highway accident.
Contrary to rumor, nothing has been decided.
Leave the empty cartons *back of* the garage.

The meaning of a preposition must be completed by a noun or a pronoun, called the *object of the preposition*. The entire group of words, beginning with the preposition and ending with the object of the preposition, is called a *prepositional phrase*.

Mark that date *on your calendar.*
Did you see the play *from the beginning?*

Prepositional phrases usually fulfill the functions of modifiers in sentences. A prepositional phrase may do the work of a single adjective or a single adverb.

The rocket *on the pad* is ready to be launched. *(On the pad* modifies the noun *rocket* and is, therefore, used as an adjective.)

The rocket was launched *according to schedule. (According to schedule* modifies the verb phrase *was launched* and is, therefore, used as an adverb.)

Since prepositions must be completed by nouns or pronouns, prepositions serve as structural signals in sentences. Prepositions signal noun (or noun substitute) structures. The usual pattern of a prepositional phrase is preposition–modifier–noun (or noun substitute).

Some of the words that may be used as prepositions may also be used as adverbs. When these words pattern with following nouns or pronouns, they are prepositions; when they are used alone as modifiers, they are adverbs. When two words that are commonly used as prepositions are used together with only one object, the first word is usually an adverb. Study the following example sentences:

I'll meet you *in* the lobby. *(In* is a preposition showing relationship between its object *lobby* and the verb *meet.)*

Come *in*. *(In* is an adverb modifying the verb *come.)*

He went *out for* a walk. *(Out* is an adverb modifying the verb *went. For* is a preposition showing relationship between its object *walk* and the verb *went.)*

A prepositional phrase is diagramed under the word that the phrase modifies. The preposition is written on a diagonal line with its object on a connected horizontal line. Modifiers of the object of the preposition are written on slanting lines below the object.

The members *of the victorious team* were elated.

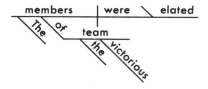

A prepositional phrase may be separated in a sentence from the word it modifies.

After the eliminations only two *of our representatives* remained *in the contest.*

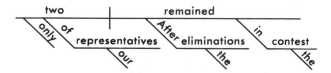

A prepositional phrase may modify the object in another prepositional phrase.

I heard *from him on Monday of last week.*

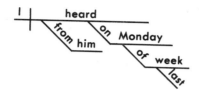

A prepositional phrase may modify all parts of a compound construction. In such a case the slanting line on which the preposition is written is attached to the main line of the compound structure.

In the morning we rowed to the middle of the lake and fished in the quiet waters.

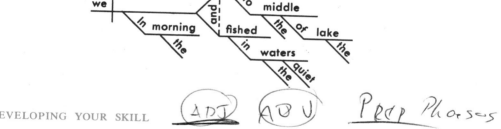

DEVELOPING YOUR SKILL

A. Pick out the prepositional phrases in the following sentences. Tell what word or words each phrase modifies. Name the part of speech whose function each prepositional phrase fulfills.

1. In most short stories the author begins with the exposition and builds carefully to the climax.
2. The new bridge across the river will be completed before winter.
3. Toward sunset we stopped at a service station and asked about nearby motels.
4. According to the latest reports the weather will change again before morning.
5. Within a few minutes everyone but Lenore had left for the Fishers' house.

B. Write a paragraph of about 150 words describing a football, basket-ball, or some other game you either watched or took part in. Begin each sentence on a new line and leave a blank line after each line of writing. Underline the prepositional phrases in your paragraph. Draw an arrow from each prepositional phrase to the word it modifies. Above each prepositional phrase write the part of speech whose function the phrase fulfills.

C. Write on a sheet of paper the italicized words that follow. After each word write its part of speech.

1. *After* the game we drove *out to* a stand just *outside of* town *for* hamburgers.   *Prep Phase*
2. *In the past* half hour I have seen Herb drive *by* five times.
3. Walk *past* the corner and you will see the name above the door of the second building *on* your right.
4. I shall go *along with* your plan; it has proved successful *before.*
5. *In spite of* your reluctance I wish you would come *inside* and tell my parents *about* your scholarship *to* the university.

D. Diagram the five sentences in Exercise A.

Conjunctions

Conjunctions join single words, phrases, or word groups called *clauses.* A clause is a group of words that contains a subject and a predicate verb.

A conjunction is a word used to connect words or groups of words. [8]

They were tired *but* happy. (The conjunction *but* connects the single words *tired* and *happy.*)

I shall see you in the library *or* at home. (The conjunction *or* connects the two prepositional phrases *in the library* and *at home.*)

Toni wrote the music *and* I wrote the lyrics. (The conjunction *and* connects the two clauses *Toni wrote the music* and *I wrote the lyrics.*)

The most commonly used conjunctions include *and, but, or, nor, for, because, since, that, after, if, where, when,* and *while.*

Sometimes conjunctions are used in pairs to connect sentence elements. Such pairs of conjunctions are called *correlative conjunctions.* The most frequently used correlatives are *both...and, either...or, neither... nor,* and *not only...but also.*

Our team is playing *both* tonight *and* tomorrow night.
Either Lucy *or* Joan will let you know.

I have *neither* the energy *nor* the desire to go.
He plays *not only* the piano *but also* the guitar.

Conjunctions are diagramed on dotted lines that join the words, phrases, or clauses connected by the conjunction.

Miss Kenny spoke abruptly *and* angrily. (*And* connects single words.)

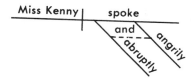

The picture will be exhibited *either* in the display case *or* in the library. (*Either . . . or* connects phrases.)

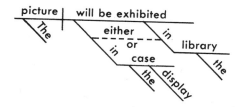

Is the work interesting *or* is it just routine? (*Or* connects clauses.)

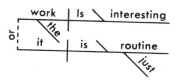

In sentences in which two clauses are linked by a semicolon and a conjunctive adverb, the conjunctive adverb is diagramed, like any other adverb, on a slanting line under the word it modifies. An (x) is written on the connecting line between the clauses.

The test seemed very difficult to me; *moreover,* it was unusually long.

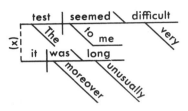

   DEVELOPING YOUR SKILL

A. Write the following sentences on a sheet of paper. Underline each conjunction and conjunctive adverb and put parentheses around the words or word groups that the conjunctions and conjunctive adverbs connect.

1. I either shall write for tour information or shall stop at the travel bureau.
2. Last winter George, Dick, and I worked at the ski lodge on weekends.
3. Clare has just returned from the hospital; therefore, we should not stay very long this time.
4. The weather in Florida has been warm and sunny throughout our vacation.
5. For a time we were swept up and carried along by the enthusiastic crowd, but we finally slipped away.

B. Write sentences to fit the following formulas. The nouns used as subjects are marked N^1. Prepositional phrases are enclosed in parentheses. The key will help you interpret the formulas.

N—Noun (or noun substitute)   Adj—Adjective
V—Verb   Adv—Adverb
LV—Linking Verb   P—Preposition
Aux—Auxiliary   C—Conjunction
   SC—Conjunctive adverb (Sentence Connector)

1. Adj N^1 V (P Adj N) C (P Adj N).
2. (P Adj N) N^1 Aux LV Adj C Adj.
3. N^1 C N^1 V (P Adj N), C N^1 C N^1 V Adv.
4. Aux N^1 V (P N), C Aux N^1 V Adv?
5. N^1 Aux Adv V (P N); SC, N^1 LV Adj (P Adj N).

C. Diagram the sentences in Exercise A.
D. Diagram the sentences you wrote for Exercise B.

INTERJECTIONS

An interjection is a word that shows strong feeling. [9]

My! I didn't know she was so talented.
What! Are you serious?

Interjections are frequently followed by exclamation points. Sometimes, however, they are merely unrelated words separated from the rest of the sentence by commas. The choice of an exclamation point or a comma after an interjection depends upon the strength of the emotion expressed.

Why, that possibility hadn't occurred to me.
Oh! It can't be true!

An interjection has no grammatical relationship to the rest of the sentence in which it appears. It is, therefore, an independent element and is diagramed on a line that is separate from the rest of the diagram.

Whee! My letter of acceptance came this morning.

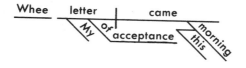

 DEVELOPING YOUR SKILL

A. List on a sheet of paper the interjections in the following sentences.

1. Heavens! This soup is hot.
2. Now, don't be nervous about your interview.
3. Why, when did he leave for Europe?
4. Oh dear! How did she sound?
5. Whew! This Latin translation is hard.

B. Write five sentences in which you use interjections.
C. Diagram the sentences in Exercise A.

COMPLEMENTS

The subject–verb pattern, or N^1–V pattern is the basic framework of most English sentences and expresses the essential meaning of the sentence. In many sentences, however, an additional word or additional words are needed for completeness and clarity. If, for example, someone were to say to you, "He mailed," you would not understand what was meant. However, if the speaker were to say, "He mailed the announcements," the meaning would be clear. The word *announcements* is called a *complement* because it completes the meaning of the verb *mailed*.

A complement is a word or a group of words that is added to another word or group of words to complete a meaning.   **[10]**

Predicate nouns, predicate pronouns, predicate adjectives, direct objects, indirect objects, objective complements, and retained objects are all complements. Each is added to another word or group of words to complete a meaning. As complements are added to the basic subject–predicate framework of sentences, new sentence patterns are created.

Predicate nouns, pronouns, and adjectives

After such verbs as *seem, become, appear, grow, remain, sound, feel, taste, smell,* and forms of the verb *be,* a predicate noun, pronoun, or adjective is used as a complement to complete the meaning of the verb. [10a]

Tina is my *cousin*. (Predicate noun)
The culprit was *he*. (Predicate pronoun)
Mr. Stark seems *irritable*. (Predicate adjective)

Both predicate nouns and predicate pronouns are often given the name *predicate nominative*. The pattern of sentences that contain predicate nominatives is one of the basic patterns of English sentences—*subject–linking verb–noun (or noun substitute) complement*. The pattern may be written with the formula $N^1–LV–N^1$. The superior number 1 after both N's indicates that the subject and the complement refer to the same thing.

Sentences that contain predicate adjectives follow another of the basic sentence patterns—*subject–linking verb–adjective complement*. The formula for this pattern is N^1–LV–Adj.

Predicate nouns, pronouns, and adjectives are all diagramed in the same manner. A slanting line separates the complement from the predicate verb.

Miss Thomas is my English *teacher* and my curriculum *adviser*. (Compound predicate noun)

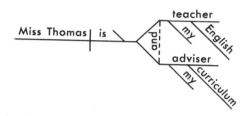

The speaker could not have been *he*. (Predicate pronoun)

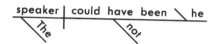

That story sounds *familiar*. (Predicate adjective)

> DEVELOPING YOUR SKILL

A. List on a sheet of paper the complements in the following sentences. Label each complement according to whether it is a *predicate noun*, a *predicate pronoun*, or a *predicate adjective*.

1. Mr. Hall is an electrical engineer.
2. Carla has seemed rather aloof lately.
3. It must have been either Stewart or I.
4. The fair grounds soon became crowded and noisy.
5. According to the nurse on duty, his condition is much better today.
6. Of all our friends it could only have been they.

7. Automobiles have become necessities for many persons.
8. My sister is the one on the right.
9. Doris and Al are charter members of the club.
10. All the contestants appeared relaxed and self-assured.

B. Diagram the first five sentences in Exercise A.

Direct and indirect objects

Many verbs, called *transitive verbs,* pass their action to a noun or pronoun either directly or indirectly. The complements of such verbs are called *direct objects* and *indirect objects.*

A direct object is a noun or a pronoun that receives the direct action of a verb.   [10b]

A direct object always answers the question *what* or *whom* after the verb.

> Agnes is filing the *cards.*
> Pat is helping *her.*

The formula for sentences with a *subject–verb–direct object* pattern is N^1–V–N^2. The superior numbers indicate that the referents of the two nouns are different.

An indirect object is a noun or pronoun that receives the indirect action of the verb and answers the question *to whom* or *what* or *for whom* or what.   [10c]

> Aunt Elaine sent *me* a check for my birthday.
> Have you told *Bea* the good news?

An indirect object always appears between the predicate verb and the direct object. In the first of the preceding sentences, *me* is the indirect object of *sent; check* is the direct object. In the second sentence *Bea* is the indirect object of *Have told; news* is the direct object.

If the preposition *to* or *for* is expressed with an object, the word group is a prepositional phrase, not an indirect object.

> I brought *Gloria* some cake. (Indirect object)
> I brought some cake *for Gloria.* (Prepositional phrase)

The formula N^1–V–N^2–N^3 is used for sentences that have a basic *subject–verb–indirect object–direct object* pattern.

A direct object is diagramed on the base line, separated from the predicate verb by a short perpendicular line extending up from the base line. An indirect object is diagramed on a line below the verb, with (x) taking the place of the understood preposition *to* or *for*.

The rules allowed each *team* three *minutes* for rebuttal.

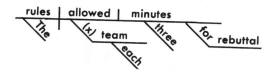

DEVELOPING YOUR SKILL

A. List and label the direct and indirect objects in the following sentences.

1. Lynn has apparently given you an accurate picture of the situation.
2. Mr. Malone always brings his family souvenirs of historic places on his route.
3. The waitress offered us a choice of either rolls or biscuits with dinner.
4. The panel included a university professor, a banker, and a clergyman.
5. Not once did anyone ask me for my opinion.
6. Will you bring me that box of envelopes?
7. The salesman sold Mother and Aunt Mary identical draperies.
8. Did you ask me a question?
9. The busy executive allotted Alex fifteen minutes for an interview.
10. His tone and gestures gave his words a different connotation.

B. Diagram the first five sentences in Exercise A.

Objective complements

Another kind of complement that is often used in sentences is the *objective complement*. An objective complement completes the meaning of the verb by amplifying the meaning of the direct object. It may be either a noun or an adjective. When a noun is used as an objective complement, it names the same person or thing as the direct object; when an adjective is used, it describes the direct object.

An objective complement is a noun or an adjective that completes the meaning of the verb by explaining or describing the direct object. [10d]

Mr. Murphy appointed Ted's father administrative *assistant*. (Noun)
Mr. Murphy considers Ted's father highly *competent*. (Adjective)

Two more of the basic patterns of English are formed in sentences that contain objective complements. The formula for the *subject–verb–direct object–noun objective complement* pattern is N^1–V–N^2–N^2. The formula for the *subject–verb–direct object–adjective objective complement* pattern is N^1–V–N^2–Adj.

Objective complements are diagramed on the base line following the direct object and separated from it by a diagonal line that slants toward the direct object.

They named the baby *Joan*.   He made me *angry*.

 DEVELOPING YOUR SKILL

A. Write the following sentences on a sheet of paper. Underline the direct objects and enclose the objective complements in parentheses. After each sentence write the formula for its basic pattern.

1. My employer considers my knowledge of French an asset.
2. Did you think his portrayal of the role realistic?
3. Has she really dyed her hair black?
4. The long period of inactivity made Joe restless.
5. The Honors Society elected Jean chairman of the annual banquet and dance.

B. Diagram the sentences in Exercise A.

Retained objects

In most sentences the subject is the performer of the action expressed in the verb. The verb is then said to be in the *active voice*. Sometimes, however, the subject is the receiver of the action expressed in the verb.

The verb is then said to be in the *passive voice*. Compare the following sentences:

> Yvonne and Corrine *arranged* the program. (Active voice)
> The program *was arranged* by Yvonne and Corrine. (Passive voice)

Since they pass their action to the subjects of sentences, verbs in the passive voice do not have direct objects. They may, however, be followed by nouns or pronouns that complete the meaning of the verbs. Such complements are called *retained objects*. Compare the sentences in the following pairs:

> They gave us an *hour* between sessions. (*Hour* is the direct object.)
> We were given an *hour* between sessions. (The direct object *hour* from the preceding sentence is retained as the complement of the passive verb *were given* and becomes the retained object.)

> We considered it a *privilege*. (*Privilege* is the objective complement.)
> It was considered a *privilege*. (The objective complement *privilege* from the preceding sentence is retained as the complement of the passive verb *was considered* and becomes the retained object.)

A noun that completes the meaning of a verb in the passive voice is called a *retained object*. [10e]

Since the pattern of sentences containing retained objects is exactly the same as that of sentences containing direct objects, the formula is the same N^1-V-N^2.

Retained objects are diagramed exactly like direct objects.

Mr. Sieller's poem was awarded first *prize*.

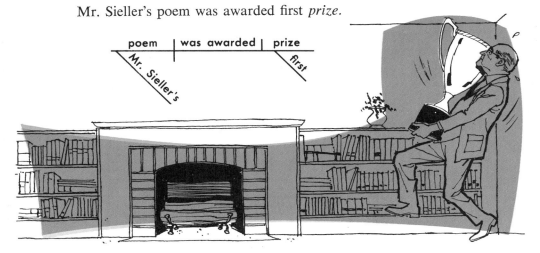

A. List the retained objects in the following sentences:

1. We were sold several worthless items.
2. Sandra was offered an unusually high salary for a beginner.
3. During his stay in the hospital, Kevin was considered an ideal patient.
4. By tomorrow Stan will certainly have been told the entire story.
5. Mr. Boyd has been appointed director of the combined chorus.

B. Diagram the sentences in Exercise A.

Sentence patterns

The basic patterns of English sentences are built on the framework of a subject and a predicate verb. As various complements are added to the basic framework, the sentence patterns change. The following chart is a summary of the seven basic patterns in English. The items in parentheses indicate the elements that constitute each pattern.

PATTERN 1
N^1 V
Lions   roar.
(subject)   *(verb)*

PATTERN 2
N^1 V N^2
Elaine   enjoys   music.
(subject)   *(verb)*   *(direct object)*

PATTERN 3
N^1 V N^2 N^3
Claire   bought   us   tickets.
(subject)   *(verb)*   *(indirect object)*   *(direct object)*

PATTERN 4
N^1 LV N^1
Tomatoes   are   fruit.
(subject)   *(linking verb)*   *(predicate nominative)*

PATTERN 5
N^1 LV   Adj
He   looks   healthy.
(subject)   *(linking verb)*   *(predicate adjective)*

PATTERN 6
N^1 V N^2 N^2
We   elected   Betty   secretary.
(subject)   *(verb)*   *(direct object)*   *(objective complement)*

PATTERN 7
N^1 V N^2 Adj
I   believe   her   wrong.
(subject)   *(verb)*   *(direct object)*   *(objective complement)*

All the basic sentence patterns may be varied without changing the basic pattern. Modifiers may be added, inverted order may be used, interrogative words may be added to introduce questions, and the subject may be understood rather than expressed. Study the following examples of Pattern Two and some of its possible variants:

N¹	**V**				**N²**	
Sue	likes				Jerry.	
Our team	won	their	last		game.	
Your friend	is taking	the	bad		news	well.
Who	chose	this			color?	
Have you	seen	her	new		coat?	
Why did Bob	take	your			car?	
(You)	Write	your			name	clearly.

Conjunctions may be used to expand the basic patterns and to avoid needless repetition and a choppy style. Read the following sentences:

Lynne went to the yearbook office early. She worked for an hour before class. Theresa went to the yearbook office early, too. She also worked for an hour before class.

Notice how much smoother the style becomes when the ideas are combined into a single sentence. Notice, too, that the basic N¹–V pattern of the preceding sentences has been retained, but has been expanded N¹–C–N¹–V–C–V.

    N¹   **C**   **N¹**   **V** **(P Adj**   **Adj**   **N)**   **(Adv)** **C**   **V**
Lynne and Theresa went to the yearbook office early and worked
(P Adj N)   **(P**   **N)**
for an hour before class.

Conjunctions and conjunctive adverbs (sentence connectors) may be used to combine two complete sentence patterns into a single sentence.

   N¹ **LV** **Adj**   **N¹** **V**   **N²**
Leo was tired. He visited David.

   N¹ **LV** **Adj** **C** **N¹** **V**   **N²**
Leo was tired, but he visited David.

   N¹ **LV** **Adj**   **SC**   **N¹** **V**   **N²**
Leo was tired; nevertheless, he visited David.

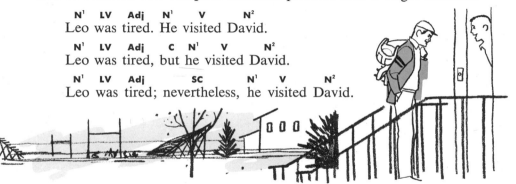

A. Your teacher may wish to have you do this exercise orally. For each of the basic sentence patterns, build a basic sentence and at least five variants of the basic sentence. Use the examples on page 263 as a guide, but try to work out other variants as well.

B. Write five sentences in which you use compound elements. Above each word in your sentences write the symbol for its function in the sentence. Underline the words that constitute the expanded basic pattern in each sentence.

C. Write the numbers from 1 to 5 on a sheet of paper. After each number write the complete formula for the corresponding sentence. Underline the symbols that represent the basic or expanded basic pattern of each sentence.

1. Certainly, someone besides Marcia must have given you some ideas on the subject.
2. The highlights of the holiday will be a sleigh ride and a square dance.
3. Tony studied architecture at the university, but he went into the advertising field.
4. We consider Jim capable; therefore we made him manager of the team.
5. The sketches of the posters for the safety campaign are both appropriate and clever.

VERBALS

Verbals are verb forms that function in sentences as nouns, adjectives, or adverbs. They retain their verb characteristics in that they may be followed by complements and may be modified by adverbs.

Words derived from verbs but used as other parts of speech are called verbals. The verbals are participles, gerunds, and infinitives.   [11]

A participle is a verb form used as an adjective.   [11a]

He is a *swimming* champion. *(Swimming* is a participle modifying the noun *champion.)*

The time *spent* at the library proved profitable. *(Spent* is a participle modifying the noun *time.* The prepositional phrase *at the library* modifies *spent.)*

In the preceding examples, *swimming,* the *ing* form of *swim,* is a present participle; *spent,* the third principal part of *spend,* is a past participle.

Participles may also be formed with *having* or *having been* and the third principal part of a verb.

> *Having completed* their work, Roger and Alan left.
> *Having been recognized,* the celebrity stopped to speak to his admirers.

A verbal used as a noun is called a *gerund.*

A gerund is a verb form ending in *ing* that is used as a noun. It may, then, be the subject of a verb, the direct object of a verb, the indirect object of a verb, a predicate noun, the object of a preposition, or an appositive.
  [11b]

> *Dancing* is my favorite pastime. (Subject)
> I like *dancing.* (Direct object)
> I give *dancing* my vote for the most pleasurable pastime. (Indirect object)
> My favorite pastime is *dancing.* (Predicate noun)
> I do have some other interests besides *dancing.* (Object of a preposition)
> I look forward to opportunities to enjoy my favorite pastime, *dancing.* (Appositive—explains *pastime*)

The third kind of verbal is called an *infinitive.*

An infinitive is a form of a verb that is preceded by the word *to.* Infinitives may be used as nouns, adjectives, or adverbs. **[11c]**

> *To reach* the shelter was their only hope. (Noun—subject)
> I have decided *to leave* now. (Noun—direct object)
> Your aim should be *to succeed.* (Noun—predicate nominative)
> We have two weeks *to spend* there. (Adjective—modifies the noun *weeks*)
> I shall be happy *to help.* (Adverb—modifies the adjective *happy*)

After such verbs as *hear, help, let, make, please,* and *see,* the word *to* is usually omitted from the infinitive.

> Did you let her (to) know?
> Please (to) help me (to) do this.

Verbals are diagramed in the positions of the parts of speech whose functions they perform.

Participles, like other adjectives, are diagramed below the words they modify.

The doctor's *encouraging* words cheered the *worried* mother.

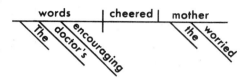

Gerunds are diagramed along an angled line placed on a stand. The base of the stand appears at the point where a noun fulfilling the same function would appear. Notice that the gerund curves along the angled line.

Bowling is a pleasant form of exercise. (Subject)

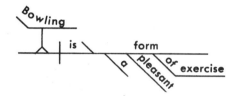

She was well known for her *acting* on television programs. (Object of a preposition)

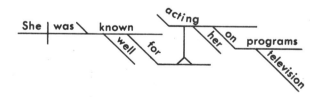

Her one bad habit, fingernail *biting,* mars her appearance. (Appositive)

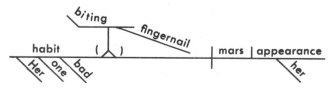

Infinitives used as nouns are diagramed like gerunds.

To sing professionally is her ambition. (Noun)

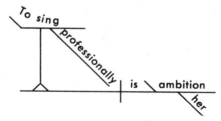

Infinitives used as modifiers are diagramed along an angled line below the words they modify.

I shall go there *to see* for myself. (Adverb)

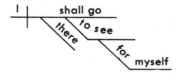

DEVELOPING YOUR SKILL

A. List on a sheet of paper the verbals in the following sentences. Label each according to whether it is a *participle,* a *gerund,* or an *infinitive.* If the verbal is used as a noun, write its noun function; if it is used as a modifier, write the word it modifies.

1. The sun setting behind the mountains was a beautiful sight to see.
2. Speaking in public is an ordeal for many people.
3. To picnic in a shaded spot in the woods is particularly pleasant in hot weather.
4. Having studied hard throughout the year, Nancy is sure of graduating next month.
5. The features of the people standing in the last row in the photograph are too blurred to recognize.

B. Diagram the sentences in Exercise A.

APPOSITIVES

An appositive is a noun or pronoun—often with modifiers—that follows another noun or pronoun to explain or identify it. [12]

Our neighbor, *Mr. Julian,* has a new automobile. (*Mr. Julian* is in apposition with *neighbor.*)

In the preceding example, the appositive is set off from the rest of the sentence by commas. Commas are not necessary if an appositive is closely related to the word it explains or identifies.

I like Robert Frost's poem *"Birches."*
His brother *Burt* is an honor student.

Appositives may have modifiers.

An appositive phrase is made up of an appositive and its modifiers.
[12a]

Mrs. Harbeck, *the director of the Foreign Relations Program,* has prepared a booklet for distribution abroad.

Appositives may be used to avoid wordiness in writing. Clauses—word groups that contain subjects and predicates—may often be condensed to appositives.

Avoid wordiness by reducing clauses to appositives.   [12b]

Mr. Shelby, *who is the president of our local university,* presented the scholarship award to Martha Erwin. *Martha is the valedictorian of our class.*

Mr. Shelby, *the president of our local university,* presented the scholarship award to Martha Erwin, *our class valedictorian.*

Appositives are diagramed in parentheses immediately following the words they identify or explain.

My sisters *Betsy* and *Laura,* the *ones* in Miss Byron's class, wrote amusing compositions about their Siamese cat, *Sami.*

A. List the appositive phrases in the following sentences. Underline the appositive in each phrase. Following each phrase write the word that the appositive explains or identifies.

1. Richard discussed his plans for the future with Mr. Griffin, an electrical engineer.
2. Helen Traubel and Patrice Munsel, singers of operatic music, also sing popular music.
3. I usually mispronounce the words *strength* and *height.*
4. Will you bring me that vase, the one on the buffet.
5. Mr. Richman, a member of the council for many years, was recently elected mayor of the town.

B. Rewrite the following sentences in concise English. Use appositives to overcome the problem of wordiness.

1. Mrs. Benton lectured at the last Parent-Teachers Association meeting. She is an authority in the field of education.
2. Synge wrote *Riders to the Sea.* The setting of the play is the Aran Islands.
3. Miss McHenry, who is our new mathematics teacher, taught at Seneca Academy, which is a school in the eastern part of the state.
4. Tom Markham set a new record in the last swimming meet. Tom is the best swimmer on our team.
5. We have just finished studying *Hamlet,* which is a Shakespearean tragedy.

C. Diagram the sentences in Exercise A.

Review Exercises—Word Functions in Sentences

A. Write the following sentences on a sheet of paper. Underline the simple and compound subjects once and the predicate verbs twice.

1. *Ballet* slippers *and* leotards are *standard rehearsal* attire at the *dancing* school.
2. The fables *written by* James Thurber appeal to almost *everyone* in our *English class.*
3. I consider him and his friends churlish, and I *have no* intention of *associating* with them.
4. The members of *our* class voted Dennis the boy most likely to succeed.
5. *Oh!* Never *before* has anything *seemed* so *completely* hopeless to me; *however,* Mr. Morrison gave *me* some encouragement *today.*

B. List the complements in the sentences in Exercise A. Label each according to the kind of complement it is.

C. List and label the verbals in the sentences in Exercise A.

D. List the italicized words in Exercise A. After each, write its part of speech.

E. Write the formula for the basic or expanded sentence pattern in each of the sentences in Exercise A.

3. Word Groups in Sentences

In many sentences word groups perform the functions of single words. Word groups within sentences may be predicate verbs, they may be modifiers, or they may be noun structures. The two kinds of word groups that are used within sentences are *phrases* and *clauses*.

PHRASES

A phrase is a group of related words that does not have a subject and a predicate. A phrase performs the function of a single part of speech. [13]

Phrases that are used as predicate verbs are called *verb phrases*.

A verb phrase is a phrase that contains a main verb and one or more auxiliary verbs.   [14]

The verb phrases in the following sentences are in italics.

> Nothing *has been decided.*
> *Have* you *finished* your work?
> They *have been* quietly *observing* the deer.

Adding auxiliaries to the main verb in a sentence does not change the basic sentence pattern. The pattern in all the following sentences is N^1–V–N^2–N^3. The predicate verb in each sentence is in italics.

> Dolores *sent* Bob an invitation.
> Dolores *has sent* Bob an invitation.
> *Has* Dolores *sent* Bob an invitation?

A prepositional phrase is a group of related words beginning with a preposition and ending with a noun or a pronoun object.   [15]

> The new books *in the library* were purchased *by the Parent-Teachers Association.*

Prepositional phrases may be used as adjectives or adverbs in sentences.

A prepositional phrase may serve as an adjective in a sentence. [15a]

Most *of the students* have purchased tickets *for all the athletic events.* (*Of the students* modifies the pronoun *Most; for all the athletic events* modifies the noun *tickets.*)

A prepositional phrase may modify the noun or pronoun that is the object of an immediately preceding prepositional phrase.

The lesson *at the beginning of the book* is easy. (*At the beginning* modifies the noun *lesson; of the book* modifies *beginning,* the object of the preceding prepositional phrase.)

Since a prepositional phrase may be used as an adjective, it may be used as a predicate adjective in a sentence without changing the basic sentence pattern. The basic pattern in both sentences that follow is N^1–LV–Adj. The predicate adjectives are in italics.

The quality of the material is *inferior.*
The material is *of inferior quality.*

A prepositional phrase may also be used as an adjective objective complement without changing the basic N^1–V–N^2–Adj pattern of a sentence. The adjective objective complements in the following sentences are in italics:

I consider such a survey *pointless.*
I consider such a survey *of little value.*

A prepositional phrase may serve as an adverb in a sentence. [15b]

Dr. Williams has lectured *throughout the country.* (*Throughout the country* modifies the verb phrase *has lectured.*)

Prepositional phrases may be used to avoid wordiness in writing.

Avoid wordiness by reducing clauses to prepositional phrases. [15c]

Each of the new staff members has been assigned to a desk. *All their desks are in the outer office.*

Each of the new staff members has been assigned to a desk *in the outer office.*

A verbal phrase is a group of related words that contains a participle, a gerund, or an infinitive. [16]

Participles, gerunds, and infinitives may be modified by other words and may be followed by complements.

A participial phrase is a group of related words that contains a participle.
[16a]

Speaking calmly but firmly, she made her point. *(Speaking* is a participle. *Calmly* and *firmly* are adverbs modifying *speaking. Speaking calmly but firmly* is a participial phrase modifying the subject *she.)*

The man *driving that convertible* is my brother-in-law. *(Driving* is a participle. *Convertible* is the object of the participle *driving. That* modifies *convertible. Driving that convertible* is a participial phrase modifying *man.)*

A gerund phrase is a group of related words that contains a gerund.
[16b]

Writing a good composition involves *careful planning.*

In the preceding example, *writing a good composition* is a gerund phrase used as the subject of the sentence. *Composition* is the complement of the gerund *Writing. Careful planning* is a gerund phrase used as the direct object of *involves. Careful* modifies the gerund *planning.*

An infinitive phrase is a group of related words that contains an infinitive.
[16c]

The Wilsons decided *to postpone their trip. (Trip* is the object of the infinitive *to postpone.* The entire infinitive phrase *to postpone their trip* is the direct object of *decided.)*

An infinitive used as a noun may have a subject as well as a complement. The infinitive phrases in the following sentences are in italics:

Barbara asked *Lenore to go with her. (Lenore* is the subject of the infinitive *to go.)*

Let *me help you with that. (Me* is the subject of the infinitive *help,* with *to* understood. Notice that the subject of an infinitive is in the objective case.)

Verbals that are formed from the verb *be* may be completed by predicate nouns, pronouns, or adjectives.

272

Being an *expert* in his field, Mr. Mills is frequently called upon for consultations. *(Expert* is a predicate noun that completes the participle *Being.)*

Having been *famous* in his youth was his constant boast. *(Famous* is a predicate adjective that completes the gerund *Having been.)*

Your mysterious caller has to be *he.* *(He* is a predicate pronoun that completes the infinitive *to be.)*

Verbals change form to show differences in time (tense) and in voice. The following list includes all the forms of the verbals formed from the verb *drive.*

	ACTIVE VOICE	PASSIVE VOICE
Present Participle	driving	being driven
Past Participle	driven	(none)
Perfect Participle	having driven	having been driven
Present Gerund	driving	being driven
Perfect Gerund	having driven	having been driven
Present Infinitive	to drive, to be driving	to be driven
Perfect Infinitive	to have driven, to have been driving	to have been driven

Since verbals and verbal phrases fulfill the functions of single parts of speech in sentences, they may substitute for single words in sentence patterns without changing the basic pattern. Compare the basic patterns in each of the following pairs of sentences:

Overconfidence may be a fault. (N¹–LV–N¹)

To be overly confident may be a fault. (N¹–LV–N¹)

I enjoyed my *trip* to Mexico. (N¹–V–N²)

I enjoyed *traveling through Mexico.* (N¹–V–N²)

His outstanding quality is his *honesty.* (N¹–LV–N¹)

His outstanding quality is *his being honest.* (N¹–LV–N¹)

Verbal phrases may be used to avoid wordiness in writing.

Avoid wordiness by reducing clauses to verbal phrases.   [16d]

Martin doesn't know *what he should do about the situation.*

Martin doesn't know *what to do about the situation.* (Infinitive phrase)

After she had finished her homework, Carla went out.

Having finished her homework, Carla went out. (Participial phrase)

Prepositional phrases used as complements are diagramed on a stand in the place of the complement whose function they fulfill.

Which of these diamonds is *of greater value?* (Predicate adjective)

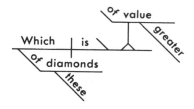

I consider his ideas *of great importance.* (Adjective objective complement)

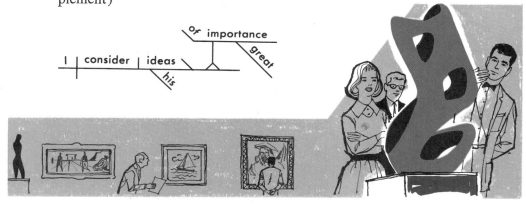

Verbal phrases used as modifiers are diagramed along an angled line below the words they modify. The verbal is separated from its object by a short vertical line and from its predicate nominative or predicate adjective by a diagonal line.

Being tired, we were quiet on the way home. (Participial phrase—adjective)

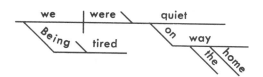

Have you gone *to see the counselor about your problem?* (Infinitive phrase—adverb)

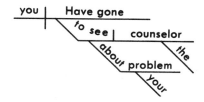

Verbal phrases used as nouns are diagramed along an angled line on a stand. The base of the stand appears at the point where a noun fulfilling the same function would appear. The verbal is separated from its object by a short vertical line and from its predicate nominative or predicate adjective by a diagonal line.

Not having been present seems *to have been a mistake.* (Gerund phrase—noun; infinitive phrase—noun)

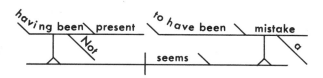

An absolute expression, which contains a participle, is an independent element; therefore, it is diagramed on a line that is separated from the rest of the sentence diagram.

Everyone having left, I washed the dishes and cleaned the recreation room.

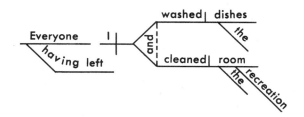

The infinitive *to let* in the following sentence has an infinitive phrase as its object. *Sue* is the subject of the infinitive *to let; him* is the subject of the infinitive *(to) use*. Notice the diagraming.

He asked *Sue to let him use her pen.* (Infinitive–noun)

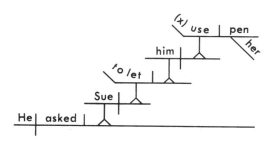

 DEVELOPING YOUR SKILL

A. List the phrases in the following sentences and label each according to whether it is a *verb phrase,* a *prepositional phrase,* a *participial phrase,* a *gerund phrase,* or an *infinitive phrase.* After each phrase used as a modifier, write the word the phrase modifies and the part of speech whose function the phrase fulfills. After each phrase used as a noun, write its noun function.

1. Having made his point, Jeff has decided to take no further part in the debate.

2. No one had ever expected our team to make such a good showing against the champions.

3. Have you made any arrangements to interview the speaker before-hand?

4. You must have heard me ask you to stop playing records for a few minutes.

5. Being a conscientious chairman, Howard has already left for the auditorium to supervise the final arrangements for the program honoring Miss Evans.

B. Rewrite the following sentences, using verbal phrases to overcome the problem of wordiness.

1. The way you should have done that was clearly explained in the instructions.

2. Jerry has investigated all the colleges in which he is interested. Now he is ready to make a choice.
3. Mark expects that he will work as a counselor again next summer.
4. We have decided that we should start work early since we should be prepared for the possibility of unforeseen delays.
5. After he had made his last delivery, Andy returned to the store where he turned in the day's receipts.

C. Write the numbers 1 to 5 on your paper. After each, write the formula of the basic pattern in the corresponding sentence in Exercise A.

D. Do as directed in each of the following:

1. Write two sentences with the basic pattern N^1–V–N^2. Use a gerund phrase as the subject of one sentence and an infinitive phrase as a direct object in the other.
2. Write two sentences with the basic pattern N^1–LV–N^1. Use a gerund phrase as the predicate nominative in one sentence, and an infinitive phrase as the predicate nominative in the other.
3. Write one sentence with the basic pattern N^1–LV–Adj. Use a verbal phrase as the predicate adjective.

E. Diagram the sentences in Exercise A.

CLAUSES

A clause is a group of related words that contains a subject and a predicate. [17]

Some clauses may stand alone as complete sentences; others are used as parts of larger sentence patterns.

An independent clause is a clause that expresses a complete thought and can stand alone as a sentence. [18]

Robert has always been a good student.
He has led the honor roll for the past four years.

A dependent clause is a clause that depends on the rest of the sentence for its meaning. [19]

Unless you have a better idea, I suggest *that we follow the original plan.*

Dependent clauses may be classified as adjective, adverb, or noun clauses.

An adjective clause is a dependent clause that modifies a noun or a pronoun.   [19a]

Adjective clauses are usually introduced by relative pronouns *(who, whose, whom, which, that)* or by subordinating conjunctions *(where, when, why)*. A relative pronoun may be used as the subject, the direct object, the object of the preposition, or as a possessive modifier in an adjective clause. A subordinating conjunction that introduces an adjective clause usually modifies the verb in that clause.

> The man *who spoke to us* is our new principal.
> The woman *whose child was lost* was hysterical.
> Is that the office *to which we are to report?*
> This is the place *where we are meeting the others.*

An adverb clause is a dependent clause that modifies a verb, an adjective, or an adverb.   [19b]

Adverb clauses are introduced by subordinating conjunctions, such as *when, where, before, since, as, as if, if, so, unless, because, in order that, so that, than, though, although,* and *as though.*

> She spoke *before she thought.* (Adverb clause modifying the verb *spoke)*

> It was cold *when we went out.* (Adverb clause modifying the predicate adjective *cold)*

An adverb clause may come at the beginning of a sentence.

> *If you are not careful,* you will slip on the ice. (Adverb clause modifying the verb *will slip)*

A noun clause is a dependent clause that is used as a noun.   [19c]

Noun clauses are usually introduced by words such as *who, which, what, that, when, where, whether, how,* and *why.* Since noun clauses fulfill the functions of single nouns in sentences, they may be used in the same ways that nouns are used.

> *What he does* is his business. (Subject)
> That question is *what we are here to decide.* (Predicate nominative)
> I believe *that you have met Laurie.* (Direct object)
> Tell *whomever you wish* that story. (Indirect object)
> The company reimbursed me for *what I had spent.* (Object of a preposition)

The fact *that she blushes easily* annoys her. (Appositive)

I have not convinced Miss Rushton *that I am capable.* (Objective complement)

Miss Rushton cannot be convinced *that I am capable.* (Retained object)

Sometimes the introductory word *that* is omitted before a noun clause.

He said *he would be delayed. (That* is understood.)

Mary said, *"You are wrong." (That* is never used before a direct quotation.)

A noun clause is always part of an independent clause. In each of the preceding examples of noun clauses in sentences, the entire sentence is the independent clause. When noun clauses are used as basic elements in sentences, they do not change the basic sentence pattern. Compare the following pairs of sentences. Remember that *N* in a sentence pattern stands for a *noun* or a *noun substitute.*

That is interesting. (N^1–LV–Adj)

What you said is interesting. (N^1–LV–Adj)

Edith believes *you.* (N^1–V–N^2)

Edith believes *that you are right.* (N^1–V–N^2)

The following facts will help you to recognize and understand dependent clauses.

An adverb clause may be elliptical; that is, some of the words may be omitted but may be understood from other parts of the sentence.

An elliptical adverb clause is an adverb clause in which one or more words are understood but not expressed. [19d]

She works more efficiently *than he.* (The complete adverb clause is *than he works.)*

While cooking, she burned her hand. (The complete adverb clause is *While she was cooking.)*

The relative pronoun is sometimes omitted before an adjective clause.
[19e]

The program *I watched* on TV was particularly good.

This is the book *I want.*

In both of the preceding sentences the relative pronoun *that* is understood.

Do not mistake an absolute expression for a dependent clause. [19f]

The train having been delayed, we left an hour late. (Absolute expression)

Since the train had been delayed, we left an hour late. (Adverb clause)

While waiting for the train, we drank coffee and chatted. (Elliptical adverb clause)

An adjective clause is diagramed below the independent clause. The word modified by the adjective clause is connected to the related word by a broken line. When the relative pronoun is understood, it is written in parentheses in the position that indicates its use in the dependent clause.

The story describes a European family *that settled in the Midwest.*

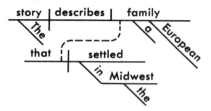

The article *I mean* appeared in yesterday's newspaper.

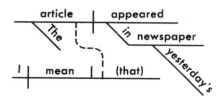

Do you know the place *where they had the accident?*

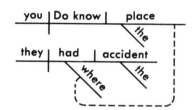

An adverb clause is diagramed below the independent clause. A broken line, on which the subordinating conjunction is written, connects the adverb clause to the word it modifies. The understood words in an elliptical clause are written in parentheses in the places where they would normally appear in the diagram if they were expressed.

I'll try to be ready *when you get here,* but don't count on it.

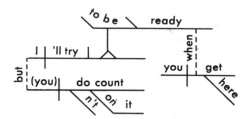

I am even more anxious *than you.*

A noun clause is diagramed on its own base line, but is attached to the main clause at the point where a noun with the same function would be written. When the only function of the introductory word is to connect the clauses, the connective is written on the connecting line. Otherwise, it is diagramed according to its function in the noun clause.

What you ask is impossible. (Subject)

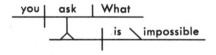

The answer is *that that is his choice.* (Predicate nominative)

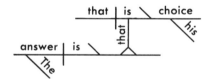

Do you know *which is her coat?* (Direct object)

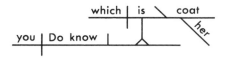

Send *whomever you wish* invitations. (Indirect object)

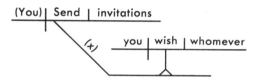

You can talk with him about *whatever interests you.* (Object of a preposition)

The conviction *that he would succeed* sustained him. (Appositive)

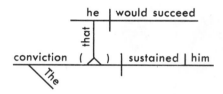

Have you convinced him *you are serious?* (Objective complement)

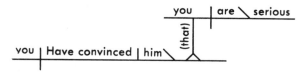

The diplomat was assured *that there would be no delays.* (Retained object)

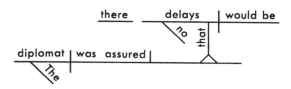

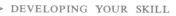

DEVELOPING YOUR SKILL

A. List on a sheet of paper the dependent clauses in the following sentences. Label each clause according to whether it is an *adjective clause,* an *adverb clause,* or a *noun clause.* If a clause is used as a modifier, write the word that the clause modifies; if it is used as a noun, write its noun function.

1. The result of my taking private Spanish lessons is that my speaking ability has improved.
2. This is the house where my parents lived during the first years of their marriage.
3. He told whomever he met the story.
4. When dawn broke, we packed our equipment and started out again.
5. Whether you agree is immaterial at this point.
6. Success depends, in part, upon what your attitudes are.
7. Because she is allergic to so many things, her enjoyment of food is limited.
8. Tina will read the letter that was sent by the superintendent.
9. The idea upon which this story is based was taken from a news item.
10. I don't understand why he is so antagonistic.

B. Write the formulas for the basic sentence patterns in Exercise A.
C. Diagram the first five sentences in Exercise A.

Review Exercises—Word Groups in Sentences

Do as directed in each of the following:

1. Write four sentences with the basic pattern N^1–V–N^2. In the first sentence use a gerund phrase as the N^1 element; in the second, use an infinitive phrase as the N^2 element; in the third, use a noun clause as the N^1 element; in the fourth, use a noun clause as the N^2 element. You may use a verb phrase for the V in any of the sentences.
2. Write one sentence with the basic pattern N^1–V–N^2–N^3. Use a noun clause as the N^2 element.
3. Write two sentences with the basic pattern N^1–LV–N^1. In the first sentence use a gerund phrase as the N^1 element that completes the verb. In the second, use a noun clause as the N^1 complement.
4. Write two sentences with the basic pattern N^1–LV—Adj. In the first sentence use a prepositional phrase as the adjective complement; in the second, use an infinitive phrase as the adjective complement.
5. Write one sentence with the basic pattern N^1–V–N^2–N^2. Use a noun clause as the second N^2 element.

4. The Entire Sentence

FUNCTION AND STRUCTURE

A sentence may be classified according to its function.   [20]

The four classifications of sentences according to function are *declarative, interrogative, imperative,* and *exclamatory.*

A declarative sentence makes a statement. It ends with a period. [20a]

Mr. Hoke is an excellent teacher.

An interrogative sentence asks a question. It ends with a question mark.
[20b]

Why have you decided to stay home?

An imperative sentence gives a command or makes a request. It ends with a period.   [20c]

Think carefully before you give your answer.

An exclamatory sentence expresses strong feeling. It ends with an exclamation point.   [20d]

What a difficult day this has been!

A sentence may be classified according to its structure. [21]

The second classification of sentences is based upon the number and kinds of clauses a sentence contains.

A simple sentence is made up of one independent clause. [21a]

Along the banks of the river stand picnic tables and benches.

A compound sentence is made up of two or more independent clauses.
[21b]

I have written her three letters, but *she hasn't answered any of them.*

A complex sentence is made up of one independent clause and one or more dependent clauses. [21c]

Since no one else is here, I shall do *whatever is necessary* myself. (One independent and two dependent clauses)

A compound-complex sentence is made up of two or more independent clauses and one or more dependent clauses. [21d]

When the school tax was increased, many taxpayers complained; but most people agreed *that a new school should be built.* (Two independent and two dependent clauses)

DEVELOPING YOUR SKILL

A. Write the numbers 1 to 5 on a sheet of paper. After each number write the classification according to function and structure of the corresponding sentence.

1. The first American college to confer degrees on women was Oberlin College in Ohio.
2. What unusual experiences you have had, and how vividly you describe them!
3. Please help me decide which of these suits I should wear while I am traveling.
4. Will you travel by plane when you go to France, or will you enjoy a leisurely crossing by ship?
5. On the way to his office, June's father had a flat tire, remembered that his spare tire was home in the garage, and discovered he had forgotten his wallet.

B. Write the formulas for the basic patterns in the sentences in Exercise A.

COMPLETENESS

Prepositional phrases and other phrases cannot be used as complete sentences.   [22]

More volunteers are needed in hospitals. *Because of the shortage of trained personnel.* (Fragment)

More volunteers are needed in hospitals because of the shortage of trained personnel. (Complete)

Verbal phrases cannot be used as complete sentences.   [23]

Having left high school in his third year. Raymond had difficulty finding and keeping a job. (Fragment)

Having left high school in his third year, Raymond had difficulty finding and keeping a job. (Complete)

Sentence fragments may occur when a sentence is carelessly divided.   [24]

After a while I began to see his point of view. *A point of view based on study and experience.* (Fragment)

After a while I began to see his point of view, a point of view based on study and experience. (Complete)

Dependent clauses cannot stand alone as sentences.   [25]

The valuable papers were locked in the vault. *So that they would not fall into the wrong hands.* (Fragment)

The valuable papers were locked in the vault so that they would not fall into the wrong hands. (Complete)

 DEVELOPING YOUR SKILL

Some of the following word groups are complete sentences; some contain fragments. If a group of words is a sentence, write *complete* on your paper opposite the appropriate number. If a word group contains a fragment, rewrite it so that it becomes a complete sentence.

1. Representatives of many countries appearing in official uniforms and wearing their medals.
2. Tell Loretta that I want to talk to her as soon as possible.
3. While Bob Merrill was in North Carolina, he took many beautiful photographs. Some of which he will show us this afternoon.
4. Leaving home for the first time and starting college in a strange city.
5. By the time I had heard the music for the fifth time, I began to develop an appreciation of the strange harmonies.

6. Mr. Magner, who is an avid student of local history, has just completed the first volume of a series about our town. According to a report I read in last night's newspaper.
7. First of all, the scholastic requirements are unusually high.
8. Being one of eight children. Sandy has had to learn to be self-sufficient.
9. More people are able to enjoy plays and to hear good music. Than was possible before the invention of the radio and television.
10. While Sybil was in college, she received many honors. One of them being election to Phi Beta Kappa.

Review Exercises—The Entire Sentence

Write a composition of about 150 words in which you give directions for making something. Start each sentence on a new line. Exchange papers in class. After each sentence on the paper you are checking indicate whether the sentence is *complete* or is a *fragment*. Write the classification of each of the complete sentences according to *function* and *structure*.

UNIT SUMMARY

Sentence mastery is essential to good writing; an understanding of grammar is essential to sentence mastery. When you understand the elements that constitute sentences and how these elements may be combined in sentence patterns, you are well on your way to achieving sentence mastery.

Since sentences are composed of words—used singly or in groups—it is essential that you understand how words function in sentences. The following chart summarizes the functions of the parts of speech and their substitutes in sentences.

STRUCTURE	PART OF SPEECH	SUBSTITUTE FOR PART OF SPEECH
Subject	noun pronoun	gerund or gerund phrase (n.) infinitive or infinitive phrase (n.) clause (n.)
Predicate	verb	verb phrase (v.)
Modifier	adjective adverb	prepositional phrase (adj., adv.) participle or participial phrase (adj.) infinitive or infinitive phrase (adj., 　adv.) clause (adj., adv.) adverbial objective (adv.)
Complement	noun pronoun adjective	gerund (n.) infinitive (n., adj.) prepositional phrase (adj.) clause (n., adj.)
Connective	conjunction preposition	conjunctive adverb (conj.)
Appositive	noun	gerund or gerund phrase (n.) infinitive or infinitive phrase (n.) clause (n.)
Independent elements Direct address Expletive Nominative absolute	interjection noun	

UNIT REVIEW EXERCISES

DISCUSSION TOPICS

A. How does an understanding of the basic patterns in English sentences help you to master the fundamentals of grammar?

B. Is it true that independent elements have no relationship to the rest of the sentence? Explain your answer.

WRITTEN WORK

A. Write a brief, but carefully organized, paragraph beginning with the following topic sentence: A writer must always keep his reader clearly in mind. Begin each sentence on a new line, and leave a blank line after each line of writing.

B. For this exercise use the composition you wrote for Exercise A. Draw one line under each subject and two lines under each predicate verb. Enclose the complements of verbs in parentheses. Above each word write the abbreviation for its part of speech. Following each sentence write the formula for its basic or expanded sentence pattern, whichever applies.

VOCABULARY

Did you know the meaning of all the words in this unit? The following sentences use some of the words in different contexts. Write the numbers 1 to 5 on your paper. After each number, write the letter of the word or phrase that could best be substituted for the italicized word in each sentence. Before making your choice, find the word on the page indicated to see how it is used in the unit.

1. Kenneth admitted that he had already *partially* rejected my thesis. [p. 223]
   (*a*) comparatively; (*b*) completely; (*c*) somewhat; (*d*) relatively
2. If you did that, you would be *compounding* your error. [p. 227]
   (*a*) correcting; (*b*) overcoming; (*c*) establishing; (*d*) increasing
3. Each *expletive* was stronger than the preceding ones. [p. 229]
   (*a*) ejaculation; (*b*) example; (*c*) utterance; (*d*) expression
4. Try to *amplify* the sound further. [p. 232]
   (*a*) augment; (*b*) prolong; (*c*) produce; (*d*) condense
5. No one ever made a more definite *assertion*. [p. 227]
   (*a*) calculation; (*b*) declaration; (*c*) refutation; (*d*) protestation

SPELLING

The following spelling words appeared in the unit or were chosen because they are commonly misspelled. Study these words so that you will be prepared to write them from dictation.

1. partially	11. philosopher
2. compounding	12. masterpiece
3. expletive	13. primarily
4. amplify	14. aisle
5. assertion	15. depreciate
6. disputants	16. predecessor
7. formidable	17. corrugated
8. hostile	18. neutrality
9. diffidently	19. debris
10. allocated	20. inimitable

UNIT SELF-TEST

A. List in three separate columns on a sheet of paper the *Subjects, Predicate Verbs,* and *Complements* in the following sentences. Label each complement of a verb according to whether it is a *direct object,* an *indirect object,* a *predicate nominative,* a *predicate adjective,* an *objective complement,* or a *retained object.* In your lists include elements of both independent and subordinate clauses.

1. *Neither* Gerda *nor* Francine would reveal her ideas for the *publicity* campaign for the variety show.
2. *Why,* water skiing has become a *very* popular sport.
3. *Why* you *acted* as you did is *no* concern *of* mine.
4. The driver who appeared *to be* at fault was given every opportunity to present his side of the story.
5. The *fact* that he has a penchant for *getting* into trouble is *obvious.*
6. Despite his irritating mannerisms, I consider *him my* friend.
7. Upon *entering* the room, Loretta paused for a moment, *choosing* the group she would join.
8. Has he told you *whether* he will write a factual account of his travels or a fictional one, or *is* he keeping it a secret?
9. *Unless* everyone *has* a good time, I feel *that* a party has not been a success.
10. Of the many *paintings that* are on exhibit, this *abstract* is the one I like best.

B. List the verbals and verbal phrases in the sentences in Exercise A. If a verbal is used as a modifier, write the word it modifies; if it is used as a noun, write its noun function.
C. List the dependent clauses in the sentences in Exercise A. If a clause is used as a modifier, write the word it modifies; if it is used as a noun, write its noun function.
D. List the italicized words in Exercise A. Label each word according to its part of speech.
E. Write the numbers 1 to 10. After each, write the formula for the basic or the expanded basic sentence pattern of the corresponding sentence.

Unit 11

Grammar and Usage

You may have noticed that you do not always use your language in just the same way in different situations; that is, you tend to be more careful of your speech in certain situations than in others. For example, when you are applying for a job or when you are being interviewed for admission to college, you tend to be more careful of your choice of words and of your usage than when you are speaking casually and informally with your friends.

There are several levels of expression; and when the occasion calls for the use of formal English, informal or colloquial English is not acceptable, any more than sneakers would be at graduation ceremonies. Thus it becomes important that you learn how to use English on various levels and that you avoid illiterate usage at all times.

Correct formal English is based upon the usage of educated people. Such usage, in turn, is based upon certain grammatical principles; therefore, a knowledge of these principles can help you improve your usage. But there are many exceptions to the grammatical rules; and language, both spoken and written, keeps changing, with written English lagging behind spoken English. If you were to compare the accepted English of Washington's day with the accepted usage of today, you would readily see that accepted patterns of English do change.

In this unit you will study correct usage and points of grammar that will help you improve your use of formal English, thus helping you to feel confident when you speak and write. Wherever there are acceptable variations for informal usage, these are pointed out also.

After you complete the Check Yourself section that follows, you will have an idea of how much you already know and how much you still have to learn about correct usage.

CHECK YOURSELF

Write the numbers from 1 to 25 on a sheet of paper. After each number write the word or words from the parentheses that will make the sentence correct.

1. Did you hear about (Tom, Tom's) going to camp with Bob and (I, me)?
2. That pilot is said (to fly, to have flown) more than one million miles.
3. Your watch is different (than, from) mine, and Anne has still another (kind of, kind of a) watch.
4. (May, Can) I (sit, set) this vase on (that, that there) table?
5. There (go, goes) Alice and Mary with (Charles's and Sally's, Charles and Sally's) mother.
6. You (had better, had ought to) take in (Bill's and Don's, Bill and Don's) bicycles before it begins to rain.
7. Ham and eggs (is, are) my favorite breakfast, but Lisa likes waffles (more better, better).
8. I (expect, suppose) that you know that the bell has (rang, rung).
9. I can't agree (to, with) your plan, and Mr. White agrees with Father and (me, myself).
·10. I should have liked (to have ridden, to ride) with (you and him, he and you).
11. Did you read (where, that) they (blamed the accident on Bob, blamed Bob for the accident)?
12. Michael said, "I don't know (whose, who's) sweater this is, but I think perhaps (it's, its) (John's, Johns').
13. Politics (don't, doesn't) interest me very much, but we should all take some interest in (them, it).
14. (My brother, My brother he) says that he is taller than (any, any other) boy in his class.
15. The clock fell (off of, off) the mantel, but Mother says that she (doesn't, don't) think that it is beyond repair.

16. Neither Mother nor Father (like, likes) the cold weather; they say that they wish they (was, were) going south this winter.
17. You would have (less, fewer) problems with your foreign language if you prepared your lesson each day more (careful, carefully).
18. (The house's roof, The roof of the house) was damaged by the storm.
19. Dave is taller than (me, I), and Alice is shorter than (he, him).
20. (Who, Whom) do you compete with (more often, most often), Kim or Carl?
21. Alan is a better skier than (any, any other) boy in our class, and he skates (well, good), too.
22. Is that (he, him) (who, whom) you see in the picture?
23. He is a boy (who, whom) I think will make a good class president.
24. I was just about to (lie, lay) down when you called; I usually don't (lie, lay) down in the afternoon, but I (took sick, became ill).
25. Neither the boys nor their father could find (his, their) money.

1. Verbs and Their Use

Every sentence contains a word that expresses an action or a state of being. Such words are verbs. You should know the various forms of verbs and the principal, or essential, parts from which they are derived.

PRINCIPAL PARTS OF VERBS

The principal parts of a verb are the *present*, the *past*, and the *past participle*. [26]

The *present participle* is another important part of a verb. It is formed by adding *ing* to the present form *(working)*.

The principal parts of a regular verb are formed by adding *d* or *ed* to the first principal part to form the past and the past participle forms. [26a]

PRESENT	PAST	PAST PARTICIPLE
move	move*d*	move*d*
play	play*ed*	play*ed*

The principal parts of an irregular verb are formed in different ways. The pronunciation of a vowel sound may be changed, or the spelling of the second and third principal parts may be different from the spelling of the first principal part. [26b]

PRESENT	PAST	PAST PARTICIPLE	PRESENT	PAST	PAST PARTICIPLE
arise	arose	arisen	lend	lent	lent
awake	awoke	awaked	let	let	let
be	was	been	lie	lay	lain
bear	bore	borne	lose	lost	lost
begin	began	begun	mean	meant	meant
bend	bent	bent	raise	raised	raised
bid	bade	bidden	ride	rode	ridden
bite	bit	bitten	ring	rang	rung
blow	blew	blown	rise	rose	risen
bring	brought	brought	run	ran	run
burst	burst	burst	say	said	said
buy	bought	bought	set	set	set
catch	caught	caught	shake	shook	shaken
choose	chose	chosen	shoot	shot	shot
cling	clung	clung	show	showed	shown
come	came	come	shrink	shrank	shrunk
creep	crept	crept	sing	sang	sung
dig	dug	dug	sink	sank	sunk
do	did	done	sit	sat	sat
draw	drew	drawn	slay	slew	slain
drink	drank	drunk	speak	spoke	spoken
drive	drove	driven	spin	spun	spun
eat	ate	eaten	steal	stole	stolen
fall	fell	fallen	sting	stung	stung
fight	fought	fought	strew	strewed	strewed
forget	forgot	forgotten	strive	strove	striven
forsake	forsook	forsaken	swear	swore	sworn
freeze	froze	frozen	swim	swam	swum
get	got	got, gotten	swing	swung	swung
give	gave	given	take	took	taken
go	went	gone	teach	taught	taught
grow	grew	grown	tear	tore	torn
hang	hanged	hanged	throw	threw	thrown
hang	hung	hung	tread	trod	trodden
hide	hid	hidden	wake	waked	waked
know	knew	known	wear	wore	worn
lay	laid	laid	weave	wove	woven
learn	learned	learned	wring	wrung	wrung
leave	left	left	write	wrote	written

A. Find and list the following verbs:

1. Three verbs that have the same principal part for all three forms.
2. At least ten verbs that have a different vowel sound in each of the three principal parts, such as *rise, rose, risen*.
3. Ten or more verbs that have the same form in the past and the past participle forms.

B. Choose five irregular verbs that you use often. Write two sentences for each of these verbs, using the second principal part in one and the third principal part in the other.

EXPRESSING TIME IN VERB FORMS

Tense is the time expressed by a verb. [27]

The six tenses are: *present, past, future, present perfect, past perfect,* and *future perfect*. The principal parts of a verb are the basis upon which all of these tenses are formed. The present (first principal part) is the form upon which the present and future tenses are made; the past (second principal part) is the basis of the past tense; and the past participle (third principal part) is the basis of the three perfect tenses.

The *present* tense expresses an action or a state of being in the present, or a habitual action.

He *plays* the piano well, doesn't he? (Action)
He *is* a very competent pianist. (Being)
I always *take* my art lesson on Saturday morning. (Habitual action)

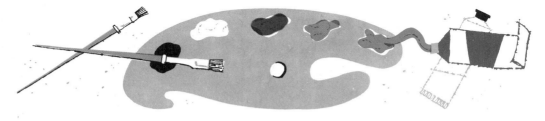

The third person singular of the present tense is always formed by adding an *s* to the present form, or the first principal part (play*s*). The other forms (first person singular, second person singular, first, second, and third persons plural) all use the present form (play).

The *past* tense expresses an action completed in the past or a state of being in the past.

> My brother *worked* on a ranch last summer. (Action)
> He *told* us many interesting facts about the ranch. (Action)
> He *was* very brown by the end of the summer. (Being)

The past tense is formed from the second principal part. The past tense *worked* is the second principal part of the regular verb *work*. The past tense *told* is the second principal part of the irregular verb *tell*. The past tense *was* is the second principal part of the irregular verb *be*.

The *future* tense expresses an action that will take place at some time in the future.

> I *shall call* you promptly at seven o'clock.

The future tense is formed from the first principal part (call) and one of the auxiliaries *shall* or *will*.

The *perfect* tenses include the *present perfect,* the *past perfect,* and the *future perfect.* To form any of the forms in the perfect tenses, you must use some form of the auxiliary *have* with the past participle.

The *present perfect* tense expresses an action that was begun in the past and completed at the time of speaking; an action begun in the past and extending to the present; and a habitual or repeated action carried out at no definite time in the past.

> We *have completed* our required reading. (Begun in the past and completed at the time of speaking)
> He *has been* here for an hour. (Begun in the past and extending to the present)
> I *have* always *walked* home by that route. (Habits or repeated action in the past)

The *past perfect* tense expresses a past action completed before another indicated time in the past. The auxiliary *had* is used with the past participle.

> I *had* already *begun* to get supper when you called.

The *future perfect* tense expresses an action to be completed before another indicated time in the future. The auxiliaries *shall have* and *will have* are used with the past participle.

By this time tomorrow, we *shall have traveled* over two thousand miles.

I feel sure that he *will have returned* the book before you need it.

A *conjugation* of a verb is a complete list of all its forms in all its tenses. The conjugation of the verb *hear* is on pages 304 to 307.

A *synopsis* is a listing of the forms of a verb in all six tenses in one person and number, such as the third person singular. Following is the synopsis of the verb *work* in the third person singular, masculine gender.

Present	He works
Past	He worked
Future	He will work
Present Perfect	He has worked
Past Perfect	He had worked
Future Perfect	He will have worked

The six preceding forms are the *simple* forms of the verb *work*. There are also *progressive* and *emphatic* forms, which are expanded verb forms. The progressive forms, made up of some form of the auxiliary *be* and the present participle, show continuing action. (He *is working*, he *was working*, he *will be working*, he *has been working*, he *had been working*, he *will have been working*.)

The emphatic forms are made by using *do, does,* or *did* with the first principal part of the main verb. Emphatic verb forms are used only in the present and past tenses. They are used for emphasis, in negative statements, and in questions.

He *does study,* but not very efficiently.

I *do* not *want* to walk very far in the cold weather.

Does he *play* the piano or any other instrument?

Did you *see* the game on Saturday?

DEVELOPING YOUR SKILL

A. Write the numbers 1 to 5, and after each number write the word or words in parentheses that will complete the sentence correctly. Then write the tenses of all the verbs you selected.

1. The bell (had rung, rang) before we (ran, run) into the building.
2. The first arrivals (had been waiting, were waiting) for almost two hours before the gates opened.
3. We (stayed, staid) there until the storm (blew, blowed) over.
4. Mary has (wrote, written) two articles for the paper, and Charles has (drawn, drawed) the illustration for the cover.
5. Mother had (awaked, awakened) early and had (begun, began) to cook breakfast when we finally (awoke, awaked).

B. Write a synopsis of the verb *explain* in the third person singular, feminine gender. Include also the emphatic and progressive forms.

C. Write the numbers 1 to 10 and the verb forms as indicated:

1. *lend*—future tense, first person, singular
2. *catch*—present tense, third person, singular, feminine, progressive form
3. *go*—past perfect tense, second person, plural
4. *leave*—past tense, first person, plural, emphatic form
5. *begin*—future perfect tense, first person, singular
6. *play*—present perfect tense, third person, plural, progressive form
7. *walk*—past perfect tense, second person, singular
8. *interrupt*—present tense, first person, plural, emphatic form, negative
9. *like*—future tense, third person, singular, masculine
10. *set*—present perfect tense, first person, plural, progressive form

CORRECT USE OF AUXILIARY VERBS

There is a tendency, in current informal usage, to use the auxiliaries *shall* and *will,* as well as *should* and *would,* in all persons. Careful speakers and writers, however, make distinctions in the use of these auxiliaries. Such distinctions should always be made in formal writing.

Use *shall* in the first person and *will* in the second and third persons to express a simple future (expectation). *Should* is usually used like *shall,* and *would,* like *will.*   [27a]

We *shall* be home by six o'clock.
You *will* be able to see quite well from these seats.

I *should* prefer to complete the work by myself.

If he has the time, I am sure that Bob *would* be happy to help you.

To express strong feeling, command, determination, or promise on the part of the speaker, use *will* in the first person and *shall* in the second and third persons.

I promise that I *will* finish what I set out to do, even if it takes all afternoon. (Promise)

Ron is determined that he *shall* save a great part of his earnings. (Determination)

Use *should* in all persons to express obligation, duty, or a condition.
                       [27b]

You *should* really try to co-operate a little better. (Obligation)

If you *should* find my gloves, please call me. (Condition)

Use *would* in all persons to express habitual action.   **[27c]**

The old judge *would* always retire early every night.

We *would* always sit around the fire for a while.

DEVELOPING YOUR SKILL

On your paper write the numbers from 1 to 5. After each number write the word from the parentheses that makes the sentence correct.

1. If he (shall, should) go, I (would, should) like to go also.
2. I promise you that I (will, shall) have the props ready on time.
3. Jan says that she (shall, will) be eighteen next October.
4. Roger and I (shall, will) bring the sandwiches.
5. He promised that he (should, would) hurry.

INFINITIVES AND PARTICIPLES

Use the *present infinitive* except when you wish the infinitive to express time before the time of the main verb.   **[27d]**

He wants *to go* to State University next year. (Present)

I should have liked *to explain* the matter myself. (Present)

The President had been invited *to throw* the first ball. (Present)

That man is said *to have invented* a silent air conditioner. (Perfect)

Use the *present participle* to express action taking place at the same time as the action expressed by the main verb.   **[27e]**

The man *throwing* the ball is the manager.

While *searching* for the luggage, I lost my ring.

Use the *perfect participle* to express action that began before the action expressed by the main verb.   **[27f]**

Having spent my allowance, I tried to find a way to earn some money.

 DEVELOPING YOUR SKILL

Write the following sentences, completing them with the correct word or words from those in parentheses. Then write the tense of the participles or the infinitives you have used to complete the sentences.

1. I should have liked (to have studied, to study) in the library.
2. (Having finished, Finishing) their work, they started for home.
3. Mary is said (to have won, to win) a golf trophy.
4. Ben wanted (to study, to have studied) engineering.
5. In (having talked, talking) with the caller, they forgot the time.

KINDS OF VERBS

Verbs may be classified as *transitive* or *intransitive*. It should be remembered, however, that many verbs may be transitive in one sentence and intransitive in another, depending upon their use in the sentences in which they occur.

A transitive verb is a verb that passes an action to a noun or a pronoun.

[28]

A transitive verb must always be a verb of action. Usually transitive verbs are followed by direct objects.

The fireman *saved* the child.

The transitive verb *saved* passes its action to the noun *child,* the direct object of the verb.

Sometimes, however, transitive verbs pass their action to the subject of the sentence, rather than to a direct object.

The child *was saved* by the fireman.

In the sentence above, the noun *child,* which is the subject of the sentence, receives the action of the verb *was saved.* The voice of a verb tells you whether the subject of a sentence receives the action of the verb or performs the action.

Voice indicates whether the subject of a sentence completes the action or receives the action of a verb. Only transitive verbs have voice. [29]

There are only two voices—*active* and *passive.*

A verb is in the active voice if a direct object is the receiver of its action. [29a]

A verb is in the passive voice if its subject is the receiver of its action. [29b]

The class *chose* the trophy. (Active voice)
The trophy *was chosen* by the class. (Passive voice)

The synopsis of the verb *save* in the first person singular, active and passive voices, is shown below. Notice that the passive voice of a verb is formed by adding forms of the verb *be* to the past participle of a verb. The tense is shown in the form of the auxiliary *be.*

	ACTIVE VOICE	PASSIVE VOICE
Present	I save	I *am* saved
Past	I saved	I *was* saved
Future	I shall save	I *shall be* saved
Present Perfect	I have saved	I *have been* saved
Past Perfect	I had saved	I *had been* saved
Future Perfect	I shall have saved	I *shall have been* saved

In many sentences, verbs in the active voice lend greater force to a sentence than verbs in the passive voice. Notice that "The class chose the trophy" seems more forceful than "The trophy was chosen by the class."

There are occasions, however, when it is preferable to use a verb in the passive voice. When you wish to emphasize the receiver of the action rather than the doer, use the passive voice. Also, if the doer is unknown, unnamed, or obvious, use the passive voice.

Mr. Smith *was presented* with a citation.

He *is considered* the leading authority on that type of rocket.

This kind of transport plane *is* no longer *used*.

 DEVELOPING YOUR SKILL

A. Write the following sentences, underlining the verb in each and drawing an arrow from the verb to the noun or pronoun that receives the action of the verb. After each sentence write whether the verb is in the active or the passive voice.

1. The reporters asked many troublesome questions.
2. One of those lots was bought by our neighbor.
3. The evidence had been destroyed by the only witness.
4. Letters were sent by the contest judges to all the winners.
5. A transcript of your credits will be sent by the registrar.

B. Rewrite the sentences in Exercise A, changing the voice of the verb in each sentence from active to passive or from passive to active.

C. Write five sentences in which the passive is the preferable voice—sentences in which you wish to emphasize the receiver of the action or sentences in which the doer of the action is not known.

MOOD

The mood of a verb shows the mood or manner in which the speaker thinks of the action.   [29c]

The three moods in English are the *indicative,* the *imperative,* and the *subjunctive.*

A verb in the indicative mood states a fact or asks a question.   [29d]

Newton *discovered* the law of gravity.

Did Fulton *invent* the steamboat?

A verb in the imperative mood expresses a command or makes a request.   [29e]

Bring your color photographs along, if you will.

Help me with this package, please.

A verb in the subjunctive mood expresses a condition contrary to fact or a wish.   [29f]

If Don *were* here, I could go. (The statement expresses a condition that is contrary to fact: Don is *not* here.)

I wish that I *were* not so busy. (This is the subjunctive mood after a wish.)

It should be remembered that not all clauses beginning with *if* require the subjunctive mood. In some sentences there is no condition that is contrary to fact.

If Mr. Smith was dissatisfied with the job that was done, he would have spoken to you about it. (The speaker is willing to accept the fact that Mr. Smith was *not* dissatisfied.)

The forms of the indicative mood and the subjunctive mood are similar except for the third person singular, which does not add *s* in the subjunctive mood (see the complete conjugation on pages 304 to 307) and for the present and past tenses of the verb *be,* which are given below in both the indicative and the subjunctive moods.

Note that *be* is used with all persons in the present subjunctive of the verb *be* and that *were* is used with all persons of the past subjunctive.

PRESENT INDICATIVE		PRESENT SUBJUNCTIVE	
I am	we are	(if) I be	(if) we be
you are	you are	(if) you be	(if) you be
he is	they are	(if) he, she, it be	(if) they be

PAST INDICATIVE		PAST SUBJUNCTIVE	
I was	we were	(if) I were	(if) we were
you were	you were	(if) you were	(if) you were
he was	they were	(if) he, she, it were	(if) they were

Use the subjunctive in clauses beginning with *that* and expressing necessity, mild command, or a parliamentary motion. [29g]

It is necessary that he *be* here when we sign the papers.

I move that the discussion *be limited* to five minutes.

Use the subjunctive *were* after *as though* or *as if* to express doubt or uncertainty. [29h]

She acted as though she *were* hurt.

He talks as if he *were* the only one who had been left out.

Following is a complete conjugation of the verb *hear.* You will note that not all tenses have emphatic and progressive forms, and that the subjunctive mood has no future or future perfect tenses.

Conjugation of the Verb *To Hear*

Principal Parts: hear   heard   heard

INDICATIVE MOOD, ACTIVE VOICE

PERSON	SINGULAR	PLURAL

PRESENT TENSE

PERSON	SINGULAR	PLURAL
First	I hear, am hearing, do hear	we hear, are hearing, do hear
Second	you hear, are hearing, do hear	you hear, are hearing, do hear
Third	he, she, it hears, is hearing, does hear	they hear, are hearing, do hear

PAST TENSE

PERSON	SINGULAR	PLURAL
First	I heard, was hearing, did hear	we heard, were hearing, did hear
Second	you heard, were hearing, did hear	you heard, were hearing, did hear
Third	he, she, it heard, was hearing, did hear	they heard, were hearing, did hear

FUTURE TENSE

PERSON	SINGULAR	PLURAL
First	I shall hear, shall be hearing	we shall hear, shall be hearing
Second	you will hear, will be hearing	you will hear, will be hearing
Third	he, she, it will hear, will be hearing	they will hear, will be hearing

PRESENT PERFECT TENSE

PERSON	SINGULAR	PLURAL
First	I have heard, have been hearing	we have heard, have been hearing
Second	you have heard, have been hearing	you have heard, have been hearing
Third	he, she, it has heard, has been hearing	they have heard, have been hearing

PAST PERFECT TENSE

First   I had heard, had been hearing — we had heard, had been hearing

Second   you had heard, had been hearing — you had heard, had been hearing

Third   he, she, it had heard, had been hearing — they had heard, had been hearing

FUTURE PERFECT TENSE

First   I shall have heard, shall have been hearing — we shall have heard, shall have been hearing

Second   you will have heard, will have been hearing — you will have heard, will have been hearing

Third   he, she, it will have heard, will have been hearing — they will have heard, will have been hearing

INDICATIVE MOOD, PASSIVE VOICE

PRESENT TENSE

First   I am heard, am being heard — we are heard, are being heard

Second   you are heard, are being heard — you are heard, are being heard

Third   he, she, it is heard, is being heard — they are heard, are being heard

PAST TENSE

First   I was heard, was being heard — we were heard, were being heard

Second   you were heard, were being heard — you were heard, were being heard

Third   he, she, it was heard, was being heard — they were heard, were being heard

FUTURE TENSE

First   I shall be heard, shall be being heard — we shall be heard, shall be being heard

Second   you will be heard, will be being heard — you will be heard, will be being heard

Third   he, she, it will be heard, will be being heard — they will be heard, will be being heard

PRESENT PERFECT TENSE

First	I have been heard	we have been heard
Second	you have been heard	you have been heard
Third	he, she, it has been heard	they have been heard

PAST PERFECT TENSE

First	I had been heard	we had been heard
Second	you had been heard	you had been heard
Third	he, she, it had been heard	they had been heard

FUTURE PERFECT TENSE

First	I shall have been heard	we shall have been heard
Second	you will have been heard	you will have been heard
Third	he, she, it will have been heard	they will have been heard

IMPERATIVE MOOD

Active Voice	Passive Voice
(you) hear	(you) be heard

SUBJUNCTIVE MOOD, ACTIVE VOICE

PERSON	SINGULAR	PLURAL

PRESENT TENSE

First	(if) I hear	(if) we hear
Second	(if) you hear	(if) you hear
Third	(if) he, she, it hear	(if) they hear

PAST TENSE

First	(if) I heard	(if) we heard
Second	(if) you heard	(if) you heard
Third	(if) he, she, it heard	(if) they heard

PRESENT PERFECT TENSE

First	(if) I have heard	(if) we have heard
Second	(if) you have heard	(if) you have heard
Third	(if) he, she, it have heard	(if) they have heard

PAST PERFECT TENSE

First	(if) I had heard	(if) we had heard
Second	(if) you had heard	(if) you had heard
Third	(if) he, she, it had heard	(if) they had heard

SUBJUNCTIVE MOOD, PASSIVE VOICE

PRESENT TENSE

First	(if) I be heard	(if) we be heard
Second	(if) you be heard	(if) you be heard
Third	(if) he, she, it be heard	(if) they be heard

PAST TENSE

First	(if) I were heard	(if) we were heard
Second	(if) you were heard	(if) you were heard
Third	(if) he, she, it were heard	(if) they were heard

PRESENT PERFECT TENSE

First	(if) I have been heard	(if) we have been heard
Second	(if) you have been heard	(if) you have been heard
Third	(if) he, she, it have been heard	(if) they have been heard

PAST PERFECT TENSE

First	(if) I had been heard	(if) we had been heard
Second	(if) you had been heard	(if) you had been heard
Third	(if) he, she, it had been heard	(if) they had been heard

DEVELOPING YOUR SKILL

Write the following sentences, completing them with the correct verb form of those in parentheses. Then after each sentence write the mood of the verb you used to complete the sentence.

1. I move that the meeting (is, be) held tomorrow.
2. If Mary (was, were) too busy to help, she would have said so.
3. I wish that the box (was, were) not so heavy.
4. It is desirable that you (are, be) there early.
5. If I (was, were) you, I shouldn't say that.

INTRANSITIVE VERBS

An intransitive verb is a verb that does not pass an action to a noun or a pronoun.   [30]

There are two kinds of intransitive verbs: *complete intransitive* and *linking intransitive.*

A complete intransitive verb is an action verb that is complete in itself. It does not pass an action to a noun or a pronoun.   [30a]

The sun *sank* slowly into the sea.
The storm clouds *gathered* quickly and ominously.

A linking intransitive verb is a verb that links, or joins, a predicate noun, a predicate pronoun, or a predicate adjective to the subject of the sentence.   [30b]

Mrs. Harris *is* an authority on Early American furniture. (Notice that the verb *is* links the predicate noun *authority* to the subject *Mrs. Harris.)*

That *is* she in the dark costume. (Notice that the verb *is* links the predicate pronoun *she* to the subject *that.)*

The apples *tasted* sour. (The verb *tasted* links the adjective *sour* to the subject *apples.)*

Some of the more common verbs that are used as linking verbs are the following: *appear, become, feel, grow, look, remain, smell,* and *taste,* as well as the many forms of the verb *be.*

It is sometimes difficult to distinguish a form of *be* that is used as a linking verb from a form of *be* that is used as an auxiliary verb with the main verb.

Our dog *has been* sleepy all day. *(Has been* is a linking verb that links the adjective *sleepy* to the subject *dog.)*

He *has been sleeping* all day. *(Has been sleeping* is a complete intransitive verb. *Has* and *been* are auxiliaries used with *sleeping* to form the present perfect progressive form.)

DEVELOPING YOUR SKILL

A. Write the numbers 1 to 10 and after each number write the verbs in that sentence. Indicate whether each is complete intransitive or linking intransitive. If it is a linking intransitive verb, write the predicate noun, pronoun, or adjective linked by the verb to the subject.

1. No mail has come for you today.
2. Several current plays are opening this week.

3. An innovation in the celebration will be the parade.
4. These are the books.
5. That may be Jill in the first car.
6. The boys worked late last night on their radio set.
7. Were the girls late for school?
8. Ted won, but with great difficulty.
9. The old fisherman sat quietly by the river, deep in thought.
10. Father has been looking for a good place to stop for dinner.

   B. Write five sentences in which you use complete intransitive verbs and five in which you use linking intransitive verbs.

USING VERBS CORRECTLY [31]

Mistakes in the use of verbs are very common. Confusion often arises in the use of verbs that are similar in spelling, in meaning, or in both spelling and meaning.

Learn the meanings and the principal parts of the verbs *lie* and *lay* and *sit* and *set* to use the verbs correctly. [31a]

Lay (to put into place) and *set* (to put into place) are transitive verbs. The action of a transitive verb may be passed to a direct object; or the verb may be in the passive voice, with the subject receiving the action of the verb.

Study the table below and the illustrative sentences that follow.

PRESENT	PAST	PAST PARTICIPLE	PRESENT PARTICIPLE
lay	laid	laid	laying
set	set	set	setting

Lay the papers here.
He *laid* his glasses there.
He *has laid* the book on the shelf.
She *was laying* the book on the table.

Set the bench on the porch.
She *set* the vase on the table.
They *have set* the chairs in the kitchen.
He *was setting* the boxes in a corner.

There are some meanings of the verb *set* in which there may be no direct object.

The gelatin must have time to *set*.
The sun *sets* at five o'clock today.

The verbs *lie* (to recline) and *sit* (to rest) are complete intransitive verbs. Intransitive verbs do not have objects, nor are they used in the passive voice.

PRESENT	PAST	PAST PARTICIPLE	PRESENT PARTICIPLE
lie	lay	lain	lying
sit	sat	sat	sitting

Mother *is lying* down, and I think that I *shall lie* down for a while too.

She never *has lain* down in the afternoon before.

Do you *lie* down often during the daytime?

I *had* just *sat* down when the curtain went up.

He *has been sitting* in the same place for a long time.

She *sat* down gracefully and quickly.

He always *sits* in the last row.

Rise is a complete intransitive verb. It never has a direct object. Raise is a transitive verb and may have a direct object or may be in the passive voice.   **[31b]**

PRESENT	PAST	PAST PARTICIPLE	PRESENT PARTICIPLE
rise (to go up)	rose	risen	rising
raise (to cause something to go up)	raised	raised	raising

He always *rises* at seven o'clock each morning.

A gentleman *rises* when he is introduced to a woman.

Will you please *raise* the window shades?

The flag *is raised* each morning at sunrise.

Frequently errors are made in the use of auxiliary verbs.

Avoid using *better* for *had better* as a synonym for *ought to*. [31c]

I *had better* (not *better*) finish this chapter before lunch.

Do not use an auxiliary with *ought*. [31d]

You *ought* (not *had ought*) to get to school on time every day.

Do not use the preposition *of* for the verb *have* after *could, should, would, may, might,* or *must.*

Do not use *would have* in an *if* clause. [31e]

If I *had* (not *would have*) seen you, I would have stopped.

Learn to use *borrow* and *lend* correctly. *Borrow* implies receiving; *lend* implies giving. [31f]

I can *lend* you a book, if you want to *borrow* one.

Learn to distinguish between *bring* and *take*. *Bring* implies motion toward the speaker or listener; *take* implies motion away from the speaker. [31g]

Please *bring* me some cream. (Motion toward the speaker)
I can *bring* you some flowers tomorrow. (Motion toward the listener)
Please *take* these plates away. (Motion away from the speaker)

Do not confuse the meanings of *learn* and *teach*. *Learn* means "to receive knowledge"; *teach* means "to impart knowledge." [31h]

If you will *teach* me, I would like to *learn* to skate.

Learn to use *let* and *leave* accurately. *Let* means "to allow" or "to permit"; *leave* means "to go away" or "to allow to remain." [31i]

Please *let* me pay for this.
I shall *leave* at four o'clock.
You may *leave* your boots on the mat.

Learn the correct use of *may* and *can*. *May* implies permission; *can* implies physical or mental ability. [31j]

You *may* help me lift this sofa if you wish. (Permission)
He *can* write legibly if he tries. (Ability)

A possibility or a wish are also expressed by the word *may.*

We *may* get there early. (Possibility)
May you always keep those good intentions! (Wish)

Might is the past form of *may*. Use *might* after a verb in the past tense; use *may* after a verb in the present tense.

He said that he *might* be able to repair the faucet easily.
She says that she *may* make some cookies.

Do not use a verb when you should use a noun.   [31k]

We gave her an *invitation* (not an *invite)* to the party.

Do not omit the *ed* from the past tense of such verbs as *ask*.   [31l]

Has he *asked* (not *ask)* them to help serve?

Avoid usages that are not acceptable English.   [31m]

The following usages should be avoided:

Say, listen, look as introductory words
Take (or took) *sick* for *become* (or became) *ill*
Says for *said*
Allow, calculate, expect, guess, and *reckon* for *think, suppose, be-lieve,* and *assume*
Ain't and *aren't I*

I have an idea (not *Listen,* I have an idea).
He became ill (not *took sick).*
He said, (not *says)* "That is too high a price."
I think (not *calculate)* the monthly bill is about six dollars.
I suppose (not *expect)* that you think me unwise.
I am late, am I not (not *aren't I)?*
We aren't (not *ain't)* late.

DEVELOPING YOUR SKILL

Write the numbers 1 to 10, and after each number write the word or words needed to complete the sentence correctly

1. I think you (ought, had ought) to (lie, lay) down and rest.
2. You have been (lying, laying) in the hot sun too long.

3. You (had better, better) (learn, teach) the children to (sit, set) very still during the performance.
4. (Might, May) I (sit, set) this down here?
5. Will you please (take, bring) these with you when you leave?
6. He said that he (might, may) be able to (lend, borrow) you some money.
7. He (says, said), "(Let, Leave) them solve their own problems."
8. Yes, you (can, may) bring me some milk.
9. You (ought, had ought) to (raise, rise) the flag at sunrise.
10. I (should have, should of) gone if I (should have, had) known.

Review Exercises—Verbs and Their Use

A. Write the numbers 1 to 5 on a sheet of paper and list every verb in the following sentences. After each verb tell its tense and voice. Also tell whether each verb is transitive, complete intransitive, or linking intransitive.

1. We had already finished our breakfast when the sun came up.
2. They will have won ten straight games if they win this one.
3. John and Mary have bought new bicycles, and I shall buy one next week.
4. That man is the coach of the team.
5. Mr. Brown has always been happy to help people.

B. Write the person, number, tense, voice, and mood of all transitive verbs in Exercise A.
C. Write the numbers 1 to 10 and select the word or words from the parentheses and write them after the appropriate numbers.

1. Carelessly, I had (lain, laid) my glasses on the coffee table.
2. He (would have, would of) helped you if you (had, should have) asked him.
3. (May, Can) we (sit, set) here for a few minutes?
4. You may (borrow, lend) my book to Anne; but she (had ought, ought) to remember to (take, bring) her own when she comes to class.
5. Were you (lying, laying) down when I called to you to (bring, take) those books to me?
6. I (better, had better) (take, bring) my books back to the library.
7. I (guess, think) that perhaps as many as twenty people can (set, sit) down at that table.
8. Would you (learn, teach) me how to ski?

9. Dick (says, said), "I (should of, should have) studied longer."
10. We had (set, sat) there for a few minutes when the dog came and (laid, lay) down at our feet.

D. Write a synopsis of the verb *lie,* meaning *to recline,* in the third person singular, masculine gender, active voice, indicative mood. Include the emphatic and progressive forms.

2. Nouns and Pronouns

Nouns and pronouns have qualities called *person, number, gender,* and *case.* Pronouns, especially, should be given careful study, since they have many different forms to indicate these qualities.

PERSON, NUMBER, AND GENDER

Person is the quality of a noun or a pronoun that indicates the speaker (first person), the person spoken to (second person), or the person or thing spoken about (third person).   [32]

Nouns do not change their form to show person and, except for nouns in direct address, are always third person. Pronouns, however, do change form to show person.

Number is the form of a noun or a pronoun that indicates whether it refers to one person, place, or thing (singular) or to more than one person, place, or thing (plural).   [33]

Gender is the quality of a noun or a pronoun that indicates whether the noun or pronoun is *masculine, feminine, neuter,* or *common.*   [34]

Study the following table, which gives the person, number, and gender of the most commonly used pronouns.

	SINGULAR	PLURAL
First Person	I, me, my, mine	we, us, our, ours
Second Person	you, your, yours	you, your, yours
Third Person		
masculine	he, him, his	they, them, their, theirs
feminine	she, her, hers	they, them, their, theirs
neuter	it, its	they, them, their, theirs

Nouns and pronouns of common gender are those that may be either masculine or feminine, as *they, them, their, theirs, friend, enemy,* and *cousin.*

DEVELOPING YOUR SKILL

List the following nouns and pronouns on a sheet of paper, and after each one write its person, number, and gender.

1. actor	6. book
2. she	7. king
3. their	8. actress
4. her	9. mine
5. his	10. theirs

CASE OF NOUNS AND PRONOUNS

The case of a noun or a pronoun is determined by its use in a sentence. The three cases are the *nominative,* the *possessive,* and the *objective.*

Nominative case [35]

Nouns in the nominative case will cause you no difficulty, since there is no distinctive form for the nominative case of nouns. The personal pronouns that you may use as substitutes for nouns do have various forms in the nominative case, according to the person and number of the nouns they stand for.

Following is a list of the personal pronouns in the nominative case.

	SINGULAR	PLURAL
First Person	I	we
Second Person	you	you
Third Person	he, she, it	they

A noun or a pronoun that is the subject of a verb is in the nominative case. [35a]

That *house* has an imposing entrance.
Mary and *she* are going in our car.
You and *I* should leave promptly at one o'clock.
We students pay half fare on the bus.

Note that *we* is the subject. The noun *students* is in apposition with the subject.

A predicate noun or a predicate pronoun is in the nominative case.

[35b]

Predicate nouns or pronouns are sometimes called *predicate nomina-tives* because they appear in the complete predicate of a sentence and are in the nominative case. A predicate noun or a predicate pronoun follows a linking verb and names the same person or thing named by the subject.

Mrs. Adams is the *woman* in the navy blue dress.

It is *she* whom I wish to talk with.

In informal speech frequently you hear "It's me" or "It's him." Such usage is becoming so widespread that it is accepted in informal or col-loquial speech; but the substitution of the objective case *(me, him, her, us,* and *them)* for the nominative case should never be made in written work or in formal speech.

A noun or a pronoun is in the nominative case if it is in apposition with a noun or a pronoun in the nominative case.   [35c]

The brothers, *he* and *David,* are pilots. *(He* and *David* are in appo-sition with the subject *brothers.)*

That is our club president, *Ricky. (Ricky* is in apposition with the predicate noun *president.)*

Notice that commas are used to set off the appositives in each of the preceding sentences. No commas are necessary, however, when the ap-positive and the noun it refers to are closely connected.

We *girls* are going in Jim's car.

A noun of direct address is in the nominative case.   [35d]

Look out for the ladder, *boys!*

A noun or a pronoun used in an absolute expression is in the nominative case. [35e]

The *boys* having finished their projects, they were eager to get started on new ones.

DEVELOPING YOUR SKILL

A. Write the following sentences, completing them with the correct word from those in parentheses. Choose the form that is correct in written work or in formal speech.
1. (We, Us) seniors are giving the banquet.
2. Gordon and (him, he) are good students.
3. (He, Him) and (me, I) are working on the same problem.
4. Are (we, us) girls supposed to go, too?
5. Is that (them, they) in the blue car?
6. That is (he, him) standing near the doorway.
7. The prop men, David and (me, I), must be there early.
8. The directors of the play are (her, she) and Carol.
9. Jill and (me, I) are the alternates.
10. (We, Us) boys have learned our parts.

B. Number from 1 to 5 and list the nouns and pronouns in the nominative case in each of the following sentences. Then label each as subject, predicate nominative, appositive, direct address, or nominative absolute.
1. Linda and I have decided to take typing.
2. Mr. Martin is the first pilot to have completed such a trip.
3. The organist is Mr. Wright, a member of the faculty.
4. Kim, why do you prefer that lighting effect?
5. The girls having finished their rehearsal, they decided to make some candy.

Objective case [36]

Although nouns do not make any change in form to indicate the objective case, there are certain changes in personal pronouns to show the objective case. Study the following table, which shows the changes in all three persons of personal pronouns in the objective case.

PERSONAL PRONOUNS IN THE OBJECTIVE CASE

	SINGULAR	PLURAL
First Person	me	us
Second Person	you	you
Third Person	him, her, it	them

A noun or a pronoun that is a direct object is in the objective case [36a]

The members of the team chose a *captain.*
Mary's cousin visited *her* for a week.
Mr. White chose *Tim* and *me* as group leaders.

A noun or a pronoun that is the indirect object of a verb is in the objective case.   [36b]

Grandmother showed *us* the ring.
Father gave *Linda* and *me* detailed directions.

A noun or a pronoun that is the object of a preposition is in the objective case.   [36c]

Many of *us* have already taken the competitive examinations.

A noun or a pronoun is in the objective case if it is in apposition with another noun or pronoun in the objective case.   [36d]

I saw *John* and *Bill,* our *neighbors,* at the market. *(Neighbors* is in apposition with *John* and *Bill,* which are the direct objects of *saw.* Since *John* and *Bill* are in the objective case, the appositive *neighbors* is also in the objective case.)

They asked us—*Don* and *me*—to the party. (The noun *Don* and the pronoun *me* are in apposition with *us,* which is the direct object of the verb *asked.)*

A noun or a pronoun that is the subject of an infinitive is in the objective case.   [36e]

I expect *them* to come early. (The pronoun *them* is in the objective case because it is the subject of the infinitive *to come.* The entire infinitive phrase *them to come early* is the direct object of the verb *expect.)*

A noun or a pronoun that is the object of a gerund, a participle, or an infinitive is in the objective case.   [36f]

Finding *them* at home was unusual. *(Them* is the object of the gerund *finding.)*

Having greeted *them,* I hurried on. *(Them* is the object of the participle *having greeted.)*

I would like to see *them* again. *(Them* is the object of the infinitive *to see.)*

A noun used as an objective complement is in the objective case. [36g]

We elected her our *president*.

A noun used as a retained object is in the objective case. [36h]

The winner was given a blue *ribbon*.

A noun or a pronoun used as the complement of the infinitive *to be* is in the objective case when the subject of the infinitive is expressed. [36i]

They took him to be *me*. (If you remember that the infinitive *to be* is linking, and that it is always followed by the same case that precedes it, you will have little difficulty with this construction. The pronoun *him* is the subject of the infinitive *to be,* and is therefore in the objective case. The pronoun *me* follows the infinitive *to be* and is an objective complement, also in the objective case.)

If the subject is not expressed, as in the sentences below, the pronoun after the infinitive *to be* is in the nominative case.

I was made up to be *Lincoln (he)*. (As you see, there is no subject of the infinitive *to be;* therefore, the noun *Lincoln* and the pronoun *he* are both in the nominative case.)

I might wish that I were *she*. (Notice that the pronoun *she* is in the nominative case, since the form of the verb is *were,* and not the infinitive form.)

Notice that the pronoun complement *me* in the diagram of the following sentence is separated from the infinitive *to be* by a slanting line.

They took him to be *me*.

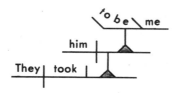

DEVELOPING YOUR SKILL

Write the numbers 1 to 10 on your paper and list the nouns and pronouns in the following sentences that are in the objective case. After each, tell why it is in the objective case.

1. Please close all the windows.
2. Mrs. Hayes showed us the costumes.
3. I have never known her to be unpleasant.
4. Many of us had never seen a rocket.
5. I called the girls, Jane and her, after supper.
6. We rather expected you to win.
7. They selected you to be him in the play.
8. We chose Dan leader of the group.
9. We thought them to be superior in every way.
10. Hearing him was not easy, since we sat in the last row.

Possessive case   [37]

Both nouns and pronouns make changes in form to indicate possession. Pronouns that are in the possessive case, such as the possessive pronoun *my,* also serve the function of an adjective in a sentence. For that reason, possessive pronouns are also called *possessive adjectives* and *pronominal adjectives.* In the table below are the possessive case forms of the personal pronouns that may be used as adjectives.

	SINGULAR	PLURAL
First Person	my	our
Second Person	your	your
Third Person	his, her, its	their

That is *his* hat.

Nouns show possession by the use of an apostrophe and *s* (*'s*) or just an apostrophe (*'*). The following rules will help you learn how to form the possessive case of nouns.

Form the possessive of a singular noun by adding an apostrophe and an s ('s) to the singular form. [37a]

SINGULAR	SINGULAR POSSESSIVE
teacher	teacher*'s*
author	author*'s*
Mr. Lynes	Mr. Lynes*'s*
lady	lady*'s*

Form the possessive of plural nouns ending in s by adding only an apostrophe. [37b]

PLURAL	PLURAL POSSESSIVE
teachers	teachers'
authors	authors'
the Lyneses	the Lyneses'
ladies	ladies'

Form the possessive of plural nouns not ending in s by adding an apostrophe and an s ('s). [37c]

PLURAL	PLURAL POSSESSIVE
children	children*'s*

To indicate separate ownership, make all words show possession. [37d]

Don*'s*, Bob*'s*, and Dave*'s* fathers are all here tonight.

To indicate joint ownership, make only the last word show possession. [37e]

Loveman and Berger*'s* store is closed today.

Form the possessive of a compound noun by adding an apostrophe and an s ('s) to the last word in the compound. [37f]

SINGULAR	SINGULAR POSSESSIVE	PLURAL	PLURAL POSSESSIVE
son-in-law	son-in-law*'s*	sons-in-law	sons-in-law*'s*

In using the possessive case of nouns and pronouns, you need to pay special attention to several points.

Use the possessive case of a noun or a pronoun before a gerund. [37g]

Did you hear about Barbara*'s* playing the lead in the play?
I can't understand *his* not knowing what to do.

Do not confuse the possessive pronoun *its* with the contraction *it's* (it is).
[37h]

The committee made *its* report quickly.

It's (it is) difficult to tell the twins apart.

A noun in the possessive case may be used as a limiting adjective. [37i]

Miss Smith*'s* cousin bought some property near my uncle*'s* cabin.

Use a phrase with *of* in place of an apostrophe when you wish to show possession by inanimate objects, except for the following: (1) expressions of time and measurement; and (2) an organization that is thought of as being made up of people.
[37j]

the roof *of the house*

two years' absence

the police department*'s* annual benefit

DEVELOPING YOUR SKILL

Rewrite the following sentences, completing them with the correct word or words from those in parentheses.

1. (Paul's, Pauls') and (Charles's, Charles') grades are high.
2. The (ladies', ladie's) blouses are on the main floor.
3. (Men's, Mens') and (children's, childrens') shoes are on the second floor.
4. (The top of the desk, The desk's top) is made of hand-tooled leather.
5. These are the (teacher's, teachers') desks.
6. (Mary and Jane's, Mary's and Jane's) father made a model submarine.
7. His (father-in-law's, father-in-laws') house is opposite ours.
8. (His, Him) knowing about the change in schedule was helpful to us.
9. The store asked (its, it's) customers to use the parking lot.
10. Did you hear about (Ann's, Ann) taking first place in the contest?

KINDS OF PRONOUNS [38]

According to their form and function, pronouns may be classified as *personal, relative, interrogative, demonstrative, intensive, reflexive, indefinite,* and *reciprocal.*

A personal pronoun is a direct substitute for a noun. The form of a personal pronoun usually indicates its person, number, gender, and case.
[38a]

The following table shows all the forms of the personal pronouns:

PERSON	NOMINATIVE	POSSESSIVE	OBJECTIVE
		SINGULAR	
First	I	my, mine	me
Second	you	you, yours	you
Third	he, she, it	his, her, hers, its	him, her, it
		PLURAL	
First	we	our, ours	us
Second	you	your, yours	you
Third	they	their, theirs	them

A relative pronoun is a pronoun that introduces a dependent clause.
[38b]

The function of a relative pronoun is to connect or relate a dependent clause to the antecedent of the pronoun. The most common relative pronouns are *who, which,* and *that. Who* refers to persons only; *which* refers to inanimate objects and animals, and to persons considered as a group; *that* may refer either to persons or to things.

I know the boy *who* is driving the car.
That book, *which* is the last in the series, tells about the Orient.
The person *that* I spoke with is the head of the department.
The house *that* he bought is near the lake.

Others sometimes used include *whoever, whichever,* and *whatever.*

You may choose *whatever* you wish as a gift.

An interrogative pronoun is a pronoun that introduces a question. [38c]

Who, which, and *what* are the most common interrogative pronouns. Others sometimes used include *whoever, whichever,* and *whatever.*

Who gave you those flowers?
Which is your favorite book?
What is the meaning of that word?
Whoever would volunteer for such a task?

A demonstrative pronoun is a pronoun that points out and identifies.
[38d]

This, that, these, and *those* are *demonstrative pronouns.* They have number but no gender or case.

This is the kind of shoe I prefer. *(This* is singular number. It refers to *kind,* which is singular.)
This is my pencil. *(This* is singular number. It refers to *pencil,* which is singular.)
That is my scarf. *(That* is singular number. It refers to *scarf,* which is singular.)
Those are my papers. *(Those* is plural number. It refers to *papers,* which is plural.)
These are the kinds of flowers I like. *(These* is plural number. It refers to *kinds,* which is plural.)

This, that, these, and *those* also may be used as modifiers of nouns and pronouns. When they are so used, they are adjectives, or determiners, signaling noun structures.

This is my book. (Pronoun)
This book is mine. (Adjective)
This kind of apple is good. (Adjective)

Two kinds of pronouns that have the same form but different functions are the *intensive* and *reflexive* pronouns. They are formed by adding *self* or *selves* to the personal pronouns: *myself, yourself, himself, herself, itself, ourselves, yourselves, themselves.*

An intensive pronoun is a pronoun that is used for emphasis.   [38e]

You *yourself* must decide what to do.

A reflexive pronoun is a pronoun that is used to refer to the subject of a sentence.
[38f]

The clown saw *himself* in the mirror.

An indefinite pronoun is a pronoun that refers to a person, place, or thing generally rather than specifically. Indefinite pronouns are less exact in meaning than are the other pronouns. [38g]

Following is a list of the more commonly used indefinite pronouns:

all	both	few	one
another	each	many	several
any	either	neither	some
anybody	everybody	nobody	somebody
anyone	everyone	none	someone
anything	everything	nothing	something

Note that a word that is used as an indefinite pronoun also may be used as an adjective, as in the second sentence that follows.

Each of us has his own recollections of the trip. (Pronoun)
He selected *each* picture with great care. (Adjective)

A reciprocal pronoun is a pronoun that indicates persons, places, or things mutually affected by the action suggested by the verb. There are only two reciprocal pronouns in English: *each other* and *one another*.

[38h]

Tim and I have helped *each other* all year.
The three boys have helped *one another*.

In the preceding sentences, and in formal speech or writing, *each other* is used to refer to two persons, places, or things, and *one another* to more than two. In informal speech, however, the tendency is to use *each other* in all situations.

DEVELOPING YOUR SKILL

A. Write the following sentences, completing them with the correct word or words from those in parentheses.

1. (These, This) is the kind of paper that I like.
2. Dick and I helped (each other, one another) put on his skates.
3. He is the man (that, which) I saw yesterday.
4. He knows the person (who, which) appraises the worth of the paintings.
5. Mother gave some cake to Ted and (we, us).

B. List the pronouns in the following sentences and after each pronoun tell what kind it is, whether *personal, relative, interrogative, demonstrative, intensive, reflexive, indefinite,* or *reciprocal.*

1. Who helped you find the book that you need?
2. The book that I mentioned is concerned with the progress that is being made in some of the backward countries.
3. All the members of the cast have helped one another; and the play, which was a great success, is the result of their combined efforts.
4. The book itself is entertaining; but you must judge for yourself whether it is the kind of book that you are looking for.
5. What is your purpose in reading that?

USING PRONOUNS CORRECTLY   [39]

It is important to use pronouns carefully if you are to attain clarity and exactness of meaning in your writing and in your speech. The antecedents of pronouns should be clear, and the pronouns should agree with their antecedents.

Every pronoun should refer clearly to a definite antecedent.   [39a]

In the following sentence it is not clear whose car is being talked about.

John talked with Dad about *his* car.

This sentence can be made clear by repeating the name of the person whose car is referred to.

John talked with Dad about Dad's car.

The antecedent of a pronoun should always be definitely stated. [39b]

In the following sentence, it is not clear whether *they* refers to the classes or to the students.

Mr. Brown took away a favorable impression of our classes and our students, saying that *they* were interesting and stimulating. (Unclear)

The sentence could be reconstructed in several ways so that the antecedent of *they* is clear.

Mr. Brown took away a favorable impression of our classes and our students, saying that *the classes* were interesting and *the students* stimulating. (Clear)

Mr. Brown took away a favorable impression of our classes and our students, saying that both *the classes* and *the students* were interesting and stimulating. (Clear)

The case of a pronoun after *than* or *as* is determined by the use of the pronoun in the understood clause. [39c]

Betty plays better than *I*. (In this sentence the understood words are *can play*. The nominative case *I* is used, because *I* is the subject of the understood verb phrase *can play*.)

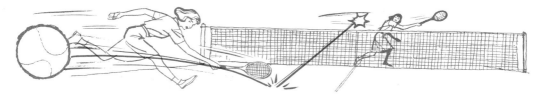

The notes you took helped them more than *me*. (The objective case *me* is used because *me* is the direct object of the understood clause *they helped*.)

Use *who* in the nominative case, *whose* in the possessive case, and *whom* in the objective case. [39d]

In the following sentences, notice the nominative case form *who* used as the subject of a verb and as a predicate nominative.

Who has been nominated? (Interrogative use of the pronoun *who;* subject of the verb phrase *has been nominated.*)

The man *who* was nominated is not here. *(Who* is used here as a relative pronoun, as the subject of the verb phrase *was nominated.)*

I don't know *who* the nominee was. (In this sentence the pronoun *who* is a predicate nominative after the verb *was,* since the natural order of the relative clause is *the nominee was who.)*

In the following sentences the possessive form *whose* is used as a relative pronoun and as an interrogative pronoun. In both uses, the word *whose* is used as a modifier.

Whose book do you have?
The woman *whose* book you have is my cousin.

The possessive form *whose* should not be confused with the contraction *who's (who is).*

Whose pen is that?
Who's writing with my pen?

328 *Grammar and Usage*

The objective case form *whom* may be used in each of the following ways: as the *direct object of a verb*, as an *indirect object*, as the *object of a preposition*, as the *subject of an infinitive*, or as the *complement of an infinitive*.

> The boy *whom* you see on the platform won first place. *(Whom is the direct object of see,* since the natural order of the relative clause is *you see whom.)*

> The woman *whom* you gave the message is my mother. *(Whom is the indirect object of the verb gave.)*

> Those are the people with *whom* I went to the concert. *(Whom is the object of the preposition with.)*

In informal usage the preposition in such a construction is placed at the end of the sentence. (Those are the people I went to the concert *with.)* In formal usage, however, the preposition should precede the objective case.

In colloquial or informal speech, too, the nominative case *who* is often used in place of the objective case *whom* when the pronoun precedes the preposition; but the substitution of the nominative for the objective form is not accepted formal usage.

> *Who* did you speak with? (Informal usage)
> With *whom* did you speak? (Formal usage)

The objective case form *whom* is used as the subject of the infinitive or as the object of the infinitive.

> *Whom* do you want to substitute for you? *(Whom is the subject of the infinitive to substitute.* The natural order of the sentence is *You do want whom to substitute for you.)*

> *Whom* do you wish to send as a substitute? *(Whom is the object of the infinitive to send.* The natural order of the sentence is *You do wish to send whom?)*

Sometimes parenthetical expressions such as *I think, I believe, I am sure,* or *do you think* are inserted between the relative pronoun and the rest of the clause. Such parenthetical expressions do not affect the case of the relative pronoun. Learn to recognize these expressions. If a sentence still makes sense when read without such expressions, they are parenthetical and should not affect the case of the relative pronoun.

Note the parenthetical expressions in parentheses in the following sentence:

Mr. White is a writer who (I think) will go far. (The pronoun *who* is the subject of the verb *will go*. The sentence makes sense without the words *I think;* therefore these words are parenthetical and do not affect the case of the relative pronoun *who.*)

Avoid using reflexive and intensive pronouns in place of personal pronouns.   [39e]

They asked to speak with Jane and *me.* (Not *with Jane and myself.*)

Avoid using the illiterate pronoun forms *hisself*, *theirself*, and *theirselves.*   [39f]

He wanted to go by himself. (Not *hisself)*

The order of personal pronouns in compounds is second person, third person, first person.   [39g]

You, Jill, and I can go together.

Avoid using *them* as a demonstrative pronoun.   [39h]

Those are my flowers. (Not *Them* are my flowers.)

Avoid using redundant pronouns.   [39i]

Redundant pronouns are pronouns that are not needed.

My brother stayed home. (Not My brother *he* stayed home.)
Let's get ready to go. (Not Let's *us* get ready to go.)

Avoid the indefinite use of *you, it,* and *they.*   [39j]

Say: This *play gives* a good picture of life in the nineties.
Do not say: In this play *it* gives a good picture of life in the nineties.
Say: That *school has* a fine library.
Do not say: *They* have a fine library in that school.

Use pronouns to keep the thought of a paragraph flowing smoothly from sentence to sentence.   [39k]

Notice how the pronoun *these* in the second illustrative sentence that follows helps to link the thought in the second sentence to that in the first. These two sentences are the first two of a paragraph.

There are many kinds of designs that may be used. Of *these*, only three have proved to be of any measurable value.

DEVELOPING YOUR SKILL

A. The following sentences contain unnecessary pronouns, errors in the form of pronoun used, and errors in pronoun-antecedent agreement. Some sentences contain more than one kind of error. Rewrite these sentences, correcting all errors.

1. Jim and Don talked about his flight to San Antonio.
2. Mary plays the piano better than me, and I play the accordion better than him.
3. In this book it gives a good description of the Rockies.
4. Father gave the keys to John and I; he told us hisself that he had confidence in our ability to drive safely.
5. Mary and Beth brought some samples of the fudge they had made, and she said that she would give Donna and I the recipe.
6. Mother brought each of we girls a bracelet, and she said that they made them by hand in Mexico.
7. Let's us hurry so that we can go with Barry and he.
8. The program interested Diane more than I.
9. My sister she likes those kind of shoes.
10. In that house they have a charcoal broiler in the kitchen.

B. Write the following sentences, completing them with the correct form of the pronoun in parentheses. Choose the form for formal usage or written work.

1. (Who, Whom) has been chosen as treasurer?
2. The man (whose, who's) book you are reading is a neighbor of ours.
3. (Who, Whom) do you want to take your place?
4. With (who, whom) did you speak?
5. The people to (whom, who) this message is broadcast are unhappy.
6. I don't know (who, whom) the leader is.
7. The candidates (who, whom) were elected are listed on this paper.
8. (Who, Whom) do you think will win the cup this year?

9. He is an athlete (who, whom) I think will be very successful.
10. (Whom, Who) did they elect?

Review Exercises—Nouns and Pronouns

A. Write the numbers 1 to 10 on a sheet of paper and list every italicized noun or pronoun in the following sentences. After each, give its number and case and the reason for the use of that case. When you list a pronoun, also tell what kind of pronoun it is.

1. *Gordon* and *I* have decided to take the *trip* with Carol's father.
2. John and *Anne's father* is *my mother's uncle.*
3. *We* saw *him,* but my brothers, *John* and *Tom,* visited *Mr. Carnes's brother.*
4. *I* cannot understand *his* calling so late; but *he* wanted to tell *me* about *Joan's* leaving early in the morning.
5. Everybody except *him* and *me* has paid *his dues.*
6. *They* believed the *clown* to be *me.*
7. *I* am supposed to be *George Washington* in the play, and *Don* was cast as an army *officer.*
8. *He himself* admitted that *he* talks to *himself.*
9. Robert, *whom* did *you* ask to collect the *money?*
10. *We* saw the twins, *David* and *Bill,* in *Charles's* car.

B. Write five sentences in which you use pronouns. Include *demonstrative, reciprocal, indefinite, relative,* and *interrogative* pronouns. Label the pronouns and draw an arrow from each pronoun to its antecedent.

C. Write the following sentences, completing them with the proper word or words from those in parentheses.

1. (In that book they tell, That book tells) about life in the Congo.
2. (Whose, Who's) cap is that lying (on the table's top, on top of the table)?
3. The council made (its, it's) recommendations.
4. (We, Us) teachers will help (Ron and you, you and Ron) decorate the room.
5. Would you lend John and (I, me) your ladder?
6. They gave free tickets to (we, us) students.
7. (Who, Whom) do you believe will win the tournament?
8. (The boys they, The boys) decided to build a model rocket for (themselves, theirselves).

9. Mrs. Brown gave the recipe to (Linda and me, Linda and myself);
   it had been given to her by her (mother-in-law's, mother-in-laws') aunt.
10. Does he know the person (whom, who) they think started the rumor?

3. Adjectives and Adverbs

DEGREES OF COMPARISON

You may use adjectives or adverbs to show the degree to which the adjective or adverb modifies a particular word. Adverbs and adjectives may change form to show degree of comparison.

The three degrees of comparison are the *positive*, the *comparative*, and the *superlative*.   [40]

The basis of the formation of these degrees is the positive form. This is the simple form of an adjective or an adverb, such as the adjective *warm,* or the adverbs *drowsily* or *often.*

The comparative degree of most adjectives, and of adverbs not formed by adding *ly* to an adjective, is formed by adding *er* to the positive degree. The superlative degree is formed by adding *est* to the positive degree.

	POSITIVE	COMPARATIVE	SUPERLATIVE
Adj.	small	smaller	smallest
Adj.	lazy	lazier	laziest
Adv.	soon	sooner	soonest
Adv.	early	earlier	earliest

Note that when an adjective or an adverb ends in *y,* the *y* is changed to *i* before the *er* is added.

Keep in mind that it is the *use* of a modifier that determines whether it is an adjective or an adverb. Some words, such as *early* or *deep,* may be used as either adjective or adverb.

That is an *early* train. (Adjective)
He leaves *early* each morning. (Adverb)

Form the comparative and superlative degrees of adjectives of more than two syllables, and adverbs that end in *ly,* by prefixing the positive form with *more* and *most.*

	POSITIVE	COMPARATIVE	SUPERLATIVE
Adj.	interesting	more interesting	most interesting
Adv.	pleasantly	more pleasantly	most pleasantly

Use *less* and *least* with the positive form to make comparisons that show a diminishing degree.

	POSITIVE	COMPARATIVE	SUPERLATIVE
Adj.	happy	less happy	least happy
Adv.	often	less often	least often

Some adjectives and adverbs follow no rule in the formation of the comparative and superlative degrees; you must memorize such forms.

POSITIVE	COMPARATIVE	SUPERLATIVE
good, well	better	best
bad, ill (adj.), badly	worse	worst
little (quantity)	less	least
many, much	more	most
late (adj.)	latter	last
near	nearer	nearest, next

Use the comparative degree in comparing two persons or things. [40a]

Of the two of us, Betty is the *more capable* pianist.
I am absent *less often* than Julie.

Use the superlative degree in comparing more than two persons or things.
[40b]

John is the *best* skier in the group.

In comparing a person, place, or thing with the rest of its class, use *other* **or** *else* **with the comparative degree in order to exclude from the class the person, place, or thing compared.** [40c]

Mary is always sleepier than anyone *else*.

This slope is steeper than any *other* I have encountered.

A few adjectives such as *round*, *square*, *unique*, *straight*, and *equal* are incapable of comparison.   [40d]

When a word has an absolute meaning, such as those listed above, it cannot be compared. A thing cannot, for example, be more round than *round*. It is possible, however, to modify such adjectives with words such as *almost* and *more nearly*.

That ball of clay is *more nearly* round than this one.

Avoid double comparatives and superlatives.   [40e]

He plays *faster* than the others. (not *more faster*.)

DEVELOPING YOUR SKILL

Read the following sentences and find any errors in the comparison of adjectives and adverbs. Write the numbers 1 to 10 on your paper and write *correct* after the number corresponding to each sentence that is correct. Rewrite correctly each sentence that contains an error.

1. My project is more nearly complete than his.
2. The new Mart is taller than any other building in the downtown area.
3. Your group collected more money than any group.
4. I am reading this biography because it is the shorter of the twelve on the list.
5. Of the two poems, I like the one about the phantom boat the best.
6. This figure is squarer than that one.
7. The negotiators tried both threats and action, but action seemed to get the best results.
8. Whom do you compete with oftenest, Tim or Joe?
9. That curtain should hang straighter than this one.
10. Hawaii has a pleasanter climate than any state in the United States.

USING MODIFIERS CORRECTLY   [41]

In learning to use adjectives and adverbs correctly, it is most important that you be especially careful not to use an adjective when an adverb is needed.

Learn to distinguish between adjectives and adverbs.   [41a]

I am *surely* (not *sure* or *real*) hungry. (An adverb is needed to modify the adjective *hungry*.)

He is *really* (not *real*) happy. (An adverb is needed to modify the adjective *happy*.)

Words with the same spelling that can be used either as adverbs or as adjectives are often troublesome. One such word is *well*, which can be used as an adjective meaning *healthy* or as an adverb telling *how*.

I feel very *well* today. (*Well* is an adjective here. The adjective *healthy* could be substituted for the word *well*.)

David plays tennis very *well*. (*Well* is an adverb here. It tells something about the quality of David's playing; it tells *how* he plays.)

Predicate adjectives and adverbs are often confused. Some verbs, such as *be, seem, become, appear, grow, remain, sound, feel, taste,* and *smell,* may be completed by predicate adjectives or they may have an adverb in the predicate. If the modifier refers to the subject, it is an adjective. If the modifier tells something about the action of the verb, it is an adverb.

These peaches taste *ripe*. (*Ripe* is a predicate adjective modifying the subject *peaches*.)

Those trees have grown *rapidly*. (*Rapidly* is an adverb modifying the verb *have grown*.)

Less refers to a quantity of something and is always used to modify singular nouns. Fewer refers to the number of something and is always used with plural nouns. [41b]

I have *less* money than I thought I had.

He has had *fewer* problems with his car this spring.

Avoid using a double negative construction in sentences. [41c]

We haven't *ever* (not *haven't never*) played more than eighteen holes.

Avoid using unnecessary adverbs. [41d]

I *seldom* (not *seldom ever*) go to lunch alone.

WHERE FRIENDS MEET TO EAT! WILL'S GRILL

Certain adverbs are often used, as in the preceding sentence, where they are unnecessary. Such adverbs include *again, back, ever, over, up,* and *with.*

> You ought to *reread* those pages. (Not reread those pages *again*)
> You will probably *end* with the best grade in class. (Not end *up* with)

Use *this* and *that* to modify singular nouns and *these* and *those* to modify plural nouns. [41e]

> *This* type of shoe feels comfortable.
> *That* kind of picture is effective on that wall.
> *These* kinds of books are difficult to read.
> *Those* types of hangers are sturdy.

The words *here* and *there* should not be used directly after the adjectives *this, that, these,* or *those.*

> They do *this* (not *this here*) *kind of* play quite well.

Do not use *a* or *an* after expressions such as *this kind, that kind, these kinds,* or *those kinds.*

> That *kind of* (not that *kind of a*) tire is best on snow-covered roads.

Avoid the illiterate use of modifiers. [41f]

Do not add *s* to words such as *anywhere, nowhere, somewhere, every-where.*

> The book ought to be here *somewhere* (not *somewheres*).

Do not use *never* to mean *did not.*

> We *did not play* (not *never played*) that team even once.

Place modifiers as close as possible to the words they modify. [41g]

> I *only* want a half dozen oranges. (Not clear)
> I want *only* a half dozen oranges. (Clear)

Avoid squinting modifiers. [41h]

A modifier that is placed in such a position that it may refer to either of two parts of a sentence is said to be squinting.

> Anne told me *often* she had trouble with algebra. (Not clear)

As you see, this sentence may mean two different things:

> *Often* Anne *told* me that she had trouble with algebra. (Clear)
> Anne told me that she *often had trouble* with algebra. (Clear)

Avoid dangling verbal phrases. [41i]

Notice that the following sentence seems to say that the bracelet is doing the rummaging.

I found my bracelet *rummaging around in the trunk.*

This sentence could be corrected by changing the dangling participial· phrase to a clause, or by relating the participial phrase to the subject *I.*

While I was rummaging around in the trunk, I found my bracelet.
While rummaging around in the trunk, *I* found my bracelet.

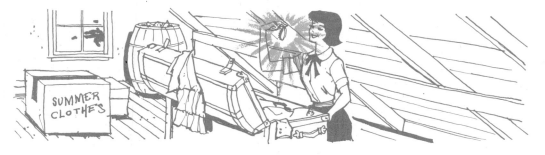

Do not use dangling adverbial clauses. [41j]

An adverbial clause is dangling when it is not clearly attached to the word or words that it modifies.

They told me *before they left* she had found the ring.

The adverbial clause *before they left* should be placed so that it is clear which word it modifies. The sentence can be corrected so that it reads:

Before they left, they told me she had found the ring.

Avoid using elliptical expressions that dangle. [41k]

An expression from which the subject, the verb, or both the subject and the verb have been omitted is an *elliptical expression.* In the following sentence the elliptical expression, shown in italics, dangles.

While writing the letter, someone knocked at the door.

In this sentence it sounds as if the person who knocked at the door were writing the letter at the same time. This sentence can be corrected by inserting the words *I was* in the elliptical expression.

While I was writing the letter, someone knocked at the door.

Avoid wordiness by reducing phrases or clauses to single-word modifiers.

[411]

The living room was *rectangular* (not *rectangular in form).*

We will send you *all available* pamphlets (not *all the pamphlets that we have available).*

DEVELOPING YOUR SKILL

Each of the following sentences contains an error in the use of modifiers. Some of the sentences contain more than one such error. Rewrite the sentences, correcting all errors.

1. We seldom ever see you, but we are real glad you came today.
2. I like that kind of a shoe better than this here kind.
3. I only ordered a dozen oranges, but they sent more.
4. There are less people here today than there were yesterday.
5. He doesn't sing very good, but he told me often he is asked to sing.
6. We never played those kind of teams.
7. While emptying the wastebasket, the wind blew the contents all over.
8. After his summer in the country, he should feel real good.
9. The errors he made were many in number.
10. I found the watch walking along the street.

Review Exercises—Adjectives and Adverbs

A. Write the following sentences, completing them with the correct word or words of those in parentheses.

1. Of the two boys, I found John the (more, most) co-operative.
2. The coach gave me three bats and told me to use the (better, best) one.
3. We can't hear very (good, well) with so much noise on the street.
4. Try to talk as (quiet, quietly) as you can.
5. The overripe figs taste (bad, badly).
6. I believe that he is the (more, most) capable of the two.
7. Ann is always hungrier than (anyone, anyone else).
8. This room is (squarer, more nearly square) than the other.
9. Of the three poems, I like this one (better, best).
10. It is a taller building than (any, any other) building in town.

B. Write the positive, comparative, and superlative degrees of the following adjectives and adverbs.

capable	well	angry	soon	good
wise	happy	often	few	fast

C. Each of the following sentences contains one or more errors in the use of modifiers. Rewrite each sentence, correcting all errors.

1. Our old car looks well and runs good.
2. Bob sure doesn't neglect his work, and he is more busier than anyone.
3. The sun rises more earlier these days, and each and every day is getting longer.
4. That table is squarer than this one, but I need one absolutely square in shape.
5. Those peaches taste badly, but these here apples taste wonderful.
6. I don't like those type of fruits, but these kind are my favorites.
7. While looking at furniture in the window, the fire engine went by.
8. I saw an accident mowing the lawn last Saturday.
9. I don't like that kind of a shoe for walking, but these kind feel real good.
10. I only asked for a few apples.

4. Prepositions and Conjunctions

Prepositions and conjunctions are words that are used to join or connect words to other words or groups of words in a sentence. For this reason they are sometimes called *connectives*.

USING PREPOSITIONS CORRECTLY [42]

When a pronoun is used as the object of a preposition, the pronoun should be in the objective case. [42a]

Sally went with *me* to the library.

No one except *Ron* and *her* were invited.

Use *between* when the object or objects of the preposition refer to two persons or things; use *among* when the object or objects refer to three or more. [42b]

Charles sat *between* Robbie and me.

We divided the candy *among* the three children.

Do not confuse the preposition *in* with the preposition *into*. *In* expresses being within a place; *into* expresses entrance to a place. [42c]

We sat *in* the airport lobby for an hour.

He fell *into* the pool.

She rushed *into* the room.

Do not use the preposition *of* for the verb *have* after *could, should,* *would, may, might,* or *must.*   **[42d]**

I *must have* (not *must of*) misunderstood you.

Use *beside* to mean *at the side of.* Use *besides* to mean *in addition to.*   **[42e]**

Won't you come and sit *beside* me?
What else do you need *besides* milk and oranges?

Use *at* to show *where* something or someone is. Use *to* to show the idea of *motion toward* someone or something.   **[42f]**

David is *at* (not *to*) home this morning.
Mother went *to* the store.

Distinguish between the prepositions *to* and *with* when used with the verb *agree.* You agree *to* a proposal and *with* a person.   **[42g]**

They agreed *to* the plan, though somewhat reluctantly.
All the students agreed *with* me that the plan seems sound.

Use *from,* not *than,* with the adjective *different.*   **[42h]**

That house is quite different *from* (not *than*) any other house in the block.

Distinguish among the prepositions *by, for,* and *with* when used with the verb *reward.* You are rewarded *by* a person, *for* something, *with* a gift.   **[42i]**

I was rewarded *with* a prize *by* the committee.
He received an award *for* his painting.

Use the preposition *for* with the verb *blame*. [42j]

They blamed him *for* the accident. (Not *blamed the accident on him*)

Use *in* and *on* with the verb *live* to mean to live *in* a town or city but *on* a street. [42k]

Joan lives *in* River Forest, Illinois, *on* Gale Avenue.

Place a prepositional phrase as close as possible to the word it modifies. [42l]

I found a table for our picture window *with a hand-toolea leather top.*

The prepositional phrase, shown in italics in the preceding sentence, should be placed next to the word *table,* which it modifies.

I found a table *with a hand-tooled leather top* for our picture window.

Do not use unnecessary prepositions. [42m]

The children were *inside* (not *inside of*) the tent.
They arrived *about* (not *at about*) noon.
Where did he go? (Not *Where did he go to?*)
The vase was knocked *off* the mantel. (Not *off of* the mantel)

Use *with,* not *to,* with *identical*. [42n]

Your hat is identical *with* (not *to*) Ruth's.

Use *for,* not *on,* with *wait* when the meaning is *to await*. [42o]

Please wait *for* (not *on*) Ricky and me.

Distinguish among the prepositions *with, from, about,* and *over* when used with *differ*. One differs *with* a person *about* or *over* a question. Something differs *from* something else. [42p]

Dad differs *with* Uncle Fred *about* the way to make a barbecue pit.
His plan differs somewhat *from* Uncle Fred's.

Distinguish among the prepositions *for, with, of,* and *at* when used with *impatient*. One is impatient *for* something desired, *with* someone else, *of* restraint, and *at* someone's conduct. [42q]

He was quite impatient *for* some news of the astronauts.
The child was impatient *of* any kind of control.
I was impatient *at* having to wait so long and I fear that I was quite impatient *with* Dennis.

Distinguish among the prepositions *for*, *with*, and *against* when used with *contend*. One contends *for* a principle, *with* a person, and *against* an obstacle.   [42r]

I contended *with* the group *for* my right to say what I wished.
We had the huge heating costs to contend *against*.

Distinguish between the prepositions *to* and *with* when used with *compare*. One compares something *to* something similar and *with* something dissimilar.   [42s]

He compared the paintings of Degas *to* those of other impressionist painters.
He compared the traditional *with* the modern styles of furniture.

Use of, not *about*, after *unmindful*.   [42t]

Unmindful *of* others' wishes, he opened the window wide.

In certain idiomatic expressions, a preposition is retained at the end of a sentence when the verb becomes passive and the object of the preposition becomes the subject of the sentence.   [42u]

They laughed at him. (Active voice)
He was laughed *at*. (Passive voice)

In informal speech it is considered acceptable and sometimes preferable to use a preposition at the end of a sentence. In the following sentence, for example, the preposition *for* is correct at the end of the sentence.

Whom did you vote *for*?

DEVELOPING YOUR SKILL

Write the numbers 1 to 20 on a sheet of paper. After each number write the word or words from the parentheses that will make the sentence correct.

1. Everyone except Lucy and (she, her) went with (Phil and I, Phil and me).
2. The money was divided (among, between) Mr. Jones's three nephews.
3. No one could (have, of) been more excited than we were.
4. The emblem of my sweater is different (than, from) yours.
5. What would you like for breakfast (beside, besides) orange juice?
6. They are (at, to) school now.

7. I cannot agree (with, to) your plan.
8. Jean lives in Batavia (on, in) Main Street.
9. When the boat capsized, Robin fell (in, into) the lake.
10. They searched for the treasure (inside, inside of) the boat.
11. Do not (blame me for the delay, blame the delay on me).
12. The artist compared his drawings (with, to) those of another modern painter.
13. The crowd became impatient (at, with) the singer.
14. Your coat is identical (with, to) mine.
15. The child dashed (in, into) the crowded street.
16. Do you have much to contend (with, against) in getting the work done?
17. The books fell (off, off of) the table.
18. Where is (he, he at)?
19. He was rewarded (with, by) a box of candy.
20. Please come sit beside (Jean and I, Jean and me).

KINDS OF CONJUNCTIONS

When conjunctions are used skillfully, they add to the effectiveness and clarity of your writing. They help to show the exact relationship between ideas in a sentence. It will be worth your careful study to learn how to use just the right conjunction to express your thoughts exactly.

There are three kinds of conjunctions—co-ordinating, subordinating, and correlative.
[43]

A co-ordinating conjunction joins words, phrases, and clauses of equal rank.
[43a]

The most important simple co-ordinating conjunctions are the following: *and, but, or, nor,* and *for. And* is used to connect similar ideas. *But* is used to connect contrasting ideas. *Or* and *nor* connect alternate ideas. *For* is used to introduce evidence for a preceding statement or an explanation of a preceding statement.

Bruce made out the list, *and* I bought the groceries. (Similar equal ideas)

I tried to reach the top shelf, *but* I'm not tall enough. (Contrasting equal ideas)

Should I return the call, *or* will she call me? (Alternate equal ideas)

You should not give an opinion in writing, *nor* should you express one orally. (Alternate equal ideas)

They could hardly keep quiet, *for* they knew we had found out a part of their secret. (The second clause introduced by *for* explains the preceding idea and is equal to it.)

A subordinating conjunction joins a dependent, or subordinate, clause to an independent clause.   **[43b]**

Subordinating conjunctions are used to show that one idea in a sentence is subordinate to another idea in that sentence. Commonly used subordinating conjunctions include *because, before, after, since, if, when, while, although, as, as if, unless, where,* and *that.*

> The game was called *because* it was getting dark.
> *If* he can finish his work in time, he will have dinner with us.
> *Unless* you can help me, I shall never finish.
> *Since* it is getting so late, perhaps we should stop working now.

Correlative conjunctions are conjunctions that are used in pairs. **[43c]**

The most commonly used correlative conjunctions are *both...and, either...or, neither...nor,* and *not only...but also.*

Correlative conjunctions should be placed in such a way that they clearly link the words, phrases, or clauses that are equal. Notice the way words, phrases, and clauses are linked together in the following sentences by the conjunctions shown in italics.

> *Both* Marge *and* I are wearing red dresses today. (The noun *Marge* is linked with the pronoun *I.)*
> I plan to leave *either* on Friday *or* on Saturday. (The phrase *on Friday* is linked with the phrase *on Saturday.)*
> *Neither* Dick *nor* Pete has his boots with him. (The noun *Dick* is linked with the noun *Pete.)*
> The girls brought *not only* sandwiches *but also* cookies and fruit. (The noun *sandwiches* is linked with the nouns *cookies* and *fruit.)*
> *Either* we must work faster *or* we must give up the idea of finishing the project on time. (The clause *we must work faster* is linked with the clause *we must give up the idea of finishing on time.)*

An adverb used as a conjunction is called a conjunctive adverb. [43d]

Sometimes adverbs are used like conjunctions to connect equal ideas. Some commonly used conjunctive adverbs are *however, moreover, nevertheless, consequently, therefore, so, still,* and *likewise.*

When such adverbs are used to link independent clauses, the clauses are separated by a semicolon, as in the sentence below.

We had not sold enough tickets; *therefore,* we did not win a prize.

Notice also that there is a comma after the conjunctive adverb in the sentence above. A comma is usually used after a conjunctive adverb.

DEVELOPING YOUR SKILL

A. Write the following sentences, underlining the conjunctions and placing parentheses around the words or word groups that are connected by the conjunctions. After each sentence indicate the kind of conjunction used in the sentence, whether *co-ordinating, subordinating,* or *correlative.*

1. Either she or I made the error.
2. Bill and Ruth painted the scenery, and Betty and I assembled the props.
3. Should I finish this work first, or would you prefer that I help you with yours?
4. I should like to visit the campus, but it is too far away.
5. You should not throw away lighted matches, nor should you leave a campfire smoldering.
6. Although our team is faster, theirs is heavier.
7. The project was a success because everyone worked well together.
8. If I can, I will sell twenty tickets.
9. Both Don and I brought sandwiches to the picnic.
10. Neither Lisa nor Sally wants to visit the zoo.

B. Using the ideas in the clauses below, write sentences in which you use co-ordinating and subordinating conjunctions. Write two sentences for each pair of clauses.

1. The weather was unfavorable. The day of the launching was postponed.
2. He finished his homework. He went to Dick's house to play records.
3. Alan and Dave played a duet on the piano. Miriam and I sat quietly and listened.
4. I want to go to that college. I haven't taken the necessary courses.
5. Don tried out for the basketball team. I went to the swimming meet.

C. Write five sentences in which you use conjunctive adverbs such as *however, nevertheless, consequently, therefore,* and *yet.*

USING CONJUNCTIONS CORRECTLY [44]

Do not confuse a preposition with a conjunction. Use a preposition to introduce a phrase and a conjunction to introduce a clause. [44a]

> Anne looks *like* her grandmother. (Preposition)
> It seems *as if* (not *like)* everyone is going to the game. (Conjunction)
> We cannot win *without* you. (Preposition)
> We cannot win *unless* (not *without)* you help us. (Conjunction)

The preposition *like* in the first illustrative sentence introduces the prepositional phrase *like her grandmother.* The conjunction *as if* introduces the clause *as if everyone is going to the game.* The preposition *without* introduces the prepositional phrase *without you.* The conjunction *unless* introduces the clause *unless you help us.*

In informal and colloquial English the preposition *like* is often used as a conjunction; however, the best speakers and writers still prefer to use *as* or *as if* to introduce a clause.

> It looks *like* it's going to snow. (Colloquial or informal)
> It looks *as if* it's going to snow. (Formal)

Sometimes *like* is substituted erroneously for the conjunction *that.*

> She feels *that* (not *like)* there may be others who could help.

The word *as* may be used as a preposition when it means "in the role of." Notice the difference in meaning when *like* and *as* are both used as prepositions in the following sentences.

> He acted *like* a dictator. (Preposition)
> He acted *as* a dictator in the play. (Preposition)

Use *that,* not *because,* to introduce a noun clause. Use *because* to introduce an adverb clause. [44b]

> The reason I didn't come was *that* I had too much work to do. (Noun clause)
> I didn't come *because* I had too much work to do. (Adverb clause)

Use *that*, not *where* or *as*, in sentences such as the following.   [44c]

I read *that* (not *where*) the astronaut will go up tomorrow.
I don't know *that* (not *as*) I've read about it.

Use *if* to introduce a conditional clause. Use *whether* to introduce a noun clause used as the direct object of a verb.   [44d]

If we can get a permit, we will visit the plant. (Conditional clause)
I don't know yet *whether* I can go. (Noun clause)

Use connectives that express relationships between co-ordinate ideas exactly.   [44e]

The meaning of a sentence can be greatly changed by the co-ordinating conjunction that is used to join its parts. Co-ordinating conjunctions may be used to add one idea or word to another; to point up contrast; to indicate choice; and to show result. The conjunctions that follow show the relationships indicated.

Addition: *and, both . . . and, also, besides, furthermore, likewise, more-over, then*
Contrast: *but, however, nevertheless, still, yet*
Choice: *or, nor, either . . . or, neither . . . nor, otherwise*
Result: *therefore, consequently, accordingly, hence*

Both Mary *and* I will go to the meeting. (Addition)

I prefer this kind of typewriter; *but* the rest of the class prefers that kind. (Contrast)

I shall have to hurry; *otherwise* I shall be late. (Choice)

Don can't play in the game; *consequently,* we shall have to find a substitute. (Result)

Be especially careful in the use of the co-ordinating conjunctions *and, but,* or *or.* Do not use conjunctions such as *and, but,* or *or* to connect a relative clause and an independent clause. Do not use *and which, but which, and who,* or *but who* unless there is a preceding clause beginning with *which* or *who.*

Tim is a strong-willed person *and who* usually gets his own way. (Incorrect)

Tim, who is strong-willed *and who* usually gets his own way, was not successful this time. (Correct)

Use subordinating conjunctions that express exactly the relationship between subordinate adverbial clauses and main clauses.   [44f]

The following conjunctions show the relationships indicated.

Time: *when, before, after, while, until, as*
Place: *where, wherever*
Manner: *as, as if*
Result: *that, so that*
Purpose: *in order that, so that*
Cause: *because, since, as*
Condition: *if, unless, provided that*
Concession: *although, though, even if*
Degree or comparison: *than, as much as, just as*

As we were coming in, they were leaving. (Time)

Wherever we went, we found suitable land on which to camp for the night. (Place)

She spoke *as if* she were in a great hurry. (Manner)

He adjusted the blinds *so that* the light would not glare in his eyes. (Result)

Our examinations will be held a week early *in order that* we may have time for senior class activities. (Purpose)

Since you have an A average in all of your studies, you will not have to take the examinations. (Cause)

If you wish, you may help the librarian shelve books. (Condition)

Although I have tried very hard, I have not succeeded in making the first team. (Concession)

I haven't finished *as much as* I had thought I could. (Comparison)

DEVELOPING YOUR SKILL

A. Write the numbers 1 to 5 on a sheet of paper. After each number write the word or words from the parentheses that will make the sentence correct.

1. It seemed (like, as if) everyone were out of town.
2. We won't be able to lift this package (without, unless) you help us.
3. He feels (that, like) he ought to take a short vacation.
4. They acted (like, as) they should have in such a situation.
5. The reason she fell was (because, that) she was wearing very high heels.

B. Number from 1 to 10 and opposite the appropriate number write the subordinate clause. Draw a line under the subordinating conjunction in the clause and indicate the adverbial idea expressed, such as *time, place, manner, result, purpose, degree* or *comparison, cause, condition,* or *concession.*

1. As the boat neared the dock, Diane's friends greeted her.
2. Although we didn't expect that we would need them, Mother insisted that we take some sandwiches.
3. When help finally came, the fisherman was so tired that he could not assist his rescuers.
4. Since the plane was losing altitude, the pilot lightened his load of cargo.
5. Wherever they went, they were welcomed.
6. He greeted us as if we were invaders in his laboratory.
7. He cannot finish the posters until the time for the game is set.
8. The field was lighted so that games could be scheduled at night.
9. He can read faster than he thinks he can.
10. Even if the road should be opened in time, the tar and gravel would be likely to harm the finish of the car.

Review Exercises—Prepositions and Conjunctions

A. Write the numbers 1 to 20 on a sheet of paper. After the appropriate number write the correct word or words of those in parentheses in each of the following sentences.

1. The treasure was found (inside, inside of) an old shoe.
2. Your problem is different (than, from) mine.
3. Mrs. Jones divides her time (between, among) her three daughters.
4. They went with Tim and (me, I) to the market.
5. Carol fell (off, off of) the pier.
6. Where did Jerry (go, go to)?
7. Pete fell (in, into) the river; he must not (have, of) looked where he was going.
8. What else did you order (beside, besides) flour and coffee?
9. He is not (to, at) home; but I can tell you that he does not agree (to, with) the plan.
10. They (blamed him for the accident, blamed the accident on him).

11. The visitors arrived (at, at about) midday; they were impatient (at, with) the long delay.
12. The lecturer compared Dickens's characters (to, with) those of other novelists of his period.
13. It looks (like, as if) we are going to be on time after all.
14. I read in the paper (that, where) you won a scholarship.
15. I don't know (that, as) I blame you.
16. It begins to look (as if, like) Anne, (as, like) many others, will also be late.
17. A little crowd had gathered (outside, outside of) the church.
18. I can't see you in this fog; where did you (go, go to)?
19. Jan rushed (in, into) the room.
20. If we (had, had of) known in time, we could (have, of) helped you.

B. Most of the following sentences contain errors in the use of prepositions and conjunctions. Rewrite those sentences that contain errors. If a sentence is correct, write the word *correct* after the appropriate number.

1. Between the candidates being considered, I believe the incumbent is the best of the three.
2. While sailing, Joe fell off of the boat and in the shark-infested water.
3. Your design is different than the model in the textbook.
4. I read in the paper where the President will discuss that issue in his next press conference.
5. I don't know as I agree with your proposal.
6. We cannot complete the tennis court without you help us.
7. Do you know where they went to?
8. Mr. Brown finally consented to speak to our class with an air of resignation.
9. He compared our work to that of other students of our ages.
10. It looks like we're going to win.
11. The reason she didn't answer was because she hadn't yet decided quite what she wished to say.
12. Our team is a good one and which hasn't lost a game this season.
13. There was another package inside of the larger one.
14. They talked to us like we were small children.
15. No one except Susan and I have been asked to the party.
16. Just between you and I, I think that painting is ugly.
17. Is there anything more to do beside what you have already told us?
18. He lives in Main Street in a house that is almost identical to yours.
19. Mother differs with us about the best way to make barbecue sauce.
20. I slipped and fell in the pool.

5. Making Words Agree

SUBJECT-VERB AGREEMENT

There are many opportunities for errors in the use of verbs, and mistakes in agreement are very common. Even in the speech of well-educated persons you are likely to hear such errors. Mistakes in written work, however, are much more serious, and since you have an opportunity to reread and correct what you have written, you should be able to find and correct errors in agreement.

The following facts about the agreement of verbs with their subjects will help you if you study them carefully and apply the rules to your speaking and writing.

A verb must agree with its subject in person and number. [45]

He always *speaks* distinctly and succinctly. (Third person singular subject and third person singular verb)

We shall leave in a moment. (First person plural subject and first person plural verb)

A singular subject requires a singular verb. [45a]

Sometimes a prepositional phrase comes between the subject and the verb. When this happens, the number of the verb is not affected. Notice that in the following sentences the subjects are separated from the verbs by prepositional phrases, but that the verbs agree with their subjects. A verb always agrees with its subject, never with the object of a preposition.

A *man* from the insurance company *wishes* to speak with Father.

One of the prize winners *is* Tom.

Words joined to a subject by *with, together with, including, accompanied by, in addition to,* or *as well as* do not change the number of the subject. If the subject is singular, the verb is singular. [45b]

Mr. Brown, as well as the boys, *is enjoying* the trip.

Note that the phrase *as well as the boys* is set off by commas from the rest of the sentence.

Singular subjects joined by *or* or *nor* require a singular verb. [45c]

Neither the *paint* nor the *paper* was the right color.

Plural subjects joined by *or* or *nor* require a plural verb. [45d]

Neither the *boys* nor the *girls* were on time.

If two subjects connected by *or* or *nor* differ in person or number, the verb agrees with the nearer subject. [45e]

Either a large building or several smaller *buildings are* to be built.
Either several smaller buildings or a large *building is* to be built.

***Each, each one, either, neither, everyone, everybody, anybody,* and *nobody* are singular and require a singular verb.** [45f]

Neither of the girls *is* a good swimmer.
Each of the boys *has* his own bicycle.

***All, none,* and *some* may be either singular or plural.** [45g]

When these words are used to mean an amount, a singular verb is used. When these words refer to several, a plural verb is used.

Some of the garden *has been watered.* (Amount)
Some of the flowers *are* in full bloom. (Several)

When a fractional number is used, a singular verb is used if the total amount is implied, and a plural verb is used if individuals are referred to.

One half of the room *is* already painted.
One half of the girls present *are* in favor of the plan.

Another word that may take either a singular or a plural verb is *number.* When *number* is used to mean *many,* it takes a plural verb; when it refers to an arithmetical number, it takes a singular verb. When *number* is preceded by the article *a,* it is frequently plural; when it is preceded by the article *the,* it is frequently singular.

A *number* of people *have signed* their names. (Many, plural)

The *number* of absences *is* too great. (Arithmetical number, singular)

Subjects joined by *and* usually require a plural verb. [45h]

Are you and *Mary leaving* now?

Mary and *the author are having* lunch together.

But if the parts of the subject refer to the same person or thing, the verb is singular.

The *author and editor,* Mr. Brown, *is* our neighbor.

Subjects joined by *and* and preceded by *every* require a singular verb.
[45i]

Every house and street *was checked*

Every nook and corner *is being searched.*

Note that the word *every* is understood in front of the words *street* and *corner.*

The pronoun *you,* even when it refers to one person, requires a plural verb. [45j]

Are you coming now, Susan?

Are you going to the game, boys?

In sentences having inverted order, the subject must be kept clearly in mind. [45k]

Here *comes* Charles.

There *go* Alan and Ted.

Are there any books in that box?

A collective noun requires a singular verb if the group is thought of as a unit; a plural verb is required if the individuals in a group are considered.
[45l]

The jury *has made* its decision. (Unit)

The jury *have disbanded* and *have left* for their homes. (Individuals)

The word *doesn't,* which is a contraction of *does not,* is third person, singular number. The word *don't,* which is a contraction of *do not,* must never be used with a singular subject in the third person. [45m]

She *doesn't* (not *don't*) understand English.

He *doesn't* (not *don't*) enjoy boating.

It *doesn't* (not *don't*) matter what you say.

Words that are plural in form but singular in meaning take a singular verb.   **[45n]**

The following categories of words should be studied carefully:

1. Words such as *physics, mathematics, mumps, news,* and *politics*

    The *news is* both bad and good.
    Physics is a difficult subject.

2. Subjects plural in form but considered as a unit, such as words describing a quantity or number

    Thirty dollars is as much as I will pay.
    Ten from forty leaves thirty.

3. The titles of books, plays, paintings, musical compositions, or other such works

    "The Reapers" is the name of a painting.

A compound subject considered as a unit rather than as two distinct things takes a singular verb.   **[45o]**

   Spaghetti and meat balls is his favorite dish.

In a compound subject if one subject is used affirmatively and the other negatively, the verb agrees with the subject that is used affirmatively.
                                                                    [45p]

   Frances, not Dave or I, *deserves* the prize.
   He, not you nor I, *is* the logical candidate for this job.

When the subject and the predicate nominative are different in number, the verb agrees with the subject, not the predicate nominative.   **[45q]**

   My favorite *dessert is* crackers and cheese.

The number of the relative pronoun that is used as the subject of a clause determines the number of the verb.   **[45r]**

The number of a relative pronoun depends upon the number of the word to which it refers.

   The boy *who is sitting* in the first seat is my brother. (The antecedent of the relative pronoun *who* is *boy,* which is singular in number. Therefore the relative pronoun *who* is singular and the verb *is sitting* is singular.)

The boys *who are talking* with Mr. Brown are the leaders of the group. (The antecedent of the relative pronoun *who* is the noun *boys*. Therefore, the relative pronoun *who* is plural and the verb *are talking* is plural.)

Use a plural verb with the plural forms of some nouns that come from foreign languages, even though the nouns look as if they are singular.

[45s]

These *are* the *data* that you requested.

Note that the singular is often used with this plural form.

This *is* the *data* that you requested.

DEVELOPING YOUR SKILL

A. Write the following sentences, completing each with the correct word of those in parentheses.
   1. One of the boys from our school (have, has) been elected to direct the activities of the whole group.
   2. Bacon and eggs (are, is) a favorite breakfast of many millions.
   3. A number of women (have, has) taken turns as crossing guards.
   4. The number of people involved in the project (are, is) great.
   5. There (go, goes) John with his new car.
   6. Mr. Jones, as well as the rest of the family, (has, have) enjoyed the game.
   7. Neither the bread nor the cookies (was, were) for sale.
   8. Neither the men nor the women (has, have) made their quota of sales.
   9. Either a single large cake or many smaller ones (is, are) to be baked.
   10. Each of you (has, have) his own bicycle.

B. Many of the following sentences contain errors in subject-verb agreement. Rewrite correctly those sentences that contain errors. If a sentence is correct, write the word *correct* after the appropriate number.

1. None of the flowers is in bloom.
2. None of the room has been painted, but some of the plaster is dry.
3. One half of the cake has been eaten.
4. A number of girls has signed up for the course, but the number of people are not large enough yet.
5. Mr. White, accompanied by his two sons, is taking a pack trip through the Smokies.
6. Aunt Sally's lawyer and adviser, Mr. Jones, is a friend of Father's.
7. Every letter and postcard has been readdressed.
8. Here comes Charles and Miriam.
9. Half of the boys have decided to work this summer.
10. Are you coming with us, girls?

PRONOUN-ANTECEDENT AGREEMENT

A pronoun must agree with its antecedent in person, number, and gender.
[46]

John will finish *his* work sooner if *he* doesn't take too many breaks.

Note that the pronouns *his* and *he* refer to *John*. *John* is third person singular, masculine; therefore, *his* and *he* must also be third person singular, masculine. A pronoun does not have to agree with its antecedent in case. The case of a pronoun is determined by its function in a sentence.

The boys will take *their* fishing equipment with *them*.

The pronouns *their* and *them* refer to *boys*. *Boys* is third person plural. *Their* and *them* must also be third person plural.

Pronouns referring to the singular pronouns *each*, *everyone*, *anyone*, *one*, *no one*, *nobody*, *someone*, *somebody*, *anybody*, and *everybody* must be singular.
[46a]

Everyone wants to win; *no one wants* to lose.

A singular pronoun is used to refer to nouns like *mumps*, *measles*, *news*, and *mathematics*, all of which are plural in form but singular in meaning.
[46b]

Although *mathematics* is not too difficult for me, I don't especially like *it*.

A plural pronoun is used to refer to two antecedents joined by *and*.
[46c]

Dick and *Ed* have *their* sweaters with them.

A singular pronoun is used to refer to singular antecedents joined by or or nor. [46d]

Either *Ellen* or *Barbara* will give us *her* pen.

A plural pronoun is used to refer to plural antecedents joined by or or nor. [46e]

Neither the *Cubs* nor the *White Sox* have begun *their* spring training.

A pronoun should agree with the nearer of two antecedents joined by or or nor. [46f]

Neither the leader nor the *children* brought *their* lunches.

A pronoun must be in the third person if its antecedent is a noun or an indefinite pronoun. [46g]

If a *boy* wishes to succeed, *he* must work hard.

If *anyone* wishes to succeed, *he* must work hard.

A phrase that comes between the pronoun and its antecedent may mislead one into using an antecedent in the wrong person.

Neither of you has bought *his* (not *your)* tickets.

The prepositional phrase *of you* does not affect the agreement of the pronoun with its antecedent, *neither.*

When the antecedent of a pronoun is a noun or pronoun of common gender, the masculine pronoun should be used, unless it is clear that a girl or a woman is meant. [46h]

Every *member* of the club has paid *his* dues. (The word *member* is common gender. It may mean boys or girls, or both.)

Every *member* of the girls' swimming team did *her* part to make a winning team. (The word *member* in this sentence clearly refers to *girls.)*

Do not use what to refer to an expressed antecedent. [46i]

The flowers *that* (not *what)* you sent me are still fresh. *(Flowers* is the antecedent.)

I cannot hear *what* you are saying. (No antecedent is expressed.)

Do not use a possessive noun as the antecedent of a pronoun. [46j]

I wore my aunt's dress *who* lives in New York.

This sentence can be corrected by avoiding the possessive case.

I wore the dress *that belongs to my aunt who* lives in New York.

A. Write the following sentences. On your paper draw a line under each italicized word and an arrow from that word to its antecedent. After each sentence give the gender and number of the antecedent of each italicized word.

1. Larry and Bruce are working on *their* boat.
2. Lisa would like to have *her* bicycle repaired quickly so that *she* can use *it* tomorrow.
3. Each participant in the meet must sign *his* name in the register.
4. The news *that* I heard was very good.
5. Do Scott and Peter have *their* books with *them?*
6. Each member of the club has been asked to bring *his* contribution to the club house tomorrow.
7. Nobody brought *his* rod and reel.
8. One of the girls left *her* notebook here.
9. If anyone wishes to buy a ticket, please ask *him* to see me.
10. Ricky and Ed have sent in *their* applications to that college.

B. Number from 1 to 10 and after each number write the correct word or words from the parentheses.

1. Each student must hand in (his, his or her) book report by this afternoon.
2. If anyone asks for (his, his or her) money back, take (their, his) name.
3. Either Mother or Aunt Janice will lend us (their, her) sewing machine.
4. Has anybody found (their, his) boots yet?
5. Neither the scouts nor the leader forgot (their, his) money.
6. In those days, everyone brought (their, his) own bat and ball to school.
7. Neither of them has (their, his) equipment.
8. Each of the boys gave (his, their) version of the accident.
9. If anyone finds (their, his) ticket, will (he, they) please tell me?
10. Anyone may go to the library if (they need, he needs) a book.

Review Exercises—Making Words Agree

Write the numbers 1 to 20 on a sheet of paper. After the appropriate number write the word or words from those in parentheses in each of the following sentences.

1. She, as well as other faculty members, (try, tries) to avoid overloading the classes.
2. One of the boys lives with (their, his) grandfather.
3. Either Mother or Father always (meet, meets) us at the bus station.
4. Neither the principal nor the students (understand, understands) the new ruling.
5. Neither the plants nor the small shrubs (was, were) harmed by the storm.
6. (Has, Have) anyone an application blank that (he, they) (don't, doesn't) need?
7. Some of us (was, were) left standing on the platform.
8. Some of the greenhouse (has, have) been repaired.
9. Neither of us (like, likes) to study on weekends.
10. Each of the topics (has, have) been assigned.
11. Every applicant must have (his, his or her, their) birth certificate.
12. A number of students (has, have) filled out their applications.
13. If either Mr. Howard or Mr. Jones (thinks, think) that you are wrong, (he, they) will tell you.
14. Will everyone bring (his, their) compass to class?
15. One of the workmen (have, has) left (his, their) tools here.
16. Mr. Brown, as well as his neighbors, (want, wants) the road paved.
17. Each of these problems (require, requires) an hour's work.
18. Father's old friend and classmate (is, are) coming to visit him.
19. Here (come, comes) the team and the cheerleaders.
20. Mathematics (are, is) a difficult subject for me.

UNIT SUMMARY

Knowing the accepted usage and the grammatical principles upon which such usage is based should give you a solid foundation for your own use of English. If you have mastered the principles that were presented in this unit, and if you remember the examples of noteworthy exceptions to these rules, you should now be able to avoid some of the more common errors in usage. Specifically, you should be able to avoid errors in verb forms, in subject-verb agreement, in pronoun-antecedent agreement, and in the cases of nouns and pronouns. You should be able to use, with confidence, troublesome verbs such as *lay* and *lie,* and you should have learned how to use modifiers and connectives so that they add meaning and clarity to your speech and writing.

UNIT REVIEW EXERCISES

DISCUSSION TOPICS

A. What is wrong with the following signs that were copied from delivery trucks and shops of advertisers?

MENS CLOTHING   CHILDRENS' SHOES
WOMENS APPAREL   FOOD AT IT'S BEST
ITS ALWAYS FIRST CLASS

B. Why is the choice of a connective important to clarity and exactness of meaning? Give examples of variation in meaning that can be achieved by different kinds of connectives.

C. What is a *squinting modifier,* and how do you avoid using one?

D. Why are *good* and *well* sometimes used incorrectly? Give examples of the correct use of these words.

E. What is meant by "levels of usage"? Is it ever proper to use colloquial or informal English?

WRITTEN WORK

A. Write synopses of the following:

1. *Eat,* third person singular, masculine, active voice, indicative mood
2. *Am,* first person singular, indicative mood
3. *Dive,* first person plural, active voice, indicative mood, progressive forms
4. *Hear,* first person singular, active voice, indicative mood, emphatic forms
5. *Leave,* third person singular, feminine, active voice, subjunctive mood

B. Write the principal parts of the following verbs:

1. begin	6. get
2. catch	7. grow
3. choose	8. know
4. drink	9. lay
5. fall	10. write

C. Write the numbers 1 to 10 on your paper. After the appropriate number write the correct word or words of those given in parentheses.

1. Everybody in the play knows that (he, they) will have to work hard.
2. The boys (neither had, had neither) the experience nor the training for the jobs they wanted.
3. Charles and (I, myself) are on the same committee.
4. I do not know (who, whom) my opponents will be.
5. Only one of the players (was, were) supposed to have (their, his) picture in the paper.

6. They took Tom to be (I, me).
7. (John and Bob's, John's and Bob's) cousin went with (Joan's, Joans') sister to the class play.
8. Neither Dianne nor (she, her) (has, have) (their, her) keys.
9. Did you know about (his, him) going to Alaska?
10. I read (that, where) (the broken window was blamed on Tim, Tim was blamed for the broken window).

VOCABULARY

Did you know the meaning of all the words that were used in this unit? In the following sentences, some of the words are used in different contexts. Write the numbers 1 to 5 on your paper. After each number write the letter of the word or phrase that could best be substituted for the italicized word in each sentence. Before making the choice, find the word on the page indicated to see how the word is used in this unit.

1. The work was filled with *redundant* expressions.   [p. 329]
   (*a*) high-sounding; (*b*) superfluous; (*c*) incorrect; (*d*) doubtful
2. The *incumbent* was chosen by unanimous consent.   [p. 350]
   (*a*) office-holder; (*b*) representative; (*c*) leader; (*d*) impostor
3. The tax assessor *appraises* property at definite intervals.   [p. 325]
   (*a*) places a value on; (*b*) looks at; (*c*) levies a tax on; (*d*) confiscates
4. The boys left the playground *reluctantly*.   [p. 440]
   (*a*) unwillingly; (*b*) slowly; (*c*) disapprovingly; (*d*) noisily
5. The senator had an *imposing* manner.   [p. 315]
   (*a*) impressive; (*b*) dictatorial; (*c*) importunate; (*d*) grandiose

SPELLING

The following spelling words appeared in the unit or were chosen because they are commonly misspelled. Study these words so that you will be prepared to write them from dictation.

1. redundant
2. incumbent
3. appraises
4. reluctantly
5. imposing
6. recollections
7. pronominal
8. phantom
9. ominously
10. concession
11. rehearsal
12. sullen
13. dissimilar
14. astronaut
15. resignation
16. capsized
17. scholarship
18. interviewed
19. connective
20. subjunctive

UNIT SELF-TEST

Write the numbers 1 to 25 on a sheet of paper. After each number write the word or words from the parentheses that will make the sentence correct.

1. I would have liked (to have been, to be) the first astronaut to fly in the space capsule.
2. Nobody except Carol and (me, I) (have, has) the keys to the library.
3. Without help he (could not have, could not of) (swam, swum) so far.
4. Invite anyone (who, whom) you think is interested in playing chess with (Ruth and myself, Ruth and me).
5. If you had to choose (between, among) those three men, (who, whom) would you choose as sponsor?
6. Neither he nor his parents (was, were) aware of the danger.
7. That mountain is higher (than any, than any other) point in this area.
8. Neither of the two passengers had (his, their) (life belt, life belts) fastened.
9. Do you know (where they went, where they went to)?
10. The reason our uniforms are not here is (because, that) we were late in sending in our order.
11. Everybody congratulated (he and I, him and me) on our victory.
12. They believed me to be (him, he), and they gave the books to (John and I, John and me).
13. Grandmother gave my brother and (I, me) a camera.
14. (Who, Whom) do you think gave the better review, Tom or (I, me)?
15. (Who, Whom) do you want to be captain?
16. (Who's, Whose) taking the money for the tickets?
17. Mathematics (is, are) difficult for Betty and (me, I).
18. Each applicant should have (his, their) list of credentials ready for the interview.
19. I am very sorry about (you, your) losing your billfold.
20. I saw in the paper (where, that) they are moving to New York.
21. She talks (like, as if) she (was, were) happy to be here.
22. Gloria was rewarded (for, with, by) a prize (for, with, by) the committee (for, with, by) her painting.
23. I cannot agree (with, to) the plan, but I am (sure, surely) glad to talk with (you and him, you and he).
24. The papers have been (lain, laid) carefully on his desk.
25. Mrs. Brown (don't, doesn't) like skiing and she feels (miserably, miserable) in cold weather.

Mechanics in Writing

In conversation you ordinarily have little difficulty in making yourself understood and in understanding another person. This ease of communication derives from the nature of speech. The spoken language has a multitude of resources for clarifying meaning—resources which you use almost unconsciously and automatically. Some of these resources are stress, pitch, and pause. Even facial expressions and gestures convey meaning.

The written language does not have nearly so many ways for conveying meanings. But one of the ways the written language does have to establish clear meanings is a system of devices that approximates the resources of the spoken language. These devices may be grouped under the general heading of punctuation. To understand how punctuation approximates the spoken language, consider the following sentence. Imagine that you were reading it aloud.

The year before [pause] the harvest was good.

In speaking this sentence you automatically pause between the words *before* and *the* to indicate that a certain meaning is intended. To indicate this same meaning in writing, you would place a comma between the words *before* and *the*.

The year before, the harvest was good.

Though the devices of punctuation are never so accurate as the resources of speech, you must master these devices if you are to express yourself clearly in writing. In this unit you will have the opportunity to master them.

Before you begin your study of this unit, answer the following questions in the Check Yourself exercise. Your answers will indicate how much you already know of punctuation and mechanics in writing.

CHECK YOURSELF

A. Rewrite each of the following sentences, correcting errors in capitalization.

1. "It's not worth it!" he shouted. "why should I pay?"
2. The committee of our Club passed the following resolution: no member who has not paid his dues will be allowed use of the gym.
3. This set of the Novels of Dickens is bound in Morocco leather.
4. The secretary of state is going to tour western europe next month.
5. Jack Kelly got his degree in Journalism from the university of Missouri.

B. Write the misspelled words in the following sentences correctly.

1. Our libary specializes in quality, not quanity, of books.
2. What was the lessen she assined for homework?
3. Ted and Norm are great friends; their allways together.
4. Mike finely admited that he was wrong.
5. What a combineation they make.

C. Rewrite each of the following sentences, correcting all errors in punctuation.

1. When we were finished painting George began to eat.
2. At the beginning of this project I thought the work would go easily.
3. We found that Frank when all the returns were counted was the real winner.
4. During the first years after his graduation from school he worked for a printer.
5. Tom, Dick, Harry and I are planning a little trip.
6. Do what you want: I no longer care.
7. The capital of Oregon Salem is on the Willamette River.

8. The Samuel Butler who was born in the nineteenth century not the one of the seventeenth century is the author of The Way of All Flesh.
9. His talk about Africa which lasted two full hours was not particularly interesting.
10. A good book; a satisfying meal; some interesting company; what more can a man want out of life!

1. Capitalization

Capital letters have two principal uses in English writing. First, they may be used to mark the beginnings of statements. Second, they may be used to distinguish between particular and general classes of persons, places, and things. In addition, there are some special situations that call for the use of capital letters.

Careless capitalization marks a writer as uneducated. By studying this section and by working the exercises, you should become familiar with nearly all the situations in which capital letters are required.

Capitalize the first words in most situations.   [47]

Capitalize the first word in every sentence.   [47a]

*H*ow much does that poodle cost?
*W*hat good luck!

Capitalize the first word in a quotation.   [47b]

Socrates said, "*T*he unexamined life is not worth living."
Wilma pleaded, "*T*urn on the television set."

Do not capitalize the first word in a continuing quotation that does not begin a new sentence.   [47c]

"No young man," wrote William Hazlitt, "*b*elieves he shall die."

When the continuing quotation does begin a new sentence, a capital letter is needed.

"Can you go?" Jim asked. "I mean, can you leave right now?"

Capitalize the first word of a line of poetry.   **[47d]**

> *M*ine honor is my life; both grow in one;
> *T*ake honor from me, and my life is done.
>
> —SHAKESPEARE

Some contemporary poets do not observe this rule. As an illustration of this usage, consider the following poem.

so much depends

upon

a red wheel

barrow

glazed with rain

water

beside the white

chickens

—WILLIAM CARLOS WILLIAMS

Whenever you quote lines of poetry, remember to reproduce them exactly as they were written.

Capitalize the pronoun *I* and the interjection O.   **[47e]**

If *I* were she, *I* should be much happier.
O death, where is thy sting?

The interjection *O* is mainly restricted these days to solemn or poetic writing. The form *oh* is much more common. The interjection *O* is always capitalized and is not followed by punctuation. On the other hand, the interjection *oh* is capitalized only at the beginning of a sentence or when it stands alone.

Oh, I don't care. Do what you like.
I asked Jim—*oh* no, I mean Harry—to come around and see you.

Capitalize the first letter of each main point and each subhead in an outline. [47f]

   I. *I*ndoor active sports
     A. *H*andball
       1. *O*ne-wall game
       2. *F*our-wall game
     B. *S*quash
     C. *R*acquets

Capitalize the first word of a formal statement following a colon. [47g]

The committee proposed that the following question be considered by the full assembly: *W*hat steps shall be taken in regard to the present laws regulating the import of goods into this country?

Capitalize the first word of a resolution following *Resolved* or *Whereas*. [47h]

Resolved: *T*hat a thorough physical examination be given every five years to all licensed drivers.

Whereas is often used in formal and legal documents to introduce conditions or principles of action.

Whereas: *T*he court has found both defendants financially liable for the accident, it hereby orders them to pay the following damages.

Capitalize the first word in each item of a list. [47i]

His essay was divided into the following sections:
    1. Prefatory remarks
    2. Exposition of main ideas
    3. Conclusions

In letter writing capitalize the first word and all nouns in the salutation. Capitalize only the first word of the complimentary close. [48]

| Gentlemen: | Dear John, | *M*y dear *M*argaret, |
| *V*ery truly yours, | *Y*our pal, | *A*s ever, |

Capitalize all proper adjectives. [49]

We drink *Brazilian* coffee from *English* cups and stir it with *Danish* spoons.

Some adjectives derived from proper nouns are no longer capitalized—*morocco* leather, *india* ink. These adjectives have outgrown the proper names from which they were originally derived.

His scheme is *utopian* and will not work.

The information is enclosed in that *manila* folder.

Still other adjectives are in the process of outgrowing their derivations so that it is difficult to tell whether or not they should be capitalized. In such cases you should consult a reliable dictionary.

Capitalize all proper nouns.   [50]

Patrick is going to *Ireland* next summer.

Marge read *Homer's Odyssey* in translation.

Some nouns, once proper nouns, have become with usage common nouns and are no longer capitalized. When you are in doubt about the status of a noun, consult a reliable dictionary.

His *odyssey* began last March and is not yet finished.

Capitalize the names of the days of the week, the months of the year, and holidays. Do not capitalize the names of the seasons of the year.   [50a]

*M*onday, *F*riday, *J*anuary, *D*ecember, *N*ew *Y*ear's, *C*hristmas, *s*pring, *s*ummer, *a*utumn, *f*all, *w*inter

Capitalize all specific geographical or place names, as well as sections of the country. Do not capitalize directions of the compass.   [50b]

*M*ount *V*ernon, *N*ew *Y*ork	the *A*rctic	the *P*acific
the *M*iddle *W*est	*P*earson *S*treet	the *M*iddle *E*ast

When *north, south, east,* and *west* refer to specific sections of the country or when they precede the name of a thoroughfare, they are capitalized. However, when they refer to directions of the compass, they are not capitalized.

You can tell by Mary Lou's accent that she is from the *S*outh.

My address is 3525 *S*outh Michigan Boulevard.

The fighting began five miles *s*outh of Stanleyville.

Do not capitalize a common noun used with proper nouns or adjectives unless it is a part of a specific name.

The American and Canadian *a*rmies shared transportation.

The United States *A*rmy shared its transportation.

Capitalize personal titles and all titles of officials in government, business, and the professions when those titles precede the name of the person [50c]

*M*r. Cooke	*P*resident Johnson	*J*udge Hand
*S*uperintendent Wills	*M*ayor Worth	*D*ean Wilt

Titles immediately following names or those used alone in place of names are only capitalized in order to show distinction and high rank.

Frank Thomas, *p*resident of the Actors' Club, will lecture tonight.
The *S*ecretary of the *T*reasury testified before the Senate today.
Adlai E. Stevenson, *V*ice-President under Grover Cleveland, was the running mate of William Jennings Bryan in 1900.

Notice that *president* and *vice-president* are capitalized when they refer to those officers of the national government. Certain prefixes and suffixes of these terms, however, are not capitalized.

President-*e*lect Eisenhower   *ex*-President Eisenhower

Capitalize the first word, the last word, and all important words of titles of books, plays, poems, songs, short stories, and essays. Do not capitalize articles, short conjunctions, or short prepositions unless they are the first or last words in the title. [50d]

*T*he *R*ed *B*adge *of C*ourage (Book)
*A*n *E*nemy *of the P*eople (Play)
"*T*he *M*an with the *B*lue *G*uitar" (Poem)
"*I*'ve *G*rown *A*ccustomed to *H*er *F*ace" (Song)
"*A D*iamond as *B*ig as the *R*itz" (Short Story)
"*O*n *L*iberty" (Essay)

If a short conjunction or preposition within a published title is capitalized, then you must capitalize it when you refer to this title. Do not, however, capitalize the articles *a, an,* or *the* when they are not part of the title.

I enjoy reading the *New York Times (the* not part of title) and *The Atlantic (The* part of title).

Capitalize the names of famous historical events and documents. [50e]

the *B*attle of *B*ull Run	the *D*eclaration of *I*ndependence
the *T*reaty of *V*ersailles	the *M*iddle *A*ges

Capitalize references to the Deity and the names of religions and races.
[50f]

| the *A*lmighty | Protestant | *B*aptist | Mongolian |
| *J*udaism | Roman Catholic | *O*ld Catholic | *N*egro |

The word *god* is not capitalized when it refers to a pagan deity, but the names of these deities, being proper names, are capitalized—*O*din, *Z*eus, *J*upiter. Pronouns that refer to the Deity are capitalized.

> And God saw every thing that *H*e had made, and, behold it was very good.

The adjective *Christian* is capitalized, but *unchristian* is not. Do not confuse *unchristian* with *non-Christian*.

Capitalize the names of religious books of all religions. Do not underline or use quotation marks. [50g]

| the *O*ld *T*estament | the *T*orah | the *H*oly *G*ospel |
| the *K*oran | the *A*pocrypha | Revelation |

Capitalize the words *father, mother, brother, sister,* and other family relationships whenever they are used in place of the person's name or in connection with that name. [50h]

> *M*other asked *U*ncle Tim to dinner tonight.

When these words are preceded by possessive pronouns, they are not capitalized.

> My *m*other asked my *u*ncle to dinner tonight.

In the names of school subjects, capitalize specific subjects offered in the curriculum (Algebra IA or Radio 2) and all names derived from proper names of countries or languages (English, Latin, German). [50i]

> Frank is doing well in *M*echanical *D*rawing II.
> Frank is good at *m*echanical *d*rawing.
> Next semester we are going to study American *h*istory and *a*lgebra.

Capitalize the names of political parties and of specific governmental bodies, departments, bureaus, or other divisions. [50j]

| Democratic party | the *H*ouse of *R*epresentatives | the *C*ongress |
| Republican party | Department of the *I*nterior | the *S*upreme *C*ourt |

Capitalize the names of buildings, business firms, and brand names of products.

[50k]

the *Prudential Building*   *Wilson and Sons*

When a common noun follows a brand name, it is not usually capitalized, except in some advertisements.

Phazt *spot remover*   Krunchey *candies*

Capitalize the names of organizations, institutions, and special groups.

[50 l]

International Association of Lions Clubs   the *Ford Foundation*

Do not capitalize such words as *high school, college, university, hotel,* or *theater* unless they are part of a proper name.

My father was graduated from the *University of Chicago.*
My father was graduated from a *university* in Chicago.

The names of classes in a school are capitalized only when the word *class* accompanies them.

The Senior class contributed generously to the scholarship fund.

Capitalize the names of special events.

[50m]

Senior Class Picnic   *Ground Hog Day*

Capitalize the names of ships, trains, planes, missiles, and rockets. [50n]

the *Friendship 7*   *Twentieth Century Limited*
S. S. *United States*   *Spitfire*

Capitalize epithets that are used with or in the place of proper nouns.

[50o]

Billy the Kid   *Alexander the Great*

Capitalize nouns used to personify some abstraction.   [50p]

Personification is a device, chiefly practiced by writers of verse, whereby objects or ideas are given the character of a person. It is the usual practice to capitalize nouns which are personified.

O wild *West Wind,* thou breath of *Autumn's* being

—SHELLEY

DEVELOPING YOUR SKILL

A. Be ready to tell in class which words in the following sentences should be capitalized. Give the reason for each use of a capital letter.

1. you arrived in the nick of time.
2. "There's one thing about milly," Ray said. "she's a good sport."
3. It was william prescott, at the battle of bunker hill, who said, "don't fire until you see the whites of their eyes."
4. My sister is going to attend the university of Nebraska this fall.
5. Have you read Joseph Conrad's *lord Jim?*
6. Oliver Goldsmith wrote, "o memory! Thou fond deceiver."
7. Augustana college at Rock island is a lutheran college.
8. My parents took *the city of San Francisco* to the west coast.
9. I think easter falls in the last week of april this year.
10. Did i show you the present aunt Mary sent me for my birthday?

B. Write the numbers 1 to 10 on a sheet of paper. After each number write the words in the following sentences that should not be capitalized.

1. Phil signed up for a course in Solid Geometry for the Winter.
2. "Lend me five dollars," Jim said, "And I'll pay you back with interest in a week."
3. Agnes signs all her letters, "Forever Yours, Ag."
4. That volume is beautifully bound in Morocco leather.
5. We live twenty miles East of Albany.
6. I always enjoy the movie reviews in The *New Yorker*.
7. There is a new book out by Ex-President Truman.
8. Athena was the Goddess of Wisdom.
9. My Father met yours at the Elks last night.
10. I chew Wiggley's Gum because I'm nervous.

Review Exercises — Capitalization

Rewrite the following sentences—using necessary capital letters and changing unnecessary capital letters to small letters.

1. Have you ever been to Atlantic city?
2. The junior class is going to play the senior class in a softball game next tuesday.
3. I enjoy studying American Literature.
4. The United States navy usually accepts only volunteers.

5. My family and I attend st. Luke's episcopal church.
6. My mother is a republican, but my father is a democrat.
7. Who was secretary of state under president Wilson's last administration?
8. You can reach him at the Chase hotel, st. Louis, Missouri.
9. I think north Michigan avenue is about six blocks east of here.
10. My Brother was graduated from High School last Fall.

2. Spelling

The ability to spell correctly can be acquired with a little persistent practice. Though the spellings of many words simply have to be memorized, thousands of others can be deduced from the application of a few rules. In this section you will learn how and when to apply these rules. You will also find that your spelling begins to improve if you practice the following procedures:

1. Pronounce your words correctly.
2. Try to visualize the spellings of difficult words.
3. Employ mnemonic (memory) devices to remember easily misspelled words.
4. Learn the rules of spelling and how and when to apply them.
5. Write words carefully.

Learn to pronounce words correctly. [51]

Pronounce words carefully so that you do not omit vowels, consonants, or syllables. [51a]

When pronunciations are slurred, sounds are often dropped. When these words are written, the dropped sounds are omitted and the words are misspelled. The person who pronounces the word *candidate* without the first *d* is likely to write *canidate*. Similar misspellings which are the result of mispronunciation are the following:

Artic for Arctic	libary for library
goverment for government	probaly for probably

Pronounce words carefully so that you do not add extra vowels.   [51b]

Just as words are misspelled because sounds are dropped from their pronunciations, so they may also be misspelled because sounds are added where none are written. Thus, the person who pronounces the word *grievous* with a second *i* will probably spell that word *grievious*. Some other words that are commonly misspelled as the result of pronouncing an extra vowel are the following:

athalete for athlete   disasterous for disastrous

Pronounce words carefully so that you do not transpose sounds.   [51c]

Words like *cavalry, hundred, prefer,* and *prescription* should be pronounced carefully so that the letters are not transposed. Do not pronounce or spell these words *calvary, hunderd, perfer,* or *perscription.*

Learn both the pronunciation and spelling of foreign words in common use in English.   [51d]

Because most foreign words used in English are not pronounced according to English rules, you must learn both their pronunciation and spelling.

au gratin (ō' grä'tăn')	*mañana* (mä·nyä'nä)
bon voyage (bôn' vwä'yàzh')	*pizza* (pēt'sà)
hoi polloi (hoi' pŏ·loi')	*Weltansicht* (vĕlt'än'zĭkt)

Visualize words in your mind.   [52]

An excellent way of distinguishing between words of similar sound or spelling is to form a picture of these words in your mind. By this means you can avoid confusing such words as *corps* and *corpse, dual* and *duel, finally* and *finely, personal* and *personnel.* Visualization is also helpful in learning to spell words with silent letters—words like column, calm, knife, and wrap.

Use memory devices to help remember correct spellings.   [53]

Many spellings that are ordinarily difficult to remember can be mastered once and for all through the use of mnemonic devices. Memorizing by principles of association is both easy and effective. For example, if you have difficulty with the word *forty*—adding an unnecessary *u*—the following sentence may help you: There were *forty* soldiers in the *fort.* If you are often uncertain about the spelling of the word *loose,* this rhyme may help: a *moose* is *loose.*

It is unnecessary for a mnemonic device to be serious and formal since it is for your own private use. The device that helps you to retain the spelling of a word is the best device. Mnemonic devices are easy to make up, and you will find them efficient short cuts to memorizing the spellings of difficult words.

Learn and apply the rules for spelling.   [54]

You will find that the knowledge of a few rules will forestall many mistakes in your spelling. Of course, you must be careful in applying these rules. A rule incorrectly applied will cause you a great deal of trouble. And, unfortunately, there are many exceptions to the following rules. In all, however, there are many more words governed by these spelling rules than there are exceptions to them.

Avoid confusing *ei* and *ie*.   [54a]

The vowels *e* and *i* frequently combine to form a single sound. When the sound these vowels form is pronounced *ē* as in the word *bleed,* then the sound is spelled *ie,* unless the letter *c* immediately precedes it. If the letter *c* does precede this sound, it is spelled *ei.*

bel*ie*ve	ch*ie*f	gr*ie*f
rec*ei*ve	conc*ei*t	c*ei*ling

If you pronounce the vowels *ei* as *ē* in the following words, then these words are exceptions to the above rule.

*ei*ther	l*ei*sure	s*ei*ze

When the vowels *e* and *i* are pronounced *ā* as in the word *mate,* then the sound is spelled *ei.*

fr*ei*ght	n*ei*ghbor	w*ei*gh

When the vowels *e* and *i* are pronounced neither as *ā* nor *ē,* then the sound is usually spelled *ei.*

counterf*ei*t	h*ei*ght	h*ei*r

The words *friend* and *sieve* are two of the exceptions to this rule.

When *e* and *i* do not combine to form a single sound—that is, when each of these vowels is in a separate syllable—these spelling rules no longer apply. For instance, consider the following words:

de-*i*-ty   so-*ci-e*-ty   spon-ta-n*e-i*-ty

You can usually trust your pronunciation to give you the spelling of such words. Otherwise, you must look them up in a dictionary.

Drop the final e before a suffix beginning with a vowel.   [54b]

If a word ends in a single consonant followed by a silent *e,* the *e* is dropped when a suffix beginning with a vowel is added.

din*e*+*i*ng=dining   defin*e*+*a*ble=definable
hat*e*+*i*ng=hating   writ*e*+*i*ng=writing

In the case of words like *singe* and *dye,* the final *e* is retained to distinguish these words from forms of other words that have similar spelling: for example, *singeing* and *singing, dyeing* and *dying.*

Retain the final e before a suffix beginning with a consonant.   [54c]

refin*e*+*ment*=refin*e*ment   remot*e*+*ness*=remot*e*ness

The words *acknowledgment, argument, awful, duly, judgment,* and *truly* are exceptions to this rule.

Double a final consonant before a suffix beginning with a vowel (a) if the consonant ends a word of one syllable or a word that is accented on the last syllable *and* (b) if the consonant is preceded by a single vowel.   [54d]

bat (the final consonant is preceded by a single vowel in a one-syllable word), *batter, batting*

excel (the final consonant is preceded by a single vowel in a word in which the final syllable is accented), *excelling, excelled*

If the accent shifts to an earlier syllable when the suffix is added, the final consonant is not doubled.

refer'+ence=ref'erence   defer'+ence=def'erence

Words ending in y preceded by a consonant usually change y to i before any suffix except one beginning with i.   [54e]

y preceded by a consonant: *busy, busily, busier; carry, carries, carried; rely, reliable, reliance*

y preceded by a consonant before a suffix beginning with *i: carry, carrying; rely, relying*

Single-syllable adjectives like *dry* usually retain the *y* before *ly* and *ness: dryly, dryness*. The *y* is also retained before the suffixes *like* and *ship*. The *y* of proper names is always retained in the plural: the William *Kellys*. The *y* is retained in the possessive case: *everybody's*.

Words ending in y preceded by a vowel generally retain the y unchanged before any suffix. [54f]

y preceded by a vowel: *buy, buying; joy, joyous; relay, relayed*

Several common words are exceptions to this rule, and the spelling of these words should be memorized: *day, daily; pay, paid; say, said*.

Words ending in ce or ge usually keep the e before suffixes that begin with a, o, or u. [54g]

When the suffix begins with *a*, *o*, or *u* and is immediately preceded by a "soft" *c* or *g*, the final *e* is retained.

change+*a*ble=change*a*ble   peace+*a*ble=peace*a*ble
courage+*o*us=courage*o*us   trace+*a*ble=trace*a*ble

The final *e* is dropped, however, after a "soft" *c* or *g* when the suffix begins with *i* or *e*.

change+*i*ng=chang*i*ng   trace+*i*ng=trac*i*ng

Words ending in c usually add k before a suffix beginning with e, i, or y. [54h]

In words like *bivouac*, which end in a "hard" *c*, you add *k* to show the retention of this sound: *bivouacked, bivouacking*. There are a few exceptions to this rule, like the word *arc: arced, arcing*.

Words ending in c usually add ally to form an adverb. [54i]

alphabetic, alphabetic*ally*   geographic, geographic*ally*
emphatic, emphatic*ally*   poetic, poetic*ally*

Only three English words end in ceed; one in sede. All others with the same pronunciation end in cede. [54j]

ceed: *exceed, proceed, succeed*
sede: *supersede*

Words whose final suffix is preceded by a "soft" c or g may end in *ence*, *ency*, or *ent*; words whose final suffix is preceded by a "hard" c or g may end in *ance*, *ancy*, or *ant*.   [54k]

final suffix preceded by "soft" *c* or *g:* benefi*c*ence, negli*g*ence
final suffix preceded by "hard" *c* or *g:* mendi*c*ant, extrava*g*ant

There is no general rule to determine whether a word should end in *able* or *ible*.   [54 l]

Consult your dictionary when you are not sure whether a word ends in *able* or *ible*.

***Full* is a prefix; *ful* is a suffix. The prefix *full* is usually separated by a hyphen from the other part of a compound. The suffix *ful* is usually joined without a hyphen to the other part.**   [54m]

full-bodied   cup*ful*

Learn the following rules that will help you to form the plural of nouns correctly.   [55]

To form the plural of most nouns, add an s to the singular.   [55a]

Unrestricted attack*s* on Allied ship*s* by submarine*s* helped bring about the first of two world war*s*.

To form the plural of nouns ending in s, x, z, ch, and sh, add es.   [55b]

boss, boss*es;* ax, ax*es;* quiz, qui*zz*es; march, march*es;* crush, crush*es*

In the case of the word *quiz*, notice that you must also apply rule 54d and double the final consonant. If a word ends in *ch*, but has a *k* sound instead of a *tch* sound as in *march,* you do not add *es* to form the plural: *patriarchs.*

To form the plural of nouns ending in y preceded by a consonant, change the y to *i* and add *es.* Most nouns ending in y preceded by a vowel add an s.

[55c]

     y preceded by a consonant: ally, all*ies;* lady, lad*ies*
     y preceded by a vowel: alley, all*eys;* chimney, chimn*eys*

To form the plural of many nouns ending in f or fe, change the f or fe to ves.

[55d]

     knife, kni*ves;* loaf, loa*ves*

Among the exceptions to this rule are the following words: belief, be-liefs; fife, fifes; tariff, tariffs. Some words of this kind have two plurals, either one of which is correct: wharf, whar*ves,* wharfs.

To form the plural of letters, figures, and signs, add the apostrophe and s ('s).

[55e]

     k's, 1960's, &'s

Words discussed as words add an apostrophe and *s ('s)* to form the plural.

     Her praise was all *oh's* and *ah's.*

To form the plural of many compound words, make the most important words plural.

[55f]

     attorney at law, attorney*s* at law
     commander in chief, commander*s* in chief

To form the plural of nouns compounded with ful, add s at the end of the word.

[55g]

     handful, handful*s;* tablespoonful, tablespoonful*s*

If in doubt about the plural of nouns ending in o, use your dictionary.

[55h]

Nouns ending in *o* preceded by a vowel, add *s.*

     boo, boo*s;* folio, folio*s;* kangaroo, kangaroo*s;* radio, radio*s*

Common nouns ending in *o* preceded by a consonant usually add *s,* but frequently add *es.*

     albino, albino*s;* buffalo, buffalo*es;* piano, piano*s;* potato, potato*es*

The plurals of some nouns are formed irregularly. If in doubt about a plural form, use your dictionary.   **[55i]**

child, *children*	mouse, *mice*
goose, *geese*	ox, *oxen*
louse, *lice*	tooth, *teeth*
man, *men*	woman, *women*

Compound words using the noun *man* form their plurals by changing the vowel.

Dutchmen   Englishwomen   gentlemen

The following words do not change the vowel to form the plural because these words are not compounds of the noun *man*.

Germans   Normans   Romans

Some nouns have the same form in both the singular and the plural. **[55j]**

Most of these nouns are the names of animals or fish:

bass, cod, deer, perch, trout

Other of these nouns are the names of nationalities ending in *ese*:

Japanese, Portuguese

Two Latin words have the same singular and plural:

series, species

Some nouns taken from foreign languages retain their foreign plurals, some have English plurals, and some have both.   **[55k]**

Foreign words that are thoroughly "naturalized" into the English language usually have English plurals. Those that are still in the process of naturalization may have only foreign plurals. Still other words have both an English and a foreign plural.

In the case of words having an English and a foreign plural, you should use the English form, unless you have a special reason for using the foreign form. For example, the word *index* has an English plural, *indexes,* and a Latin plural, *indices.* When you wish to refer to mathematical exponents, you must use the Latin plural.

The following list gives the plurals of some of the commonly used words in English that are derived from foreign languages.

Words with Foreign Plurals

Singular	Plural
alumnus	alumni (masculine)
alumna	alumnae (feminine)
analysis	analyses
axis	axes
basis	bases
datum	data
stimulus	stimuli
synopsis	synopses
thesis	theses

Words with English and Foreign Plurals

Singular	English Plural	Foreign Plural
appendix	appendixes	appendices
cactus	cactuses	cacti
curriculum	curriculums	curricula
formula	formulas	formulae
index	indexes	indices
nucleus	nucleuses	nuclei
radius	radiuses	radii
stratum	stratums	strata

Proper nouns preceded by titles may form their plurals in either of two ways. [55 l]

the Miss Mohr*s* or the *Misses* Mohr
the Mr. Green*s* or the *Messrs.* Green
the Commander Cooke*s* or the *Commanders* Cooke

Proofread carefully everything that you write. [56]

Many spelling errors are the result of carelessness or impatience, and not of ignorance. Those who make such errors simply do not take the time to proofread what they have written. You should cultivate the habit of proofreading everything that you write—even personal letters. And you should read at least once for spelling mistakes alone. Whether you are a good speller or a poor speller, you will find in a short time that you can reduce the number of spelling errors by habitually proofreading what you write.

A. Be prepared in class to make up mnemonic devices which will help you to remember the correct spelling for each of the following words. For example, you may remember that there are two *r*'s in *embarrass* by recalling the following sentence: Embarrassment is a ba*rr*ier to frankness. Those parts of the following words that frequently cause spelling errors are italicized.

add*ress*	mo*r*tgage
d*e*scription	nick*el*
d*iary*	pygmy
hypoc*risy*	sep*a*rate
incident*ally*	su*r*prise

B. Write the numbers 1 to 5 on a sheet of paper. After each number write the word in parentheses which is appropriate for the meaning of the sentence.

1. The principal gave his (ascent, assent) to our plan for raising money.
2. Changes in circumstance will (altar, alter) the terms of your contract.
3. There used to be hundreds of (heards, herds) of buffalo roaming the prairies.
4. The sun (shone, shown) bright on my old Kentucky home.
5. Aren't you (threw, through) with your homework yet?

C. Correct the misspelled words in the following sentences on a sheet of paper. Beside each correction write the number of the spelling rule that applies to the correction.

1. They swam to his rescue, but he had drownded before they reached him.
2. Bob's nieghbors gave him a farewell party.
3. Do you beleive in installment buying?
4. How many days did the seige of the Alamo last?
5. This job requires a combineation of skills.
6. Our school is droping athaletics next year.
7. Is he carfull or carless about his work?
8. George exceled in the study of mathematics.
9. A truck like that carryies four tons of goods.
10. The most recent order superceeds all previous ones.

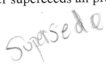
Supersede

D. Write the plural form of each of the following words on a sheet of paper.

basis	bacterium	criterion
Molly	sister-in-law	taxi
1800	teaspoonful	hero
YMCA	fox	ray
baby	life	Chinese

Review Exercises — Spelling

A. Write the following words on a sheet of paper, inserting *ie* or *ei* to complete their spelling.

cash__r	gr__f	p__rce
conc__t	l__sure	r__gn
fr__ght	n__ther	retr__ve

B. Correct the misspelled words in the following sentences on a sheet of paper.

1. Mark was beatten so severely he decided to give up playing handball.
2. The governor is going to intersede on behalf of Jeremy Williams.
3. It's not exactly a grievious error.
4. Niether the King nor his hiers were much disturbed at the news of a new invasion.
5. Let's go out and have some peetza.
6. Have you noticed latly how strangely Marlon has been acting?
7. The term *honor* is not really defineable.
8. The police were not properly equiped to put down a rebelion.
9. All was in readyness for Bea's surprise party.
10. Bob could always describe a football game graphicaly.

3. Punctuation

The purpose of punctuation is to show the reader how sentences and parts of sentences are related. In conversation a speaker has many resources for showing such relations—a change in facial expression or in pitch of voice, for example. In writing, the resources are less numerous. And the writer must use them with accuracy if the reader is not to be confused. Remember that in most cases you will not be present when your writing is read. You will not have the chance to clear up distortions in meaning caused by faulty punctuation. You must therefore be able to say in writing what you *really* mean.

In this section you will study the chief devices for making your writing clear and lucid. You will study the comma, the semicolon, the colon, and the period. You will learn the correct use of each mark of end punctuation and of quotation marks, apostrophes, dashes, parentheses, and brackets.

THE COMMA

Probably the most frequently used mark of punctuation in English is the comma. It is also the mark of punctuation most frequently *misused*. Originally the term *comma* referred to a part of a sentence that was distinct, a part that should be marked off by a comma-sign. Over the years this term has come to be applied only to the sign itself. If the part to be marked off occurs in the middle of the sentence, as it does in this sentence, a pair of commas is used. If the part occurs at the beginning or the end of the sentence, only one comma is used.

In the section to follow, you will learn the rules governing the correct use of the comma.

Use commas in your writing in all the situations established through usage.   [57]

Insert a comma between sentence elements when the thought might be incorrectly interpreted if no punctuation were used.   [57a]

Instead of thirty, eight cartons were delivered.
When they had eaten, the children went to bed.

If the commas were omitted from these sentences, confusion would result. For example, if the comma were omitted from the second sentence, one would read *When they had eaten the children* before the structure of the sentence became clear.

Use a comma to set off an introductory adverbial clause.   [57b]

If I were in your place, I would go to the game with Jim.

When we started up the side of the mountain, I wasn't sure that we would ever reach the top.

If the introductory adverbial clause is short, the comma may be omitted if no misinterpretation would occur. In the following sentence, for example, a comma is not needed.

If he asks he will receive a prompt reply.

Use a comma to set off introductory participial phrases and introductory infinitive phrases used as adjectives or adverbs.   [57c]

Finally finishing our work, we turned out the lights and went home.

To graduate next June, you must pass this English course.

Use a comma to set off a succession of prepositional phrases at the beginning of a sentence.   [57d]

At the end of this book, you will find the index.

Agreement on the placement of commas after introductory elements is not unanimous. However, if you place a comma after an introductory element of five or more words, you can avoid one type of overpunctuation.

On the whole I agree with what you say. (No comma needed)

After twenty days of zero temperatures, even a slight warming feels good. (Correct use of comma)

Use a comma to set off a single word like yes, no, well, indeed, alas, or single words obviously out of their natural order in the sentence.   [57e]

No, I think you're wrong there.

Indeed, there were only two left.

Lately, our luck's been very good.

Use a comma to set off words of direct address, whether they come at the beginning, the middle, or the end of the sentence. [57f]

> *Frank*, will you come here and help me!
> Tonight, *my friends*, the winner of our contest will be announced.
> Where are you going, *Toni?*

Notice that in the second sentence the expression of direct address occurs near the middle and requires a pair of commas to set it off.

Use commas to set off parenthetical words or phrases. [57g]

An expression which has a grammatical function in a sentence, but does add an idea, is said to be *parenthetical.* Because such expressions are felt to interrupt the normal order of the sentence, they are set off by commas.

> Mitchell was, *according to the evidence*, guilty on both counts.

> I, *therefore*, knew that she no longer cared to go.

Sometimes the writer wishes to achieve a different emphasis, and he will omit the commas and not set off the parenthetical expression.

> I *therefore* knew that she no longer cared to go.

Some adverbs which occur in main clauses are considered parenthetical and are set off by commas.

> Mike, *however*, has no other plan to offer.

Use commas to set off words in apposition. [57h]

Words set beside nouns and pronouns for the sake of explanation or identification are called *appositives.*

> Aaron Burr, *Vice-President under Jefferson,* was tried for treason.
> Carol Coogan, *my sister's best friend,* is going to be a nurse.
> Which would you like to see tonight, *a movie or a play?* (Here the appositive is separated from the pronoun *which* because of the interrogative structure of the sentence.)

Some appositives, like some clauses, are restrictive in meaning and are not set off by commas. For example, if the writer of the following sentence had more than one brother, the appositive would be essential to the meaning, or restrictive, and would not be set off by commas.

> My brother *Tom* works in California.

Use a comma to set off a final clause when the thought turns aside; if the thought continues, use no comma. [57i]

To determine whether a comma should be used before a final clause, examine the final clause to see if it introduces a new idea or continues the idea presented in the main clause. Study the following sentences and the explanations of their punctuation.

I regretted having spoken, *even though what I said was true.* (The final clause introduces a new idea and is therefore preceded by a comma.)

I shall send you a card *when your order arrives.* (The final clause continues the idea begun in the main clause. No comma is needed.)

Use commas to set off the elements of a series of words, phrases, or clauses. [57j]

Commas are used to separate three or more elements in a sentence that are similar in structure or function.

Anne bought an apple, two pears, and a peach. (Three words in a series)

Our men travel by train, by plane, and by ship. (Three phrases in a series)

She told us how she planned to raise the money, who would contribute, and how much they would give. (Three clauses in a series)

Some writers would omit the final comma before the word *and* in the previous sentences. It is both correct and wise, however, to include this comma. Often the omission of the final comma in a series will lead a reader to mistake the last two items for a compound.

Hank's favorite subjects are algebra, English literature, and history. (If you omit the final comma in this series, you are saying that one of Hank's favorite subjects is English history.)

If two items in a series are compound, then they should not be separated by a comma.

We had *bacon and eggs,* coffee, and toast for breakfast.

Inserting a comma before the first word or after the last word in a series is incorrect.

I like, to fish, to hunt, and to camp, during my summer vacations.

All the commas in a series may be omitted if a connective is supplied before each item except the first.

He came *and* saw *and* conquered.

All the connectives may be omitted in a series if a comma is supplied before each item except the first.

He came, saw, conquered.

Use a comma before a co-ordinating conjunction that connects two independent clauses.   [57k]

Two independent clauses joined by a co-ordinating conjunction, such as *and, but, for, or,* or *nor,* form a compound sentence. A comma is usually used before the co-ordinating conjunction.

I should like to do him a favor, *for* he has often helped me.

When the independent clauses are short and have the same subject, the comma may be omitted, and the conjunction alone joins them.

I liked the movie *and* I enjoyed the book even more.

When a comma appears in either of the independent clauses, a semicolon rather than another comma may be used before the co-ordinating conjunction.

Lucy, a very bright girl, has won a scholarship to Radcliffe College; *and* she will major in history there next year.

Use commas to set off nonrestrictive phrases and clauses.   [57 l]

A restrictive clause or phrase limits the application of the word it modifies to an individual or to a specific class. A nonrestrictive clause or phrase modifies a word, but does not limit that word to an individual or to a specific class.

Everyone *who mails his entry before midnight next Sunday* will receive a special bonus.

The italicized clause in the preceding sentence modifies the pronoun *Everyone* and, at the same time, limits this word to a particular class. This clause is therefore restrictive. It cannot be omitted from the sentence without changing entirely the main thought of the sentence.

Clara Wilson, *who is very pretty,* is going to enter the beauty contest.

The italicized clause in this sentence modifies the proper noun *Clara Wilson,* but it is not essential to the main thought of the sentence. The main thought of this sentence would still be preserved—that Clara Wilson is going to enter a beauty contest—even if the nonrestrictive clause were omitted. Compare the changes in meaning brought about by the omission of clauses in these two sample sentences:

Everyone . . . will receive a special bonus.

Clara Wilson . . . is going to enter the beauty contest.

Because nonrestrictive clauses and phrases can be omitted from the sentence without changing the essential meaning of the sentence, they are set off by commas. Because restrictive clauses and phrases are part of the essential meaning of the sentence, they are not set off by commas.

George will pass the exam *if he studies.* (The essential idea of this sentence is not that George will pass the exam, but that he will pass it only if he performs a certain action. The italicized clause is therefore restrictive and not set off by a comma.)

George will pass the exam, *whether or not he studies.* (The essential idea of this sentence is that George will pass the exam. The italicized clause is therefore nonrestrictive and must be set off by a comma.)

Sometimes a clause or a phrase will be either restrictive or nonrestrictive, depending upon which meaning the writer intends.

The new student *from Hawaii* likes the climate here. (By making the italicized phrase restrictive, the writer intends to show that this student is one of several new students, but the one referred to is the one who is from Hawaii.)

The new student, *from Hawaii,* likes the climate here. (By making the italicized phrase nonrestrictive, the writer intends to show that there is only one new student and that he is from Hawaii.)

The following clues may be of help to you in distinguishing between restrictive and nonrestrictive elements.

1. Nonrestrictive elements may be removed without changing the essential meaning of the sentence.
2. Restrictive elements do not usually modify proper nouns.
3. Dependent clauses introduced by *that* are usually restrictive.
4. Nonrestrictive elements are usually indicated by a pause when read aloud.

It might be difficult to determine whether a modifier is restrictive or not in a sentence taken out of context. But you should have little difficulty in determining this when you are writing a composition. If you have clearly in mind what you want to say, you ought to know how to punctuate it.

Use commas in letter writing between the day and the year, between the city and the state, after the salutation in a social letter, and after the complimentary close. [57m]

> December 7, 1962
> Halfway, Oregon   97834
> Dear Cynthia,
> Yours truly,

The zip code should always be placed after the state. There is no comma between the state and the zip code.

> Detroit, Michigan   48214

Avoid using only a comma to splice, or join, two independent clauses. [57n]

A comma fault occurs when independent clauses are joined together with only a comma, as in the sentence to follow.

> We asked Jim for some money, he gave us none.

There are four ways to correct a comma splice. First, you may substitute a semicolon for the comma.

> We asked Jim for some money; he gave us none.

Second, you may add a co-ordinating conjunction.

> We asked Jim for some money, *but* he gave us none.

Third, you may make each main clause into a separate sentence.

We asked Jim for some money. He gave us none.

Fourth, you may subordinate one of the independent clauses.

Even though we asked Jim for some money, he gave us none.

Which of these methods you choose will depend upon the thought you wish to express. If, for example, you find that two independent clauses differ widely in ideas, you would probably do better to cast them as separate sentences, rather than as a compound sentence.

There is one exception to these methods for correcting a comma splice error. Short, independent clauses having the same subject, and closely related in form, may be separated by only a comma.

We ran, we sang, we danced.

It is not incorrect, however, to separate such clauses with a semicolon.

We ran; we sang; we danced.

Use a comma between co-ordinate adjectives.   [57o]

When a series of co-ordinate adjectives modifies a single noun, commas are used to separate the adjectives.

Good, bad, and *indifferent* people will be found in every organization.

Not all adjectives in a series are co-ordinate. Some adjectives are so closely related to the noun that they nearly form compounds.

The *little old* lady came down the steps of her huge, modern, recently built mansion.

Use commas to separate the parts of an address.   [57p]

Our new address is 1245 N. Astor Street, Chicago, Illinois 60610.

Use commas to separate the parts of a date.   [57q]

I was born on January 15, 1945.

When only the month and the day are given, no comma is used.

Our project will be finished by August 18.

When the month and the year are given, commas are usually used—though they may be omitted.

George Washington was inaugurated in April, 1789, in New York City.

George Washington was inaugurated in April 1789 in New York City.

Commas are not used when the items of a date are joined by a preposition.

George Washington was inaugurated in April of 1789 in New York City.

Use a comma to set off the exact words of a speaker from the rest of the sentence, except when a question mark or exclamation point is required.
[57r]

He told me, "There's no train till midnight."
"What's on TV?" she asked.

Use a comma to set off a short final clause that changes a statement to a question.   [57s]

It's about time we were going, *don't you think?*

Use a comma to separate contrasted co-ordinate elements in a sentence.
[57t]

Diane worked *quickly,* but *efficiently.*
A written contract, not only a verbal agreement, is absolutely necessary.

Use a comma or commas to set off transposed modifiers.   [57u]

It was a successful party, *gay and happy.*
His expression, *dark and gloomy,* caught my attention.

Use a comma or commas to separate an absolute expression from the rest of the sentence. 　　　　　　　　　　　　　　　　　　　　　　[57v]

The waves being six feet high, we decided to stay out of the water.

For the first time, *the supply being exhausted,* he had to refuse orders.

Use a comma to show that a part of a clause has been omitted. 　[57w]

Rather than immediately repeat a word or a group of words, you may sometimes use a comma to show that such words are understood.

Frank was reared in Dayton; John, in Columbus. (The comma in this sentence shows that the verb *was reared* has been omitted from the second clause.)

DEVELOPING YOUR SKILL

A. The italicized clauses in the following sentences may be either restrictive or nonrestrictive—depending upon the meaning intended. Be prepared in class to explain the different meanings that would result from changing these clauses from restrictive to nonrestrictive.

1. Members *who have not attended* will not be charged.
2. Even statisticians *who have analyzed the facts* cannot agree on a solution to the problem.
3. The aircraft *which was first sketched by Leonardo da Vinci* is in mass production today.
4. The members of our basketball team *who are exceptionally tall* have a decided advantage over their opponents.

B. Determine where commas are necessary in each of the following sentences. After the proper number, write the words on a sheet of paper that should be followed by commas. Be sure to place a comma after each of these words.

1. In addition to these there are four more requirements.
2. If I were in his place I guess I would do the same.
3. To be on time you must get up an hour earlier.
4. At the beginning of the story I was very puzzled.
5. I knew even though he lied to me what the real situation was.
6. Which do you prefer coffee or tea?
7. We the people of the United States in order to form a more perfect Union establish justice insure domestic tranquility provide for the common defense promote the general welfare and secure the blessings of liberty to ourselves and our posterity do ordain and establish this Constitution for the United States of America.

8. Joan Wilson the president of our class voted against the new assessment of dues.

9. Frank who is an expert mechanic repairs his own car and for a small charge will repair yours.

10. On cold windy nights like these I would rather stay at home.

C. Correct the errors in the use of commas in the following sentences.

1. Mike and George are brothers; Tom and Phil cousins.
2. I'm going to buy a ticket aren't you?
3. Louise was born on Lincoln's Birthday; February, 12.
4. We didn't buy a new car last year, we bought two used cars this year.
5. "Did you inquire" she asked "whether we are going to be on time or not?"
6. We left having shut down our summer cottage for the city.
7. We telephoned grandmother long distance, she was not at home.
8. The exams were tough, I managed to pass.
9. Yes I'll go with you if you hurry and get ready.
10. This document *The Declaration of Independence* is cherished by all Americans.

THE SEMICOLON

A semicolon is used where a mark of punctuation stronger than a comma is needed. It is most often used in sentences that have two or more parts of equal rank.   **[58]**

Use a semicolon to separate related independent clauses that are not connected by a co-ordinating conjunction (*and*, *but*, *or*, *for*, *nor*).   **[58a]**

I don't care which car you buy; they are both good cars.

If a co-ordinating conjunction had been used to connect these clauses, a comma, not a semicolon, would have been required.

Do not forget that the clauses to be joined by a semicolon must be independent. A subordinate clause may be joined to an independent clause by a comma, but not by a semicolon.

I don't care which car you buy; *because they are both good cars.* (Incorrect)

Use a semicolon between independent clauses connected by a co-ordinating conjunction if the clauses contain commas or are long. [58b]

Our neighbors, the Grahams, are going to Martha's Vineyard for their vacation; and we are thinking of accompanying them.

Use a semicolon to separate independent clauses connected by such conjunctive adverbs as *however, therefore, consequently, nevertheless,* and *moreover.*

[58c]

James is very bright; *however,* he is not a good worker.

A conjunctive adverb may also be used as a pure adverb, without serving to connect independent clauses. When used as adverbs, such words as *however* and *therefore* are not preceded by semicolons; instead, they are set off by commas.

I did not go, *however,* for I could not afford a ticket.
I shall, *nevertheless,* vote for him for mayor.

Use a semicolon between items in a series if any of the members of the series contain commas. [58d]

On his fact-finding trip, he visited Davenport, Iowa; Rockford, Illinois; and Madison, Wisconsin.

Use a semicolon before such words of explanation as *for example, namely,* and *that is.* [58e]

Boston was the center for many famous American artists; namely, Winslow Homer, John Singer Sargent, and Gilbert Stuart.

DEVELOPING YOUR SKILL

Determine where semicolons are necessary in each of the following sentences. After the proper numbers write the words on a sheet of paper that should be followed by semicolons. Be sure to place a semicolon after each of these words.

1. Milly Adams, the girl next door, enjoys attending parties, however, she often stays at home to do her homework.

2. My friend, the postmaster, says that mail is rather light this time of year, and he ought to know, if anyone does.
3. There are eight national holidays in the United States, namely, New Year's Day, Washington's Birthday, Memorial Day, Independence Day, Labor Day, Veterans Day, Thanksgiving, and Christmas.
4. Our game was called off at the last minute, it was raining hard, and the field was soaked.
5. I think we ought to go home, moreover, I think we ought to go home right now.
6. All grammar rules must be based on the way people talk, for, when you come right down to it, there is no other standard.
7. The discussion was held on television, the best medium for such events, it can show the participants' reactions in detail.
8. Volcanoes are active in warm climates, such as South America and Africa, and they are even active in areas of extreme cold, such as the Antarctic.
9. My dentist advised me not to eat so much candy, he said that too much candy causes tooth decay.
10. They held a conference, the pitcher and the catcher, out at the mound, they decided to walk the next man up.

THE COLON

The chief function of a colon is to introduce something that will follow.
[59]

The colon is used mainly as a mark of formal introduction. It directs the reader's attention to something that will follow: a list of details, an explanation or a restatement, a quotation.

Use a colon to introduce a list when the items follow such words as *the following* **and** *these*.
[59a]

Poetry is usually divided into the three following types: dramatic, lyric, and narrative.

You should avoid using a comma after forms of the verb *be*, or when it will interrupt a sentence or a prepositional phrase.

Three types of poetry are: dramatic, lyric, and narrative. (Incorrect)
The three types of poetry consist of: drama, lyrics, and narratives. (Incorrect)

Use a colon after the salutation in a business letter.   [59b]

Dear Sirs: Dear Madam:

Use a colon to separate hours from minutes when expressing a time in figures. [59c]

   8:54 P.M.   7:30 A.M.   12:00 P.M.

Use a colon before a long, formal statement or a formal quotation [59d]

Hughes maintains that the following situation has come about: the conflict in the world between hostile ideologies is reflected in a new tenseness and anxiety in the emotions of every person living in this century.

In circumstances such as these, the Secretary always liked to recall a sentence from a letter by John Adams: "All great changes are irksome to the human mind, especially those which are attended with great dangers and uncertain effects."

Use a colon after a statement which is followed by an explanatory clause or expression. [59e]

Henry James was never really a popular novelist: none of his novels ever attained the sales of a modern best-seller.

Use a colon to separate the act from the scene of a play. [59f]

Some of the most eloquent lines in all of English poetry occur in Marlowe's *Doctor Faustus,* V:2. (Act V, Scene 2)

Use a colon to separate chapter and verse when referring to a specific Biblical selection. [59g]

Lincoln's reference to the "house divided" is from Mark 3:25. (Chapter 3, verse 25)

Use a colon to separate the title of a book or an article from its subtitle. [59h]

The Shadow Line: A Confession, by Joseph Conrad

"Death and Forever: Some Fears of War and Peace," by Sanford Gifford

DEVELOPING YOUR SKILL

Rewrite the following sentences, inserting colons where they are needed and removing them where they are incorrectly placed.

1. This year I'm taking courses in: English; algebra; history; and physics.
2. One of my favorite passages is Genesis 12;3-6.

3. Advertising is effective only if the following requirements are carried out; ads planned for a particular market, ads appear in the appropriate medium, distribution of the product adequate to meet increased demand brought about by ads.

4. The following quotation is from *Hamlet,* II, 2; "Use every man after his desert, and who shall 'scape whipping? Use them after your own honor and dignity."

5. You must present your birth certificate; your diploma, and two letters of recommendation.

6. His letters always began, "Dear Sir, I am pleased to write to you. . . ."

7. The full title of Mr. Aldridge's book is: *After the Lost Generation; A Critical Study of the Writers of Two Wars.*

8. Tom was always optimistic; he continually saw the bright side of every bad situation.

9. His idea was the following; to add five new words each day to build his French vocabulary.

10. So far as Jack understood, there were only two kinds of books in the world, those he read and bad books.

END PUNCTUATION

The period, the question mark, and the exclamation point all have one thing in common: they may be used to terminate or to end a sentence. For this reason all three marks are called *terminal* or *end punctuation.* The period, in addition to marking the end of a sentence, has several other uses, each of which will be described in this section.

Use a period at the end of a statement.   [60]

Phil knows all the words to all the latest songs.

Avoid writing *run-on* sentences caused by the omission of a period. [60a]

A sentence which consists of at least two independent clauses joined together without adequate punctuation is called a run-on sentence. Such sentences are fairly common in student writing.

Agnes was rather unhappy for she had not been invited to the party.

A period may be used to correct the punctuation of a run-on sentence. The conjunction is then dropped.

Agnes was rather unhappy. She had not been invited to the party.

A run-on sentence may also be corrected by using a semicolon, a comma and a co-ordinating conjunction, or a subordinating conjunction.

Agnes was rather unhappy; she had not been invited to the party.
Agnes was rather unhappy, *for* she had been not invited to the party.
Agnes was rather unhappy *because* she had not been invited to the party.

Use a period after abbreviations. [60b]

All but a few abbreviations should be avoided in formal writing. A period is required after the following abbreviations.

Dr.	M.A.	etc.	P.O. Box
Mr.	M.D.	Jr.	R.R. (Rural Route)
Mrs.	Ph.D.	Sr.	R.F.D.

Abbreviations occurring after a proper name are usually separated from the name by a comma: *Arthur Norman, Ph.D.* But when an abbreviated title appears before a name, it is not separated by a comma: *Dr. Stephen A. Mitchell.*

Some titles may not be abbreviated and should be written out in full:

Bishop	Professor
General	Senator
President	Reverend

Some abbreviations are written with no periods:

AAA	NATO
CBS	UN
APO	per cent

Use a period to end a mild imperative sentence.   [60c]

Please follow me.

Use a period at the end of an indirect question.   [60d]

I wonder whether you would care to go.

Use a period at the end of a simple request that is stated in the form of a question for the sake of courtesy.   [60e]

Would you tell the doctor that I am waiting.

Use a period after each number or letter in an outline, except for those enclosed in parentheses.   [60f]

> I.
> > A.
> > > 1.
> > > 2.
> > > > a.
> > > > b.
> > > > > (1)
> > > > > (2)
> > B.
> II.

Use periods to indicate ellipses.   [60g]

You may often wish to cite a quotation—but sometimes not all of it. In such cases you must indicate what has been deleted by using points of ellipses—a series of three dots. If you delete material from the end of a sentence, you must add a period, making four dots in all.

"The public buys its opinions as it buys . . . its milk, on the principle that it is cheaper to do this than to own a cow. . . . but the milk is more likely to be watered."

—Samuel Butler, *Note-Books*

Use a question mark at the end of a question.   [61]

How soon will you deliver my new car?
We all asked, "Are you going now?"

Use a question mark enclosed in parentheses to express uncertainty or doubt.　　　　　　　　　　　　　　　　　　　　　　　　　　　**[61a]**

Geoffrey Chaucer was born in London in 1340 (?).

The question mark shows that you have searched for a particular fact and that the authorities are uncertain about it. Do not use a question mark to indicate merely that you are uncertain.

For indicating the uncertainty of dates, you may prefer to use the abbreviation *c.*

Geoffrey Chaucer was born in London c. 1340.

The abbreviation *c.* stands for the Latin word *circa,* which means *about.* This abbreviation cannot be used to express doubt about anything other than a date. It cannot be used, for example, to express doubt about a person's place of birth.

Use question marks after elliptical questions in a series.　　　**[61b]**

Have you seen Ned? Or Jim? Or Bill?

Use an exclamation point at the end of an exclamatory sentence.　　**[62]**

What a fine job you've done!

An exclamation point may also be used after an interjection.

O! What a beautiful day it is!

Whether an exclamation point or period is used after an imperative sentence depends upon the intensity of emotion the writer wishes to convey. A period follows a mild imperative; an exclamation point follows a strong imperative.

Please hurry. (Mild imperative)
Hurry up! (Strong imperative)

DEVELOPING YOUR SKILL

A. Rewrite the following sentences, correcting whatever mistakes you find in the use of abbreviations, periods, question marks, and exclamation points.

1. "Where did the fire begin," asked the chief?
2. "Stop where you are," shouted the guard.
3. That's William Mills Ed D, not William Mills M D.

4. How many books have you? Two Three Four.

5. Jane asked whether she could come with us?

B. Rewrite the following sentences, making sure that the proper marks of punctuation are present and correctly placed.

1. Will you please take me to your leader?

2. Hey there, You with the red hat, where are you going?

3. I've finished all my work now I can relax a little.

4. His address is the following: "Gen. C. G. Stewart, Far East Command, APO 971, San Francisco, California 94100."

5. Pres. Roosevelt and Prime Minister Churchill declared the *Atlantic Charter* in August of 1941.

6. Men are said to be the best cooks in the world, I doubt very much that they are.

7. We inquired whether the flight from New York would be on time?

8. Born in (?) 1494 near Chinon, the French writer Rabelais became famous for his satire *Gargantua*.

9. A team of C.B.S. and N.B.C. newsmen were on hand to interview Sen. Smythe.

10. Would you please close the door?

QUOTATION MARKS

Quotation marks are used to enclose direct quotations—a speaker's exact words.   [63]

There are four basic ways in which these marks may be used. The following situations illustrate each of these ways:

Type A: "___," he said.
Type B: He said, "___."
Type C: "___," he continued, "___."
Type D: "___," he concluded. "___."

The first word of a direct quotation is always capitalized. The first word in the second part of a broken quotation is not capitalized (Type C) unless a new sentence begins (Type D). Material which is directly quoted is usually separated from the main text by some mark of punctuation—one or more commas, a period, an exclamation point, a question mark.

Do not use quotation marks with indirect quotations.   [63a]

Pete said, "I have a new job." (Direct quotation)
Pete said that he had a new job. (Indirect quotation)

Quotation marks always follow commas and periods and precede semi-colons and colons. The position of quotation marks with exclamation points and question marks varies with the particular situation.　　　**[63b]**

"Let's go and investigate," said Harry.

Lou sat further back in his chair. "I think I'll stay here."

Harry asked me, "Coming?" (Only the quotation is a question.)

Lou's response puzzled me. Why did Lou say, "I'll stay here"? (The question mark applies to the whole sentence.)

I said to Harry, "You bet I am"; and I arose, moving toward the door. (The semicolon applies to the whole first clause.)

Begin a new paragraph each time the speaker changes in dialogue (two or more persons speaking).　　　**[63c]**

"What time have you?" Irene asked.

"My watch isn't running," Arthur replied, unstrapping it from his wrist and tapping it gently against the desk.

"Well, how am I going to find out what time it is?"

"There's a sundial in the garden, you know." Arthur smiled.

If you have a quotation that runs continuously for several paragraphs, you should place quotation marks only at the beginning of the first paragraph, and at the end of the final paragraph.

Use quotation marks with titles of short stories and poems, and titles of chapters, articles, and other parts of books and magazines.　　　**[63d]**

Somebody once remarked that "The Ancient Mariner" would not have been so successful a poem if Coleridge had called it "The Old Sailor."

Use single quotation marks to set off a quotation within a quotation.

[63e]

"Wordsworth wrote that poetry is 'emotion recollected in tranquillity.' "

Use quotation marks to enclose words or expressions used in a special sense.   [63f]

The "diaphragm" on the lens of the camera helps the photographer to determine his exposure. (A technical word used in non-technical writing)

The pile drivers were going "ka-phoom" outside my window all day long. (A coined word)

Lucy "jumped for joy" when Naomi told her. (A colloquial expression)

Some authorities object to colloquialisms enclosed in quotes. These authorities argue that if a word or an expression is so inappropriate to the context that it requires quotes, it should not be used at all. Before you use such an expression, consider whether another expression would not be more suitable.

 DEVELOPING YOUR SKILL

Rewrite the following sentences, making sure that they are punctuated correctly.

1. The unicorn is a mythical beast, said her husband. such an animal simply does not exist.
2. Yvonne always refers to her costume jewelry as goldry.
3. Bob thought that "we ought to stay at home."
4. His chapter "on rockets" is the best one in the book.
5. "What Churchill really said," our teacher continued, "was "blood, toil, tears, and sweat," not "blood, sweat, and tears."
6. Katherine Anne Porter's fine story 'Flowering Judas' is about a political bandit in Mexico.
7. "If I agree to go with you?" he said, "then will you come."
8. "No more"! he shouted. "I've had enough."
9. Frank asked, "where did you park the car"?
10. Hemingway's short story *The Killers* is thought to be one of his best.

THE APOSTROPHE

The apostrophe is used with the possessive forms of nouns, with contractions, and with the plurals of letters and numerals.

Use the apostrophe (') to indicate omitted letters, to indicate certain possessives, and to form certain plurals.   **[64]**

The apostrophe is used to indicate that one or more letters have been omitted in a contraction.   **[64a]**

they have	becomes	*they've*
do not	becomes	*don't*
is not	becomes	*isn't*
he will	becomes	*he'll*

When *will not* is contracted, the letter *o* is dropped and the spelling is changed: *won't.*

Use the apostrophe with a noun to indicate possession.   **[64b]**

SINGULAR	PLURAL
lady's	ladies'
man's	men's

Singular nouns and plural nouns that do not end in *s* add an apostrophe and *s* (*'s*) to form the possessive; plural nouns that end in *s* add only an apostrophe (*'*).

For a complete discussion of the formation of the possessive case, see rules 37a through 37j in this text.

Use the apostrophe to form certain plurals.   **[64c]**

Plurals of letters, figures, and other symbols are shown by adding *'s*.

Dot your *i*'s and cross your *t*'s.
Naomi writes her *5*'s like *6*'s.

For additional information, see rule 55e, page 379.

Some organizations of living persons may be considered possessive.
[64d]

Our *firm's* business is mainly in South America.
The *states'* sovereignty is protected by the Constitution.

With the exception of a few idioms, the names of non-living things form their possessive with the preposition *of*.

the handle *of* the door (not, the door's handle)
a *stone's* throw (idiomatic exception)

Certain expressions of time, words indicating amount in dollars and cents, and certain idiomatic expressions may be possessive.   [64e]

SINGULAR	PLURAL
a week's pay	two weeks' pay
a penny's worth	two pennies' worth

Use an apostrophe to show the omission of figures in a date or of letters in a dialectal word.   [64f]

the class of '*64*

When a writer wishes to show a dialectal pronunciation, he may omit letters from words. Where these omissions occur, he should indicate by an apostrophe.

"You go '*bout* two miles '*fore* you come to a fork in the road."

Use an apostrophe to form the plural of words referred to as words.
[64g]

My teacher told me I used too many *and's* in my compositions.

Do not use an apostrophe with pronouns ending in *self* or *selves*.   [64h]

Some things one must learn for *oneself* (not *ones'elf*).
They can only hurt *themselves* (not *themselves'*) by acting like that.

 DEVELOPING YOUR SKILL

Rewrite the following sentences, making sure that each has the necessary apostrophes and that they are correctly placed. Correct any errors in the use of contractions.

1. The childs eyes widened as he opened his birthday presents.
2. Willn't you come home, Bill Bailey?
3. "Minding your ps and qs" is a very old-fashioned expression.
4. We received a bonus of three month's pay last Christmas.
5. The class of 54 is going to play this years graduating class.
6. "We hardly knew whether we were comin or goin."
7. Our house's roof leaks.
8. Your too late to be of any use.
9. A womens committee was formed to raise funds for our church.
10. On Messrs. Johnsons recommendation, I am offering you the job.

THE DASH

The chief use of a dash is to indicate to the reader that a sudden shift in structure or thought is occurring. The dash is most effective when used sparingly.

Use the dash (—) to show changes or interruptions in the thought of a sentence.   [65]

Use the dash to indicate a sudden change in the direction of thought.
                                                                [65a]

His dogs—there are only two of them left now—don't seem to thrive on peanuts and vitamin pills.

Use a dash to indicate a suddenly interrupted bit of conversation.   [65b]

When a sentence in dialogue is broken off in the middle, only a dash and quotation marks are needed to end the sentence.

Mac's face flushed red, "Do you mean to say—"
"Yes, that's exactly what I mean."

Use a dash to set off long, complicated appositives that are themselves punctuated with commas.   [65c]

Cornering the market—that is to say, buying up all the available shares of a company in anticipation of a demand for those shares—is such an expensive operation today that it rarely happens.

Use a dash to give emphasis or suspense to parenthetical material. [65d]

A boy becomes a man when he no longer walks through puddles—but around them.

Use a dash to set off a summarizing clause.   [65e]

Sixty-seven cents in change, a broken pocket knife, an old newspaper clipping—these were all he had left in the world.

Use a dash in dialogue to indicate hesitation.   [65f]

"Well, are you for us or against us?"

"I—I—I just can't say."

DEVELOPING YOUR SKILL

Rewrite the following sentences, inserting dashes where they are required. It will be necessary for you to alter some of the other marks of punctuation.

1. If you take a trip it would have to be a short one why don't you borrow my scooter?
2. Three French hens, two turtledoves, a partridge in a pear tree, these my true love gave to me.
3. "No, I," his voice broke off.
4. We finally sold our car, a fine, old rattletrap with many interesting noises.
5. My project on which I had worked for months was completed at last as I slipped the final section of the ship into the bottle.

THE HYPHEN

The hyphen is used chiefly to bind words and word elements into compounds. It has other uses—such as dividing words into syllables—which will be explained in this section.

Use the hyphen in compound adjectives, after certain prefixes, and in words that must be divided at the ends of lines.   [66]

Use the hyphen between the parts of compound numbers from twenty-one to ninety-nine.   [66a]

forty-three   one hundred eighty-five

Use the hyphen between the words in a compound adjective—words that, used together, form a single modifier of a noun or a pronoun.   [66b]

his off-the-record comments

his grief-stricken widow

When two or more compounds modify the same noun, the noun may be given only once.

second- and third-year students

Use a hyphen between certain prefixes and the proper nouns or adjectives that are used with them. [66c]

pro-American

ex-governor Stevenson

neo-classical

post-Victorian

Use a hyphen to divide a word between syllables at the end of a line. [66d]

prepara-

tory

prob-

able

Use a hyphen between the numerator and denominator of a fraction used as an adjective. [66e]

Gould owned a *two-thirds* interest in the company. (Adjective)

Gould owned *two thirds* of the company's stock. (Noun)

Use a hyphen to join the parts of certain compound nouns, adverbs, and verbs. [66f]

NOUNS	ADVERBS	VERBS
brother-in-law	full-throatedly	dry-clean
light-year	hot-temperedly	hand-wash

Use a hyphen to distinguish words of similar spelling, but of different meanings. [66g]

re-creation from *recreation*   *re-cover* from *recover*

Use a hyphen to show the omission of a connecting word. [66h]

pages 65-73 (The word *through* omitted)

DEVELOPING YOUR SKILL

Rewrite the following sentences, making any changes necessary so that the words in these sentences will be correctly hyphenated.

1. There are forty four beans in every cup of our coffee.
2. His booming, pear shaped tones quickly put the audience to sleep.
3. The troops reformed their lines for a new attack.
4. The movie was advertised as a never to be forgotten experience—but I can't remember its name.
5. The preVictorian world now seems to have been much more easy going.

ITALICS (UNDERLINING)

Italics are used to distinguish titles, words and letters used out of context, and foreign words. Occasionally italics are used for the sake of emphasis.

Italic type (in which the letters slant upward and to the right) is simulated by underlining in writing and typing.   [67]

Use italic type for the titles of books, newspapers, magazines, works of art—such as statues, musical compositions, pictures—and the names of airplanes, ships, trains, missiles, and rockets.   [67a]

> The House of Mirth (Title of a novel)
> Washington Post and Times Herald (Name of a
>   newspaper)
> Vogue (Name of a magazine)
> An Arrangement in Grey and Black (Title of a
>   painting)
> U.S.S. Enterprise (Name of a ship)
> Twentieth Century Limited (Name of a train)
> Atlas (Name of a guided missile)

Use italic type for words, letters, and numerals referred to as such. [67b]

> He'll say *but* once too often.
> That is a *4*, not an *H*.

Use italic type for foreign words and phrases.   [67c]

> Oliver Cromwell wasn't noted for his *joie de vivre*.

Italics are sometimes used for emphasis.   [67d]

> I will *not* give up the ship!

 DEVELOPING YOUR SKILL

On a sheet of paper write all the words in the following sentences that should be in italic type. Be sure to underline these words.

1. Do not use the word consul when you mean council.
2. Homer's Odyssey has been the basis for a famous Victorian poem and a modern novel.
3. The word referred has three r's in it.
4. What does it mean to be au courant?
5. The Normandy was converted to a troopship during the war.
6. How much are twelve 7's?
7. That's a funny way to spell convenience.
8. They can always raise a large army—i.e., gather a large number of untrained men to wear uniforms.
9. Which do you prefer—Newsweek or Time?
10. It seems as though a de facto recognition of their government is impossible to avoid.

PARENTHESES

Matter which is incidental or explanatory (comments, dates, details, page references) may be set off by parentheses. Frequently dashes may be used instead; often commas may be used.

Use parentheses to enclose material that is explanatory or incidental.
[68a]

The Duke's country estate (loaded down as it was with back taxes) was thrown open to the public for tours, at two shillings per person.

Parenthetical material is not capitalized unless it would be normally— for example, if it included a proper noun. Punctuation which belongs with such material is included within the parentheses.

Often in his defense of freedom of expression (see his *Areopagitica,* pp. 31-35), Milton would claim as his right what he would not allow others.

Use parentheses to enclose material that gives directions or references.
[68b]

Read Dr. Wolf's discussion (Chapter 3) of the duties of his commission.

Use parentheses to mark numbered or lettered divisions within sentences or paragraphs. [68c]

Numbers and letters enclosed in parentheses are not followed by periods.

A player shall lose the rally if he: (a) fails to return the ball legally to the front wall, (b) intentionally interferes with his opponent, (c) is struck with the ball after it has rebounded from the front wall.

DEVELOPING YOUR SKILL

Write the following sentences on a sheet of paper, enclosing any parenthetical material within parentheses.

1. If you run into Jan at the meeting I'm sure she'll be there, ask her to phone me some time next week.

2. Bricks are usually manufactured by one of the three following processes: 1 stiff-mud process, 2 soft-mud process, or 3 dry-press process.
3. If you look up the rule see Chapter 12, you will learn how to punctuate that sentence.
4. I can't pick him out can you? in all that crowd.
5. This book remember I told you to read the first chapter? is now a best
   seller.

BRACKETS   [69]

Brackets are a somewhat specialized mark of punctuation, and not used
in informal writing. Their function is to enclose material added by the
writer to clarify quotations he has used.

**Use brackets to enclose material that has been interpolated by someone
other than the original writer or speaker.**   [69a]

In his narrative he noted that, "Though several newspapers took the
side of Cook against Peary [in the dispute about who had reached the
North Pole first], Danish scientists proved Cook's claim false."

**Use brackets enclosing the word *sic* to show that an error in quoted mate-
rial is one that occurs in the original material.**   [69b]

Kempf writes, "This apparati [*sic*] is not likely to operate effectively
under the extremes of lunar temperatures."

DEVELOPING YOUR SKILL

Write the following sentences on a sheet of paper, inserting brackets
where they are needed. In some places you may also have to insert the term
sic.

1. Richard began his letter of application, "I am hopping to work for you
   because . . . ."
2. The word *goyim* original meaning a *tribe* or a *nation* is now commonly
   used in a derogatory sense.
3. His biographer said, "He Burns was more interested in writing poetry
   than in enforcing the laws of the customs office."
4. The burglars left a note saying, "We liked your food. Butch injoyed
   the apple pie best."
5. "In 1854 she Florence Nightingale arrived in the Crimea with a group
   of nurses to tend the British soldiers wounded in the Battle of Bala-
   clava."

Review Exercises — Punctuation

A. Rewrite each of the following sentences, inserting or omitting punctuation, underlining what should be written in italics, and correctly capitalizing words.

1. To top it all off I caught a bad cold and had to stay in bed for a week.
2. This evening gentlemen we are going to discuss only business.
3. He left moreover without saying good-by.
4. I don't care if Liz is going to the dance I must stay home and study.
5. Go to either island, you will have a fine time whichever you choose.
6. If you leave at 730 A.M. you should be there in an hour.
7. Al felt great for he had won first place.
8. Life on the Mississippi, you've read it haven't you? is now published in an inexpensive paperback edition.
9. Quite a few preVictorian notions about psychology have proved correct; much to our amazement
10. Would you rather read Look than Life?

B. Rewrite the following paragraphs so that they are correctly punctuated.

J P Morgan who had helped to organize the United States steel corporation in the early 1900s was probably the most powerful and influential financier of his time. Like other very rich men of that era Morgan liked to do things on a grand scale but he insisted on doing them well. His yacht Columbia for example was four time winner of the America's Cup.

Educated in Germany at the University of Goettingen Morgan early developed a strong interest in rare books and manuscripts an interest that he kept up all his life. He accumulated one of the finest private collections in the world. In 1923 Morgans' son, John Pierpont jr, dedicated his fathers library to research scholarship.

4. Form in Writing

Letter writing is the one form of writing practiced almost universally. Nearly everyone at some time or other has written a letter—and most people have written many. The conventions of form for this type of writing are not subject to much variation. A deviation from the standard is quite noticeable and usually distracting. The writer should strive therefore to observe the conventions of form so that his reader may fully concentrate on the content of the letter.

In this section you will also learn to observe the conventions of making outlines and writing paragraphs.

SYLLABICATION

In order to keep the right-hand margin of your writing fairly even, you will often find it necessary to "break" words at the end of a line. Such breaks, or divisions, must be done correctly. Most dictionaries and most publishers break words into syllables according to their pronunciation, not according to roots and affixes.

Syllabication is the division of words into syllables. [70]

The following rules will help you to determine the correct syllabication of words. If you are in doubt about where to divide a word, consult your dictionary.

Divide a word at the end of a line only between syllables. A one-syllable word may not be divided. [70a]

> prayer (not pray-er)   scratched (not scratch-ed)

Do not divide a word so that a single letter stands by itself at the end of the line or at the beginning of the next line. [70b]

> April (not A-pril)   many (not man-y)
> oblige (not o-blige)   showy (not show-y)

Do not carry over a group of letters that contains only a silent vowel sound. [70c]

> handle (not han-dle)   rustle (not rus-tle)

Usually, divide a word after a prefix or before a suffix. [70d]

> con-fide   friend-ship
> sub-mit   knight-hood

Usually, divide a word between two consonants. [70e]

Words that contain double consonants are usually divided between the double consonants.

> drop-ping   but-ter
> bat-ter   fun-ny

Double consonants that are part of the root are not divided.

guess-ing   cross-ing
will-ing   pass-ing

Two consonants that occur between two vowels may be divided if each consonant is separately pronounced.

ab-solve   in-nate
gos-sip   in-fil-trate

If two consonants are pronounced as a single sound, they should not be divided.

assi*gn*-ment   no*th*-ing

Do not divide proper names into syllables.   [70f]

Raymond (not Ray-mond)   Beckman (not Beck-man)

Do not divide words that would cause difficulties in pronunciation. [70g]

raging (not rag-ing)   women (not wo-men)

DEVELOPING YOUR SKILL

Hyphenate the words in the following list to show where they may be divided at the ends of lines. Some words may be divided at more than one place. If a word should not be divided, write that word without hyphens on your sheet of paper beside the appropriate number.

1. erupt   6. Johnson
2. hearth   7. revolt
3. satiety   8. wonderful
4. against   9. understand
5. leprosy   10. cordial

THE PARAGRAPH

A paragraph is an orderly arrangement of sentences, all of which are related to a single topic.   [71]

Each paragraph you write should have unity, coherence, and proper emphasis. Unity may be obtained through use of a topic sentence, either expressed in the paragraph or understood. Coherence may be obtained by arranging the sentences in a logical order and by using transitional devices. Proper emphasis is obtained by proportioning your treatment to the importance of your ideas and by placing the most important ideas in the most emphatic positions—the beginning and the end of the paragraph.

Depending upon the nature of your material, you will choose one of three general methods for developing individual paragraphs and series of paragraphs within a composition. You may arrange your material in chronological order, in spatial order, or in the order of importance.

Chronological development is probably the most commonly used of these three methods. In developing paragraphs chronologically, you simply record events in their order of occurrence. This is the method frequently used by sports writers in reporting a game or an event.

Spatial development is reserved almost exclusively for describing the physical appearance of a person, an object, or a scene. You may develop paragraphs describing a landscape, for example, by first mentioning objects that are far away, then those in the middle distance, then those close at hand. Or, you may exactly reverse this procedure. The point to remember in developing a paragraph spatially is that you must arrange your details into a pattern that enables your reader to form a clear idea of what you are describing.

Development by importance is chiefly used in argument and persuasion. In using this method, you will usually proceed by stages from the least important idea to the most important idea. You will not jump back and forth between major and minor ideas. The one notable exception to beginning with a minor idea occurs in news writing. Many newspapers and some magazines begin their stories with the most important idea in order to catch the reader's attention. This style is not recommended for your general writing.

Indent the first line of every paragraph, except in letters written in block form.   [71a]

Paragraphs of letters written in the indented and semiblock styles are indented about three fourths of an inch or, if you are using a typewriter, about seven spaces. Letters typed in the block form are not indented, and each paragraph begins at the left-hand margin.

Do not leave blank space on a line unless a new paragraph is to begin on the next line.   [71b]

Each line of a paragraph after the first line should begin at the left margin and continue across the page until the line is filled. Only the last line of a paragraph may be partially filled.

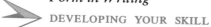

The following sentences make up two complete paragraphs. But their original order has been scrambled. On a sheet of paper rewrite these sentences, restoring the paragraphs to their original order. Be sure to consider the principles of unity, coherence, and emphasis as well as those of form when you rewrite these paragraphs. After you have rewritten these paragraphs, tell whether they follow a chronological order, a spatial order, or an order of importance.

The President's secretary and the secret service men had warned him against such a public reception. The day at the Pan-American Exposition in Buffalo was boiling hot. But McKinley liked to meet people and, most of all, he liked to shake hands. Only the President seemed cool and energetic, as he stood in the Temple of Music, shaking hands with the public. Everyone had his handkerchief out in an effort to soak up some of the heat.

A week later McKinley was dead, the third President of the United States to be assassinated. The first bullet struck a button on McKinley's vest and was deflected; the second went deep into his body. McKinley noticed that the right hand of the next man in line was wrapped in a handkerchief. At just that moment two shafts of fire darted out from the bandaged hand, striking the President full in the chest. Instinctively he shifted his position to reach out for the man's left hand.

OUTLINES   [72]

An outline is a plan for a piece of writing. It shows in skeleton form the sequence and the relative importance of each idea in a piece of exposition or argument. (Description and narration are not usually outlined.)

The main headings in an outline are labeled with Roman numerals. Subtopics are indented and labeled with letters and numbers. A major subtopic is labeled with a capital letter; a minor subtopic, with an Arabic number. If further subdvisions are needed, Arabic numbers in parentheses and, then, lower case letters in parentheses are used. Each division of an outline must have at least two subtopics. You cannot divide something into only one part.

The only heading in your outline that will not have a letter or a number in front of it is the title.

Two types of outlines are in common use—the *topic outline* and the *sentence outline*.

A topic outline is one in which each heading and subheading is a word, a phrase, or a dependent clause. [72a]

In the following topic outline, notice that each entry begins with a capital letter, but does not end with a period. The topics and subtopics in this outline are key words and phrases.

English as a Universal Language

  I. History and potentialities of universal languages

     A. Two types of universal language

        1. Manufactured language

            a. Volapük

            b. Esperanto

            c. Ido

        2. Modification of a living language

     B. English best chance of becoming universal language

  II. Basic English a systematic modification of English

     A. Make-up of Basic English vocabulary

     B. Level of Basic English vocabulary

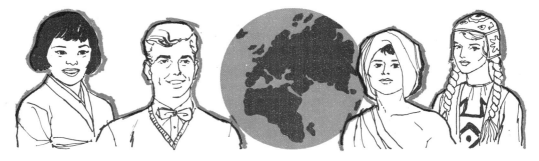

When you wish to have a more detailed outline, you should make a sentence outline rather than a topic outline.

A sentence outline is one in which each heading and subheading is a complete sentence. [72b]

The numbering and lettering in a sentence outline is the same as that in a topic outline. Since each topic and subtopic is a complete sentence, each entry in this outline must begin with a capital letter and end with terminal punctuation, usually a period. Follow the style of the following sentence outline.

English as a Universal Language

I. Since the fall of the Tower of Babel, men have sought to dissolve the barriers between them by creating a universal language.
  A. Attempts at creating a universal language are of two distinct kinds.
    1. The first type of universal language is manufactured on logical principles. There are three such languages that have met with some degree of success.
      a. Volapük was constructed from Latin roots still in use in European languages.
      b. Esperanto uses roots of other European languages and allows no grammatical irregularities.
      c. Ido is a modification of Esperanto.
    2. The second type of a universal language is a modification of some existing, popular language.
  B. Of all existing languages, English probably has the best chance of becoming a universal language.

II. Basic English is a systematic modification of Modern English.
  A. Basic English is made up of 850 English Words—600 nouns; 150 adjectives; 16 verbs; 20 prepositions. The remaining words "operate" with nouns and adjectives. There are about 250 idioms that must also be memorized.
  B. The majority of these words are used by six-year olds. By mastering Basic English, a foreigner can make himself easily understood by a native speaker.

DEVELOPING YOUR SKILL

Choose one of the following titles as your subject for a topic or a sentence outline. Construct an outline for this title.
1. The Monroe Doctrine and Latin America Today
2. When I Ran away from Home
3. Some New Rules for Football
4. Outside Support for Art and the Theater

LETTER WRITING

There are three general styles for both business and social correspondence—the *indented*, *block*, and *semiblock styles*. The indented style is usually reserved for social letters; while the block and the semiblock styles are usually reserved for business letters.

In letters written in indented style, the second and third lines of the heading, the first word in each paragraph in the body, and the signature are indented.   [73a]

Letters written in block style have no indentions in any part of the letter.
                                    [73b]

Letters written in semiblock style have only the first word in each paragraph in the body indented; the rest of the letter is in block style.   [73c]

The diagrams that follow illustrate the form of the block, semiblock, and indented styles. An additional diagram illustrates the *full block style*, which is really a modification of the block style.

FULL BLOCK   BLOCK

SEMIBLOCK   INDENTED

Business letters are usually typed; social letters are usually written in longhand. The name of the sender of a business letter is usually typed under his signature.

Every letter is made up of distinct parts. The business letter usually has six parts; the social letter usually has five parts.

The heading of a letter contains the sender's street address, city, state, zip code, and the date. [73d]

INDENTED STYLE	BLOCK STYLE
215 E. Chestnut Street	215 E. Chestnut Street
Clifton, Idaho 83228	Clifton, Idaho 83228
April 17, 19—	April 17, 19--

Business letters are often written on stationery that has the name of the firm printed across the top. When stationery contains a letterhead, it is not necessary to duplicate this information, and only the date is written in the place of the heading.

Though it is best to confine a business letter to a single page, it is not always possible to do so. When more than one page is required, a special heading is used across the top of each additional page. This heading contains the name of the person to whom the letter is addressed, the page number, and the date:

Mr. R. J. Wilkes   2.   April 17, 19--

The inside address, which is used only in business letters, contains the name of the person (or company) to whom the letter is written, the street address, the city, the state, and the zip code. [73e]

INDENTED STYLE	BLOCK STYLE
Mr. R. J. Wilkes	Mr. R. J. Wilkes
Division Sales Manager	Division Sales Manager
Western National Rubber Co.	Western National Rubber Co.
704 Graves Street	704 Graves Street
Seattle, Washington 98102	Seattle, Washington 98102

Abbreviations are not usually used in the inside address. When, however, the official title of a business firm includes an abbreviation, the abbreviation should be used. For example, most firms using the word *incorporated* in their title use the abbreviation *Inc.*

The salutation is the writer's greeting to the recipient of the letter. [73f]

In social letters the salutation is informal and is followed by a comma; in business letters the salutation is more formal and is followed by a colon. The salutation always begins in the left margin. The first word and all nouns in the salutation are capitalized.

SOCIAL LETTERS   BUSINESS LETTERS

Dear Roy,   Dear Mr. Wilkes:

The body of the letter is that part in which the sender writes his message or states his business.   [73g]

In both business and social letters, extra space is left between the salutation and the line preceding the salutation. In business letters extra space is left between the salutation and the body of the letter; in social letters and in letters written in longhand, no extra space is left.

The complimentary close is a concluding expression of regard for the recipient of the letter.   [73h]

The wording of the complimentary close should be appropriate to the tone of your letter and to the relationship which exists between you and the person who is to receive your letter. The first word of the complimentary close begins with a capital letter and the last word is followed by a comma.

SOCIAL LETTERS   BUSINESS LETTERS

Your pal,   Yours truly,
As ever,   Sincerely yours,
Yours,   Respectfully yours.

The signature is the sender's handwritten name.   [73i]

You should sign your letter in ink, whether it was written by hand or typewritten. In a social letter you may sign your first name only if you are sure that it will be recognized. In a business letter you should sign your full name. If your letter is typewritten, leave four spaces below the complimentary close and type your name. Between the complimentary close and the typed name, write your signature.

INDENTED STYLE　　　　　　　BLOCK STYLE

Your pal,
Al

Yours very truly,

Albert F. Kempf

Albert F. Kempf

Though the title *Mr.* is never used in a signature, a woman may use *Miss* or *Mrs.* to indicate how a reply should be addressed to her. If a woman signs her name without any title, it is assumed that she is unmarried. She may, however, write *Miss* in parentheses before her signature. A married woman may write *Mrs.* in parentheses before her signature, or she may write her married name in parentheses under her signature.

UNMARRIED WOMAN　　　　　　MARRIED WOMAN

Yours truly,
Diane Cherin

Yours truly,
(Mrs.) Agnes Bishop

or　　　　　　　　　　　　　*or*

Yours truly,
(Miss) Diane Cherin

Yours truly,
Agnes Bishop
(Mrs. James Bishop)

Two addresses appear on the envelope. The first is the *return address* and the second is the *mailing address*. The style in which these addresses are written should match that used in the letter.

The return address on the envelope contains the sender's full name and address. [73j]

The return address is usually placed in the upper left-hand corner of the envelope. The name of the city, the name of the state, and the zip code should all be written on one line. Do not use commas at the ends of the lines. Abbreviations may be used.

The mailing address on the envelope contains the full name and address of the person (or company) to whom the letter is being sent.   [73k]

The mailing address is usually placed about halfway down from the top of the envelope and is usually begun a little left of the center. Abbreviations should not be used unless they are a part of the name. Again, commas are not used at the ends of lines.

> Diane Cherin
>   1115 W. Washington Blvd.
>   Chicago, Ill. 60631
>
>
>
>   Mrs. James Bishop
>   1545 Lake Shore Drive
>   Chicago, Illinois 60610

DEVELOPING YOUR SKILL

A. Write one of the following business letters:
   1. A request to your representative in the legislature to bring about certain improvements in your neighborhood.
   2. A request to the circulation manager of a magazine to change your mailing address.

B. Write one of the following social letters:

   1. An answer to a friend's inquiry about a course you are taking in school this year.
   2. An invitation to a friend to spend the week end with you.

Review Exercises—Form in Writing

A. Hyphenate the following words to show where they should be syllabicated. Not all of the following words may be syllabicated.

sentinel	probate	arbitrate
their	absolve	preparation

B. Prepare a topic outline or a sentence outline for one of the following subjects. If your teacher wishes, you may use a subject of your own.

1. Houses I Have Lived In
2. The Results of the TVA Program
3. Dixieland Jazz *vs.* Progressive Jazz
4. Military Service in Peacetime

C. Write two letters—one a social letter, the other a business letter—to be submitted to your teacher. You should also indicate the form for addressing the envelopes for the letter.

D. Read the following paragraph. The original order of the sentences has been scrambled. On a sheet of paper rewrite this paragraph, restoring it to its original order. Tell whether this paragraph was developed spatially, chronologically, or by importance.

On his second day in the trenches, he decided to try it out. It was a remarkable shot, considering that the sniper had a target only about an inch square. And the damaged periscope would make quite a souvenir—and perhaps, an interesting story. She said that she had returned the periscope to the store where he bought it and made them refund its price in full. A few weeks later, he received a note from his mother. No sooner had he begun to look around than an enemy sniper, over four hundred yards away, put a bullet through the center of the top eyepiece. He arrived back in France with a new trench-periscope that he had purchased on leave in England. He wrapped it up carefully and sent it home to his mother in England.

UNIT SUMMARY

The devices of punctuation are an attempt to approximate the resources of the spoken language for clarifying meaning. Unless you learn to punctuate correctly, you continuously run the risk of distorting your meaning.

In this unit you saw how the standard marks of punctuation are used to clarify meaning. You have learned to use the comma, the semicolon, the colon, and the marks of terminal punctuation. You have learned to recognize when a dash or parentheses or brackets is needed.

In addition, you have learned to observe the correct form in writing. You have learned the mechanics of letter writing and of paragraphing.

UNIT REVIEW EXERCISES

DISCUSSION TOPICS

A. Explain the relation of punctuation to the spoken language. Give examples.
B. Discuss paragraphing in relation to the principles of unity, coherence, and emphasis.
C. What is the importance of proofreading what you write?

WRITTEN WORK

A. Arrange the following numerals and letters into the correct form for an outline. Do not change their sequence.
I, A, 1, a, b, 2, a, b, 3, B, 1, 2, II, A, 1, 2, 3, B, 1, 2
B. Write the form requested in parentheses after each of the following words:

father-in-law (plural)	trace (add *able*)
data (singular)	ox (plural)
trace (add *ing*)	kangaroo (plural)
thesis (plural)	carry (add *ing*)

C. Rewrite the following sentences, correcting all errors in mechanics and spelling.

1. I ask for your attention ladys so that I may conclude my remarks.
2. Alice was dissappointed for she had spent much time memorizing her part.
3. The notice read as follows; "No smoking alowed sic. in this area.
4. Frazer's explanation of the primitive ritual of the scapegoat see volume 2 has I think it is safe to say a bearing on some of our contempory problems.
5. Eighty seven guests were present at her weding.
6. The class of 61 will hold its meeting April 23 1964 at the Sheraton hotel at 8,30 PM
7. The tail of my dog is too short.

8. "Take five more minutes" he said. "then we leave whether you're ready or not."
9. "What fun. Let's do it again."
10. Would you please close the window?

VOCABULARY

Words from this unit are used in different contexts in the following sentences. Write the numbers 1 to 5 on a sheet of paper. After each number write the letter of the word or phrase that could be best substituted for the italicized word in each sentence. Before making your choice, turn to the pages in this unit on which these words were used.

1. Mr. Bascome *derived* pleasure from giving to charity. [p. 368]
   (*a*) sought; (*b*) received; (*c*) looked for; (*d*) expected
2. His plan is *utopian,* but it might just work. [p. 368]
   (*a*) new; (*b*) experimental; (*c*) visionary; (*d*) complicated
3. Mike *deduced* from the powder burns on her fingers that Jill had fired a pistol recently. [p. 373]
   (*a*) observed; (*b*) inferred; (*c*) thought; (*d*) speculated
4. Spies always try to *infiltrate* the enemy's ranks. [p. 415]
   (*a*) demoralize; (*b*) penetrate; (*c*) disrupt; (*d*) augment
5. Some people claim that the ability to think logically is *innate* and cannot be learned. [p. 415]
   (*a*) inborn; (*b*) unteachable; (*c*) unlearnable; (*d*) unattainable

SPELLING

Some of the following spelling words appeared in this unit. All of these words were chosen because they are commonly misspelled. You should study these words so that you will be able to write them correctly when your teacher dictates them to you.

1. derived	11. achievement
2. utopian	12. approaching
3. deduced	13. decision
4. infiltrate	14. dissatisfied
5. innate	15. interesting
6. hundred	16. miniature
7. forestall	17. partner
8. preserved	18. sacrifice
9. bivouac	19. source
10. ancient	20. strenuously

UNIT SELF-TEST

Rewrite the following sentences, correcting all errors in mechanics and spelling that you find.

1. I asked, "how much does it cost"?
2. Three presidents of the United States were born in Massachusetts, John Adams, John Quincy Adams, and John F. Kennedy.
3. Virtually all milk sold in the United States is Pasteurized.
4. He lives on Tower road in Winnetka.
5. My aunt Sally and my cousins are comming to dinner tonight.
6. One of the best libaries in the Middle West is that of the university of Illinois.
7. After Jenny sang the song never sounded the same to me again.
8. I prefer doing my work now and then resting later.
9. We were disappointed for all the critic's reviews were favorable.
10. I will pay this bill, however, this is the last I will pay for you.
11. Mr. Cyril our teacher for the last five years has resined his position and is going to work for the goverment.
12. I'm sorry he's ill though I didn't especially want to meet him.
13. During the winter I like to: ski, skate and tobaggan.
14. I should like to see a good play but I never seem to have the time.
15. Dick will work hard, only if he is paid well.
16. Would you come this way, please?
17. Fran is a quick worker but not a very accurate one.
18. Who wrote that song can you remember, it's called 'Night and Day.'
19. Hes a law abiding citizen when everyone is watching.
20. His novels though brilliant and complex had very poor sales.

Unit 13

Style in Sentences

Have you ever stopped to think that almost everything you write is meant to be read by someone? Very likely, it will be read because you are not personally present to express the ideas orally. Your writing should, however, express your personality as clearly as your physical presence would. And one of the primary influences your writing will have on the reader is its style.

Your style of writing is that quality which makes your writing distinctively yours, and it is directly related to the style of the sentences in your writing. In this unit you will learn how to improve your sentence style by writing sentences that have clarity, unity, variety, and parallelism.

CHECK YOURSELF

Each of the following sentences has a particular style weakness. Rewrite each sentence, eliminating its weakness in style.

1. His father asked him was he going to be home that night.
2. The new wrestling team captain acts as brave as a lion.
3. The Dean of Boys gave me some good advise about college.
4. We had better begin to get ready to start to go.
5. The meat platter is on the stove but has been eaten.
6. The room is a perfect square in shape.
7. Mr. McCoy has just returned from South America, and he is the president of the Wire and Tube Company.
8. Was the rules committee able to affect a change in the procedures?
9. His work was interesting, exciting, and with challenge.
10. The player with the most points either was Arthur or Bob.

1. Basic Problems in Style

CLARITY IN SENTENCES [74]

One of the characteristics of good sentences is clarity. Perhaps you have read or listened in class to the compositions of some of your friends. Did you understand what the person was saying at all times, or did you find that the expression of the ideas in some sentences was hazy, making the sentences difficult to understand? Very likely, this lack of clarity made the compositions less interesting to you, also.

You can write clear sentences more easily if you understand the parts of a sentence and the logical relationship of one part to another.

The subject of a sentence must be clearly defined. [74a]

Writing humorously is the most outstanding characteristic of Twain's book. (The subject *Writing humorously* is not clearly related to the rest of the sentence.)

The humor in his writing is the most outstanding characteristic of Twain's book. (The subject of the sentence is now clearly defined.)

The subject of a sentence must make sense in relation to the predicate. [74b]

The grocery list is on the table and will be needed before dinner. (In this sentence the grocery list, not the groceries, will be needed before dinner.)

The groceries on the list on the table will be needed before dinner. (In this sentence the subject is clearly related to the predicate.)

Adjust the form of an indirect quotation to the rest of the sentence. [74c]

He wanted to know could he renew his subscription. (Illogical)
He wanted to know whether he could renew his subscription. (Clear)

A sentence sometimes becomes unclear when it presents too many details. *Rambling sentences* are those in which words like *and* and *so* are used to add certain details that would be better placed in a separate sentence.

Avoid the use of too many details in a single sentence. [74d]

Because great amounts of snow began to fall, the city sent out many snowplows and salt trucks, *and so* the streets were cleared by morning, and most commuters arrived at work on time. (Rambling)

Because great amounts of snow began to fall, the city sent out many snowplows and salt trucks. They cleared the streets by morning, and most commuters arrived at work on time. (Improved)

Wordiness is often the result of superfluous words in sentences.

Avoid the use of superfluous words. [74e]

His new jacket is blue in color. (This sentence is *redundant* because of the unnecessary repetition of the same idea in the words *blue in color.*)

His new jacket is blue. (Clear)

Superfluous words in sentences also include *circumlocution* (talking around the point), *prolixity* (putting emphasis on unimportant details), and *verbosity* (using many words where a few words would do).

She accepted the gift with exuberant joyfulness. (Circumlocution)
She accepted the gift happily. (Clear)

He bought a new jacket with a hood-like headpiece lined with fur. (Prolixity)
He bought a new jacket with a parka. (Clear)

My most amiable and esteemed acquaintance has moved to Beloit. (Verbosity)
My best friend has moved to Beloit. (Clear)

The effectiveness of a clear sentence is often lessened by the use of *trite expressions*. Such expressions are figures of speech that have lost their effectiveness through excessive use.

Avoid trite expressions.

The following list includes trite expressions that should be avoided.

aching void	busy as a bee	good as gold
add insult to injury	cold as ice	green with envy
all work and no play	cool as a cucumber	heated argument
almighty dollar	deadly earnest	hungry as wolves
apple of his eye	easier said than done	ignorance is bliss
at a loss for words	eyes like stars	pretty as a picture
beat a hasty retreat	fools rush in	red as a rose
beautiful but dumb	fly in the ointment	sings like a bird
brave as a lion	furrowed brow	staff of life
brown as a berry	goes without saying	wee, small hours

Avoid mixed figures of speech.

Figures of speech can add effectiveness to your writing, but two figures of speech must not be mixed in the same sentence. Notice the mixed comparisons in the following sentence:

> The story of life is paved with cobblestones.

The preceding sentence mixes the idea of life being both a story and a rough road. The sentence may be improved in the following way:

> The road of life is paved with cobblestones.

DEVELOPING YOUR SKILL

Write each of the following sentences so that the idea in the sentence is expressed clearly. After your sentence write the number of the rule that applies to that sentence.

1. His sister is as pretty as a picture.
2. The hunter shot a specimen of the bovine family.
3. The fire started in a skillet in the kitchen, and then other grease on the range started to burn, and so the chef called the fire department and then began to use the fire extinguisher.
4. By directing traffic was the way he helped the week-end activities.
5. She asked was I going to help her with her studies tonight.
6. With dark glasses on at night makes a man an unsafe driver.
7. This water is as cold as ice.
8. He walked like a man on a treadmill who was rowing against the current.
9. The blissful infant engaged in recreation by spontaneously arranging the multicolored cubes.
10. Sharon wanted to know was I selected to serve on the committee.

UNITY IN SENTENCES

In addition to being clear, your sentences should also have unity.

A sentence has unity when all the ideas expressed are closely related and contribute to a single impression. [75]

Abraham Lincoln was a great President, and he was born in Kentucky. (Faulty)

Our school won the state basketball championship last year, our enrollment being one of the smallest in the state. (Faulty)

If the ideas in a sentence are related, the sentence may be rephrased in a way that will make the relationship clear.

Unity is sometimes achieved by subordinating one idea to the other.
[75a]

Abraham Lincoln, who was a great President, was born in Kentucky.

If the ideas expressed in a sentence are not closely related, they should not be in the same sentence. Unrelated ideas should be expressed in separate sentences.

Unity is sometimes achieved by the complete separation of ideas. [75b]

Our school won the state basketball championship last year. Our enrollment is one of the smallest in the state.

DEVELOPING YOUR SKILL

Rewrite the following sentences to attain unity.

1. The captain of our team is a senior, and his name is Don Nitz.
2. He was leaving the building, and he heard the telephone ring in his office.
3. Mr. Hanback attended the national conference, and he is the principal of our school.
4. Visitors at the World's Fair in Seattle want to see the space needle, and Mt. Rainier is also a beautiful sight.
5. My uncle lives in Evanston, and his name is Howard.
6. My brother has just left for college, and he is eighteen years old.
7. Many colleges now have traveling representatives, and their primary job is to find qualified students.
8. Last week I read *Julius Caesar* again, and it was written by William Shakespeare.

9. Miami is the site of many national conventions, and it is not the capital of Florida.
10. Our new car is red, and we bought it last night.

EASILY CONFUSED WORDS   [76]

There are four reasons why certain pairs or groups of words are often confused. First, certain words are homonyms; they have the same pronunciation but they differ in meaning and, often, in spelling: *bear* (animal), *bear* (to carry), and *bare* (without covering). Second, some words are easily confused because they are similar in appearance: *advice, advise; allusion, illusion*. Third, some words are confused because they are similar in pronunciation; they are not homonyms, but sloppy pronunciation often makes them sound alike: *accept, except; whether, weather; formally, formerly*. Last, some words are confused because they have similar meanings: *about, around; aggravate, annoy*.

The following list of words and explanations is included to help you become familiar with words that may be easily confused. Also, the list provides a reference aid that you may use easily and quickly. The only way, however, that you can learn to use each of these words correctly is to master the pronunciation, spelling, and meaning of each word.

about—approximately. There were *about* twenty people at the meeting.
around—along the circumference of; on all sides of. He swam *around* the edge of the pool.

accept—to receive (a thing offered) with a consenting mind. I shall *accept* your invitation happily.
except—(v.) to omit; (prep.) with the exclusion of. Shall we *except* (v.) his name from the list? Everyone is going *except* (prep.) me.

advice—(n.) recommendation regarding a decision. Some people are always giving unsolicited *advice*.
advise—(v.) to recommend a course of action to someone. I *advise* you to explain the entire situation. NOTE: Avoid using *advise* to mean *inform* or *tell*. Please *tell* us when the shipment will be sent. Do not say, "Please *advise* us when the shipment will be sent."

affect—(v.) to influence; to assume the character of; to feign. Did the injury *affect* your movement in any way?
effect—(v.) to bring about; to accomplish; (n.) a result; consequence. Did the new rules *effect* (v.) any change in the members' attitudes? What *effect* (n.) on the audience did his speech have?

aggravate—to make worse. Sitting in a draft may *aggravate* your cold.

annoy—to disturb or irritate, especially by repeated acts. My nephews *annoy* me with their endless questions.

all together—everyone or everything in one place. The cups were *all together* on one shelf.

altogether—wholly. There are *altogether* too many discrepancies in this report.

altar—raised structure in a place of worship. One usually finds candles on an *altar*.

alter—to change in some particular respect. The architect was able to *alter* the specifications without increasing the cost.

beside—(prep.) by the side of. She set the spoon *beside* the knife.

besides—(adv. and prep.) in addition; over and above. I don't know her; *besides* (adv.), I've never even seen her. How many *besides* (prep.) you and me are going?

capital—first; chief; principal city of a state or country. Olympia is the *capital* of Washington.

capitol—when capitalized, the building in which Congress holds its sessions; often not capitalized, the building in which a state legislature meets. We visited the *Capitol* when we were in Washington, D. C. The state legislators hurried from the *capitol* at the end of the session.

character—the total of an individual's distinctive qualities. The mayor's *character* has never been questioned.

reputation—the opinion others hold of one's character. The *reputation* of a person in public life is especially important.

coarse—rough; rude; crude. The jacket was made of *coarse* cloth.

course—series of studies; progress. Which English *course* will you take in college next year?

complement—that which completes. This black purse will be a perfect *complement* to your attire.

compliment—a flattering speech or attention. I wish to *compliment* you on your taste in clothes.

consul—an official who represents his government in a foreign country. The Ethiopian *consul* was introduced to us at the party.

council—an advisory or legislative body. How many members are there on the student *council?*

counsel—(n.) advice; adviser; (v.) to advise. He asked his attorney for professional *counsel* (n.). If you want me to *counsel* (v.) you, I shall try to do my best.

decent—fitting; proper. Helping that family was the most *decent* thing he ever did.

descent—downward movement. The *descent* of the space capsule was observed on radar.

des' ert—(n.) arid region. The downed pilot was miraculously found in the *desert.*

de sert'—(v.) to abandon. Why did you *desert* your friends just when they needed you?

dessert—(n.) course served at the end of a meal. We had cherry pie for *dessert* on George Washington's birthday.

device—(n.) a mechanical apparatus; a scheme. This new *device* for use in the kitchen will save you many hours of work.

devise—(v.) to think out; invent; plan. The consultant will try to *devise* a new way to expedite our billing procedures.

discover—to find or find out about something not previously known but already in existence. I am sure that you will *discover* the benefits of this new drug as soon as you start taking it.

invent—to produce for the first time; to create something new. Our top research scientist hopes to *invent* a smaller transistor.

famous—well-known, generally for admirable achievement. Lincoln is one of our most *famous* Presidents.

notorious—well-known, generally for an unfavorable reason. Jesse James became *notorious* for his train robberies.

formally—in a conventional or ceremonious manner. He was *formally* presented with the citation.

formerly—in time past. The instructor was *formerly* a physician.

healthful—serving to promote health of body or mind. Vacations and recreation are thought to be *healthful* for an individual.

healthy—being in a state of health; well; showing good health; conducive to health. Gloria is a *healthy* person.

human—characteristic of man. Jealousy is a *human* attribute.

humane—kind; benevolent. He is one of the most *humane* persons I have ever met.

illusion—an unreal or misleading image; a deceptive appearance. The glaring sun presented an *illusion* of water.

allusion—an indirect reference by passing mention or by quotation to something generally familiar. His *allusion* to the life of Poe helped make his point more definite.

imply—to express indirectly; to hint or hint at. I did not mean to *imply* that he is dishonest.

infer—to draw a conclusion from facts or premises. From your comments, I can only *infer* that my work is inferior.

liable—answerable; exposed to the danger or risk of something undesired. The court found that the company was *liable* for accidents on the company's property.

likely—probably. It is *likely* that there will be trouble over the claim.

apt—suitable; quick to learn. He gave an *apt* answer to the leading question.

maybe—(adv.) perhaps. *Maybe* he was lost.

may be—(v.) conditional probability. I *may be* able to go out if you call my mother.

most—(n.) the greatest or largest quantity or amount; (adj.) greatest in number, quantity, size, or extent; nearly all. *Most* (n.) of the people liked the show. *Most* (adj.) physicians enjoy their profession.

almost—(adv.) nearly. We had *almost* reached the station when the car ran out of gas.

nauseated—disgusted; sick at the stomach. Several persons became *nauseated* during the flight.

nauseous—disgusting; causing nausea. The *nauseous* sight caused her to turn her head.

persecute—to cause to suffer because of belief; to annoy; harass. The ruler will probably *persecute* them because of their faith.

prosecute—to carry out legal action against. My uncle decided that he had to *prosecute* one of his best friends.

personal—pertaining to a particular person; not public or general. I do not care to express my *personal* feelings.

personnel—employees of a service or a company. The *personnel* received large salary increases this year.

practicable—feasible. Your idea to rent books seems to be a *practicable* one.

practical—proved to be useful. Jet planes provide a *practical* means of rapid travel.

precede—to go before. The bride's mother will *precede* the bride down the aisle.

proceed—to go forward; to advance. They will *proceed* with the construction as soon as the contracts are approved.

principal—(adj.) first; chief; (n.) a sum of money due to a debt or used as a fund; the chief executive officer of a school. My *principal* (adj.) reason for being here is that I want to inspect your facilities. He asked the clerk to tell him how much *principal* (n.) remained on his note. Mr. Franson is the *principal* (n.) of Forest Road School.

principle—fundamental truth or rule. Honesty is a *principle* that I always follow.

prophecy—(n.) a prediction. His *prophecy* that the world would end was not true.

prophesy—(v.) to predict. I will not try to *prophesy* what the result will be.

quiet—(adj.) free from noise; (n.) silence. The motor on the electric typewriter was exceptionally *quiet* (adj.). The *quiet* (n.) of the night helped him to sleep well.

quite—(adv.) completely; wholly. NOTE: Avoid using *quite* to mean *very* or *somewhat*. Are you *quite* sure that your answer is correct?

stationary—(adj.) fixed; not movable. The buoy in the river has a *stationary* anchor.

stationery—(n.) paper for writing letters. I sent my cousin a box of *stationery* for her birthday.

to—(prep.) direction toward. My parents took me *to* the museum last week.

too—(adv.) also. I asked Jane to go, *too*.

two—a number (2). I received only *two* ties for my birthday.

weather—(n.) state of the air or atmosphere with regard to temperature, humidity, or any other meteorological phenomena; (v) to come safely through. Do you know what the *weather* (n.) will be tomorrow? I doubt that this boat can *weather* (v.) the approaching storm.

whether—(conj.) introduces an indirect question. Have you heard *whether* or not the game will be played?

if—(conj.) supposing that; in case that. *If* it rains, I won't be able to go.

Rewrite the following sentences, correcting all misused words. Write *correct* after the appropriate number if the sentence contains no errors.

1. What will you serve for desert?
2. I know of no one who can prophecy the future.
3. Are you quiet sure that he called me?
4. Because we are all humane, we all make mistakes.
5. He was formally an English teacher before he joined the theater.
6. May be you can give me some advise.
7. Will you have to altar your plans to visit the notorious recording star if it rains?
8. Many trucks, beside the railroads, help supply merchandise to cities.
9. The reaper was discovered by Cyrus Hall McCormick.
10. The people in the room filled with fumes were nauseated.
11. Am I to imply from your remarks that you want me to go?
12. How many personal do you employ here?
13. The only desk in the room contained three sheets of stationary.
14. I don't know if I shall go or not.
15. The lines he drew turned out to be an optical allusion.
16. There were most a hundred people at the reception.
17. Mr. Williams is likely for the injury I sustained in his car.
18. To people are sometimes to many people when one wants to be alone.
19. I hope that my dog's barking does not aggravate you.
20. Did the last song in the play have any effect on you?

Review Exercises—Basic Problems in Style

Write each of the following sentences, correcting any lack of clarity or unity and any misused words.

1. After each meal makes a good time for one to brush his teeth.
2. The boys were standing altogether at the end of the room.
3. She asked did I talk to you on the phone last night.
4. The rough road to success is paved with stormy waters.
5. The fact that he complemented me will not altar my opinion of him.
6. The car started quickly even though the temperature was below zero, and Dad started to back the car out of the garage, and then he noticed that the front of the car was bouncing up and down, and when he stepped out of the car and walked to the front, he noticed that one tire was flat.
7. When I looked out the window this morning, I saw that several inches of small tabular and columnar crystals of frozen water, formed directly

from the water vapor of the air when its temperature at the time of condensation was below freezing, had fallen.

8. The sudden decent of the plane frightened some of the passengers.

9. Miss Peterson is our fastest typist, and she can type ninety words per minute.

10. If you think that two much sunshine is healthy, you're laboring under an allusion.

2. Improving Sentence Style

VARIETY IN SENTENCES   [77]

Vary sentence beginnings.   [77a]

Sentences often lack variety because each one begins with the subject of the sentence. Study carefully the following ways of varying sentence beginnings.

Begin the sentence with a prepositional phrase:

John went to Smitty's after the show. (Begins with the subject.)

After the show John went to Smitty's. (Begins with a prepositional phrase.)

Begin the sentence with a single-word modifier:

Sandra happily closed the book. (Begins with the subject.)

Happily, Sandra closed the book. (Begins with a single-word modifier.)

Begin the sentence with a dependent clause:

He cleaned his car after the rain had stopped. (Begins with the subject.)

After the rain had stopped, he cleaned his car. (Begins with a dependent clause.)

Begin the sentence with a verbal phrase:

Ray stubbed his toe as he was running to catch the ball. (Begins with the subject.)

Running to catch the ball, Ray stubbed his toe. (Begins with a verbal phrase.)

Begin the sentence with a transposed appositive:

University Days, a humorous story about college days, was written by my favorite author. (Begins with the subject.)

A humorous story about college days, *University Days* was written by my favorite author. (Begins with a transposed appositive.)

Vary the length of sentences. [77b]

You know how disturbing and difficult it is to read a long sequence of short, choppy sentences, and how confusing it is to read a series of long, involved sentences. Remember these points in your own writing and use short, long, and average sentences to help keep your reader interested and to fit the mood of your writing.

Use a nominative absolute at the end of a sentence. [77c]

The cars sped around the track, *their motors roaring with the torture of the race.*

The wings of the injured duck pommeled the air, *their noise telling the location to the hunters.*

Use a variety of structures to avoid the overuse of *and* and *so*. [77d]

Notice the careless manner in which the ideas in the following sentence are connected by *and* and *so*.

We had to work on the yearbook at school last Saturday morning, *and* I knew that it would be difficult to get up early on Saturday, *so* I went to bed early, *and* I still overslept, *so* I could have stayed up late on Friday night. (Faulty)

Because we had to work on the yearbook at school last Saturday morning, I went to bed early on Friday night, knowing that it would be difficult to get up early on Saturday. Nevertheless, I could have stayed up late on Friday, for I overslept the next morning. (Improved)

Vary the types of sentences.   [77e]

Skilled writers often use two types of sentences that help add variety to their writing. These two types, the *periodic sentence* and the *loose sentence* should not be overused, but they will add variety to your writing when used sparingly and properly.

A periodic sentence is one in which the essential meaning is not completed until the end. A loose sentence is one that could end at one or more places other than at the actual end of the sentence.

Because English is used in every subject you study, it is important that you master its use. (Periodic)

It is important that you master the use of English because it is used in every subject you study. (Loose)

Use inverted sentences.   [77f]

An *inverted sentence* is one in which all or part of the verb in a sentence precedes the subject. Read the following examples of inverted sentences to see the manner in which they would add variety to a group of sentences in natural order.

All through the forest ran the small wild animals.
Rarely does one have an opportunity like this.

Use balanced sentences.   [77g]

A *balanced sentence* is one in which several parts of the sentence are similar in length and in structure. This type of sentence is often used to express a contrast.

Our team has won every game; their team has lost every game.
A penny saved is a penny earned.
Diane is a blonde; Jean is a brunette.

Use elliptical sentences.   [77h]

An *elliptical sentence* is one in which the complete thought is implied rather than specifically stated. Do not confuse an elliptical sentence with a fragment of a sentence. Elliptical sentences are often correctly used in conversation.

"Where have you been?"
"Out."
"Out where?"
"At Herb's house."

Use the position of words in a sentence to gain emphasis and variety.
[77i]

In some of your sentences you will want to emphasize a certain aspect of the idea being presented. Notice the emphasis gained in the second sentence that follows.

The lake is certainly too rough for any small craft today. (Unemphatic)

Certainly the lake is too rough for any small craft today. (Emphatic)

Use the principle of climax in sentences.
[77j]

To use the *principle of climax* in a sentence is to build to a climax in a sentence, to save the best or most important element for the end of the sentence.

The money that was collected helped pay her rent, buy her groceries, and pay for the operation to restore her sight.

 DEVELOPING YOUR SKILL

A. Rewrite each of the following sentences to vary its beginning according to the directions in parentheses after each sentence.

1. We heard the siren during the performance. (Begin with a prepositional phrase.)
2. The boy shuffled lazily toward the door. (Begin with a single-word modifier.)
3. His invention would not work until he soldered the broken wires. (Begin with a dependent clause.)
4. Four sports cars went by while we were standing on the corner. (Begin with a verbal phrase.)
5. Ling Poo, a Siamese cat, seems always to be in trouble. (Begin with a transposed appositive.)

B. Rewrite each of the following sentences, varying the sentence in the manner described in the rule whose number follows the sentence.

1. Don has brown hair; Paul is a redhead. (77g)
2. It seldom rains during this time of the year. (77f)
3. "Do you know how much Bill paid for his new car?"
   "No, I don't know. How much did he pay?"
   "He paid three hundred dollars."
   "Did he pay it all yesterday?" (77h)
4. The deadline for your story was last night. (77i)
5. Joan's birthday presents included a new car, a sweater, and a purse. (77j)

C. Write two periodic sentences, two loose sentences, and one sentence ending with a nominative absolute.

PARALLELISM IN SENTENCES   [78]

Parallelism in sentences means that similar constructions are used for similar ideas in a sentence. Read the following sentence in which the similar ideas are expressed in different ways.

The explorer discovered a valley that was deep, fertile, and of great beauty.

The preceding sentence can be improved by making the three descriptive adjectives parallel in structure.

The explorer discovered a valley that was deep, fertile, and beautiful.

Avoid unnecessary shifts in person, number, voice, and tense of verbs in sentences.   [78a]

If *they* understand the meaning of parallelism, *one* will improve his style in writing sentences. (Shift in person and number)

The students *wrote* the dialogue, and the music *was written* by the faculty. (Shift in voice)

I *emptied* the wastebaskets, and Jim *washes* the chalkboards. (Shift in tense)

Avoid unnecessary shifts in the mood of verbs.   [78b]

Go to the store and you *will buy* me some bread. (Shift from imperative mood to indicative mood)

Avoid shifts in the kinds of modifiers used.   [78c]

That boy is *honest* and *of great courage.* (Shift from single-word modifier to phrase modifier)

Avoid shifts in the kinds of verbals used.   [78d]

To follow the course is *heading* for destruction. (Shift from infinitive to gerund)

Use the same construction before and after co-ordinating conjunctions.
                                                                [78e]

My favorite forms of exercise are talking and running *(not* to run).

We washed the walls to clean the room and to give more light *(not* for more light).

We decided that you should go with us and that we should call you *(not* and to call you).

Write correlative conjunctions so that they immediately precede parallel terms.   [78f]

The workers *both* were tired *and* hungry. (Faulty)
The workers were *both* tired *and* hungry. (Improved)

The second part of a parallel construction must contain all words necessary to make the construction clear.   [78g]

He wore clothes that were better than any other boys. (Faulty—the clothes are compared with boys.)

He wore *clothes* that were better than any other boy's *clothes.* (Improved)

The tables are dusted and the floors mopped. (Faulty)
The tables *are* dusted and the floors *are* mopped. (Improved)

She was going to night school and taking English. (Faulty)
She *was* going to night school and *was* taking English. (Improved)

I like John more than Norman. (Faulty)
I like John more than *I like* Norman. (Improved)

He said that he would go and enjoy the trip. (Faulty)
He said *that he would* go and *that he would* enjoy the trip. (Improved)

Repeat an article, a pronoun, or a preposition whenever the repetition is necessary for clarity.   [78h]

We elected a secretary and treasurer. (One person)
We elected *a* secretary and *a* treasurer. (Two persons)

He bought the car that had been wrecked and needed many repairs. (Faulty)

He bought the car *that* had been wrecked and *that* needed many repairs. (Improved)

He was both flattered and took delight in the award. (Faulty)
He was both flattered *with* and took delight *in* the award. (Improved)

Use the same construction for all the members of a series.   [78i]

The performance was bright, gay, and of many colors. (Faulty)
The performance was bright, gay, and *colorful*. (Improved)

My aim is to be healthy, to be happy, and prosperity. (Faulty)
My aim is to be healthy, to be happy, and *to be prosperous*. (Improved)

The point of the pen is gold, its barrel is metal, and plastic is used for its cartridge. (Faulty)

The point of the pen is gold, its barrel is metal, and its cartridge is plastic. (Improved)

Use the same construction for all the members of a list. [78j]

The members of the class listed the following activities as their favorite forms of recreation:

1. Swimming
2. Hunting
3. Sailing
4. Hikes (Faulty—Hiking would be the correct form.)

Use the same construction for all the main topics in an outline and for all the subtopics under the same topic. [78k]

DECORATING A ROOM

I. Planning the room
   A. Draw a plan
   B. Group the furniture
   C. Budget your money
II. Using color
   A. Effects of color
   B. Schemes in color

The main topics in the preceding outline both have the same construction. The subtopics under *I.* all have the same construction, and the subtopics under *II.* have the same construction. Notice, however, that it is not necessary for the two sets of subtopics to be identical in form.

DEVELOPING YOUR SKILL

Rewrite each of the following sentences so that similar ideas are expressed in parallel form.

1. The elderly man walked slowly and with great care.
2. When a person votes, you are exercising a privilege.
3. I wrote my report while he completes his history assignment.
4. To hurry through a long assignment is rushing toward a low grade.
5. I write letters faster than reports.
6. At the end of the race he was panting and gasped for air.
7. The prize was either won by Paul or David.
8. The team is composed of the following players: Bill Bower, Herb Franson, Dave Miskelly, Barney Biestman, and Reinke, Gilbert.
9. Speeches were given by the president and secretary of the club.
10. I am unaccustomed and frightened by speaking before a large group.

Review Exercises—Improving Sentence Style

A. Write the way in which each of the following sentences varies from the normal sentence pattern.

1. Because more snow fell during the night, the tracks were covered the next morning.
2. A retired engineer, Uncle George now collects model trains.
3. The pilot fought to gain altitude, one motor having stopped.
4. Often are the results the same as these.
5. Obviously you were at fault.

B. Rewrite the following sentences, using parallel constructions wherever necessary.

1. In this case, calling a doctor would have been better than to depend on your own abilities.
2. I have found that you can never trust a person who lies to me.
3. He neither was tired nor bored during your visit.
4. The meeting was conducted orderly and with efficiency.
5. He wanted to go to school and continuing with his work.

UNIT SUMMARY

Your style in writing sentences often determines whether or not a reader can understand your meanings. If a weak style impedes the comprehension of the reader and it becomes necessary for him to reread the material several times before he can grasp your ideas, your sentences probably lack the characteristics of good style that are important in all writing. In this unit you learned ways in which you can make your sentences clear and unified. You also studied some of the words in the language that are often confused.

Other aspects of style studied in this unit include variety in the sentences you write and parallelism within the sentences. Variety in sentences adds interest to your writing and may help make meanings clear, but variety simply for its own sake should be avoided. Parallelism is necessary whenever more than one idea is presented in a sentence.

UNIT REVIEW EXERCISES

DISCUSSION TOPICS

A. Why is writing that contains many weaknesses in style difficult to read with understanding?
B. How does wordiness impede comprehension?
C. How does variety in sentences help comprehension? How might variety impede comprehension?
D. How do parallel constructions contribute to style in sentences?

WRITTEN WORK

A. Write the numbers 1 to 5 on a sheet of paper. After the appropriate number write the sentence described.

    1. Begin with a prepositional phrase.
    2. End with a nominative absolute.
    3. Begin with a dependent clause.
    4. Include two modifiers that are parallel.
    5. Include two verbals that are parallel.

B. Write sentences using each of the following words correctly: *altar, alter; coarse, course; decent, descent; des' ert, de sert', dessert; personal, personnel; practicable, practical; stationary, stationery.*
C. Write a paragraph in which you describe what you think will be the most outstanding events in your graduation exercises. Include as many of the directions in this unit as possible. After the paragraph, list the numbers of the rules you have followed in your writing.

VOCABULARY

Did you know the meaning of every word in the unit? In the following sentences, some of the words are used in different contexts. Write the numbers 1 to 5 on your paper. After each number write the letter of the word or phrase that could best be substituted for the italicized word in each sentence. Before making the choice, find the word on the page indicated to see how the word is used in this unit.

1. Use this spice *sparingly* to bring out the flavor of the meat.   [p. 446]
    (*a*) heavily; (*b*) with restraint; (*c*) additionally; (*d*) carefully
2. There was a *unity* of agreement among the delegates.   [p. 433]
    (*a*) divergence; (*b*) discord; (*c*) universality; (*d*) oneness

3. Their comments about the new building were *exuberant*.   [p. 435]
   (*a*) pleasant; (*b*) lavish; (*c*) colorful; (*d*) repulsive
4. The salesman *pommeled* the door in anger.   [p. 445]
   (*a*) slammed; (*b*) forced open; (*c*) beat; (*d*) shook
5. Poor eyesight often *impedes* one's reading ability.   [p. 452]
   (*a*) hinders; (*b*) determines; (*c*) contributes to; (*d*) regulates

SPELLING

The following spelling words appeared in the unit or were chosen because they are commonly misspelled. Study these words so that you will be prepared to write them from dictation.

1.	sparingly	11.	losing
2.	unity	12.	peninsula
3.	exuberant	13.	ceiling
4.	pommeled	14.	gymnasium
5.	impede	15.	clearance
6.	quiet	16.	description
7.	prolixity	17.	warrior
8.	circumlocution	18.	management
9.	verbosity	19.	friend
10.	recreation	20.	shining

UNIT SELF-TEST

Rewrite each of the following sentences, correcting any weakness in style.

1. The whistles were blowing and the bells rang.
2. The charcoal burner should be filled and lighted.
3. Have you decided to except her invitation?
4. Airplanes fly faster than trains.
5. Working in the garden and to paint the house occupied all his leisure time.
6. When a person breaks the law, you are looking for trouble.
7. There were around forty people in the house and on the porch.
8. We have positions for a clerk and typist.
9. It started to rain and we ran for the house and we found the door was locked, so we ran back to the car so we could get out of the rain, and we reached the car and it stopped raining.
10. We bought the dog on Monday, and he was taken home with us on Tuesday.

INDEX

References in red type indicate pages on which instructional material appears.

451

England, meaning of name, 95
English language
   Check Yourself, 94
   French influence on, 99-101, 102, 109, 110
   Greek influence on, 105, 109
   inflections, 95-98, 99, 100, 101, 102, 110, 112
   Latin influence on, 94, 95, 102, 103-104, 109
   Middle English, 99-101, 102, 103, 110, 112
   Modern English, 102-105, 106-108, 109, 111, 112
     British and American English, 106-108, 111, 112
     dialects, 102-103
     orthography, 103-104, 105, 108, 109, 110, 111
     vocabulary, 104-105, 106-107, 109, 110, 112
   natural and grammatical gender, 96-97, 102, 112
   Old English, 95-98, 99-100, 102, 105, 110, 112
   origin and growth, 94-98, 99-101, 102, 110, 112
   word order in sentences, 97-98, 99, 100, 102, 110, 112
English words. *See* English language
Equivocation, 33, 34, 35, 43, 44
Example and illustration in paragraphs, 165-167, 172, 182
Except, accept, 434, 450
Exclamation point, 401, 402, 427
Exclamatory sentence, 284, 285, 287, 401, 402, 427
Expanded verb forms. *See* Emphatic form of verb; Progressive form of verb
Expansions of basic sentence patterns, 205-208, 209, 212, 213, 214, 228, 263, 264, 289, 290
Expletive, 229, 234, 235
   diagraming, 234

Exposition, 161-163, 165, 180-182
Eye dialects, 198-199, 214

Fallacies in reasoning, 28-33, 34-35, 43, 44
   See also individual entries
False analogy, 29-30, 33, 34, 35, 43, 44
False dilemma, 31, 34, 35, 43, 44
Famous, notorious, 436
Figures of speech, avoiding mixed, 432, 439
Footnotes, 143-145, 146, 148-152, 154-156
For with *blame,* 341, 343, 349
For with *wait,* 341
For, with, and *against* with *contend,* 342, 343
For, with, of, and *at* with *impatient,* 341, 343, 350
Foreign words and phrases
   italics, 410
   plurals, 355, 380-381, 383, 426
Form class words, 199-202, 204, 214
   test frames, 201
Form in writing. *See* Writing, form in
Formal English, 291, 292, 316, 325, 328, 342, 346, 360
Formally, formerly, 436, 439
Fractional numbers, agreement with verb, 352, 356
Fractions and numbers, hyphenated, 408, 409, 426
Fragment, sentence, 286, 287
From, not *than,* with *different,* 340, 342, 349, 350

Gender
   common, 314-315
   feminine, 314-315
   masculine, 314-315
   natural and grammatical, 96-97, 102, 112
   neuter, 314, 315
Geographical dialects, 194-196, 197, 200, 214

463

465

nu
pe
phi
pre

prin
progr
3
regular
synopsis,

ADJ A

ADU